THE ADVANCE OF SCIENCE

THE ADVANCE OF SCIENCE

OF

SCIENCE

EDITED BY

WATSON DAVIS

Director, Science Service,
Washington

DOUBLEDAY, DORAN & COMPANY, INC.

GARDEN CITY   1934   NEW YORK

PREFACE

SLOW as scientific progress seems at times, and undramatic as it often is in itself, it is possible to see year by year an increase in our knowledge of man and nature.

It is the purpose of this book to outline the extent to which that knowledge has now advanced in each of the major fields of scientific endeavor. It is no exaggeration to say that every day sees new territory won by the forces of knowledge and a corresponding amount lost to ignorance. A bird's-eye view of the frontiers reached by man, a view in which man sees each part of the advance in its proper relation to every other part, may fulfill a useful purpose in a world in which many are confused by the very multiplicity of events, and in which many are pondering their individual relationship to that world and to the millions that populate it.

This record does not pretend to be exhaustive, nor does it pretend to fulfill the specialist's needs. It is for the layman who senses the latent drama in true scientific achievement and who wants to be told in his own terms what science has done, what it has attempted, and how it affects his life that *The Advance of Science* is designed.

The fact that this book attempts to summarize scientific knowledge as it exists today has not prevented the injection of research acquired by the world in an earlier period. Where background is necessary to understand the most recent scientific progress, it has been included.

In the true sense of the word, this volume is a collaboration resulting from the efforts of the editorial members of the Science Service staff.

Science Service is the institution for the popularization of science, organized in 1921 as a non-profit corporation, with headquarters in Washington and with trustees nominated by the National Academy of Sciences, the National

v

Research Council, the American Association for the Advancement of Science, the E. W. Scripps Estate, and the journalistic profession. Board of Trustees: Dr. C. G. Abbot, Secretary, Smithsonian Institution; Dr. J. McKeen Cattell, *President,* Editor, *Science;* Dr. John H. Finley, Associate Editor, New York *Times;* Dr. H. E. Howe, Editor, *Industrial and Engineering Chemistry;* Dr. W. H. Howell, *Vice-President and Chairman of Executive Committee,* Johns Hopkins University; Dr. Vernon Kellogg, Secretary Emeritus, National Research Council; Dr. Burton E. Livingston, Johns Hopkins University; Dr. R. A. Millikan, California Institute of Technology; Dr. Raymond Pearl, Johns Hopkins University; Marlen E. Pew, Editor and Publisher, New York; Robert P. Scripps, Scripps-Howard Newspapers; Thomas L. Sidlo, Cleveland, Ohio; Harry L. Smithton, *Treasurer,* Cincinnati, Ohio; Mark Sullivan, Writer, Washington; Dr. David White, U. S. Geological Survey. Honorary President: Dr. W. E. Ritter, University of California.

Acknowledgment is made to Dr. Frank Thone, for Chapters 9, 12, 13, 17, 18, 19, 20, 30; Miss Emily Davis, for Chapters 11, 26, 27, 28, 29; Miss Jane Stafford, for Chapters 21, 22, 23, 24; Miss Marjorie Van de Water, for Chapters 10, 25, 31; J. W. Young, for Chapter 14; Mrs. Miriam G. Bender and Mrs. Anne Shively for editorial assistance; Miss Minna Gill for library assistance; Dr. J. H. Williams, Dr. Morton Mott-Smith, James Stokley, and Dr. R. M. Langer for their aid as Science Service writers; and Alan C. Collins for constant constructive aid. Science Service's day-by-day gathering of scientific news for newspapers, the editing of the weekly *Science News Letter,* and the other functions of Science Service have, it is believed, brought a breadth to this volume that otherwise might not have been obtained.

It is also desired to record appreciation of the helpfulness of those eminent scientists and journalists who serve upon the Board of Trustees of Science Service.

To acknowledge the coöperation of all the scientists who have assisted by information and advice is impossible. For expert criticism of certain portions of this book, however, debt is acknowledged to: Dr. C. G. Abbot, Dr. Carl D. Anderson, Paul Appleby, Dr. O. E. Baker, Dr. W. C. Beasley, Dr. B. H. Bok, Dr. Isaiah Bowman, Dr. F. G. Brickwedde, Dr. J. McKeen Cattell, Dr. A. H. Compton, Richard Crane, Dr. Walter Freeman, Dr. Paul Hanley Furfey, Dr. William K. Gregory, D. L. Hazard, Capt. N. H. Heck, Dr. Melville J. Herskovits, Dr. E. A. Hooton, Dr. R. G. Hoskins, Dr. H. E. Howe, Dr. W. H. Howell, Dr. W. J. Humphreys, Dr. Thomas H. Johnson, Neil Judd, Paul O. Komora, Dr. George Kreezer, Dr. C. C. Lauritsen, Dr. E. O. Lawrence, Dr. James P. Leake, Dr. George W. Lewis, Dr. George Grant MacCurdy, Dr. R. A. Millikan, Miss Jenka Mohr, Dr. H. Victor Neher, Dr. Raymond Pearl, Dr. A. T. Poffenberger, Dr. Robert Redfield, L. T. Samuels, Frank Setzler, Dr. H. L. Shapiro, Dr. Harlow Shapley, Dr. S. C. Simms, Matthew W. Stirling, Ralph E. Tarbett, Dr. Warren S. Thompson, Dr. T. Wingate Todd, Dr. David White, Dr. R. C. Williams. These specialists are not to be held to account for errors, although their co-operation has prevented many.

W. D.

CONTENTS

CONTENTS

HALFTONE ILLUSTRATIONS

TEXT ILLUSTRATIONS AND FIGURES

xiii

THE ADVANCE OF SCIENCE

CHAPTER 1
UNPUZZLING THE UNIVERSE

THE MOST WIDE-FLUNG TASK in the universe is the exploration of the universe itself. To attempt it, astronomers have set up giant telescopes on mountain tops and planned even more powerful looking glasses for the heavens. Mathematicians, using the results of the astronomers, have spun theories of formulæ that probe into the possible past and future of the universe.

We who have our minds upon things here on earth have difficulty in comprehending the universe from the viewpoint of the astronomer. A hundred miles an hour is a high speed to the traveler on the surface of the earth; the astronomer uses as his yardstick light which travels 186,000 miles per second, 11 million miles per minute, or 660 million miles per hour. Miles for the astronomer become much too small a unit of length, and he uses the distance that light travels in a year, about 6 trillion miles.

Suppose we rush outward in distance away from the earth, traveling in our imagination much faster than the speed of light, which is the universe's highest possible speed. First we come to the sun eight minutes away by light express. We are, of course, ignoring the earth's satellite, the moon, and the planets which are the other members of the sun's family. The nearest star is about four light years away. Then we travel for some 50,000 light years in one direction or as few as 2,000 light years in another to reach the boundaries of the great system of stars called our galaxy, in which the sun providing the earth with energy through its light and heat is but an insignificant glowing speck. This galaxy of ours, which we see spread over the sky as the Milky Way and to which the bright stars belong, is composed of about 100 billion stars. Beyond this portion of the universe, important principally because we happen to live in it, there is the far vaster volume of the universe sprinkled with other galaxies, some of them probably as large as our own. Among the nearest of these external systems are the Magellanic Clouds which can be seen and photographed only from the southern hemisphere. They are about 1 million light years away. The Great Nebula of Andromeda is at about the same distance. So far as the present astronomical instruments can sound the depths of space, to a distance of the order of 300 million light years, the universe is dotted with great star systems or nebulæ. In that immense expanse there are millions upon millions of nebulæ, great "island universes" which each contain millions of stars.

Telescopes, as a routine, photograph galaxies 100 million light years distant. That light originated 100 million years ago. It is our only contact with this external part of the universe, yet started on its journey from the galaxy when the earth was far younger, in middle Cenozoic time, geologically speaking, when the mammals were just beginning their development. That light drifted speedily through space as the great epic of earthly evolution unfolded itself and gave rise to mankind. During the last 6,000 years, while civilization and science have been developing, that light has been within our own galaxy. When the astronomer puts a photographic plate into the camera eye of his telescope and exposes it, he is, therefore, using light which is very antique indeed. And he records upon his photograph an almost infinitesimal flash in the history of a great external galaxy of stars.

Other Galaxies

How MANY galactic systems are there? A census of the galaxies of known space has been one of astronomy's major tasks of the past few years.

There are 75 million gigantic star systems in the vast space sphere visible to the largest telescopes. This is the estimate of Dr. Edwin P. Hubble of the Carnegie Institution's Mt. Wilson Observatory that spies upon the stars from its eminence over Los Angeles, Hollywood, and Pasadena. Dr. Hubble drew his conclusions from a count of nebulæ on 1,283 photographs taken with Mt. Wilson Observatory's 60- and 100-inch telescopes. On these photographs covering 2 per cent of the three quarters of the sky seen from Mt. Wilson, Dr. Hubble found approximately 44,000 nebulæ. With even distribution of nebulæ in the universe, there would be about 75 million galaxies within astronomy's present reach. This might seem to crowd the universe. Yet if all the molecules in the universe were distributed evenly, each would be separated from its neighbor by a distance of seven feet. Prof. William D. MacMillan of the University of Chicago has arrived at this figure, using Dr. Hubble's estimate.

Not that the matter in the universe is evenly distributed or that the great galaxies are evenly spaced. Dr. Harlow Shapley, director of the Harvard College Observatory, indefatigable universe unraveler, has come to the conclusion that galaxies cluster among themselves. Our own Milky Way galaxy, joined with the two Magellanic Clouds, the Andromeda group, the Messier 33 galaxy, and other star clouds totaling seven or eight galaxies all within a million years of each other, form a supergalaxy. Other supergalaxies are not so small but are made up of hundreds of ordinary galaxies.

As Dr. Shapley and the astronomical workers who cooperate with him have piled up observations on the galaxies and the supergalaxies, measuring and counting tens of thousands of the star systems, they have found the galaxies irregularly distributed in space. There appears, from preliminary data, to be indication of a gradient of density of galaxies as we look across the Milky Way from the south to the north. Studies of selected regions of the sky show that in the south, in a given volume of space, there are so many galaxies. In the north there are more of these star systems in the same volume. This holds good for distances of about 100 million light years from us. Farther away, triple that distance, as Dr. Hubble found, the galactic counts show nearly uniform distribution.

This makes the astronomers impatient for larger telescopes with which they may conquer more distant portions of the universe. Does this irregularity of distribution continue? The individual galaxy begins to lose its isolation and importance. Like a bee in a swarm, it may be the part of a greater system. The astronomers are eager to find the destiny of the swarms of galaxies.

Milky Way Fog

IN THE farthest reaches of space where the galaxies swarm, the void is reasonably transparent and free from the obscuring fog that hides the central regions of our own galaxy. Dr. Shapley feels sure from his researches that mists of the cosmos have not distorted the observations and that the irregularities observed in the galactic distribution are real.

Veils closer to us have been raised by recent researches to reveal the real nature of our portion of the universe.

"As empty as interstellar space" is a comparison that needs revision. For the gigantic voids between the stars that shine in the night sky are not truly empty. They are filled with an extremely tenuous cloud of fog, which contains so close to nothing that physicists would pronounce it perfect as a vacuum if it were here on earth.

Astronomers know that there is something in the space that seems to be empty because the light of distant stars is dimmed and reddened in its passage through space. This was shown by Dr. R. J. Trumpler of the Lick Observatory as well as by observations made with the Yerkes 40-inch telescope. Distant stars appear somewhat more ruddy than the ones nearer to us. This suggests to the astronomers that interstellar space has an effect like that of the atmosphere of the earth upon the sun's rays. When the sun is near the horizon its rays look red because they must travel through a thick layer of air.

But do not suppose for a moment that the light that is scattered by the air is lost, for it is not. The light subtracted to make the redness of the sunlight reappears as the blue of the sky. The compensation is so exact that it can be figured out theoretically. Applying a like reasoning to interstellar space and its particles, Dr. Otto Struve, director of the Yerkes Observatory, considered what effect the space reddening of the starlight should have on the space surrounding the stars. It would cause a faint general illumination of space, a slightly radiant screen of the heavens upon which are projected the more luminous images themselves. Dr. Struve computed just how much this background illumination should be expected to contain. The result surprised him.

The total amount of light produced by space should be greater than that of all the stars combined, and the color of this general illumination should be as blue as the bluest daylight of the sky. That the night sky is actually bright and not dark can be easily proven by any observer situated far from city lights. When the eyes are sufficiently adjusted to the dark, the sky appears faintly luminous between the stars, and the outlines of near-by objects, such as trees or houses, can be easily perceived.

In certain regions of space, near luminous stars, the interstellar fog may be illuminated so much that these regions appear even brighter than the rest of the sky. This would especially be true if a local condensation in the interstellar fog happens to be near such a bright star. It can then be photographed with a telescope because of its great luminosity, and it is seen projected as a bright spot upon the faint general sky illumination. Such spots are called nebulæ. The composition of these nebulæ is not fully understood. Some of them scatter the light of the stars, and their luminosity is therefore due to reflected or scattered starlight.

If such nebulæ consist of very small particles, such as atoms of a gas or extremely fine dust, they should redden the light of the stars and appear blue to the observer. In fact, they should be as much bluer than are their neighboring stars as the sky is bluer than the yellow light of the sun. On the other hand, if the nebulæ consist of large pieces, such as particles of sand or of small stones or meteorites, they should merely dim the light of the stars without making it redder, and their own color should be similar to that of the neighboring stars. A study of the colors of the nebulæ should therefore give a clue as to the size of the particles in the nebulæ observed. Recent investigations made by Drs. Struve, C. T. Elvey, and P. C. Keenan at Yerkes Observatory, showed that the nebulæ are slightly bluer than the stars in their vicinity. But they are not nearly as blue as would be expected if they were composed throughout of very small particles. The astronomers suppose therefore that the nebulæ consist of particles of all sizes, but that the proportion of very minute particles is not sufficient to render the light entirely blue.

As a result of other researches on obscuring matter, the part of the universe in which we live will probably turn out to be "just another galaxy." Our galaxy has heretofore been considered much larger than other such systems, but an astronomical "electric eye" used by Drs. Joel Stebbins and Albert E. Whitford of the University of Wisconsin on the Mt. Wilson 100-inch telescope has furnished evidence that man does not live in an unusually large collection of stars after all.

The existence of an extensive layer of dark, obscuring material near the central plane of the Milky Way had been confirmed previously by Dr. Stebbins, who is director of Washburn Observatory. The photo-electric amplifier perfected by Dr. Whitford attached to a giant telescope detects faint stars and nebulæ which cannot be photographed because they are lost in the "sky shine" or the diffuse light of the earth's own atmosphere. With this instrument the known diameter of the famous Andromeda nebula was more than doubled, and its extension has been traced out to where the luminosity is only 1 per cent of the general surface brightness of the sky.

Our galaxy is a vast celestial pinwheel, whirling about a center we earthlings cannot see. Dr. Alfred H. Joy of the Mt. Wilson Observatory made careful measurements of the rate and direction of movement of a large number of stars and found evidence that the great wheel-shaped swarm of stars of which our sun is a member is a rotating wheel. According to his calculations, it takes some 240 million years for it to make one complete turn.

Ideas of the Cosmos

WHENCE CAME we and whither are we going?—a question that gives rise to religions—is bound up tightly with science's search for the structure of the universe. When the earth was considered the center of the universe and the stars mere lights hung in the canopy of heaven (or any variation of that idea), cosmology was simple. As telescopes reached out into the heavens to show the insignificance of the earth, man's philosophical and religious notions changed. The universe was demonstrated to be complex, at times seemingly overpowering to mentality.

Now essential simplicity is returning through the use of mathematics, physics, and astronomy. A comprehensive review of relativistic cosmology such as that made in 1933 by Prof. H. P. Robertson of Princeton University may not at first glance seem to support the idea of simplicity. But despite the complex formulæ, there is emerging out of "the attempts that have been made during the past decade and a half to solve the general problem of the structure of the universe as a whole" an understanding, which is always an approach to simplicity.

The present burst of cosmological speculations is due to Einstein, "who through his general theory of relativity advanced the view that the structure of the space-time continuum is determined causally by its material and energetic content, and who took the first step toward a solution." Einstein's was a static universe, filled with matter, and the father of this universe has now transferred his scientific affections to more advanced models. Prof. Willem de Sitter gave mathematical expression to another stationary universe, totally empty. Dr. H. Weyl, working in 1922 on the De Sitter universe, introduced the concept of expansion. The late Dr. A. Friedmann of Petrograd discovered also in 1922 the class of expanding universes now in favor, and others, Abbé Georges Lemaître and Prof. Robertson among them, have hewn out of mathematical physics an assortment of universes, of which Prof. Robertson lists some twenty.

The steps in formulating relativistic universes are detailed by Prof. Robertson and may be briefed as follows:

Astronomical data allowed the assumption of the uniform distribution of matter in the large within the visible universe, and by analogy in the universe as a whole.

Astronomical evidence shows that the relative motions of neighboring nebulæ are extremely small compared with the velocity of light, and this allows the introduction of the idea of cosmic time and simultaneity in the universe at large.

This led to a form of the structure of the universe without drawing upon the experimental astronomical observation that the light from great aggregations of stars reddens as the distance outward increases, which is interpreted to mean that the nebulæ are rushing outward at tremendous speeds and indicates that the universe is expanding. Theory thus checked the telescopes in indicating an expanding universe.

To be sure, there are difficulties. Most troublesome is the short time scale allowed, of the order of 10 billion years. But Prof. Robertson is convinced that "the underlying theory forms an integral part of the theory of relativity, and that although the choice of a particular model may for the present be influenced by the predilections of the individual, we can hope that the future will reveal additional evidence to test its validity and to lead us to a satisfying solution."

This short-time scale for the universe, compared with estimates of the age of the stars, brings the paradoxical idea that the stars may be older than the universe.

So plentiful are theories of the universe that Dr. Shapley has said that there are two more cosmologies than there are cosmologists, because there are two cosmologists who hold two different theories at the same time. While the universe as a whole may be expanding, Dr. Shapley finds that our own supergalaxy, the portion of the universe closest to man and the earth, is not expanding.

Beginning and End

THE BEGINNING and ending of the universe are even more difficult than is its continued existence. Abbé Lemaître, whose exposition of the expanding universe theory has had such vogue, visioned the universe as born literally in a flash, "an astronomical instant." He suggests a high rate of cosmic evolution during the universe's first stages of development, with a later slowing down of the rate as the galaxies formed themselves and sped apart at an explosive rate. Prof. de Sitter of the University of Leiden sees the universe as capable of contraction as cataclysmically rapid as is its present apparent rate of expansion. But he advanced mathematical reason for not believing that it will vanish, whirlpool fashion, into the single astronomical point in space, and instant in time, whence it was born. Prof. Richard C. Tolman, the American authority on thermodynamics, has extended this science of heat, energy, and motion to Einstein's relativity and concludes that there is a possibility that the universe need not be thought of as having a definite beginning, and that it will never die of an energy leveling in the sense that the old-fashioned classical physicists predicted.

Much more accessible to us than the distant galaxies are the stars of our own neighborhood, those that we see twinkling in the sky on fine, clear nights. Because our sun is a star in this Milky Way galaxy of ours, we earth dwellers have a peculiar interest in stars and their actions.

The hardest problem of all star study is the source of the energy which keeps the stars shining. Synthesis and annihilation of atoms are the only two processes so far suggested which would supply enough heat to last for the millions of years of geological time. Theories indicate that the mutual annihilation of the positive and negative particles, the protons and the electrons, would not happen except at temperatures of many billions of degrees such as do not exist in the interior of stars.

The theory of Prof. Henry Norris Russell, Princeton astronomer, is that atomic synthesis, the building of heavier atoms out of hydrogen, makes the sun and stars give off heat and light. The rate of loss of heat from a star is almost incomprehensively great. The sun radiates heat away into the depths of space at the rate of 4,200,000 tons per second—and the sun is a smallish star.

The mechanism visualized by Prof. Russell is based on

the idea that atomic nuclei are built up of protons and neutrons. The incorporation of a proton into a nucleus would in many cases change an atom into a heavier element. The important feature of this process from the standpoint of keeping the stars stoked is that when a proton or hydrogen atomic heart is built into a heavier element, about 1/130 of its mass disappears and must be represented by heat liberated in the process.

Stellar Hurricanes

GREAT WINDS blow in the atmospheres of the distant stars compared with which the hurricanes of the earth's atmosphere are mere zephyrs. Dr. Otto Struve and Dr. C. T. Elvey, of Yerkes Observatory, found that while the outer gaseous atmospheres which surround the luminous lower strata of the stars have heretofore been assumed to be relatively quiescent, the rainbow spectra of stars give evidence that powerful turbulent currents exist in the atmosphere of many stars. Spectroscopic phenomena that puzzled astronomers for years were explained, and it is possible to measure the most frequent wind velocity of individual stars. The faint star known as 17 Leporis has an atmospheric velocity of about forty miles per second. In the sun, which is a star, there is practically zero wind velocity, however. The winds in the stars may be likened to the winds on earth although the densities of stellar atmospheres are much lower than the density of earthly air.

Seeing the Invisible

STARLIGHT that cannot be seen by the eyes, brings to earth some of the astronomer's most important information. If we could go outside the earth's air and see the night sky with most unhuman eyes, sensitive only to the ultraviolet or to the infrared, the constellations would change their aspects, and stars we now call "faint" would burst into brilliance. The most intense radiations of very hot blue stars are in the ultraviolet, wavelengths too short to be seen, Dr. Paul W. Merrill, of the Carnegie Institution's

Mt. Wilson Observatory, tells us, and the most intense light of the cool, red stars is in the infrared, wavelengths too long to be seen. Not much happens to starlight in its long passage through the abysmal depths of interstellar space, but what the earth's atmosphere does to it is a crime. Ozone in our atmosphere annihilates most of the ultraviolet, while oxygen and water vapor mutilate the infrared.

In modern telescopes the observation of ultraviolet light is hindered by the opacity of glass and the transparency of silver. The use of quartz or special ultraviolet glass and of aluminum mirrors is advantageous. Recent improvements in photographic emulsions have made it possible to extend photographs of stellar spectra a considerable distance into the infrared. But there are infrared stellar radiations of wavelengths too long to be photographed. When these radiations are focused by a telescope on a small blackened receiver the rise in temperature, although minute, can be measured and interpreted, and Dr. C. G. Abbot, secretary of the Smithsonian Institution, and two Mt. Wilson astronomers, Drs. Edison Pettit and S. B. Nicholson, observing at Mt. Wilson, have obtained important results by this method.

Because the usual silver coat applied to telescope mirrors is "blind" to the extreme ultraviolet light (beyond 3,300 Angstrom units), the development of aluminum coatings for telescopic mirrors is one of the most important improvements in astronomical equipment made in recent years. Brilliant metallic aluminum films have been applied successfully to astronomical mirrors at both Cornell and California Institute of Technology and we may soon expect to have aluminum replace silver in everyday looking glasses.

Plans are under way for aluminum-coating the world's largest telescope, the great 200-inch mirror that a few years hence will be pointed at the heavens from some southern California mountain top. Dr. J. Strong of California Institute of Technology has already coated the 36-inch reflector of Lick Observatory as a sort of preliminary exercise to this larger job.

The building and erecting of the 200-inch telescope is

astronomy's major instrumental task of this decade. Since 1929 plans and actual construction of this gigantic instrument have been quietly progressing at Pasadena, and at last the nine-foot disk that will be the mirror has been cast, not of fused quartz as originally intended, but of a superior sort of pyrex glass. It will be probably the end of the decade before this great mirror is given the precise optical shape needed and set in the peak-top nest of machinery and instruments that will point it at the heavens and utilize the greatest concentration of heavenly light ever achieved.

Only in this decade has the structure of the universe been investigated by direct observations. The great task of the 200-inch telescope will be to enlarge the sample of the universe that can be brought under human observation. At present the region that can be observed is a vast sphere some 600 million light years in diameter. The 200-inch will be ten times as powerful as the 100-inch mirror at Mt. Wilson, now premier penetrator of space. It is hoped that it will penetrate more than three times as far into space and thus open for investigation an unexplored sphere of about thirty times the volume that has been sounded hitherto.

Meanwhile lesser astronomical spying-spots are being planned or have actually been placed in operation. At Corning, N. Y., there have also been poured glass disks for the 85-inch University of Michigan telescope to be set up at Base Lake, Michigan, and the 80-inch McDonald Observatory telescope that will view the stars from Mt. Locke in southwestern Texas. After they have been slowly cooled it will be the work of months to grind and polish them. The new 40-inch reflecting telescope of the U. S. Naval Observatory is about ready for service, and a new 60-inch Harvard telescope has been swung into action at the new observing site at Oak Ridge, Mass.

Radio and the development of electrical methods of detecting light have had their influence upon the astronomer. Photoelectric cells have been substituted for photographic plates just as years ago light sensitive emulsion came to the aid of astronomers' eyes. As explained earlier in this chapter Drs. Stebbins and Whitford scanned the Andromeda nebula and detected extensions of it, impossible to see or photograph, that double its size. The "electric eye" converts feeble light into electric current, and this is fed into vacuum-tube arrangements such as are used in radio sets and amplified many times.

The astronomical electric eye was used to detect the *Gegenschein,* or the counterglow, that can be seen in the dark night sky as a faint patch of light in a position directly opposite that of the sun. It is due to the reflection of sunlight from a swarm of minute particles far out in space. The "electric eye" again rivals its human counterpart, not only in permitting scientists to detect the *Gegenschein,* but also in measuring its brightness. Dr. C. T. Elvey, of the University of Chicago's Yerkes Observatory, detected it with a photoelectric cell attached to the Yerkes' 40-inch telescope, the world's largest refractor or lens telescope.

Electronic telescopes that will use electrical instead of optical amplification and have light-gathering power thousands of times greater than present telescopic giants are visualized as the result of the development of television and radio.

CHAPTER 2
WITHIN THE SUN'S FAMILY

THE EARTH is related to the sun as an infant child is to its mother. The sun's beams nourish and warm the earth. Life on earth would be snuffed out by any accident to the sun. Brothers and sisters to the earth, the other planets, numbering eight since the discovery of Pluto, are in the sun's family. Mercury and Venus swing their ellipses around the sun inside the earth's orbit, while Mars, Jupiter, Saturn, Uranus, Neptune, and Pluto are outside the earth's path, farther from the sun. Between Mars and Jupiter is the region in which asteroids or minor planets move. The moon is the earth's child, closest of other astronomical bodies, with the exception of the meteors that actually plunge into the earth's atmosphere and sometimes fall to earth.

Distances between sun and planets are immense compared with those on the earth's surface. It is more than 92 million miles from sun to earth. Contrasted with the depths of space reached by telescopes, the solar system is minute indeed. Light arrives in $1\frac{1}{3}$ seconds from the moon and in 8 minutes from the sun. By light express the orbit of Pluto, farthest planet, could be crossed in 11 hours, compared with a time of hundreds of millions of years to the galaxies. We are justified in being so intensely interested in the solar system only because we happen to live in it.

Spots on the face of the sun, sometimes visible through smoked glass when they are large, puzzled those who saw them through the centuries. Nearly every sort of earthly phenomena, from war, birthrates, and crop failures to magnetic storms and auroras, has been linked to sunspots by scientific enthusiasts and less careful observers. While there is good observational evidence that sunspots and changes in the electrical field of the earth are related, astronomers

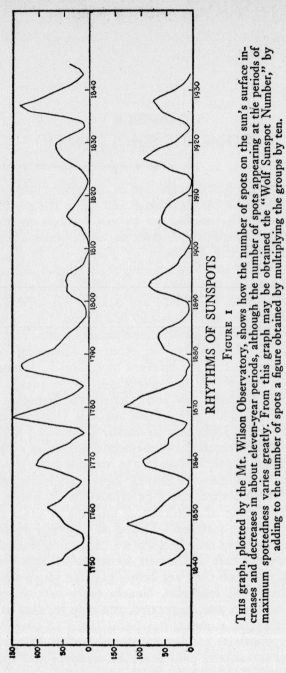

RHYTHMS OF SUNSPOTS

FIGURE I

This graph, plotted by the Mt. Wilson Observatory, shows how the number of spots on the sun's surface increases and decreases in about eleven-year periods, although the number of spots appearing at the periods of maximum spottedness varies greatly. From this graph may be obtained the "Wolf Sunspot Number," by adding to the number of spots a figure obtained by multiplying the groups by ten.

are confident that sunspots have no immediate major effect on earthly conditions.

There was no public excitement or fear, as there might have been in past ages, when in the closing months of 1933 a new cycle of sunspots was born. The spottedness of the sun was at a low ebb. A minimum was approaching. The old cycle of sunspots had nearly run its course. Then, on October 10th, Mt. Wilson Observatory astronomers saw on the sun's face the first of a new family of spots, the leader in a new cycle of spots that will last nearly eleven years. Others followed shortly, mingled with stragglers of the old cycle.

Sunspots are gigantic disturbances in the luminous layer or photosphere of the sun. The dark central part or umbra of spots varies in diameter from 500 miles to some 50,000 miles. The earth could be lost in the swirl of the larger spots. The German astronomer, Schwabe, in 1843 first discovered that the number of spots varies greatly in different years and shows an approximately regular periodicity of about eleven years. Dr. George E. Hale, now director emeritus of Mt. Wilson Observatory, discovered that when the sunspots appear in pairs the leading spot is opposite in magnetic polarity from the following spot. The spots in the northern hemisphere of the sun are also opposite in sign from the analogous spots in the southern hemisphere. He also found that the sun is a giant magnet much like the earth in this respect.

At the beginning of a new sunspot cycle, the spots appear in high latitudes and the magnetic polarity characteristic of each hemisphere is reversed, and in this way astronomers now know that a new cycle is about to begin. The appearance of the new cycle spot did not mean that the exact time of sunspot minimum had arrived, as the first spots of a new cycle often appear a month or two before the exact time of minimum.

Sunspots and Radio

THE SUNSPOT MINIMUM carries special significance for the radio fan. Observations by Dr. Harlan T. Stetson, director

ECLIPSE

THIS magnificent photograph of the eclipse of August 31, 1932, which shows the corona extending hundreds of thousands of miles from the sun's surface, was one of the few successful pictures taken on that day. Many observers experienced cloudy weather.

80-INCH TELE-SCOPE

WORK is going forward on this giant reflecting telescope to be erected in the Davis Mountains, Texas. When completed it will be exceeded in size only by the present 100-inch glass at Mt. Wilson, and the monster 200-inch mirror for the California Institute of Technology, which has been cast but which will take years to finish.

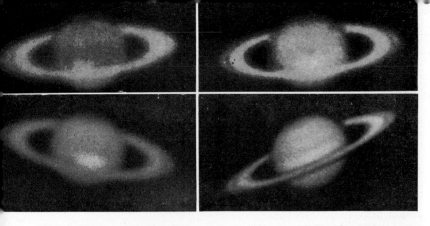

SATURN'S SPOT

Courtesy of Lick and Lowell Observatories

FOUR pictures of the great ringed planet taken under different conditions. The picture at the lower right shows the equatorial belt as it usually appears. The one at the lower left shows the spot, so large that it could engulf the earth, as it was seen soon after its discovery in early August, 1933. Only twice before have such spots been seen, once in 1876 and again in 1903. Just why they occur is unknown, although the planet being very cold (perhaps 290 degrees below zero) and not dense (one eighth that of the earth or seven tenths that of water), the spot may be a gigantic whirl on the equatorial belt. The spot was about 20,000 miles long and 12,000 miles wide. The picture at the upper left was made by violet light, and the one at the upper right by yellow light. The spots are principally useful in determining the rate of the planet's rotation.

DEAD NEBULAE?

THESE photographs by the late Dr. E. E. Barnard tend to prove that dark matter exists in space, blotting out the stars. This matter may be nebulæ of dead material. Note the winding trail in the photograph at the lower left.

STRATOSPHERE CLOUDS

THESE "mother of pearl" clouds exist in the stratosphere fifteen to nineteen miles above the earth. Discovered and photographed by a Norwegian, Prof. C. Störmer, they are twice as high as any clouds heretofore known.

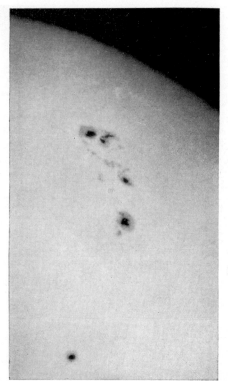

Courtesy of U. S. Naval Observatory

SUNSPOTS

THESE spots appeared on the sun when little expected, near the minimum of the sunspot cycle. They may have disturbed radio reception. When it is known why these spots act as magnets, one of science's great mysteries will be explained.

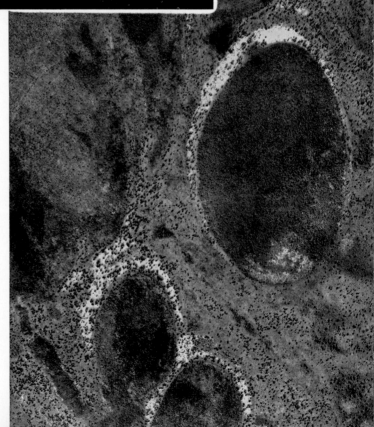

© Brown

FIREBALL

A RARE photograph, perhaps the only one ever taken, of a great fireball plunging earthward in March, 1933. The ball was visible to many in seven states of the southwest, as a New Mexico rancher, Charles M. Brown, snapped his camera. Parts of the meteor were found.

COMET'S SCARS?

AN AREA of 40,000 square miles along the south Atlantic coast is pockmarked with large elliptical depressions, known locally as "bays." Some scientists say they were made when a comet, larger than Halley's, struck the earth in pre-Ice Age days. Others doubt the cometary origin theory, and believe the "bays" are the result of wind and wave action.

of the Perkins Observatory, showed that radio broadcast field intensities as received in Ohio from a Chicago station during the last two years of feeble sunspottedness remained consistently at the highest level since the sunspot maximum in 1928–29. The few spots that occasionally appeared during the period of sunspot minimum had a comparatively small effect on the radio as compared with the effect produced by the terrific solar cyclones which raged on the sun four and five years before. Long-distance reception in the broadcast band had never been better than in 1932 and 1933 since the advent of broadcasting. Contrary to popular belief, however, this has not all been due to improvements in radio technique nor the increased power in broadcasting stations. The fifty-fold increase in intensity can without doubt be attributed to quieting activity in the solar disturbances which are chiefly responsible for the ionization of the Kennelly-Heaviside layer.

The rise in the ionized layer during 1932–33 which has been responsible for the excellent long-distance reception has, however, had a somewhat disquieting effect on those who listen to programs thirty or forty miles from a broadcasting station, for the sky wave has come through so well as to interfere with the ground wave at these critical distances, thus producing interference and mushiness in receiving sets within this critical area. With the beginning of the new sunspot cycle long-distance reception during the next few years will deteriorate, but the disturbing factors in local areas should become less troublesome. Radio fans therefore may expect to be compensated for their lack of DX reception by much improvement in the shorter range.

Sunspots and Heat

MORE IMPORTANT than the sunspots in effect on the earth are the changes in the sun's heat or the solar constant which has been the subject of study by Dr. Abbot, secretary of the Smithsonian Institution for many years.

The "weather" forecast for the sun is: Colder for 1934 and 1935. The long-range forecast of the variations of the sun's radiation made by Dr. Abbot is "solar radiation gen-

erally below normal." This is not a forecast of earthly
weather. Dr. Abbot emphatically stated that weather is
much more complex than variation of solar radiation
"owing to circumstances of mountains, deserts, vegetation,
oceans, ocean currents, snow, clouds, humidity, wind which
affect localities differently." Yet he is firmly persuaded that
the main part of the departures from normal monthly
mean temperatures at many localities is produced by the
seven periodic variations of the sun. These are intricately
woven periodicities of 7-, 8-, 11-, 21-, 25-, 45-, and 68-
month periods which he discovered as the result of observations and calculations extended over many years.

The most sensitive heat measurer known, the kampometer, was invented by Dr. Abbot, and it will aid scientists
in determining the amount of heat from the sun, from distant stars, from planets, and from feeble sources of heat
here on earth. Its sensitivity exceeds the thermopile, the
bolometer, and the radiometer, from which it differs in principle. It utilizes with great refinement the unequal expansion
with heat of two metals which allows the household thermo-
stat to operate, and magnetic fields are applied to give
control and sensitivity to the mechanism. Because he observed that a galvanometer he was using twenty-five years
ago deflected when sunlight fell upon it due to being twisted
slightly by the warmth, Dr. Abbot was led to construct the
kampometer.

While it is the heat that arrives from the sun at the
surface of the earth that affects our daily lives, astronomers
desire greatly to know how hot is the sun. Sir Arthur Eddington, the British astronomer, calculates the temperature
of the sun as an average of 12 million degrees, and a maximum of 21 million degrees Centigrade. These high temperatures represent a reduction from the 1924 Eddington
estimate, which was 40 million degrees Centigrade.

Sir Arthur considers that it is possible that the sun consists of as much as 99.5 per cent hydrogen but that a content of 35 per cent is more probable. The recognition that
a large proportion of hydrogen exists in the sun and stars
is considered by Sir Arthur to be the most important advance in stellar theory in seven years.

The Eclipse

ASTRONOMERS often travel halfway around the earth when their calculations show that the moon will completely cover the disk of the sun for a few fleeting minutes. Only during such a total solar eclipse can the sun's corona and other faintly illuminated outer portions be observed. There was only one suitable place from which the "paradox" eclipse of Feb. 14–13, 1934, could be observed conveniently. This was Losap Island in the Pacific, an island mandated to the Japanese. To it many Japanese and two Americans carried their instruments and made successful observations. According to local times, the eclipse ended the day before it began, due to the fact that the moon's shadow rushing over the sea crossed the international date line and lost a day.

One of the astronomical puzzles for many years has been the hypothetical element coronium. In 1869, when a solar eclipse path crossed the United States, green lines in the spectrum of the sun's outer envelope caused astronomers to assume an unknown element and name it after the sun's corona. Dr. D. H. Menzel, of Harvard Observatory, and Dr. J. C. Boyce, of the Massachusetts Institute of Technology, have made the first important step in unraveling this astronomical mystery that has existed since the first observations of the coronal spectrum more than sixty years ago. Their analysis identifies three of the five strongest coronal lines with neutral oxygen atoms in the high solar atmosphere. These atoms are in very peculiar states of excitation.

Thus the life-supporting gas in the earth's atmosphere promises to explain another of the mysteries of the heavens. For oxygen has heretofore been shown to be the cause of light from far-off nebulæ and from the aurora or northern lights of the earth's atmosphere. The light of the gaseous nebulæ was long attributed to the hypothetical element nebulium. A few years ago the nebulium mystery was solved by finding that highly ionized oxygen and nitrogen were largely responsible for the radiation. In recent years the mysterious light of the aurora has also been assigned to oxygen. By matching the spectral lines of light from the sun, stars, and other otherwise inaccessible sources, with those from known elements, scientists have been able to prove the existence of various earthly substances in other parts of the universe. Helium, which is now rated as a useful and fairly available elemental gas, was discovered in the sun's chromosphere during the eclipse of 1868 as a bright yellow line. Not until 1895 was it discovered here on earth chemically.

The solution of the mystery of coronal radiation was assisted greatly by the discovery at Mt. Wilson Observatory that the famous Nova Ophiuchi, which became brighter than ever before in August, 1933, showed coronal lines at one stage of its explosive outburst.

Life on Other Planets

As WE CONTEMPLATE the plan of the solar system or gaze upon a planet in the sky, we may well wonder if there is life existing upon the other planets. The probability seems to be that man is the solar system's Robinson Crusoe. The other worlds that circle around the sun will never offer him any neighbors. Even Venus, the planet most like the earth, probably has no human life on it. The verdict of Dr. Walter S. Adams, director of the Mt. Wilson Observatory, is:

"It is impossible to state definitely that life has not developed on Venus, but it is very unlikely, and the case against Mars is much stronger."

Chemical conditions of the planetary atmospheres, together with temperatures conditioned by their distances from the sun, all militate against the possibility of life as we know it on any of them. Mercury, the planet nearest the sun, and also the smallest of all the planets, is too small and too hot to hold any atmosphere at all. It reaches temperatures of 600 degrees Fahrenheit.

At the other extreme of the solar system, the large outer planets, Jupiter, Saturn, Uranus, and Neptune, with the recently discovered smaller planet Pluto, have temperatures far below zero, which alone would preclude life as we know it. Their great masses give them force of gravity to hold thick and dense atmospheric blankets, which include gases rare or unknown in the earth's atmosphere. The earth long ago lost most of its hydrogen, for example, but Dr. Adams thinks it likely that the great outer planets have retained this gas. He has also detected the poisonous gas ammonia as a fairly abundant constituent of their atmospheres. But oxygen, absolutely essential to the maintenance of life, he has not found on any of them.

Mars and Venus, our nearest planetary neighbors, are especially well situated for observation. But Mars is so small, and its force of gravity so weak, that its atmosphere is very thin. It has white polar caps, indicating the presence of water; but so far the Mt. Wilson studies have not indicated the existence of any free oxygen, not even a tenth of a percent. of that in the earth's atmosphere. Venus has neither oxygen nor water above the dense clouds that hide its surface. It does have carbon dioxide in abundance.

Dr. V. M. Slipher, director of the Lowell Observatory at Flagstaff, Ariz., is more optimistic about the planet Mars:

"Of all the planets the conditions for life as we know it are most promising on Mars. In thinking of such life we are apt to judge too narrowly by our experiences on earth. We are too prone to think of earth conditions as the ideal and to forget that the wide adaptability of life to its environment largely makes it seem so. What has come to the earth may come to another planet in our system, or even in other systems. However this may be, we must be impressed with the fact that our solar family is a beautiful and wonderful system of bodies; so much so that if it were not a living example before us we would say it could not long exist. Yet it goes on now as it did a few hundred million years ago, as we know from the fossilized remains of life existing then, and so we may rest assured that there is not much accident involved in the past or to be expected in the future. In the face of such a wonderful example of a purposeful guiding power, how can we be satisfied to think that life is an accident, and not an intended part of the whole plan?"

Small Fry of the Heavens

THE SMALL FRY of the universe from time to time provide entertainment for those of us who do not have access to telescopes. It is always good sport to go meteor hunting on a moonless, clear night out in the country away from the lights that blind stargazers. A few shooting stars per hour can always be bagged, and occasionally, if one is lucky, a bright fireball may be seen. These vagrant fragments of metal and stone that plunge into the earth's atmosphere to burn from the friction they encounter are the earth's only imports. Most of them are so minute that they are consumed before they reach the earth's surface. The Perseid meteor shower of August and the Leonid shower of November can usually be counted upon to give a good show, and because they are fragments of old comets and travel in its orbit they can be predicted with some assurance.

There were two outstanding meteor events recently. A great meteor shower that was seen from Europe on the night of October 9, 1933, for a period of four hours, seems destined to be remembered as one of the major meteoric displays of all history. And a meteor that lighted three states of southwestern United States on the morning of March 24th was a striking phenomenon.

What the March 24th meteor looked like can best be told in the words of Dr. John Strong, physicist of the California Institute of Technology, who happened to view it from a speeding railroad train:

"The meteor appeared like a rocket, and it seemed to come from the earth. Its trajectory was slightly arched and it was visible about five seconds. The first light was more intense than daylight, and it lighted up three states. The meteor seemed to wobble, leaving a luminous tail about two degrees long. [The full moon is half a degree in diameter.] The meteor and tail appeared like a rocket of burning magnesium with red streamers of granular material. At the end of the trajectory overhead the meteor forked and turned red and then was no longer visible. The cloud of smoke about a fourth of a degree wide was luminous as if a searchlight were trained on it. The smoke column broke into four or five segments which rotated ten degrees and coalesced to form a striated cloud. Highest segment remained isolated. The cloud was brightly illuminated with fringes appearing alternately rich blue, then white. The isolated segment emitted brown light. The meteor was first noticed at 5:05 A. M. when the train was at Springer, New Mexico. The sun rose at about 6 A. M. when the train I was on was at Wagon Mound. At 6:15 A. M. the cloud was still visible but somewhat diffuse. The meteor trajectory was 30 degrees from normal to the railroad track at Springer. The cloud remained at about 30 degrees elevation. The meteor appeared as large as a basket ball a fourth of a mile away. The porter of the car claimed he heard a hissing noise a few minutes after the meteor was seen."

America missed the great October 9th meteor shower because when it was at its peak at 8 P. M. Greenwich time, it was still daylight in the western hemisphere. Those who saw the storm of shooting stars witnessed a display that surpassed in brilliance the famous showers of 1833 and 1866. It was associated with a minor periodic comet that otherwise made no real stir in the astronomical world. This Giacobini-Zinner comet was seen in April, 1933, from Hamburg Observatory on its regular visit to this part of the solar system. It was very faint and within sight of only large telescopes. It was discovered in 1900, rediscovered in 1913, and was observed again in 1926. The earth was rushing through space only 370,000 miles away from the orbit of the comet when the extraordinary meteor display was seen. Small fragments traveling close to the comet's path burned with flashes in the earth's air. The extent of the display was quite unexpected, although a watch had been set in England for a minor stream of meteors that was known to be connected with the comet.

"Two hundred meteors in two minutes, and then counting became impossible," eyewitnesses reported. "The fire-stars became as thick as flakes in a snowstorm. . . . They came in flocks and gusts. . . . The sky was thick with them wherever one looked. . . . At one time as many as 100 might have been seen in any five seconds of time. . . . Literally thousands of meteors. . . . Fully 500 meteors per minute were to be seen. . . . Quite impossible to count them. . . . You could even see them through the clouds." From Odessa to Belfast such sights were seen.

Seldom in recent years has a comet made such a disturbance. Comets, those single-trip or periodic visitors to the vicinity of the sun, have been unusually demure. None has become visible to the unaided eye.

Meanwhile the earth continues to revolve on its axis day after day. The astronomer knows that these revolutions of this earth are becoming slower. Not that it will affect practically the lengths of the nights and days of those of us now living. Millions and millions of years in the future this older earth will take a longer time in turning around, there will be fewer days in the journey of the earth around the sun which defines the year, and twenty-four hours will stretch out longer than is now the case. According to the theory of tidal evolution formulated over half a century ago by Sir George Darwin, the earth's rotation is being gradually retarded by tidal friction.

Dr. Josef J. Johnson, of the department of astrophysics of the California Institute of Technology, has looked into the matter of what will happen to the relative lengths of day and month. Eventually, hundreds of millions of years hence, the day and the month will become of equal length. The earth will present always the same hemisphere toward the moon, as even today the moon presents one side continuously to the earth. The two bodies will revolve as though attached to the opposite ends of a rigid rod. Solar tidal friction, continuing to act, would make the day longer and longer, while the month would become shorter and shorter, due to the gradual dissipation of what is called the angular momentum of the system.

If this continued, eventually the month would be much shorter than the day, a relationship which now obtains between the period of rotation of Mars and the period of revolution of Phobos, its innermost satellite. The inhabitants of the earth, if any, would see the moon rise in the west, go through its various phases, and set in the east. But Dr. Johnson concludes that the day can never become longer than the month. Present-day knowledge of the earth's interior leads him to the conclusion that the "rigid-bar" situation will continue indefinitely. Tidal forces will raise a permanent tide in the body of the earth which will forever after keep the day "in step" with the month.

Half the earth will never see the moon, and the other half will always have the moon in its sky. Astronomy does not go so far as to say how that will affect the poetry of that distant day.

CHAPTER 3
THE COSMIC RAY MYSTERY

Cosmic rays bombard the earth from outer space every second of the day and night. They penetrate everything including our own bodies. They carry the mightiest packet of energy yet known to science. They give rise to bursts of material particles.

Yet cosmic rays constitute one of the great mysteries. Years of research have piled up experimental facts. Theories have been spun and debated. We are not sure whether they are particles of matter or super X-rays. We are ignorant of where they originate and what cosmic process is their progenitor. We who are their unknowing targets do not know whether they harm or benefit us, promote disease or bring health, or merely leave us untouched. They are unseen and undetectable with all but special instruments.

For thirty years physicists have known of a penetrating radiation that caused electricity to leak away from electroscopes containing two ribbons of gold or fibers of quartz which repel each other under the influence of an electric charge. Since 1925, when Millikan's researches pushed cosmic rays into the front rank of physics, the quest has been unceasing and world-spread.

Outstanding have been the surveys by Dr. R. A. Millikan and Dr. Arthur H. Compton, both Nobelists, both marshaling corps of physicists, both receiving financial support from Carnegie funds. Millikan's California Institute of Technology studies have probed atmosphere heights, plumbed lake depths, and captured cosmic rays in the laboratory. Millikan himself has toted heavy instruments to mountain tops, traveled to the far North and the tropic South, and flung marvelously ingenious balloon-lifted electroscopes to the stratosphere. Compton, from his University of Chicago base, traveled 50,000 miles, sailed many seas, and trod many continents measuring cosmic rays in 1932. Associates have covered the world collecting records and more records.

Theories Add Zest

THE COMPETITION of theories has added zest to the chase after the cosmic rays. Most diverse are the ideas about the nature of the radiation. Earliest was the photon theory, the idea that the cosmic rays are immensely powerful, short wavelength radiations of the same family as light and X-rays. It was natural after experience with X-rays and radium's gamma rays to consider cosmic rays as superradiation of the same kind. Dr. Millikan at first took this viewpoint. But because radioactive elements also give off speedy electrons and alpha particles, it was also logical to think of some of the cosmic rays as speedy particles of high energy. This is a second theory, upheld by Dr. Compton. It may take years of lively and profitable discussion and experimentation to bring in a verdict.

While interpretations may differ, there is considerable agreement in the experimental data gathered by the several investigators using different methods of detection and observing from various parts of the earth. For instance, Dr. Millikan's delicate instruments borne aloft by airplanes showed that cosmic rays increase in intensity less rapidly with elevation near the equator than in high latitudes such as in the United States. Dr. Compton's experiments on high mountain peaks in this country and in South America in the tropics showed the same effect. Dr. Millikan and Dr. Compton both agree that their experiments can be interpreted by assuming that both photons and particle rays, some of them perhaps positrons, are present in the incoming beam. Thus there is considerable agreement in interpretation as well as experiment. But the agreement is by no means complete.

As to what causes the discharging of the sensitive electrical instruments used in detecting the effects of cosmic radiation, Drs. Compton and Millikan also agree. Very energetic electrified particles produce the effect. Whereas Dr. Compton considers them the original rays, Dr. Millikan believes they are secondary radiation produced by photons smashing into the hearts of atoms. Dr. Compton suggests, on the contrary, that particle cosmic rays produce photons in the earth's atmosphere just as electrons striking an X-ray tube target produce X-rays.

Evidence that cosmic rays vary in intensity with latitude under the influence of the magnetic field of the earth was found by Dr. J. Clay, Dutch physicist, and by Dr. Compton. Cosmic rays are stronger near the magnetic poles than at the equator. Dr. Compton's survey shows that at sea level, the difference between intensity at latitude 45 degrees and the equator is roughly 16 per cent, whereas at elevation 9,000 feet the difference is about 23 per cent. Dr. Millikan and Dr. Victor Neher have also found this effect. Why cosmic rays bombard the earth less energetically near the equator was given theoretical explanation by Prof C. Störmer of the University of Oslo, by Abbé Lemaître, and Prof. M. S. Vallarta of Massachusetts Institute of Technology. Using the idea that cosmic rays are particles and are affected by the magnetism of the earth just as electrons from the sun cause the aurora in polar regions where magnetism is strong, Lemaître evolved a mathematical theory that shows that electrons of 10,000 million volts cannot reach the earth's surface at the equator. The great earth-magnet changes the paths of electrified particles in such a way as to produce lower intensities at the equator than at the two poles of the earth.

The idea that cosmic rays are the hearts of atoms of ordinary matter, principally hydrogen, positively charged by the action of starlight on interstellar gas, and accelerated in some cosmic electric field, resulted from over ten thousand observations of cosmic ray intensities in Panama, Peru, Mexico, and this country by Dr. Thomas H. Johnson, of the Bartol Research Foundation, physicist and Carnegie Institution associate. Using a sort of cosmic ray "telescope" that "sees" on a motion-picture film only the cosmic rays that pass through three Geiger-Mueller counting devices in a line, and set off in them simultaneous electrical pulses,

Dr. Johnson established that the western sky is "brighter" with cosmic rays than the eastern sky. This difference in cosmic ray brightness between the east and west is also greater at higher elevations and the closer the observer goes to the magnetic equator. That some of the cosmic rays are particles, positively charged, follows from this observation of the way the earth's magnetic field bends their paths.

This effect was predicted in 1931 by Prof. B. Rossi of Italy, although his experiments failed to show it. Dr. Johnson first found in 1932 evidence for a greater western intensity on the top of Mt. Washington, N. H., and then in 1933 more evidence was found by Dr. Johnson and L. Alvarez of the University of Chicago, working independently in Mexico City. Later Prof. Rossi as well as Dr. Johnson got confirming results from experiments nearer the equator.

Hundred Billion Volt Wallops

NO OTHER RADIATION "packs such a wallop" as cosmic rays. Compared with other energies here on earth, they rate thousands and millions of times as powerful. Cosmic ray energies seem to lie between 100 million and more than 100 billion volts. It is not possible to be any too definite and positive, because estimates necessarily change with additional experiments. Comprehension becomes difficult when energies reach billions of volts. The highest electrical pressure on high-tension power lines is 240,000 volts. The peak of artificial electricity production for experimental purposes is 10 million volts. Lightning is rated at about 1 billion volts.

The immense energies of the cosmic rays discourage the hopes of scientists that artificial cosmic radiation can be produced. Dr. Millikan estimated in his early work that some cosmic rays had energies of the order of 10 million volts, and it is understandable that plans were then being laid to make synthetic cosmic radiation. Those aspirations vanished with the increasing realization of the high energies involved.

Dr. Anderson's cloud chamber at California Institute of

Technology in which the positron was discovered (Chapter 5) has furnished much information about cosmic-ray energies. He found that some positrons are born of cosmic rays smashing into matter. The cosmic-ray energies deduced from the tracks left in the Anderson cloud chamber range from 100 million to 3 billion volts. The Lemaître-Vallarta theory, together with Dr. Johnson's asymmetry measurements, gives definite values for the energy of half of the cosmic radiation, and shows it continuously distributed between 5 billion and 50 billion volts.

The figure of 100 billion volts is a result of Dr. W. Kolhörster's measurement of penetrating radiation in the depths of the Strassfurt salt mines. He found that the minimum energy of these rays, which are a very small part of the total, is such that they can plow through the equivalent of a half mile of water, a penetration which is greater than ever before demonstrated. Dr. Axel Corlin of Sweden's Lund Observatory found radiation that still had energy after passing through somewhat greater equivalent depths and therefore the voltage figures can be made even higher. And energies of 100 billion volts or more are indicated by the great bursts set off by cosmic-ray collisions, called stösse, which have been observed particularly in Germany.

What messages are these penetrating cosmic rays bringing to earth? Whence do they come, and what clues do they give us as to happenings in other parts of the universe? There are many scientific guesses as to the origin.

Since our nearest star, the sun, has such a powerful energetic influence on the earth, it would be but natural to look to it as the originator of cosmic rays. But a cosmic or at least an interstellar origin of cosmic radiation is supported by the absence of any large or regular effect of the sun on cosmic rays. If the sun or Milky Way were responsible for any considerable portion, the intensity would rise and fall according to the position of one or the other. No measurable effect of this character has been found.

"Birth cries" of atom building in the depths of the universe. That was Dr. Millikan's suggestion as to the cosmic rays. The lower energies correspond to those which would be released in the manufacture of heavier atoms out of hydrogen. Dr. Millikan visualized a clustering of atoms into cosmic-ray dust in space's depths and then an occasional sudden formation of helium atoms, oxygen atoms, an iron atom or even a uranium atom, releasing in these atomic syntheses the penetrating radiations that seem to pervade all space.

Atomic mass measurements show that, if helium is made from hydrogen, 27 million volts of energy are released. For oxygen, iron, and uranium formation, the energy releases are figured at 100 million and 500 million and 2 billion volts, respectively.

Since some of the cosmic rays have energies of over 2,000 million volt-electrons, Dr. Millikan suggests the synthesis of highly unstable and transitory elements heavier than uranium, the heaviest discovered, but that these elements then disintegrate radioactively into the kinds found in the stars and on earth. Thus Dr. Millikan sets up synthesis instead of annihilation as playing an important part in the universe, which is admittedly a happier prospect for those of us who would like to visualize the universe a going concern eons in the future.

Astronomers are now abandoning the idea that the heat energy of the sun and stars comes from annihilation of the mass of atoms and are beginning to favor the idea that natural upbuilding of atoms within stellar bodies keeps them shining. With the origin of cosmic rays similarly explained by interstellar catastrophic formation of atoms, synthesis instead of disintegration or annihilation would play a major rôle in the universe.

Theories of Origin

OF THE RADIANT ENERGY rushing about the universe, the cosmic rays, totally unknown a few decades ago, are by far the most important in Dr. Millikan's opinion. He deduces with astronomical estimates that the universe's total radiant energy in the form of cosmic rays is from 30 to 300 times greater than that existing in heat, light, and all other forms combined. Of the imports of energy received by the earth, the cosmic rays equal approximately one half the total energy coming in from the stars, excepting the sun.

Sir James Jeans, the British physicist, has an exactly opposite suggestion of cosmic-ray origin. He sees in cosmic rays the signals to earth of the annihilation of matter somewhere in the universe.

Cosmic rays are the superradioactive outpourings of a primordial atom which Abbé Lemaître considers formed the whole universe some ten thousand million years ago, before it began to expand. He suggests that the cosmic rays are a new kind of radiation, very energetic speedy hearts of heavy atoms such as oxygen and iron.

The sun is suggested as the place of origin of cosmic rays by Prof. Alexandre Dauvillier of Paris, who sees the possibility of electrons coming from the bright spots or faculæ on the sun, being speeded up by the outer atmosphere of the sun, and then being distributed on earth by its magnetic field.

Dr. Johnson believes that action of starlight on the small residue of gas in interstellar space produces the positive particles that he finds cosmic rays to be. These would be accelerated towards the earth and given their speeds in some hypothetical cosmic electric field.

Cosmic rays originate when a star explodes into a super nova, according to a theory of Drs. F. Zwicky and W. Baade of Pasadena. A nova is a star which suddenly flares up to many times its normal brightness. Such an event happened in 1933 to a star in the constellation Ophiuchus. These novæ ordinarily become about 20,000 times as bright as our sun, but occasionally they become enormously brighter, and then they are termed super novæ. Such a one appeared in Andromeda in 1885 and lasted about 25 days, giving off 100 million times as much visible light as our sun. A super nova, according to Dr. Zwicky, would give 10 million times as much ultraviolet light as visible. That means it would give off as much energy in one second as our sun does in 100 million years. With this tremendous supply it would not be surprising if a great deal of high-energy radiation such as cosmic radiation were included. This theory therefore indicates that the rays are intermittent, since such super novæ are rare. Dr. Zwicky estimates about one in a galaxy in a thousand years. This accounts for our failure to get any appreciable cosmic radiation from our own galaxy. It also explains other puzzles which other theories bring up. The main advantage is that the rays come mainly from extremely far distances—from stars beyond the powerful telescopes of the present time.

Obviously all of these theories are not correct, and it may be that the real explanation of the what and whence of cosmic rays will be hidden in cosmic depths for many more years. Even if today all the physicists of the world decided that a certain mechanism of origin best fitted the facts observed, tomorrow new facts or more plausible theory might upset the widely accepted ideas. There would be no sorrow, for that is the method of scientific progress. When science becomes so self-complacent that it cannot change its conclusions in the face of new evidence, it ceases to be science.

No one is trying to make money out of the cosmic rays. They seem far removed from the applications of science that remake so rapidly our material environment. Far more profitable to humanity than any fanciful practical utilization is the light that cosmic rays are throwing on the structure of matter and the universe. In the riddle of cosmic rays there may be a key to the greater mystery of the universe itself.

CHAPTER 4
WITHIN THE ATOM

IF SCIENTISTS were in the habit of arguing which scientific research is most important (they do not, since they are much too busy researching), there might be as many answers as there are scientific problems. Yet when due allowance is made for the enthusiasms that are generated by the many thrilling tasks of exploring nature, there might be fairly general agreement that the attacks upon the atom, the multiple inquiries into the constitution of matter and energy, are in a fundamental sense the most important.

The extent of the problem of the constitution of matter and energy is limited only by the universe itself. The secret of life is possibly a matter of atomic or molecular arrangement. Even life would not appear so important if we could view it with unprejudiced eyes, for, so far as we know, life is limited to a satellite of a merely average star which is one of millions in one galaxy out of millions in the universe. Cancer, which kills a small percentage among one of the thousands of forms of life on that satellite, is of minor universal interest, although it may be all-controlling in the destiny of an individual human being. The atomic constitution of gold is much more interesting to scientists than its man-made economic value as a base for monetary systems.

In the alchemical days of the Middle Ages, philosophers spent their lives trying to make gold out of base metals. Scientists do not now aspire to such selfish transmutation. Nevertheless, transmutation is frequent. Dozens of artificial transmutations are known. Natural transmutations are constantly in progress in radioactive elements. None is industrially useful because of new substances produced. Some of the energy released, as in the case of radium radiation, is utilized in medicine and the arts. High hopes of tapping

34

atomic energy are as yet unrealized. The greatest value of transmutations comes from the light they shed upon what is happening within the atom.

This twentieth century has seen an extraordinary development of ideas and experimental facts relating to the nature and constitution of matter and energy. The atom has evolved from a little hard ball which was considered the ultimate particle of matter into an entity so complex and multiplex that the best advice is not to try to visualize it. The components of atoms are at some times considered particles of matter and at other times, waves of energy. The picture of an atom as a heavy but minute kernel surrounded by circling bits of negative electricity—a nucleus of tightly packed protons and electrons surrounded by orbital electrons forming a miniature solar system with nucleus as sun and electrons as planets—has given way to a dim and indistinct mathematical entity that may best be visualized, if at all, as an equation.

Before it is possible to be surrounded by the intellectual mist that envelops the atom, the mind must project itself down the scale of size from the everyday world where things are measured in feet and inches to the submicroscopic realm of millimicrons. The human eye, aided by the most highly developed lens systems of super-microscopes, is limited by the wavelength of visible light. A bit of matter smaller than the shortest visible light wave cannot reflect the light and in that way notify the eye of its existence. The ultra-microscope, using an intense beam of light at right angles to a dark field, allows particles too small to be seen directly to send out a reflected radiance that serves to detect particles as small as 1/250th of the wavelength of the shortest visible light. These excursions into science's Lilliput land are far too superficial to expose the secrets of the atoms. An atom within a microbe is of about as little significance in point of size as an individual in a nation.

X-rays and, more recently, beams of electrons have been shown capable of revealing the atomic structure within the crystals that compose all matter. Diffraction spectra of X-rays produced by layers of atoms in crystals are used in the same manner as the rainbows of visible light that are produced by finely scored surfaces or gratings. Each chemical element flies its own spectral "flags" or rainbow-like lines, whether visible light or X-rays are used.

These fruitful excursions are proving to be of industrial as well as scientific value, but they do not probe within the atom and provide understanding of the ultimate structure of matter.

Smashing Atoms

WHAT WE KNOW of the atom's structure comes from the use of violent tactics. Atoms are exploded, pulled apart, smashed, and otherwise hammered by natural and artificial projectiles. The fragments that fly out give clues as to how the atoms are put together. Radiations that are emitted hint as to what transformations of mass and energy have taken place. As is so often the case in science, observations must be remote from the actual happening that is so far down the scale of measurement. The knowledge must be gained second or third or fourth hand. This does not mean that the knowledge is not correct and permissible; for the rules of testimony of courts of law do not apply.

Some atomic fragments or radiations can be allowed to perform a chemical change that will reveal them to the scientist. They are allowed to fall upon a photographic plate. Or some can be detected when they come in contact with a chemical substance that fluoresces, that is, in this case, changes invisible "light" into visible light. Many of the atomic particles reveal themselves by their electrical properties. They plunge through a water-vapor-laden chamber (Wilson cloud or expansion chamber) and, unseen themselves, leave wakes of tiny water droplets that clearly show their paths. They burst into a gas-filled vessel in which a carefully balanced electrical system is upset by the electrical stir they create. These radiation- and particle-detecting devices take their positions of usefulness alongside the older telescopes and microscopes.

Let us call the roll of the atomic particles that now hold the center of the stage of experimental physics. Some are new actors and some are old stagers. Here they are:

Electron: Unit of negative electricity, given off when anything becomes hot. Propelled from disintegrating radioactive substances with speed approaching that of light, electrons are called beta rays; propelled by high voltage they are called cathode rays.

Proton: Nucleus, kernel or heart of the hydrogen atom, unit of positive electricity, about 1,850 times as heavy as the electron.

Positron: Positive electron, a positively charged particle with mass of electron. Discovered 1932. (See Chapter 5.)

Neutron: Electrically neutral particle, which may be elementary building block, combined with positron to form a proton. Neutron discovered 1932. (See Chapter 5.)

Deuton: Nucleus of deuterium or heavy hydrogen (isotope mass two) atom, probably constituted of one proton and one neutron. Deuterium discovered 1931. (See Chapter 7.)

Alpha particle: Nucleus of helium atom, disintegration product of radioactive substances.

Positive ions: Nuclei or kernels of the various chemical elements. Protons and alpha particles are special kinds of positive ions. Streams of positive ions, propelled by high voltage, are called positive or canal rays.

The Family of the Elements

THERE ARE ninety-two different kinds of chemical elements, from the lightest, hydrogen, to the heaviest, uranium. All or nearly all of them are now discovered and the sequences and the relationships of their properties allowed Mendeleeff and Moseley and their successors to predict many of them before they were discovered. There is indication there may be elements heavier than uranium. (See Chapter 5.) Even in the assured ninety-two, simplicity turns into complexity under the close scrutiny of science. Just as the elements were being fitted neatly into their niches, it was discovered that nearly all of them are twins, or triplets, or quadruplets, and even more multiplex. These isotopes (remember this, for it will be a word much used in these chapters), as the varieties of the same element are called, have different masses although they are considered the same element. The whole numbers of atomic weights (when expressed in multiples of oxygen taken as 16) are taken as evidence that they are aggregations of the simpler fundamental particles used as building blocks. Some of these isotopes are so different from their companions of the same element that they are practically different elements. This is notably the case with mass one ordinary hydrogen and mass two heavy-weight hydrogen (deuterium). Exploration of the isotopes is progressing steadily, and rearrangements of ideas about them will undoubtedly be necessary with the acquisition of new knowledge.

Under the famous Einstein equivalence of mass and energy, which from the present viewpoint seems to have a very solid foundation of scientific truth, mass and energy are interchangeable. Experimentally demonstrated in atomic disintegrations and syntheses which so far are not practically important, the practical equivalence of mass and energy, tapping the energy of the atom, constitutes one of the great objectives of the physicist. For the present there is a rather sharp line of demarkation between matter and radiant energy, despite the theoretical equivalence.

Radiant energy is most familiar as visible light. So important is the rainbow of the spectrum from the long-wave red light to short-wave violet that it is sometimes difficult to realize that it occupies only a small portion of the broad range of radiant energy manifestations. On the long wave, or low frequency, side of visible light are heat, radio, and electrical waves, while on the short wave, or high frequency, side are X-rays, gamma rays, and cosmic rays. In the matter of atomic transformation, it is the short-wave radiation that plays the most prominent rôles.

In the conceptions and visualizations of the physicists, radiant energy as well as particles of matter often "double in brass." Light—and when physicists speak of light they often include magnanimously the whole range of the radiant energy spectrum—is often thought of as consisting of "gobs" or packets. The light is, to use a term of the newer physics, "quantized." The unit or corpuscle of light is the photon, not to be confused with proton, which is the nucleus of the hydrogen atom. Photon and proton are not likely to be confused except when spoken. This is true of neutron and deuton.

In the radiant energy repertoire of the physicist, whether you consider them electromagnetic waves or photon corpuscles, X-rays and gamma rays are historically older than cosmic rays from the standpoint of their discovery. Gamma rays, released spontaneously from exploding radioactive atoms like those of uranium and radium, are shorter in wavelength and more powerful than X-rays. But as more powerful X-ray tubes have been devised, the separation in the spectrum between X-rays and gamma rays promises to disappear. Cathode rays or streams of electrons flung at metal targets under the impulse of high voltages create X-radiations approaching in penetration the natural gamma radiation from radium, and one tube can provide a quantity of radiation which all the radium in the world could not equal. Man-made radiation cannot yet aspire to the high voltages of that portion of the cosmic rays bombarding the earth from outer space which consists of photons. Using cosmic rays as experimental tools in attacking the atom is, therefore, a matter of a watchful-waiting gamble which has nevertheless given profitable winnings.

Electron, proton, positron, neutron, deuton, alpha particle, ions, X-rays, gamma rays, and cosmic rays—these are concerned in the investigation of the atom and the inquiries into the nature of matter and energy.

The first intimation that the atom is not a "billiard ball" ultimate particle came when Becquerel in 1896 discovered radioactivity in uranium and when Pierre and Marie Curie in 1898 discovered radium. The whole complexion of physics began to change.

The discovery of radioactivity gave the physicists their first unquiet feeling that the laws of classical physics which had served them so well in the workaday world might not express the facts of that innermost frontier within the atom. The radioactive elements that sputtered alpha particles, beta particles, and gamma rays were seized upon as heavy artillery provided by nature to be used in unraveling her secrets of the atom. A young professor of physics at McGill University, Montreal, laid siege to other atoms using the products of radioactivity as ammunition. He was Ernest Rutherford, now, as Lord Rutherford of Nelson, the presiding genius of the famous Cavendish Laboratory at Cambridge University in England. First he decisively blasted the idea that the atom was solid stuff. Some of the alpha particles flung at atoms bounced back, and from a study of the speeds of their recoil he showed that the atom is mostly space with its weight concentrated in an almost infinitesimal bit, with its diameter about one one hundred thousandth of that of the atom itself.

Knocking H out of the Atom

THE ATOM was blasted in 1919 by Rutherford when he literally knocked H out of nitrogen. The H in this case stands for hydrogen.

This was the first artificial transmutation of matter, the first realization of the alchemical dream of changing one element into another. Just what happened? The atom of nitrogen weighing 14 on the usual scale of atomic weights was bombarded by a swift charged particle of helium weighing 4, which was shot out from a radioactive substance. It momentarily coalesced with it into a mass of atomic weight 18. Then this combination split into two entirely different substances, the hydrogen nucleus or a proton weighing 1 and an unusual type of oxygen atom that weighs 17. Only about one out of a million of Rutherford's alpha-particle projectiles scored hydrogen-producing hits.

The oxygen variety of mass 17 formed in this bombardment was a quite new kind of substance, for this oxygen isotope was undemonstrated in 1919. It was not to be identified until more than a decade later.

While economic history may count the year 1919 as worth remembering because of the signing of the Treaty of Versailles which formalized the ending of the World War, that year is much more likely to live in the memory of the generations to come as the year in which Rutherford smashed the atom.

The hydrogen that Rutherford knocked out of nitrogen by bombarding it with alpha particles from radioactive disintegrations gave fresh life to a century-old hypothesis. It is that hydrogen, lightest of the chemical elements, is the stuff out of which all of them are made. Rutherford's experiment gave belated fame to Dr. William Prout, early nineteenth-century Edinburgh physician, whose contention that hydrogen was a fundamental building block of the elements was considered the height of fancy by his contemporaries.

Rutherford also bombarded sodium, aluminum, phosphorus, and other light-weight atoms. Out of some when attacked by alpha particles came hydrogen. Other experimenters seized upon this method of causing one atom's convulsions to bring destruction to another. It became a favorite field of exploration in physics. This mode of transmutation is considered proved for 13 elements, all light-weights.

Proton and electron were enthroned as the two electrically opposite particles forming all atoms and therefore all matter. Just as kings and queens and their dynasties topple, particles and theories in physics do not always continue to hold dominion.

While the idea that everything consists of protons and electrons held sway, there lurked undiscovered other particles which were to be revealed only by a proper cooperation of theoretical and experimental development.

The new deal in physics that has been developing since the turn of the century was not born of brilliant experiments alone. Physical theory, written into existence by mathematical pencils of physicists who use scintillations of their brain cells rather than the radioactivity of atoms, has guided experimentation and explained the meaning of observed experimental facts.

The Atom's New Deal

THE NEW DEAL in atomic theory has even gone beyond the relativity ideas of Prof. Albert Einstein that created the widely heralded thought revolution of the few years following 1919.

Yet strangely enough the newer deal concerning the atom began in a large measure in the brain of Prof. Einstein when in 1905 he applied the quantum theory that Prof. Max Planck had introduced earlier.

The great names in physics of today are concerned with this "new deal" for atoms. Just as the Einstein relativity theories set lay and scientific heads to buzzing, so the development of theories about the nearly infinitesimal in science, which have culminated in what is known as the "quantum wave mechanics," involve delightful paradoxes that puzzle both lay and scientific minds.

This new quantum wave mechanics is so complex that even the simplest fundamental process cannot be pictured and is expressible only by means of mathematical symbols. But there are many paradoxes that are mentally intriguing if examined and discussed in an approximate and unmathematical way.

Present atomic theory really grew out of the admirable adaptation by Prof. Niels Bohr, Danish physicist, of the bare quantum theory postulates of the early twentieth century to the problem of atomic structure. The Bohr atom as further developed by Prof. Arnold Sommerfeld served the physicists as a working model with fair success until about 1925. Then the paradoxes became overwhelming. Something had to be done to the theory.

A group of young geniuses arose. The development began in Europe with Prof. Werner Heisenberg leading a new attack that in the hands of Prof. Max Born and Prof. P. Jordan led to the "matrix mechanics." Prince Louis de Broglie began an attack from the viewpoint of wave action that was carried on by Prof. E. Schroedinger to the "wave mechanics." Both were shown to be equivalent to one general scheme now christened the quantum mechanics.

The importance of theoretical research in shaping the revolution of the new physics is emphasized by Nobel prizes in physics that have been awarded for theory: Einstein, Bohr, De Broglie, Heisenberg, Dirac, Schroedinger.

The interplay of experiment and theory seems to have banished the proton, the heart of the hydrogen atom, to a subsidiary place among the building blocks of the universe. Science seems to have arrived at a trinity in the structure of matter, and the whole universe may be thought of as composed of three elementary particles, the well-established electron, and the two new particles, neutron and positron, which were discovered only a few months ago. As Dr. R. M. Langer first suggested, the proton is composed of a neutron and a positron. To this statement there should be appended the familiar warning of railroad time tables: Subject to change without notice.

HIGHLIGHTS IN ATTACK ON THE HEART OF MATTER
FIGURE 2

1816—All elements are made up of hydrogen atoms, William Prout suggested. ENGLAND

1871—The elements were arranged in order of the weights of their atoms by D. Mendeleeff and Lothar Meyer to form the periodic table. RUSSIA, GERMANY

1895—X-rays were discovered by W. K. Roentgen. GERMANY

1896—The nucleus of the element uranium gives off radio-active rays (alpha, beta, and gamma) that penetrate all materials, A. H. Becquerel found. FRANCE

1897—The negative electron which with the proton, the positive "electron" (or hydrogen atom core), makes up all atoms was discovered by J. J. Thomson. ENGLAND

1898—Radium, whose nucleus is constantly breaking up or disintegrating by emitting alpha and beta particles, was isolated by Pierre and Marie Curie. FRANCE

1900—Foundations of the quantum theory, which is based on the idea that energy is in lumps or quanta, were laid by Max Planck. GERMANY

1904–09—Alpha rays from radioactive substances are high-speed helium nuclei, it was shown by W. Ramsay, F. Soddy, E. Rutherford, and T. R. Boyds. ENGLAND

1911—The theory of the "nuclear" atom, holding that all the weight and the positive charge are concentrated in a small central nucleus, was proposed by E. Rutherford. ENGLAND

1911—The number of negative electrons on the outside of the atom was found by C. G. Barkla from a study of the scattering of X-rays. ENGLAND

1912—The possibility of isotopes; that is, that atoms of different nuclear weights might have exactly the same chemical properties, was suggested by F. Soddy. ENGLAND

1912—The rare gas neon actually has nuclei of two different weights, J. J. Thomson showed. ENGLAND

1913—Laws of atomic disintegration which tell how the nucleus changes in the radioactive breakdown of an element were discovered by F. Soddy, K. Fajans, and A. S. Russell. ENGLAND

1913—Niels Bohr announced his famous theory of the atom which combined Rutherford's "nuclear" atom with the ideas of the quantum theory and measurements of spectra. DENMARK

1914—How to locate an atom in the periodic table from a study of X-ray wave lengths was learned by H. Moseley. ENGLAND

1919—An element was transmuted artificially for the first time when E. Rutherford knocked the hydrogen nucleus out of nitrogen nuclei with fast alpha rays, which are speeding helium nuclei. ENGLAND

1919–32—Weights of the isotopes of most of the chemical elements were measured by F. W. Aston, who thus showed that Prout had been nearly right in thinking (in 1816) that the weight of any atom is an exact multiple of the weight of the hydrogen atom. ENGLAND

1922—Boron, fluorine, sodium, aluminum, and phosphorus were artificially disintegrated by E. Rutherford and J. C. Chadwick. ENGLAND

1925—The new quantum mechanics of the atom to replace Bohr's simple theory was set up by W. Heisenberg, E. Schroedinger, P. A. M. Dirac (England), P. Jordan, and Max Born.   GERMANY, ENGLAND

1929—A high wall of force was pictured by G. Gamow (Germany) and R. W. Gurney and E. U. Condon (United States) surrounding the atom nucleus and used to explain the law of radioactive decay. Gamow is a Soviet scientist.   GERMANY, UNITED STATES

1931—Energy of the nucleus, as well as that of the outer shell of the atom, is in lumps or quanta, J. C. Chadwick, J. E. R. Constable, and E. C. Pollard showed.   ENGLAND

1931—The table of atom nuclei was systematized, and unknown isotopes, some of which have since been found, were predicted by W. M. Latimer, H. C. Urey, H. L. Johnson, R. T. Birge, and D. H. Menzel.   UNITED STATES

1931-32—The existence of a double weight hydrogen isotope (deuterium) was shown by F. G. Brickwedde, H. C. Urey, G. M. Murphy, F. Allison, and W. Bleakney.   UNITED STATES

1931—Some atom nuclei appear to vibrate in step with an approaching alpha particle, H. Pose and G. Hoffman (Germany) and J. W. Ellis (United States).   GERMANY, UNITED STATES

1931—Theory of electron, predicting positron or "anti-electron," presented by P. A. M. Dirac.   ENGLAND

1932—Neutron, a neutral particle with mass of electron, is formed by bombardment of beryllium with alpha particles, J. Chadwick (England) discovered, following experiments by W. Bothe and H. Becker (Germany) and F. Joliot and Irene Curie-Joliot (Paris).
ENGLAND, GERMANY, FRANCE

1932—Mass was converted into energy when alpha particles were given off from lithium bombarded with protons accelerated by only 600,000 volts, J. D. Cockroft and E. T. S. Walton discovered.   ENGLAND

1932—Discovery of positive electron (positron) created by cosmic rays smashing into matter, by C. D. Anderson.   UNITED STATES

1933—Positrons are created artificially by bombardment of matter with gamma rays, J. Chadwick, P. M. S. Blackett, and G. Occhialini demonstrated.   ENGLAND

1932—Electron and the magnetic poles are the fundamental particles of matter, R. M. Langer suggested.   UNITED STATES

1933—Energies equivalent to 3 million volts used to accelerate atomic particle in E. O. Lawrence's whirligig atom gun.   UNITED STATES

1933—Electrostatic generator designed to produce 10 million volts for atomic research built by R. J. Van de Graaff.   UNITED STATES

1933—Million volt X-ray tube used in atomic experiments by C. C. Lauritsen.   UNITED STATES

1934—Artificial radioactivity produced by bombardment of boron, aluminum, and magnesium with alpha particles yielding positrons by F. Joliot and Irene Curie-Joliot.   FRANCE

CHAPTER 5
THE BIRTH OF NUCLEAR CHEMISTRY

THE EXPLORATION of the atom has progressed with such rapidity that physicists and chemists have been plunged into a new branch of knowledge. It is "nuclear chemistry."

This realm is one step farther toward that unattainable of the infinitesimal. Within it physics and chemistry blend, fuse, merge, and lose their separate identities. Atoms as a whole are too large to be dealt with.

It is no longer meaningful to apply the tags of "chemist" or "physicist" to the scientists who are pushing energetically at the new frontiers. The nucleist, to coin a name for the new kind of explorer, deals with the combination and dissociation of the ultimate particles which make up the hearts of atoms in the minute world of the nucleus.

No epic of geographical exploration, no rushing of airplanes or plodding of dog teams over polar wastes has been more spectacular than the pioneering within the nucleus. Let us focus our eyes through our minds upon that invisible but very real realm of the nucleus.

Without the tentative road maps or the preliminary blueprints drawn by the reasonings of theoretical physicists, it is probable that nucleists would have been much slower in recognizing and discovering neutrons, positrons, and some of the other newer manifestations of atomic particles. If theory evolved out of intricate mathematical relationships and computations had not suggested the existence of particles and energies unidentified, the experimentalists might not have been able to distinguish and demonstrate the existence of the neutron and the positron.

As it happened, two groups of experimenters actually produced quantities of neutrons as the result of atomic bombardment but did not recognize them.

About a dozen different light elements undergo transmutation when bombarded with alpha particles, giving off an atom of hydrogen, forming a new and heavier atom. Some elements resisted attempts at this transmutation, and the scientists concluded that for this reason certain elements do not have in their internal structure a charged atom of hydrogen. Theoretically, beryllium might have belonged to either one of these two classes, and it was therefore a particular object of bombardment.

Prof. W. Bothe and his colleague, Dr. H. Becker, in Germany, when they tried the experiment, found to their surprise that beryllium, when bombarded with alpha particles from polonium, gave off what seemed to be high energy electromagnetic waves similar to the gamma rays resulting from radioactivity. So highly penetrating was this radiation that they thought at first that in this reaction there might be an explanation of origin of the cosmic rays.

The investigation was continued in Paris by Mme Curie's daughter Irene and her husband Prof. F. Joliot, who observed that the new beryllium radiation could knock hydrogen out of paraffin wax and other hydrogen containing materials that were being used to measure the radiation's penetration. This was a strange action for gamma rays.

Neutron Discovered

THE RECOGNITION that a new particle was being studied came in Cambridge's Cavendish Laboratory. Dr. James Chadwick concluded that the beryllium radiation did not have a wavelike nature. It came into impact with atoms as though it were an energetic particle, and it did not travel with the speed of light, as it should have if it had consisted of gamma rays. His conclusion, substantiated by further experiment, was that the neutron had been discovered. It was an electrically neutral particle, which in itself was unique. Because it is electrically neutral, the neutron seems to have the ability to creep into places from which it would be barred by an electrical field.

Carbon, the element that forms diamonds and coal, is a

by-product of neutrons. Beryllium weighs nine, and helium weighs four. A neutron weighs one. Carbon weighs twelve. It is simple arithmetic.

At the time that the neutron was discovered (1932), the favorite idea of its constitution was that an electron and a proton came together, their electrical charges canceled each other, and a neutron was born. But that was before the discovery of the positron gave rise to the view that the neutron may itself be an ultimate particle.

Owing to the helpful habit of physicists imagining all sorts of theoretically possible combinations, the neutron was actually named before it was discovered. A dozen years before the discovery, the idea of an electron and a proton combining to form a neutral particle had been suggested by Rutherford in England and Dr. W. D. Harkins in America. Later Dr. R. M. Langer and Dr. N. Rosen in America recognized the usefulness of the neutron in explaining atomic structure.

The neutron immediately upon its discovery was seized upon as a very welcome tool to be used in prying open the atom. So long as neutrons could be produced only by natural alpha particles resulting from radioactivity, there was a limit to the quantity to be obtained. High voltage (Chapter 6) passed through helium gas was used to create artificial alpha particles in profusion.

The experiment of flinging artificial alpha particles at beryllium was first made (Jan., 1933) at the California Institute of Technology, Pasadena, Calif., by Drs. Charles C. Lauritsen, Richard Crane, and Andrew Soltan. Artificial production of neutrons in larger quantities than the world had hitherto known was achieved.

The artificial alpha rays were given a push of a half-million volts. The slow neutrons produced probably had under a million volts of energy, but they nevertheless could penetrate two inches of lead. This was the first time that neutrons had been produced without use of radioactivity. The neutrons were measured with a small electroscope about the size of a fountain pen, which was devised by Dr. Lauritsen. Paraffin was used as a detector, the neutrons, or electrically neutral particles, plunging into this substance and giving rise to radiation that affected the roentgenometer or small electroscope.

Later the full voltage of the Pasadena giant X-ray tube, one million volts, was used in speedng the helium hearts, and correspondingly more neutrons were produced. These slow-moving helium particles were thousands of times less efficient than radioactively produced helium particles in producing neutrons. But they were so numerous that more neutrons were obtained than could be had if all the radium in the world could have been concentrated into one place.

The next step toward greater supplies of neutrons came when the hearts of heavy-weight hydrogen or deuterium (Chapter 7), known as deutons, were flung at beryllium. This might be thought to be a backward step, since the deutons have a mass of two compared with the mass four of the helium nuclei. Prof. G. N. Lewis of the University of California supplied the heavy hydrogen, in the form of heavy water, necessary for the experiment.

Imagine the delighted astonishment of the Pasadena group, when they found that the deutons produced 500 times as many neutrons as the artificial alpha particles did.

At Berkeley, Calif., Prof. E. O. Lawrence and his colleagues, Drs. M. Stanley Livingston and Malcolm C. Henderson, discovered the same effect. A deuton propelled at 3 million volts against the beryllium atom apparently penetrates its nucleus and turns it into boron. In its exuberance the newly born isotope 10 boron nucleus kicks out a neutron with ten million volts energy.

It was but natural that the nucleists tried their deutons on other elements. Lithium yielded neutrons even more copiously than beryllium, with helium as the one by-product. The heavy atoms did not react in just the same way. But the result was even more interesting.

Prof. Lawrence and his collaborators speeded deutons at 3 million volts in their whirligig atom-gun. They were the most energetic particles thus far produced by artificial means and controlled by men. These deuton atomic bullets were allowed to bombard targets of platinum, brass, wax, and many other substances. Disaster was the result of these collisions between the deuton bullets and the target atom hearts. The fragments of these atomic explosions flying out were caught and measured. One kind of fragments, protons, flew out with a speed of 5,400,000 volts. As this is 2,400,000 volts more than the deuton bullet speed, small amounts of highly concentrated energy must have been released. The companion fragments to protons were neutrons, with an energy of 2,400,000 volts.

Prof. Lawrence and his co-workers have boosted the efficiency of atomic disintegration many thousands of times during the past two years. They report that one deuton in ten thousand, striking beryllium and lithium, gives rise to a neutron and possibly 5 million volts. The scientific significance of this high yield is much more important than its possible practical application.

It will be remembered that when the two Germans, Drs. Bothe and Becker, generated neutrons and did not recognize them, thus missing the honor of being the neutron's discoverers, they thought the radiation created consisted of gamma rays such as come from radium. It turns out that they were half right after all, for mixed with the neutrons that are emitted is some gamma radiation. At Pasadena it was found that the number of gamma rays that were generated when beryllium was bombarded with deutons was about equal to the number of neutrons produced at the same time.

With a plentiful source of neutrons provided, the next problem is what to do with them. The future will answer the question, probably with many surprises. The continuation of the attack upon the constitution of matter will come first. With plenty of controllable neutrons that because of electrical neutrality are able to insinuate themselves into the hearts of atoms, the scientists will undoubtedly make even faster progress than they have in the past few years, productive as they have been.

Unlike X-rays, neutrons are stopped by light element and material that is not dense. The most effective protection against neutrons is not thick plates of lead but water or paraffin. The denser a material, the more deeply the neutrons penetrate. For instance, a 200,000-volt X-ray is stopped by one quarter of an inch of lead, but some of the neutrons generated by Prof. Lawrence's apparatus will filter through 12 inches of lead.

What Good Is a Neutron?

WE MAY EXPECT to hear that the biologists have seized upon neutrons to determine their effects upon living matter. Although neutrons are not the same kind of radiation as X-rays or radium's gamma rays, they probably would have profound effects on living organisms. It seems strange, but neutron rays due to their ability to penetrate dense material more deeply will pass through bone more easily than through flesh. Will they affect cancer cells differently from normal cells? Will they change the constitution of germ plasm as X-rays do, having an influence upon heredity? Will they some day be a therapeutic agent used by physicians in treating or diagnosing human ills?

One of the achievements of the neutron, which came shortly after its discovery, was the smashing of oxygen. Dr. N. Feather, of the Cavendish Laboratory, showed through experiments performed in an oxygen-filled expansion chamber that oxygen is transformed by neutron bombardment with the emission of an alpha particle. Oxygen was one of the elements that resisted attacks by protons or alpha particles that were so successful upon other light elements. Neutron bombardment is the only method so far known for smashing it. Nitrogen also falls before the battering of the neutron, but nitrogen was the first element to be transmuted in Rutherford's famous pioneering attempts.

The neutron is a remarkable atomic particle. Dr. W. D. Harkins of the University of Chicago has pointed out that it can be considered an additional chemical element. Its atomic number would be zero, and he suggested that it be called "neuton" when considered in this rôle.

Like all of the fundamental types of matter called elements, Dr. Harkins considers neuton made up of atoms, but these possess a remarkable, previously unknown characteristic—that is, while they are like all other atoms in being electrically neutral, they are excessively small. They are so minute that more than a million times a million of these new atoms, or neutrons, could be contained in the volume of any ordinary atom and still leave some space which is not occupied. Since a neutron has about the mass of an ordinary atom, this means that its density is excessively high. If a lady's thimble could be filled with the neutrons in contact, the material in it would have a weight greater than that of all of the warships of all the navies of the earth.

This new material could neither be held in a thimble nor in a heavy, tightly sealed metal box, since it passes easily through any known material. Neutrons are so minute that they pass very readily through other atoms without producing any disturbance or indeed any noticeable effects.

The success in artificial production of neutrons recalls the first successful application of the high-voltage method of generating fast particles for producing atomic transmutations. This was the 1932 experiment of Drs. J. D. Cockcroft and E. T. S. Walton of the famous Cavendish Laboratory. It was remarkable also because of the relatively low voltage that was used. A steady potential of about 600,000 volts was used to accelerate a stream of protons upon a lithium-coated target. Alpha particles were given off. A lithium atom struck by a proton captured the hydrogen particle and then split into two alpha particles. From the principle of momentum, the alpha particles should fly off in nearly opposite directions, and this was found to be the case when the tracks of the alpha particles in an expansion chamber were photographed. The really exciting thing about this particular transmutation was the large amount of mass that was transformed into kinetic energy. The energy emitted was several hundred times as much as that possessed by the proton whose smashing brought about the reaction.

Some twenty-five times the number of helium atomic hearts were shot off from boron when this element was attacked by a stream of protons using the same voltage and technique that successfully transmuted lithium into helium with release of energy. This was shown in 1933 by Drs. Cockcroft and Walton. In this case the result was alpha particle triplets, the proton entering the boron nucleus of atomic mass 11 and the resulting nucleus splitting into three helium nuclei. By hydrogen bombardment also, fluorine was made to break up into oxygen and helium, and beryllium was changed into lithium and helium.

Repeating the Cockcroft-Walton lithium experiment, three German physicists at the Institute for Experimental Physics at Kiel showed that there were detectable atomic breakdowns at an input of only 29,000 volts, which is a twentieth of the potential used in the British experiments.

Because of the effectiveness of protons in effecting such atomic transmutations, a Massachusetts Institute of Technology discovery was important. It assured a more plentiful supply of atomic bullets of hydrogen for shooting at other atoms.

This source of protons devised by Drs. Edward S. Lamar and Overton Luhr was nine times as prolific as any previously known. It is an electric arc operating in hydrogen at low pressure between an incandescent filament and a neighboring metal electrode. Ordinarily such an arc would produce ions of which about 10 per cent would be protons and the remainder molecular ions. However, by surrounding the arc with a third electrode maintained at a negative potential of a few hundred volts, the percentage of protons produced is immediately increased to approximately 90 per cent.

Recalling the pioneer Rutherford atomic transmutation, Prof. Lawrence at Berkeley for the first time in history knocked H out of matter by artificial means. With his whirligig atom gun he maneuvered collisions between heavyweight atom hearts (deutons) and carbon atoms, with the result that protons or hydrogen hearts were ejected.

The Positron Is Born

DISCOVERIES in atomic science leave their trails of consequences that remind one of the tracks of water droplets that are formed about the ions left by the passage of charged corpuscles through the water-saturated space of a Wilson cloud chamber. The discovery of the neutron started one sequence. So also did the discovery that the familiar negative electron has a positive counterpart.

Electrons have been known and studied for some forty years, ever since Prof. J. J. Thomson (now Sir J. J. Thomson) showed that cathode rays consisted of negative charged particles far smaller than an atom. Dr. R. A. Millikan measured the negative electric charge on these electrons.

Electrons have proved to be nearly omnipresent. They are the stuff of electrical current. Metals are believed to be full of them. They are thought to be responsible for emission, absorption, and scattering of light. No atom could be complete without them. The electron is still, despite our changing ideas about ultimate, a fundamental particle.

In all these years of acquaintance with the negative corpuscle or electron, scientists felt very, very sure that there was no positively charged particle smaller than the proton, which was nearly two thousand times heavier. The first suggestion of a positive electron came from Prof. P. A. M. Dirac in 1931, when he put forth his theory of the electron. This prediction of a positive electron made scientists alert to the possibility of finding it in nature. But they did not know where to start to look for it.

The discovery was made in the course of experiments with cosmic rays at the California Institute of Technology. Dr. Carl D. Anderson had set up a Wilson expansion or cloud chamber on its side in such a way that cosmic rays might plow through the greatest possible length. He was photographing the long tracks that the cosmic ray particles leave behind them. An intense magnetic field was used to curve the particles and the amount of curvature gave an indication of the speed and energy with which they were traveling. This investigation was a part of the extensive program of cosmic ray research that Dr. R. A. Millikan had organized. It was not a search for the positive electron.

There was one feature of this expansion chamber, besides the intense magnetic field, that was unusual. Dr. Anderson placed a thin lead plate in it so that the cosmic rays and any particles that might shoot through the chamber would have something to try their energies upon. The Russian, Skobeltzyn, and others had previously watched and photographed cosmic ray cloud tracks, and Drs. Millikan and Anderson had adapted the method because of their hope that it would give information about the nature of cosmic rays.

In 1931 Dr. Anderson found that cosmic rays disrupt atoms of the air and other matter when they plunge earthward. He made photographs that showed particles, writing their paths in water droplets, curving in opposite directions under the magnetic influence, showing that they were oppositely charged with electricity. One such curving track was made, in a pioneer photograph, by an electron of 140 million volts energy. Another was made by a positive particle, which at that time Dr. Anderson guessed was a proton of about 70 million volts energy.

Here were projectiles of much higher power than physicists were in the habit of using in their researches. Here were transmutations on a grand scale of energies. Little wonder that young Anderson gambled harder than ever, risking the exposure of foot after foot of movie film in the hope of catching the atom smashing at exactly the right instant. Only the happenings during a fiftieth of a second could be caught at each try. Since the disrupting of atoms by cosmic rays does not happen every instant, many of the films were blank.

Then came August 2, 1932, and the making of the portrait of one of the most famous particles in all history. It left a water droplet trail five centimeters long even after it plunged through six millimeters of lead. Carefully checking its curvature, inspecting the texture of the trail on the photograph, digging into the Dirac electron theory, Dr. Anderson concluded the positive electron had been caught. With due caution, he waited until two more similar photographs were obtained and then sent to *Science* the announcement of the discovery of the positive electron, a positively charged particle with a mass approximately equal to the ubiquitous negative electron.

He continued to make photographs, slowly accumulating in seven months fifteen photographs of positive electron tracks in a group of thirteen hundred photographs of cosmic ray tracks. Then in February, 1933, news came from

Cambridge that in Cavendish Laboratory, the discovery of the positive electron was confirmed. Dr. P. M. S. Blackett and G. Occhialini had arranged their expansion chamber so that the passage of a cosmic ray through the chamber set up electrical impulses in two Geiger counters, one above and the other below the chamber. Only when both counters signaled at the same instant was a photographic plate exposed. The British experimenters found that some of their photographs showed "showers" or bursts of many tracks, all radiating from a single point. It was as though there had been an explosion. In the flying particles were positive electrons. There were ordinary common old-fashioned electrons as well. Dr. Anderson, too, found these showers. In many more cases than can be accounted for by chance, a negative and a positive electron were found to come from the same point. The significance of this may have important consequences. In giving birth to electron pairs, energy may be turning into matter. But that is another story. (See Chapter 6.)

Now that the existence of the positive electron was recognized as the result of work in two laboratories, it was time for it to be christened. Dr. Anderson named the child of the cosmic rays "positron." At the same time, for the sake of uniformity, he suggested that the name of the negative electron be changed to "negatron," but since the electron for forty-odd years has been called by its old name it seems unlikely that scientists will take kindly to the new one. "Positron," in the few months since its coining, has been firmly written into the literature and promises to stick.

There was some objection to the disregard of mythology inherent in the word "positron." Prof. Herbert Dingle of Imperial College of Science and Technology in South Kensington, England, suggested the name "oreston" for the new positive particle. This is mythologically correct, for Orestes was the brother of Electra. Other English physicists had in the meantime contributed to the confusion, but not in a serious manner. The discovery of the positive particle came from the cosmic ray tracks that seemed to be bent in the wrong way. Sporting Englishmen immediately thought of cricket and the peculiar hops that the ball takes on bouncing in front of the wicket. These are called "googlies," so the new tracks and thus the particles in laboratory slang became "googlies" also.

In the early days of science's acquaintance with the positron, it was necessary to wait for cosmic rays to create them, and this made the photographic bagging of a positron quite rare and difficult. It was natural that the attempt was made to obtain positrons artificially and with some control. Success came to Dr. J. Chadwick of Cavendish Laboratory working with Blackett and Occhialini. With the ability to manufacture positrons there came a burst of research upon this latest of atomic particles.

The honor of being the shortest-lived thing in the universe was conferred upon the positron. It will be remembered that Prof. P. A. M. Dirac, as a result of abstruse mathematical calculations, predicted that the positron would be born of radiation. It is. He also foretold its life would be short. It would be immediately absorbed by surrounding matter and die giving birth to new radiation. If water were the absorbent, the interval between these two events, he estimated, would be of the order of a billionth of a second —longer if the absorbing matter were rarer, shorter if it were denser. Only in interstellar space far removed from all other sorts of matter could the positron live to a respectable old age. Its extremely short life under terrestrial conditions explained, he said, why it had never been detected.

The precise manner of a positron's death was also predicted by Prof. Dirac. If it encountered a free electron, both particles would be annihilated and give rise to two photons or gamma rays traveling in opposite directions, of a total energy of a million electron volts—the energy equivalent of the matter destroyed. If it encountered an electron firmly bound to the nucleus of an atom, only the positron would be annihilated, and only one photon would be emitted of half a million volts. So fantastic this theory seemed at the time it was promulgated that physicists doubted if Prof. Dirac himself believed it. Credulity came with the discovery of the positron.

Evidence was obtained by Dr. Anderson and Dr. Seth

Neddermeyer of Pasadena, Skobeltzyn of Leningrad, and others, that positrons are born of radiation and consequently are not preëxisting fragments of the atom that are simply knocked out, as electrons are, by the impinging radiation. Then Prof. F. Joliot and Prof. Jean Thibaud, two French physicists, reported simultaneously but independently evidence that the positron dies when absorbed by matter in the precise way that Prof. Dirac described. As a source of positrons they used aluminum bombarded by the alpha rays of polonium, a method previously discovered by the Joliots of Paris.

The positron in a few short months had even revised our opinion of the content of the universe. Reaches of "empty" cosmic space between the galaxies are not really empty. They are filled with high-energy positrons, which remain there, suspended permanently in space, because there are no electrons for them to mate with. In stars, planets, and other ponderable masses of matter, positrons, electrons, and the recently discovered chargeless neutrons are associated into atoms. Dr. Blackett of Cambridge estimates that this vast, disperse population of positrons in the incalculable oceans of intergalactic space makes up an appreciable fraction of the total mass of the universe. Basing his computations on the calculations of the Abbé Lemaître, Dr. Blackett finds that the unattached positrons account for about a thousandth part of the whole material universe.

Atoms Smash Themselves

POSITRONS wrote a new chapter in radioactivity when early in 1934 the Joliots produced artificial radioactivity.

Radium and the other chemical elements that vigorously throw off projectiles and rays as they spontaneously disintegrate are among the scientific wonders of our age. Ever since Becquerel in 1896 discovered such radioactivity in uranium, ever since M. and Mme Curie in 1898 isolated radium, the whole complexion of physical science has been changing. Radium has rendered invaluable service to medicine by combating cancer. Far more important in the long run of time has been the insight into the constitution of matter that has been obtained from the spontaneous disintegration and transmutation of elements that is called radioactivity.

The persistence and unchanging nature of radioactivity has perplexed scientists. Heat, hammering, or any other treatment has not speeded, slowed, or otherwise changed an iota the constant natural disintegration of radium or any other radioactive substance. Nature in this case resists human control. So confident are scientists that radioactivity continues uninfluenced by external means that they use radioactivity as a clock for measuring the age of the earth. Knowing the rate of the formation of helium out of uranium, determinations of the amounts of these elements in rocks can be used to compute the ages of the various layers of the earth.

In view of this stability and constancy of natural radioactivity, the achievement of artificial radioactivity by the Joliots was of great scientific importance. Considering what radium has meant to the world in a purely practical sense, there may eventually be expected new aid to medicine and perhaps even industry.

Radioactivity, created for the first time by an external cause, is not exactly the same as natural radioactivity. The essential and important point is that a radioactive disintegration is started that continues after the instigating bombardment has stopped.

Artificial radioactivity was first produced in aluminum. At a foil of this metal was flung a stream of high-speed alpha particles from polonium. From it there came neutrons, and then with great speed a stream of positrons, which continued to be flung off for many minutes after the bombardment stopped.

Atoms had been disintegrated previously. But the projectiles used have seemed to do their work like a high-explosive shell, not like an incendiary bomb. The transmutation was done in an instant and did not continue after the hit had been scored. In artificial radioactivity, the transmutation continues over a considerable period. The new atoms formed by the attack have a fairly long life but are unstable and finally break down.

There was a rush to explore artificial radioactivity. The Pasadena group of experimenters led by Dr. Lauritsen flung million-volt deutons, heavy hydrogen hearts, at carbon. Delayed emission of positrons resulted. Radioactivity that was wholly man-made had been achieved, because the atomic battering ram, the deuton, was set in motion and controlled by the experiments. Then Prof. Lawrence and his Berkeley group sprayed a variety of elements with three-million-volt deutons and proved that a dozen elements could be made artificially radioactive. At Cavendish Laboratory, Cockcroft produced induced radioactivity in carbon by smashing with high velocity protons.

The output from artificial radioactivity is different from the radiations of naturally radioactive elements. Uranium and other members of its naturally radioactive family emit three kinds of rays: Alpha rays or streams of helium atom nuclei such as were used by the Joliots in producing artificial radioactivity; beta rays which are streams of high-speed electrons; gamma rays which are radiation like radio, light and X-rays, except that they are more penetrating and shorter in wavelength. Like the beta rays, the positrons of artificial radioactivity had a distribution of speed ranges that is known as a continuous spectrum.

It is singularly appropriate that "Irene Curie," as Mme Joliot signs her name to research reports, should share the discovery of artificial radioactivity. The Joliots are a husband-wife research team that have carried on with success in the field pioneered by Mme Joliot's parents, M. and Mme Curie, discoverers of radium. Working in the Institute of Radium in Paris, where Mme Curie continued her researches until her death, the Joliots have been at the forefront of the exploration of the constitution of the atom.

The discovery of artificial radioactivity brought with it convincing chemical proof of the artificial transmutation of the elements. The Joliots used a strong polonium source for alpha particles and succeeded in getting about one hundred thousand atoms of the artificially radioactive element, nitrogen, in the case of the attack on boron. This may seem to be a large number of atoms, but it is a very small amount of material upon which to perform a chemical experiment. And they had to work fast in order to complete the chemical reactions before the activity disappeared.

They irradiated a small amount of the chemical compound, boron nitride. They then produced ammonia gas by heating this activated boron nitride with caustic soda. Tests upon the ammonia showed that it was unusual. The artificial radioactivity had forsaken the boron and had traveled away with the ammonia. This was proof that the radioactive element formed is nitrogen. Similar experiments were performed with aluminum by dissolving irradiated aluminum in hydrochloric acid and finding that the activity is carried away with hydrogen gas that can be collected in a test tube. It was chemical proof of transmutation, one element turning into another, the modern realization of the old dream of the alchemists. It was good proof also that the helium heart or alpha particle is actually captured in these reactions.

The artificial radioactivity experiments were made largely at first on light-weight elements. What would happen if one shot atomic high-speed particles at a heavy element like uranium?

Prof. Enrico Fermi, of Rome's Royal University, tried the experiment. Prof. Fermi found that by bombarding uranium with neutrons he could make one of these particles stick in the uranium nucleus. The weight of the atom was therefore increased.

He produced a superheavy element with atomic weight greater than science had previously known existed.

This new material was the 93d element. Its existence had not been suggested, and a place for it does not exist in the conventional periodic table of chemical elements which ends with 92, uranium itself.

Element 93, like uranium, was found to be radioactive, disintegrating in 12 minutes so that only half the original amount remained. If element 93 ever existed naturally on the earth, therefore, it must have been during the very early days in the childhood of what is now a pretty old world.

Neutron, positron, deuton—the new atomic particles

parade on the stage of physics and perform their tricks. Are there more actors waiting in the wings of theory, soon to be spotlighted by experiment?

Most likely to emerge and run the risk of scientific hisses or applause is a light kind of neutron, named neutret or neutrino. Its existence was suggested by Prof. W. Pauli of Switzerland, a neutral particle with the same light mass as the electron and the positron. Already there is some evidence of the existence of the neutret from careful weighings of other particles and the experiments upon artificial radioactivity. As companion to the neutret, there may be the antineutret. Each of these is thought to be half of a photon. Neutret and antineutret combine, and lo! there is a unit of light radiation. That is the theory.

Still another atomic actor waiting for its cue may be the negative proton. It would be identical in mass with the ordinary proton or nucleus of a hydrogen atom, but would have a negative rather than a positive charge upon it.

The negative proton is yet unfound, but scientists would like to find it, for its existence would help explain, in part, why the nuclei of some atoms spin one way while others spin in "reverse." It would help account, too, for certain stability conditions in atoms like beryllium and for the emission of a positron by a neutron struck with high-energy radiation. The positron coming off would leave behind a negative proton within the atom.

The bombardment of physical theories by experimental tests is as merciless and unceasing as the radiations from radium. The result of this intellectual radioactivity is more theories, more tests, more theories, with the cycle repeating over and over. As the formulæ spill over the pages of the scientific journals, as the results of tests tax the consuming power of scientific comprehension, the human mind gropes closer to a true knowledge of the great plan of the universe. That would be reward enough for our scientific strivings.

The practical by-products may be valuable. A ray of knowledge, striking we cannot predict where, may scintillate and kindle a revolution.

CHAPTER 6
ENERGY FROM ATOMS

THE GREAT GOAL of discovering the constitution of the atom has spurred the building of heavy artillery for blasting the heart of matter. In a dozen centers of research on physics, "atom guns" are being fashioned and aimed at their tasks of flinging minute particles with ever increasing energies in the hope of smashing more atoms. The primary objective of this siege is to obtain more knowledge.

In the secret places of the scientific heart, there is another hope. The release of atomic energy would be of vast practical importance. Some of the atomic artillery is being rushed to completion with the admitted intention of attempting to tap the energy of the atom.

For the purpose of attacking the atom, electricity is much better adapted than the rifles, cannon, and howitzers of armies and navies. Far more energy can be concentrated just where it is wanted. The stream of electrons that make up an electric current, whether it be the fuel for a small flashlight or the flash of lightning, can themselves be used as bullets. Electrons are lightweights. The comparatively massive nuclei of atoms, protons, deutons, alpha particles, are much more efficient as projectiles. Fed into an electrical discharge through a practically airless chamber, these particles take up speed and energy depending upon the voltage of the electrical current flowing.

Simplest of the atom guns is a vacuum tube such as used in ordinary X-ray apparatus. Voltages such as are used in medical, dental, or even X-ray analysis work are usually too feeble to be interesting to those who knock at the gates of the atom. Although atomic disintegrations have been obtained at as low as 20,000 volts, voltages of about a million or more are most interesting.

In comparing voltages, which affords an easy method of contrasting energies, the physicist, when he says "volts," really means "electron-volts," for it is understood that the volts are considered to be pushing along a unit of mass which is taken to be the minute weight of the electron.

Alpha particles produced as a result of radioactivity have energies of 4 million to 9 million volts, and one of the most powerful gamma rays, that of radioactive thorium C'', has an energy of 2,600,000 volts. The average beta particle and a typical gamma ray radioactively produced have energies of a few hundred thousand volts. These figures are recited to emphasize that radium and radioactive substances are themselves natural atom guns of no mean power. This does not mean that the development of artificial methods of speeding atomic particles is not justified. There is so little radium in the world, and it is so costly.

More Than all the Radium

ONE GIANT X-RAY TUBE will produce a larger quantity of high-power radiation than all the radium in the world. For example, Rutherford explains that by an electric discharge through hydrogen at low pressure it is not difficult to obtain a stream of protons equivalent to a current of one tenth of a milliampere. In order to produce alpha particles equal in amount to this supply of protons, 170,000 grams of radium would be required. There are only about 600 grams of radium isolated and in use in the world today. As the result of transmutations performed by high-voltage particles, neutrons at the rate of 10 million per second have been produced, and this equals the intensity of some X-rays.

Before 1932 there was no experimental justification for believing that voltages lower than about 3 million would be effective in smashing atoms. The work of Cockcroft and Walton and subsequent experimenters in transmuting lithium with protons with energy values of mere tens of thousands of volts showed that transmutation of some elements was much less difficult than had been imagined. That did not stop the push toward higher voltages. If low voltages were effective, what startling effects were to be obtained from extremely high voltages.

Largest of the more or less conventional X-ray type high-voltage tubes in active service for physical experimentation is the million-volt tube at the California Institute of Technology. Built under the direction of and presided over by Dr. Lauritsen, it has already given many useful results.

Dr. W. D. Coolidge, Director of the General Electric Research Laboratory, who is the father of the most prevalent type of X-ray tube in practical service, has built high-voltage X-ray tubes, using the cascade method of superimposing one voltage upon another or placing the voltages end to end, as it were. In this way, with three sections operating, he obtains a voltage of some six hundred thousand. Two of these giant X-ray outfits are in operation at hospitals in New York and Chicago, but they are used for treating cancer and not for exploring the atom.

In Germany, Drs. A. Brasch and F. Lange, as early as 1931, built a new type X-ray tube, constructed of alternate ring layers of paper, rubber, and aluminum, which produced 2,600,000 volts, continuing for a millionth of a second. Earlier, Drs. Lange and Brasch attempted to harness the lightning by emulating Benjamin Franklin and snatching electricity from the skies. They stretched ropes between two mountain peaks in northern Italy and obtained 55-foot sparks that measured 16 million volts. This was dangerous, and they had to wait for storms in order to conduct research. For that reason they turned to laboratory research.

In 1930 Drs. M. A. Tuve and L. R. Hafstad and O. Dahl at the Department of Terrestrial Magnetism of the Carnegie Institution, using a high-voltage apparatus involving a Tesla coil, artificially produced particles and radiations with energies of above a million volts for the first time. This achievement won the $1,000 prize of the American Association for the Advancement of Science.

"Artificial lightning" generators, apparatus capable of developing 10 million volts, have been developed in the Pittsfield, Mass., laboratory of the General Electric Company under the direction of the late F. W. Peek, Jr. These are very useful in testing transmission lines so as to make them capable of withstanding the 100 million to 200 million voltages of real lightning, but they cannot be used effectively for attacks upon the atom. The physicist wishes to have a sustained output of millions of volts, so that his attacks will not be limited to a series of impulses each a mere fraction of a second in duration. For example, the California Institute of Technology million-vote tube, while operated by alternating current, delivers a sustained flow of high voltage which allows a continued attack.

A million volts is about as much as can be applied to conventional tubes. At the limit of their resources along one line of development, it was necessary for the physicists to develop novel methods. Upon opposite coasts of America there arose two new ideas that their young originators proceeded to translate into apparatus.

Whirligig Atom Gun

PROF. E. O. LAWRENCE, at the University of California, found a way to void the troubles and expense of operating vacuum tubes at very high voltages. He worked out a method of starting off his atomic projectiles at modest voltages of a few thousand volts such as could be imparted to them by conventional, standard tubes. Then he gave them repeated pushes with an electric current that speeds them up to the equivalent of millions of volts. So far the top speeds developed are equivalent to 4,800,000 volts. With deutons and other particles speeded at energies corresponding to 3 million volts, Prof. Lawrence and his associates have performed the most advanced transmutation experiments.

This ingenious atom gun flings atomic particles in widening spirals of a magnetic field until they are accelerated to million-volt speeds, although the greatest actual potential difference between any two points in the apparatus amounts to only a few thousands of volts. The electrical whirlpool is within a round flat metal box, looking like a complicated and glorified covered frying pan. Between two sides of this box there is the voltage difference that gives each particle a kick whenever it passes from one side to the other. This voltage is reversed just after each kick, so that the next passage accelerates the particle in the opposite direction. After riding this electrical-magnetic merry-go-round for about 150 circuits and 300 reversals of voltage direction, the particle becomes so speedy that it comes to the boundary of the box and there is snatched by an electrode out of its path sufficiently to make it batter into the specimen that is to be attacked.

The giant 85-ton magnet that provides the magnetic field is one of the largest in the world. It was made to the order of a now defunct Chinese government but was never delivered. Two of four such electromagnets accompanied the American Expeditionary Force to France as part of powerful radio outfits. A similar apparatus was used for radio transmission at Bordeaux, France, for many years after the World War, but the 1,000-kilowatt arc that was designed to flash between the magnet poles is now made obsolete as a radio signaling device by the more efficient and less interfering radio vacuum tubes. Eight tons of copper wire were used in winding the magnet for functioning in the Lawrence whirligig atom gun. Its service as an essential part of a gigantic atom gun will undoubtedly be much more important to the world than any duty it might have performed flashing radio messages across the Pacific.

The other novel method of obtaining high voltage is the Van de Graaff electrostatic machine, the idea of which was born in an American mind while in England's Oxford, came to adolescence in Princeton, and now is achieving maturity in an airship hangar near New Bedford, Mass.

Van de Graaff

A FEW YEARS AGO Robert J. Van de Graaff, a young Rhodes scholar, puzzling upon the problem of power for smashing the atom, went back to the idea of the old-fashioned static generator for electricity, the sort of electrical machine used by Benjamin Franklin. Modern electrical generation had developed along the line of electromagnetism, and

Dr. Van de Graaff revived the other principle and built it into a modern machine.

The first Van de Graaff generator was a model constructed in the fall of 1929 at Princeton University, where Dr. Van de Graaff was working as National Research Fellow. It was built out of a tin can, a silk ribbon, and a small motor, and the cost of material was nothing. This model developed 80,000 volts, a limit set by the corona discharge from the edges of the tin can. He then built a small laboratory model of his generator at the cost of a few hundred dollars. It produced between 1 million and 1,500,000 volts, the highest direct voltage current ever attained up to that time. Much more expensive apparatus, upon which other scientists had worked for years, had been able to produce only 800,000 volts direct current. Working with Dr. Karl T. Compton, then professor of physics at Princeton, Dr. Van de Graaff joined the Massachusetts Institute of Technology staff when Dr. Compton became president of that great engineering school. With the aid of associates, they visualized a giant generator, an electricity-producing machine that would develop a steady current of 10 million volts.

Ten Million Static Volts

No CONVENTIONAL BUILDING at the Massachusetts Institute of Technology was large enough to house the large Van de Graaff generator. Col. E. H. R. Green offered his airship dock on his estate at Round Hill, Mass., a structure 140 feet long, 75 feet wide, and 75 feet high, with railroad track running into it and great doors that weigh over 23 tons. The 10 million-volt Van de Graaff generator consists of two large hollow columns, 25 feet high and 6 feet in diameter, which are surrounded by a hollow polished aluminum sphere 15 feet in diameter. Each column is mounted on a heavy four-wheeled truck running on railway track 14 feet wide. The spheres, which act as reservoirs into which electricity is poured by relatively small static generators at the base of the columns, rise to 43 feet above the ground.

Even while the generator is running at full potential, scientists can stay and work within the 15-foot diameter aluminum spheres, surrounded by high potential electric fields in a manner somewhat analogous to the way in which Settle and Fordney were surrounded by rare air on their stratosphere flight and Beebe was surrounded by ocean in his record bathysphere dive. The giant aluminum spherical terminals are unique in construction, the largest such structures of this metal ever produced. They were made by fabricating orange-peel sections which were welded and then polished to a bright finish so as to eliminate projections that would cause the electricity to spark away. Although built of light metal a half inch thick, each hollow ball weighs a ton and a half.

Stroke a cat or comb your hair on a dry day and see the sparks fly. This method of generating static electricity is essentially the same as that in the Van de Graaff static machine. Static electricity antedates the electromagnetic method that is used in the generation of practically all the electric power today. The Greeks knew that by rubbing a piece of amber with a cloth an electric charge could be generated. With the practical application of the discoveries of Faraday and Henry, that motion in a magnetic field can generate a current, with the development of the vast electrical industry based upon these principles, static electricity did not have the opportunity of becoming practically useful but remained within the laboratory in the bags of scientific tricks of physics professors.

In principle the Van de Graaff generator is simple. From near the surface of the ground to the elevated hollow cylinders there run moving belts. Electricity is picked up on these belts at the ground level, and it is then conveyed, like water in a bucket pump, to the hollow spheres, where it is dumped into them and travels to their surfaces. It is not even necessary to provide a source of low-voltage electricity to spray upon the belts, as the belts can create and pick up the necessary electricity without aid. One of the hollow cylinders thus has its surface charged positively, and the other is charged with negative electricity. How much electricity the hollow cylinders will hold without spilling over, or sparking like artificial lightning, one from the other, depends upon their size and the atmospheric conditions.

A relatively large amount of electricity, 1,000 kilowatts, is designed to be generated by the 10-million-volt machine when it operates at full capacity. This is as much as the power plant of a small town generates. This power would give 100 milliamperes at a potential of 10 million volts. The generator would light 90,000 ordinary 10-watt, 110-volt incandescent electric lamps, if connected in series, and there would be 10 per cent current margin to spare. If these lamps were set as close together as possible, say eight to the foot, they would string out to about two miles.

When there is merely air between the two spheres, the direct current generated flows as a flashing stream, at designed peak a combined electrical pressure of 10 million volts, with the oppositely charged spheres each at a potential of half that value. In November, 1933, the Van de Graaff generator was given its first test run and developed indoors an estimated voltage of 7 million.

When the real work of the Van de Graaff generator begins, there will be no spectacular electrical fireworks. A large vacuum tube, a foot in diameter and 40 feet long, designed by Dr. L. C. Van Atta, made not of glass, as is usual, but of laminated paper, will extend from one sphere to the other, and the electricity will discharge through it, creating the most powerful X-rays ever known by hurling millions of electrical "bullets" against a metal target. Each of these "bullets" will be moving at velocities 100,000 times greater than the speed of any rifle bullet, a speed so great that they would encircle the earth's equator three times a second.

Eager to push onward in the conquest of the atom to bombardments more intense than those already within the reach of the 10 million, Dr. Van de Graaff and his crew of scientific associates are planning on paper and in laboratories for a generator that will make the present giant seem feeble by comparison. They plan a 50-million-volt generator. It will be built within a gigantic vacuum tank. The insulation for its immense currents and voltages will be provided by lack of air. Powerful vacuum pumps and novel air traps will keep the air out. A small machine within a vacuum tank was tested to 50,000 volts in 1933.

Electrical Revolution Ahead?

As OFTEN HAPPENS in these grand-scale scientific experiments there may be brewing an industrial revolution. Electrostatics may replace electromagnetics in producing the electricity that runs our motors, lights our lamps, and keeps industry's wheels humming. Enormous disks, spinning at high speeds in an almost perfect vacuum, promise to replace the familiar generators of electrical power plants. These disks would be great electrostatic machines, producing direct current electricity at tremendously high voltages. The vacuum would be necessary to prevent the production of sparks that might wreck the machine or prevent the electricity from being led out on wires to be usefully employed. Dr. Van de Graaff had made designs for such machines, although little has been said about their practical utilization. Such direct current electrostatic generators may soon be developed and given a practical baptism. There are many advantages in generating and transmitting high-voltage direct current instead of alternating current. More power can be transmitted as direct current than as the alternating current which is now standard on power lines. Large-scales development of direct current electricity by the Van de Graaff electrostatic method might bring about a radical change in the electrical industry.

It is difficult to tell what repercussions will come of scientific experiments. The energy of the atom may not be tapped by the atomic artillery being aimed at the secret of atoms. New but more conventional methods of power production may arise as a result.

Within the atom there is energy that is far more appealing to the practical-minded scientist than the gold that the alchemists dreamed of transmuting from lead. Compared with the energy that can be extracted from coal, gasoline, explosives, and other common fuels, subatomic energy seems fabulous. Annihilate the atoms in a bucket of sea water, and there would result enough energy to drive for more than a month the engines of the merchant fleet of the world.

For matter and energy are merely different aspects of the same thing. The famous principle of relativity, formulated by Prof. Albert Einstein in 1905, included the idea of the equivalence of matter and energy. Lose mass and gain energy, or lose energy and gain mass. There is a very simple equation that allows the computation of just how much energy is equivalent to so much mass.

Expressed in symbols it is simply: $E = M c^2$ where E is the energy expressed in ergs, M is the mass in grams and c^2 is the square of the velocity of light. Light's velocity is 30 billion centimeters per second. It works out that one gram of matter is equivalent to 900 quintillion ergs.

Expressed in more understandable language, the annihilation of one pound of water would create enough energy to heat 100 million tons of water from freezing to boiling temperature.

Here are some of the startling possibilities, if and when science finds a way to annihilate matter and utilize the constitutional or sub-atomic energy of matter that would be released:

A breath of air would operate a powerful airplane for a year continuously.

A handful of snow would heat a large apartment house for a year.

The pasteboard in a small railroad ticket would run a heavy passenger train several times around the globe.

A teacup of water would supply the power of a great generating station of 100,000 kilowatts capacity for a year.

If lead could be changed into gold, the value of the energy released would exceed enormously the value of the gold produced.

Radioactivity gave the first hint of energy within the atom. Determination of weights of the various atoms of the elements provided the statistical data that allowed computation of just how much energy would be produced in transmutations of elements and in annihilations if such could be accomplished. The many tedious and difficult research steps in exploring atomic structure that led to the discovery of the periodic table, the existence of isotopes or varieties of elements, and accurate weights of atoms and their nuclei, constitute important chapters in science's progress.

Mass Equals Volts

THE CLASSIC EXAMPLE of energy release that would occur in atomic transmutation is the theoretical building of a helium atom out of four hydrogen atoms. That great discoverer of isotopes, Dr. F. W. Aston of Cambridge, England, first gave it. Taking, as the scientists do, the most common kind of oxygen atom as standard and weighing exactly 16, one hydrogen atom (here we are talking about the ordinary kind and not deuterium) weighs 1.0078 and four weigh 4.0312. A helium atom weighs 4.0022. The difference is 0.028 mass units, which would have to be released as energy. This is about equal to 28 million electron-volts, which represents a considerable amount of energy. This mass and its equivalent energy that would disappear if one element were changed into another are known as "mass defect" and "binding energy."

Astronomers have seized upon this idea of matter's conversion into energy to explain how the sun and stars keep stoked. At immense temperatures such as exist in the centers of the stars, matter may yield up its energy prolifically. Yet it is not necessary to theorize about the remote heavenly bodies to find support for the carefully developed and plausible theory of the interconvertibility of matter and energy. The transmutation experiments explained in Chapter 5 have provided convincing and encouraging demonstrations.

Rutherford, in his historic experiments of 1919, when he first artificially transmuted matter, also made the first atomic transformation yielding a gain in energy at the expense of matter. Some of the flinging of helium at nitrogen that knocked out hydrogen also released energy. The amount of energy released was not large, and the emphasis was upon the accomplishment of transmutation.

The Cockcroft-Walton bombardment of lithium with protons, resulting in the production of alpha particles with kinetic energies much greater than was fed in by the im-

POSITRON

THIS historic photograph, taken August 2, 1932, by Dr. Carl D. Anderson, at the California Institute of Technology, is famous because it constitutes the discovery of the positive electron or positron. A 63,000,000-volt positron is seen passing through a six-millimeter lead plate and emerging as a 23,000,-000-volt positron. The track consists of tiny particles of water collected along the path of the positron as it plunges through the moisture-laden atmosphere of the cloud chamber. The track is curved because the chamber is placed in a strong magnetic field. This may become one of the most famous photographs in physics.

VAN DE GRAAFF GENERATOR

THE great Van de Graaff generator, built by Massachusetts Institute of Technology physicists in an airship hangar, is the scene of one of the many present attempts to release the atom's energy. The generator works on the principle of the old-fashioned static electricity machine that Benjamin Franklin used, and will build up a steady direct current potential of 10,000,000 volts.

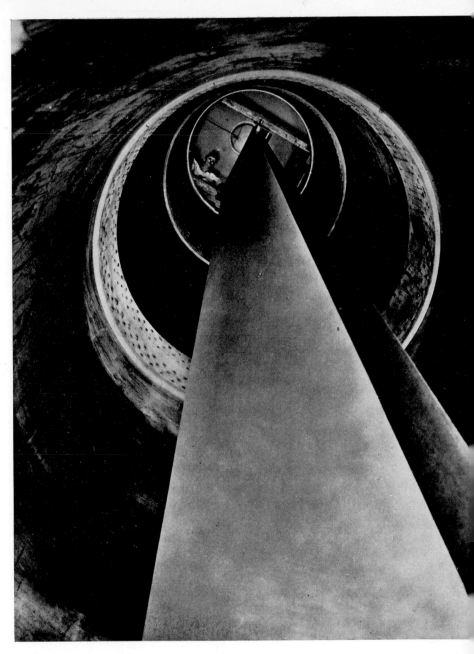

ATOM SMASHER

LOOKING up inside the Van de Graaff generator. Up this belt travel the electrical charges to the giant spheres. When charged, there flashes between the two spheres the most powerful direct current yet produced by man; yet, inside the sphere, the M.I.T. scientists work in perfect safety. In fact, the inside of the sphere is the safest place to be when the discharge takes place.

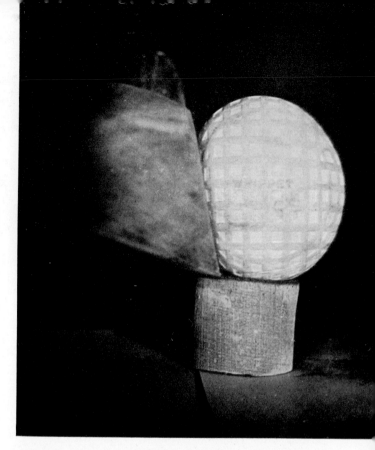

GOLF

THE stroboscope camera, operating without any shutter, can take a picture in one one hundred thousandth of a second. A light flashes just as the club hits the ball, and the ball is seen flattened on one side and elongated. An instant later the ball, beginning its flight, springs back, so that the elongation is in the opposite direction.

MILK DROP

GREAT beauty is discovered by the stroboscope camera used by Massachusetts Institute of Technology engineers, as a drop of milk falls on a hard surface. Moving film, without the start-stop motion in moving-picture cameras, is used. The pictures "read" from bottom to top of the page. Five hundred pictures may be taken in one second.

pacting protons, was the first really exciting release of energy. What is as important, the amount of energy released, as determined from the velocity of the twin alpha particles emitted, corresponds very well with the loss in mass that occurs.

Just because we may be practically interested in the obtaining of energy at the expense of matter, we must not overlook the importance of experiments that show the reverse process, the conversion of energy into the mass of matter.

The discovery of what seems to be the creation of matter out of energy came in the train of research that followed upon the discovery of the positron. In many respects, the making of matter out of energy is far more amazing and thrilling than the atom smashings that have liberated energy.

The theory, well supported by experimental facts, is that the positive electron is born out of radiant energy or "light" or photons. It is supposed that a highly energetic photon can transmute itself into a pair of electrons, one positive and one negative. Two particles of matter come into existence where only a bundle of energy existed before. That tested and famous Einsteinian equivalence of mass and energy tells that the mass of two electrons at rest is equal to about 1 million electron volts. When this is put to test by studying what happens in the formation of the electron pairs, it is found that the energy with which a pair of electrons is moving after its formation is never within a million volts of the energy contained in the creating photon. This gives strong support to the idea that "light" is changing into matter.

Atomic Energy, How Soon?

NOT ALL SCIENTISTS are confident of man's eventual tapping of atomic energy. Lord Rutherford has issued a timely word of warning. He calls the energy produced by the breaking down of the atom "a very poor kind of thing," and those who look for sources of power in atomic transmutations are "talking moonshine."

From two angles, Dr. R. A. Millikan, eminent in American science, has reassuring doubts about the tapping of atomic energy. Those who fear the too rapid advance of science and live in dread of the day when some unscrupulous or careless Dr. Faust may touch off the stupendous subatomic powder magazine and blow this comfortable world of ours into star dust, may "sleep in peace in consciousness that the Creator has realized the wisdom of introducing some fool-proof features into his machine."

What if atomic energy should come true? Even if a modest, minute part of the energy in matter were made available for mechanical use, all other forms of energy would be antiquated, such as fuels, explosives, dammed water, etc. A real industrial revolution, compared with which the present economic consequences of machines and energy replacing labor are mere minor adjustments, would result from a practical release of atomic energy. Continuous flight over continents and oceans would become commonplace. Coal mines and oil wells would be valueless. Dams and electrical transmission lines would be as outmoded as stagecoaches. Unusual metals now expensive to extract from plentiful raw materials would become cheap. Food might be synthesized instead of being raised on farms. International planning of economic and industrial life would be necessary, conventional economics would be destroyed, and if man did not master the consequences of cheap atomic energy the world would be plunged into a great sociological disaster.

If and when evolution brings such a world, the atomic energy may be used with a clear conscience without feeling that mankind is "getting something for nothing." The energy released from the atom is no more to be despised as unearned than the energy released when coal is burned.

Fire and its energy marked the rise of man above the status of the animals. Atomic energy may demonstrate the superman.

CHAPTER 7
HEAVY HYDROGEN

IF IT WERE DISCOVERED that some substantial citizen of the world was actually twins and one of these twins was twice the weight of the other although they had passed for each other to all who knew them, there would be created in everyday life a situation such as confronted the chemists and physicists when in 1931 the twin nature of hydrogen was discovered. For hydrogen is one of the most substantial of chemical elements, more important perhaps than any other except carbon.

The discovery of a heavy kind of hydrogen, about twice the weight of ordinary hydrogen, has stirred scientists to a high pitch of intellectual excitement. It is more important than any of the recent isolations or discoveries of new chemical elements. It is even now ranked "among the great discoveries of science." It is the starting point in developing a far-reaching new field in chemistry.

Discovering Deuterium

DEUTERIUM, as the heavy hydrogen has been christened, has started a fever in the chemical laboratories of the world. It has reoriented research programs, sidetracked less promising researches, and caused a rush to print that has filled the announcement columns of the chemical and physical journals. Whereas water was just water a few months ago, there is now heavy water, distinctly different from ordinary water. And there are actually nine chemical kinds of water. Biologists have joined in the race, to discover the effect of deuterium in heavy water upon living things.

"Urey, Brickwedde, and Murphy" is the way in which the scientific literature cites the research team that discovered heavy hydrogen. They are three young scientists, who were 38, 28, and 26 years old in 1931 when they acted as obstetricians to hydrogen's fission. Prof. Harold C. Urey and Dr. G. M. Murphy are at Columbia University, while Dr. F. G. Brickwedde is in charge of the Low Temperature Laboratory at the National Bureau of Standards in Washington. Urey himself had speculated on the existence of double-weight hydrogen (and also triple-weight hydrogen and quintuple helium) after he had compared the proton and electrons in the kernels of the elements lighter than oxygen and had come to the conclusion that there was a place for more than one kind of hydrogen in the scheme of elemental things. By one of the coincidences that happen in science as elsewhere, Prof. Herrick L. Johnston of Ohio State University came to the same conclusion, and his predictive paper was printed by the side of Urey's in the same number of the *Journal of the American Chemical Society*.

Acting upon Birge and Menzel's suggestion that there might be in ordinary hydrogen gas one part of hydrogen isotope 2 to 4,500 parts of mass one hydrogen atoms, Urey, Brickwedde, and Murphy decided that the best way of concentrating the heavy isotope would be to take a quantity of ordinary hydrogen gas, liquefy it, and then evaporate all but a few drops of it. The heavy hydrogen would remain mostly in the last few drops. These drops were sealed into glass bulbs by Brickwedde in Washington and sent to Urey and Murphy in New York.

The spectrograph, that useful analyzer of the rainbow of light emitted by the intense activity of the atoms, was called into service. The little ampule of hydrogen gas, in which the experimenters confidently hoped they would find heavy hydrogen, was subjected to electrical discharge. In the way the light was emitted Urey and Murphy found telltale spectral "flags" which proved the existence of heavy hydrogen.

The theory of the hydrogen atom allows the calculation of the location in the light spectrum of the lines which signal the presence of any chemical element. There, close beside the familiar lines of ordinary hydrogen, were other fainter "flags" engraved by the light on the photographic plate. They were separated only a twentieth of an inch from the more familiar lines, but they were enough to identify the existence of the atoms of heavy hydrogen beyond any doubt. Drs. Urey, Brickwedde, and Murphy were able to announce the existence of hydrogen of mass two.

Careful comparison of the new series of "Balmer" spectral lines told them that Brickwedde in his low temperature evaporation had increased the concentration of the heavy hydrogen to about five times what it is in the normal hydrogen gas. This was a larger increase in concentration than had ever before been secured in attempts to separate the isotopes of the elements. Since this enrichment had been obtained with relative simplicity, the discoverers and other scientists who eagerly read their announcement were quick to realize that in the two kinds of hydrogen they had their first real opportunity to separate cleanly the interesting and significant element varieties or isotopes that are considered the same element although they have different weights.

Another analytic instrument, much newer than the spectroscope and mass spectroscope, gave even earlier evidence of the existence of heavy hydrogen. At the Alabama Polytechnic Institute, Prof. Fred Allison had developed a magneto-optic method of chemical analysis. It had not given satisfactory results in the hands of some chemists and physicists. But in 1930 and again in 1931 Prof. Allison reported readings with his instrument that he explained by the presence of a mass two hydrogen in ordinary water.

The Race for Heavy Water

WITH THE EXISTENCE of deuterium conclusively demonstrated, there was the great urge to get it isolated in such purity as to see whether it was markedly different from ordinary hydrogen. Dr. E. W. Washburn, chief of the U. S. Bureau of Standards division of chemistry, who died early in 1934 in the midst of intensive research on deuterium, suggested and put into practice the method of separating deuterium by electrolysis. In the industrial plants that make oxygen and hydrogen gases by breaking up water with an electric current, Dr. Washburn found the first step in electrolytic separation already accomplished. The water in commercial electrolytic cells that have been operated for long periods was markedly richer in the heavier deuterium than ordinary tap water. The lighter kind of hydrogen had a tendency to go off as gas first when the water was broken up into its hydrogen and oxygen by the electricity. Further electrolysis of the water rich in deuterium gave what was, up to that time, the world's heaviest water.

Other chemical laboratories began the production of heavy water rich in deuterium in order that they might have it for experimental purposes. Almost complete separation of the isotopes was first obtained by Prof. Gilbert N. Lewis of the University of California, making use of the electrolytic method. He obtained a small amount of heavy water calculated to contain less than a hundredth of 1 per cent of the ordinary or light-weight hydrogen. This liquid cannot be distinguished by the eye from ordinary water, but it has a density of 1.1056 at 25 degrees Centigrade, boils at 101.42 degrees, freezes at 3.8 degrees, and has a maximum density at 11.6 degrees. Its heat of vaporization is 250 calories per mole greater than that of ordinary water. At Princeton even higher specific gravity was obtained, 1.1078.

Just what these figures, that differ markedly from the standard values accepted for water, mean, will be realized when it is remembered that water is the substance widely used in setting the standard values for freezing point, boiling point, and other physical constants.

Like any rare substance, the cost of heavy water was at first high. About the middle of 1933, 95 per cent heavy water was valued at $150 a gram, $150,000 a quart. Early in 1934, Princeton University scientists produced it at an estimated cost of $5 a gram. With methods already developed, it can probably be produced in quantity at from $1 to $2 per gram, a figure that is higher than the 1934 price of gold. Compared with its early production costs of one-time chemical rarities, like neon, argon, helium, and even aluminum, the cost of heavy water is not excessive.

With the enthusiasm that befits exploration of a new chemical realm, dozens of chemists laid aside less interesting problems and investigated dozens of aspects of unique deuterium, deuterium oxide, as heavy water is chemically called, and other deuterium compounds.

Now a Third Hydrogen?

WHILE HEAVY HYDROGEN was being explored thoroughly, the search for "heavy, heavy hydrogen," or a mass three isotope, proceeded. There is growing evidence that triple hydrogen does exist, although there is probably not more than one part in 10 billion parts of normal hydrogen. Lord Rutherford found evidence of the formation of triple hydrogen in bombardments involving double hydrogen. Dr. Wendell M. Latimer and Herbert A. Young at the University of California, using the methods of Prof. Allison, found evidence of triple hydrogen and so also did Prof. Allison himself. A Princeton group found triple-weight hydrogen in deuterium and made it by smashing deuterium. Drs. M. A. Tuve and L. R. Hafstad at Washington found it in very pure deuterium. The extreme scarcity of triple weight hydrogen will probably prevent its isolation or its chemical utilization.

Just as parents have the privilege of naming their children, discoverers have the right of christening new chemical babies. It was rather awkward to continue referring to "hydrogen isotope of mass two" when the infant was so lusty and needed so much writing about in scientific journals. "Heavy hydrogen," for precise scientific literature, was unsatisfactory because of the mass three hydrogen isotope. So Drs. Urey, Brickwedde, and Murphy held a scientific christening and dubbed the new heavy-weight hydrogen "deuterium." To the more common mass one isotope they gave the special name of "protium," so that the old term of hydrogen might be applied to both and specifically reserved for the mixtures of the protium and deuterium which before deuterium's discovery were the only hydrogen known. Because, as described in Chapter 5, the nucleus of the deuterium atom was useful as a particle in atomic studies, it needed a special name. "Deuton" was selected by Dr. Lewis, corresponding to "proton," the long accepted name for the ordinary hydrogen atomic nucleus.

If the existence of mass three hydrogen is conclusively proved, the number of chemical compounds in the universe is prodigiously increased. Take water, for instance. With three kinds of hydrogen and three kinds of oxygen, there can be eighteen kinds of water. When the thousands of compounds containing hydrogen are considered, the complexity becomes bewildering.

Heavy hydrogen, by introducing a dual chemical personality, had upset physical constants upon which scientists had placed great reliance. Was it to have a similar effect in the field of biology? Eagerly a few drops of the precious heavy water were diverted from physical experiments to biological tests of its effect upon life. Because deuterium is heavier and therefore slower moving, it might slow down the processes of life.

Life Slowed

THE FIRST BIOCHEMICAL EXPERIMENTS were made by Prof. Lewis with a few drops of his nearly pure heavy water. Using minute tobacco seeds, Prof. Lewis put some of them in tiny test tubes that contained ordinary water. Others he put in tubes of the special heavy water containing only double-weight hydrogen. The seeds in ordinary water sprouted. Those in the new heavy water did not. From theoretical considerations, Prof. Lewis had predicted that heavy water would not support life and would be lethal to higher organisms. This was the first chance to test his theory. When the experiment was repeated at a later time, and the seeds transferred to ordinary water after a period of soaking in heavy water, some of them did sprout, but their growth was freakish and short-lived. Part of a batch of flatworms, apparently killed by immersion in heavy water, similarly revived in ordinary water.

The first heavy-water experiment on a warm-blooded animal was made by Prof. Lewis. Heavy water failed to kill a mouse to which it was administered with a dropper, but did cause the animal to act very strangely, as if temporarily poisoned. Prof. Lewis chose three mice of "respectable ancestry." To one of them he administered the heavy water, drop by drop, because it is so costly. To the other two he gave ordinary water; these mice served as experimental "controls." The two "control" mice behaved normally, dividing their time between eating and sleeping; the one that got the heavy water did neither, but persistently leaped about, and for some mysterious reason licked at the glass walls of his cage. "The more he drank of the heavy water the thirstier he became," Prof. Lewis reported. "He would probably have drunk much more if our supply of heavy water had not given out." In spite of his evident distress, the mouse recovered.

Prof. W. W. Swingle of Princeton, using 92 per cent heavy water manufactured by Princeton chemists, found that it is lethal to certain fresh-water animals. Green frog tadpoles survived only an hour when placed in the heavy water. Tadpoles of the same sort immersed in distilled water that contained only 30 per cent heavy water lived happily and unaffected for twenty-four hours. Paramecia, one-celled organisms that are favorite biology experimental material, resisted the heavy water successfully for twenty-four hours.

Plants retain heavy water and build it into their woody tissues and into the starches and other carbohydrate foods they form. Although heavy water is present only in very minute proportions in the normal water of the soil and of rivers, the plants in some way are able to select it out, so that a larger ratio of it is present in the water bound up in wood and carbohydrate than is present in the "normal" free water which the plant takes in.

Cause of Old Age?

FAR FROM BEING a mere chemical matter of interest to scientists only, heavy water may be a matter of life and death for all of us. The hypothesis has been advanced that the cause of old age and senility is too much heavy water in the human body. Drs. Ingo W. D. Hackh and E. H. Westling of the College of Physicians and Surgeons School of Dentistry, San Francisco, have suggested that the tragedy of growing old is linked to the properties of heavy water. It has an inhibitory effect upon the normal functioning of protoplasm of which the human body and other animal bodies is largely composed.

Because the human body evaporates a large portion of the water that it consumes, it will in the course of years become enriched with heavy water. The light water, evaporating at a lower temperature, leaves the body more readily than the heavy water. This increase in the proportion of heavy water in the body fluids may account for "the increasing inhibitory action of the protoplasm during senility." If this idea is sustained, will science find the "fountain of youth" in some method of rejuvenating by removing the heavy water from our tissues?

With heavy water cast in the rôle of the poison used by the old man with the scythe to end our years, the scientific imagination can also suggest a more sweeping effect for heavy hydrogen. The earth flying through space is continually losing some of its thin layer of atmosphere. Light hydrogen, being lightest of the elements, escapes first. Perhaps 99 per cent of the earth's hydrogen has already vanished into outer space. The heavy hydrogen will be the last of the hydrogen to escape.

If heavy hydrogen kills, then the doom of mankind, if not caused earlier in some other way, will come when the light hydrogen disappears. This possible baleful theory need not worry us who are now living or those who will populate the earth in the immediate future. If this is the fate of the human race, it will not happen for at least some hundreds of millions of years.

CHAPTER 8
GREAT COLD AND STRANGE LIGHTS

LIKE THE MAKE-BELIEVE of fairy tales, physics has its Never-Never Land where everything is impossibly cold, where atoms and molecules stop their dances, and electricity flows without hindrance. It is called the absolute zero of temperature. It is difficult to visualize the "south pole" of temperature. The absolute or Kelvin temperature scale, abbreviated K., has its zero at minus 273.1 degrees on the Centigrade scale or at minus 459.6 degrees on the Fahrenheit scale, the system used generally to designate everyday temperatures.

The ingenuity and persistence of scientists have pushed the range of attained temperature downward until it extends nearly to the ultimate of absolute zero. The lowest temperature ever produced and measured by man, 85/1000 of a degree on the Absolute scale, was achieved in the Kamerlingh Onnes laboratory at the University of Leyden, Holland. This "farthest south" of temperature is extraordinarily close to the absolute zero point. Only a few months earlier, new cold records of about twenty-five hundredths of a degree had been made at both the University of California and the Leyden laboratory.

The two groups of research workers, one at the University of California and the other in Holland, used novel methods identical in principle. The University of California scientists were Drs. W. F. Giauque and D. P. MacDougall, while the Dutch scientists were Prof. W. J. de Haas and E. C. Wiersma of Leyden and Prof. H. A. Kramers of Utrecht.

Dr. Heike Kamerlingh Onnes, the pioneer in low-temperature research who worked at Leyden, Holland, used the method of lowering temperature by reducing the vapor

pressure of liquid helium. He reached a temperature of
0.82 degrees absolute, and the same method was used by
his successor, Dr. W. H. Keesom of Leyden, in 1932, to
attain 0.71 degrees.

The new low temperature records were made by taking
advantage of the fact that when a substance is magnetized
it heats up. Using liquid helium, made by cooling, liquefying, and solidifying of air, and then liquefying hydrogen to
cool the helium, a substance is cooled as low as possible.
Then it is magnetized. It heats up. Liquid helium is used to
remove that heat. Then it is demagnetized, taking care to
keep it heat insulated. It becomes colder as a result of the
demagnetization. Thus lower temperature than ever before
attained has been reached. Technically the method is referred to as "adiabatic demagnetization of paramagnetic
salts." The Americans used a gadolinium sulphate while the
Dutch physicists used cerium fluoride as the substances to
be cooled.

The world's newest cryogenic laboratory is at the California Institute of Technology with Dr. Alexander Goetz
in charge. There hydrogen has been liquefied at temperatures lower than 250 degrees below zero Centigrade
(minus 418 degrees Fahrenheit). Such frigid liquid gases
will enable the scientists to penetrate a little explored field,
the study of metals at extremely low temperatures. Because of the danger of explosion, some of the first lique-
faction runs were made at night when near-by buildings
were vacant. Success, however, proved that there is no
fault in design which would cause explosions. In liquefying
hydrogen, one of the two torpedo-shaped containers holds
a liter, slightly more than a quart, of liquid hydrogen, and
the other the same quantity of liquid air. If these combine,
the energy available is equivalent to that in fifty pounds of
TNT. They are more likely to explode than TNT, and
such a detonation would be more violent than that caused
by the equivalent amount of TNT.

By subjecting matter to unusual experiences, such as
great cold, great pressure, and high heat, scientists expect
to learn more about the properties and structure of matter.

One of the many difficulties is that in the laboratory high

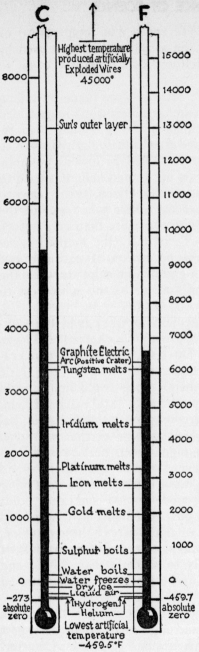

TEMPERATURE'S EXTREMES

Figure 3

A graphic representation showing the tremendous spread between absolute zero and the hottest temperature that man has been able to produce. The Centigrade scale is on the left, the Fahrenheit scale on the right.

pressures or high temperatures can be obtained separately but not together. All materials soften when highly heated and consequently will not withstand high pressure unless the temperature is moderate.

High Pressure and Heat

THE RECORD for high pressure is held by Dr. P. W. Bridgman of Harvard University, and stands around 600,000 pounds per square inch. This is the pressure at the bottom of a pile of bricks 100 miles high. Temperatures around 5,000 degrees Fahrenheit have been obtained in the laboratory, but only at moderate pressures.

Nature, however, produces vastly higher pressures and temperatures and produces them both together. Inside the stars, pressures are measured in millions of tons per square inch, and temperatures in millions of degrees. Even inside our own earth they are measured in thousands. How matter behaves under these conditions is at present entirely in the realm of hypothesis based on enormous extrapolation from experimental data. We would like to have more direct evidence.

Now comes Dr. C. Ramsauer, a German scientist, with an ingenious though simple contrivance by which high pressures and high temperatures can be produced simultaneously —but only for a fraction of a second. However, science is accustomed to phenomena of short duration. Speeding electrons and cosmic rays flash by in a millionth of a second. Yet what vast fields of new knowledge they have opened up! And materials can withstand momentarily pressures and temperatures that would be fatal if prolonged. Much may therefore be learned from Dr. Ramsauer's apparatus in which matter for the first time approaches a little way toward the conditions to be found in the stars.

The apparatus consists merely of a gun, which shoots a cylindrical projectile straight into the barrel of another similar gun. The projectile is brought to rest by compressing the air or other gas contained in the second gun. Not only is the pressure thus enormously raised, but also the temperature, for, as anyone knows who has pumped up an automobile tire, rapid compression of a gas heats it up. This is also shown by the Diesel engine, in which the explosive charge is heated by mere compression to the ignition point.

Calculation shows that if the gas is perfect and its specific heat or thermal capacity is constant, a projectile having a velocity of 300 feet per second, brought to rest in a distance of 3 feet—the length of the second tube—will compress the air therein to 375 pounds per square inch, and raise its temperature to 2,240 degrees Fahrenheit. These are very moderate figures. But if the speed of the projectile is raised to 3,000 feet per second, which may easily be done, the pressure jumps to 14 billion pounds per square inch, and the temperature to 216,000 degrees.

Of course, it is not expected that anything like these figures will actually be reached. No gas is perfect, the specific heats are not constant, and other things may happen in this as yet unexplored region, which equations based on observations at much lower pressures and temperatures cannot predict. Nevertheless, the calculation indicates that by this simple means very high pressures and temperatures can be produced, and produced simultaneously.

Preliminary apparatus as actually constructed consisted of a single long tube, the firing being done at one end and the compressing at the other end. A number of slits near the middle allowed the products of combustion to escape. For speeds up to 600 feet per second, compressed air was used to fire the gun. Under these circumstances it was found that the projectile bounced back and forth between the compression and the gun chambers as many as 24 times. Smokeless powder was used for higher speeds, but at 1,500 feet per second the apparatus was damaged. These are, of course, only preliminary trials. The real research is yet to be carried out.

Earth materials under extremely high pressures, such as they have to endure at considerable depths in the earth's interior, act structurally much as they would if subject to high temperatures. This has been learned from X-ray investigations of matter at high pressures by Dr. Willi M. Cohn working at Berkeley, Calif. In a special apparatus, pressures as high as 3,000 atmospheres, or 45,000 pounds per square inch, were attained. To resist such pressure it is necessary to make the metal walls of the cylinder thick and exceedingly strong, and this would interpose a very difficult barrier to the passage of X-rays by means of which the materials under pressure are to be studied. This difficulty is avoided by setting a window of beryllium, a very light but very strong metal, on the side where the rays are admitted. Opposite this window, on the "exit" side, is a second window of glass or bakelite. Behind this the photographic plate is placed. Photographs of the minute structure of the materials under study, made with X-rays both before and after the pressure is applied, give patterns from which it is possible to deduce the physical changes taking place.

How Fast Is Light?

THE VELOCITY of light is such an important fundamental constant of the physical world that much time has been spent in determining its value with extraordinary precision. The latest average value, which will doubtless be accepted as the world standard, is 299,774 kilometers (186,280 miles) per second. The investigation was carried on by Dr. Francis G. Pease of the Carnegie Institution's Mount Wilson Observatory and Fred Pearson of the University of Chicago, working with the mile-long vacuum pipe line at the Irvine Ranch, Santa Ana, Calif. The apparatus was designed and first used by the late Prof. A. A. Michelson. Further analysis of the observations may change the last figure by one or two units. This new value is seven thousandths of 1 per cent. lower than the Michelson 1926 result of 299,796 kilometers per second obtained as the result of observing the passage of light between two mountain peaks in California.

Unexplained variations which exceed considerably the experimental error of measurement were found in the course of the observations. One of these had for a time recurred every 14¾ days and another a longer period of about one year, but neither period persisted throughout the entire series. The range of variation in each case was about 20 kilometers (12 miles) per second.

The cause of such apparent variations is first of all to be sought in instrumental sources, in possible changes in the apparatus, the length of the lightpath, ground disturbances, errors in the timing mechanism, or a possible effect of refractive index in the path of light. The precision required in this difficult experiment is extraordinarily high. For such an investigation it would be desirable to have quartz mirrors, a much more stable pipe-line, and elaborate timing devices. In the opinion of Dr. W. S. Adams, Mt. Wilson Observatory director, it is only as a last resort that recourse should be taken to the hypothesis that the velocity of light actually varies.

Invisible Light

HUMAN EYES are capable of seeing only a portion of all the light there is in the world. Beyond the violet of the visible spectrum there are the ultraviolet radiations of shorter wavelength, and beyond the visible red there are the infrared or heat radiation of longer wavelength.

New tools for the study of invisible light rays have been placed in the hands of science as a result of researches on the optical properties of metals by two physicists at Johns Hopkins University. Prof. R. W. Wood found that thin films of the alkali metals possess the unique property of being transparent to ultraviolet light, and Prof. A. H. Pfund succeeded in preparing powder films of silver, gold, and several other metals that are transparent for the infrared or heat rays. Both types are opaque to visible light.

The value of these filters in scientific research lies in their ability to remove the visible rays from a beam of light. Visible light is almost always produced in sources of infrared or of ultraviolet light and frequently causes disturbances in measurements. Of the few materials now known which are capable of transmitting ultraviolet but not visible light one is a nickel oxide glass invented by Prof. Wood. The new alkali metal filters transmit a wider range in the ultraviolet spectrum than any filters of this type previously available. Technical applications, such as photoelectric counters operating with invisible beams, may be expected to follow.

The alkali metals, lithium, sodium, potassium, rubidium, and cæsium are soft, lustrous, highly reactive materials now used extensively in the production of photoelectric cells. A sixth member in this chemical family, element number 87, has not yet been isolated. The preparation of thin films of these metals was achieved by Prof. Wood by an ingenious method in which the metal is heated in a quartz bulb, the top of which is cooled to the very low temperature of liquid air. The metallic vapor condenses on the cold wall, forming a film whose thickness can be varied by regulating the heating of the metal. The operation is carried out in a vacuum. Films, a hundred-thousandth of an inch thick, of each of the five alkali metals were made in this way.

Prof. Wood discovered that all five of these metals were transparent to ultraviolet light, but the point in the spectrum at which they become transparent depends on the metal. Thus lithium, the lightest element in this group, transmits only the short wavelength part of the ultraviolet region, while for cæsium, the heaviest member, the transition point occurs in the visible part of the spectrum. In addition to the ultraviolet, cæsium transmits violet light, and films of this metal are described as having a rich violet color. This investigation included the study of various other optical properties of the alkali metals, such as reflecting power and interference phenomena. It was from observations of the latter that it was possible to determine the thickness of the films.

Photographing Invisible Objects

THE ORDINARY CAMERA of a few years ago was practically blind to any colors except the blues and invisible ultraviolet rays. So insensitive were photographic plates to the reds that it used to be safe to develop photographic plates and film with a red light. Advance in the science of photography has resulted in the development of photographic emulsions that are affected with more equality by all the colors of the spectrum or rainbow of colors. Photographs are less color blind than they were, and the various colors register on modern panchromatic plates with their proper light values much as the human eye sees them. The reds are no longer just black in a photograph.

Not content with making photographic plates record color values faithfully, the scientists working with photographic processes have developed emulsions that are sensitive to the invisible light rays that lie in the spectrum on the long-wave side of the visible red. These infrared rays are really just the same as heat rays. By using certain complex dyes as sensitizing agents for the silver salts in the photographic materials, plates that photograph by heat instead of light have been produced.

For several years these heat-sensitive plates have been used by scientists, especially astronomers, who have made their telescopes "see," or rather feel, stars that are invisible to both human eyes and ordinary photographic plates. Because the infrared light or heat penetrates through hazy atmosphere far better than visible light, infrared sensitive plates have been used successfully for photography at great distances. A mountain at a distance of 331 miles has been clearly recorded on such a plate. Photographs have been snapped in rooms that were in utter darkness so far as visible light and human eyes were concerned.

At first these infrared plates were specialties, available only to the specialists, many of whom sensitized their own plates. The plates often had to be kept on ice like fresh food in order that they would not be spoiled by heat before use. Now infrared sensitive plates are available commercially.

Long-distance photography provides the greatest use for heat-sensitive plates. But they allow fantastic pseudo-night effects in daylight photographs. The blue sky photographs black, and green foliage, a strong reflector of infrared, photographs a silvery white. Perhaps a new kind of portrait photography will come into style with the subject sitting "in total darkness."

If we could shut out the strong light of common day and

see things only by the fluorescence caused by ultraviolet radiation, the familiar streets and buildings around us would glow with the strange unfamiliar colors of a picture-book fairyland. The light would not be the ultraviolet itself, but visible radiations set up in various minerals and other substances by the action upon them of the invisible ultra-violet.

Ultraviolet lighting and special paints combined make possible the complete redecorating of a room with a flip of a switch. The usual room setting may be changed at will to that of a luminous Japanese tea garden or again to a dimly lit winter scene in a Swiss chalet. Ordinary non-luminous paints are used for the formal common finish that forms the standard type of decoration. Over these paints it is pos-sible for skilled artists to paint a scene of entirely different design with fluorescent paints of almost any color that will not show in daylight or with ordinary lighting fixtures. Still a third scene may be applied with phosphorescent paints that will glow in the dark. When the visible light is ex-tinguished and pure ultraviolet light is shone from con-cealed fixtures, the fluorescent and phosphorescent pigments in the special paints begin to shine, and the walls are lighted by a soft gentle light. When all the light, both ordinary and ultraviolet, is extinguished, the phosphorescent pattern be-comes visible.

Sodium Gives Light

UPON HIGHWAYS and tennis courts a strange yellow illumi-nation is beginning to be seen as sodium-vapor lamps come into experimental and semi-commercial use. Since 1932 sodium-vapor lamps for outdoor highway lighting have been installed on a large scale in Holland, Switzerland, Denmark, Sweden, and England. In 1933 both General Electric and Westinghouse installed sodium-vapor lamps of their own design on several highways, and sodium's yellow light was used to floodlight New York buildings. The great advantage of the sodium-vapor lamps is their efficiency. In them one watt of electricity will produce the intensity of light that requires $2\frac{1}{2}$ watts in an ordinary tungsten filament incandescent lamp. The great disadvantage is the singleness of color, an intense yellow, the color obtained when salt is sprinkled on an open fire. It is not likely that sodium-vapor lamps, despite their efficiency, will be popular in homes or places where people gather socially because the monochromatic light makes people take on weird appearances. But its economy and the very fact that it gives only one color of light fits sodium-vapor illuminants for service on highways, playing fields, and in factories where keenness of vision and low cost are major factors.

While engineers bathe the night-time world in new lights, there is in the making a revolution in the materials with which artists record on canvas their imaginative or realistic impressions of the world as they see it. Dr. Herbert E. Ives of the Bell Telephone Laboratories is the physicist who has been responsible for the development of so many improvements in the science of communication, including television. As a hobby, he paints. Troubled by the myriad of tubes of paints needed by an artist, Dr. Ives applied the sciences of optics and chemistry to the problem and developed three pigments, called "minus red," "minus blue," and "minus green." Each of these reflects mostly the light rays complementary to its "minus" hue, but also a large range of others. Mixing them gives all desired ranges of hues, and combining all of them gives black. Adding white, to give tints and for the actually white parts of the painting, Dr. Ives has a palette carrying only four kinds of paint, which are sufficient for every imaginable requirement of the artist.

With the difficulty of color mixing on the artist's palette simplified by Dr. Ives, the principles of art will be more easily taught and more of those who have the urge to paint for pleasure will be able to indulge their desire to place color on canvas. Science will have served art just as it has so effectively aided industry.

CHAPTER 9
THE CHANGING EARTH

Earth is a mother who changes but slowly. Man's years are but moments in her days; the oldest of us has not seen any significant wrinkles that our grandsires a hundred times removed did not also see.

Nevertheless, she does change. Wind and weather are always at work on her face, and their work of erosion never ends. We of the short lives think of that only when by our own thoughtless, selfish mischief we make possible a speeding-up of the process and then have to take desperate steps in haste to undo what we can of our own damage. One phase of man's effort to become even a small geological factor on his own account is related in this connection, in Chapter 19. But for the most part, this principal cause of change in the face of nature is so gradual that its workings cannot be recorded in the chronicle of a brief few months. The only geological events that happen quickly enough might be likened to slight nervous twitchings: earthquakes, volcanic eruptions, landslides, floods, and mud-flows. These take place in a few hours or even a few minutes, and their consequences are often awesome from the human point of view. Yet we must remember always that they are only the relatively sudden releases of forces or strains that have been accumulating for a long period: an earthquake that shakes down a city has as a rule been centuries a-making, through some such cause as the gradual loading of the adjacent sea bottom with eroded spoil from the land, until the underlying rock strata can no longer carry the burden without slipping or buckling a bit.

We must remember, too, that these things we call convulsions of nature are not really major disturbances. They seem so only to our egocentric selves: what is a tremor that destroys a row of towns compared with the slow upheaval of rock that through millennia of millennia build a mountain range?

And finally, we must remember that though we and our works may unfortunately be in the way of some of these lesser quick changes in Earth's face and so be swept away, there is nothing malevolent about the action. The legal phrase that terms such events as earthquakes, floods, and windstorms as "acts of God" is basically not as blasphemous as we like to say it is. The human race, as well as other living things, profits by the building of mountains, the cutting of river channels, the deposit of new soil by the flooding of the Nile or the ash-showers of Vesuvius.

Earthquakes

WE CAN EVEN AVOID, or at least mitigate, the consequences of some of these sudden jerks of nature. Long ago we learned to come in out of the rain, and to tame fire to keep away the cold. We have also learned to build waveproof sea walls and hurricane-proof houses. We can put up earthquake-proof office buildings and apartments as well, if we can persuade a scary Chamber of Commerce to admit that maybe an earthquake will come our way some day, and if we can exercise a little vigilance to keep building contractors up to specifications.

From the record of recent earthquakes scientists have already been deriving lessons which await only the pleasure of "practical" men to be put into effect for the general benefit. The scientists have intensified their efforts toward an eventual ability to forecast earth storms as they learned, a few generations back, to forecast air storms. Seismometers, seismographs, tiltmeters, their name is legion, but their effort is all in the same direction: the increasing of human security on a slightly uneasy earth.

Engineers have also joined in the game, in an effort to find out how much steel, how riveted or welded together, must be put into a building to make it more secure against shakes and yet not wastful of material. The newest thing is what is known as a stress recorder, and is the invention of A. C. Ruge, research associate in seismology in the department of civil engineering, at the Massachusetts Institute of Technology.

In this apparatus, when a stress is applied a beam of light is correspondingly displaced, so that the line traced on a photographic paper becomes a curve, accurately recording the degree of bending and hence the force exerted at that point. But such things are only beginnings in man's effort to avoid or protect himself from the consequences of Earth's uneasiness. Years of development must still be gone through—and in the meantime the earthquakes still go on.

Terrestrial Messengers

THE FALL OF A METEORITE from the skies is usually (and quite properly) considered an astronomical event. But when one of these masses of iron or stone from unknown outer space has been lying on or in the earth long enough, it may with equal propriety be considered from the geological point of view. Thus geologists consider themselves licensed to study and speculate about Meteor Crater, the great pit in the northern Arizona plateau believed to have been caused by the smashing impact of a massive projectile from the skies. This crater may be much older than it is commonly credited with being. Past estimates have ranged from 2,000 to 10,000 years, but on the basis of five independent lines of geological evidence Prof. Eliot Blackwelder of Stanford University is "led to suspect," he states, "that the crater was made during the last interglacial epoch, perhaps 40,000 to 75,000 years ago."

Most of Prof. Blackwelder's evidence consists of indications of a much moister climate than now prevails on the arid plateau, and of a relatively long duration of this moist climate. Most striking is his interpretation of a deep deposit of lake-bed strata at the bottom of the crater. This deposit is of such a nature that it indicates a long-standing, permanent body of water, not a mere succession of playas or seasonal ponds such as might be found in the Southwest of today. At present one must bore 200 feet below the bottom of the pit to find permanent water.

The old lake-bed deposits consist of extremely finely pulverized quartz with many remains of snail shells and diatoms, or one-celled water plants. This is interbedded with fresh-water limestone, beds of coaly material, and a single layer of volcanic ash, indicating a long-past explosive eruption somewhere in the neighborhood.

Prof. Blackwelder's other lines of evidence consist of marked indications of active erosion by the wind and also by running water, such as is furnished by the infrequent "cloudbursts" of a semi-arid region.

Less impressive now, but incomparably more terrific in their genesis, were the shallow elliptical formations called the Carolina "bays," if the meteoritic theory of their origin, put forth by Prof. F. A. Melton and Prof. William Schriever of the University of Oklahoma, is correct.

The terrors that may have attended the Doomsday brought by the small comet that the two scientists believe struck the earth in that region would require for their proper telling the imagination of a youthful H. G. Wells.

One's mind recoils from thinking about such a cataclysm, as something too dreadful to be really possible. Yet there is good evidence that such a smash occurred at least once in the history of the world, and that within comparatively recent times, as geological dates go. It happened in the states of North and South Carolina, and it possibly involved parts of several other adjoining states as well.

It is a strange thing that though the Carolinas are among the longest-populated of the white man's settlements in the United States, the significance of these scars has only just been read by geologists.

If Profs. Melton and Schriever are in error about the cause of these markings, which now bear the curious local name of "bays," doubters will have a nice job of disproving on their hands, for the two men have built up a strong case in support of their hypothesis.

The "bays" of the Carolinas are a series of elliptical depressions in the earth, scattered in hundreds throughout the flat coastal-plain country of both states, from the Georgia boundary northeastward to Cape Lookout.

The "bays" vary greatly in size, from a few yards to a

mile and a half in their longer diameter, but in all other respects they show that they belong to the same natural family.

They are all elliptical in outline, and the bigger the bay the greater is the length relative to the width. Every one of them has its long axis in a northwest-southeast direction, and every one has a raised rim of light, sandy soil at its southeastern end. Around some of them the rims run entire, but these have higher lips at the southwestern end. A few have double rims, and at least one has a triple rim. Some of the largest "bays" have lesser "bays" within them. Some of them have intersecting rims, but in all such cases it looks as though the rim of one had pushed aside the rim of its neighbor. At present they are quite shallow—only a few yards below the surrounding ground level at the deepest— but borings show that their original depth was considerably greater, and that they have been filled up with other material, different from their sandy bottoms, and from the sandy soil in their rims.

Whatever made these "bays" could not have hit the coastal plain much before the beginning of the Ice Age, roughly a million years ago, for the bottoms of most of them lie in a geological formation known to be of late preglacial date. On the other hand, their latest possible date of formation must have been quite early in the Ice Age, for the soil deposits within and around them have been identified as early glacial. So the scientists have obtained a fair "bracket" on their age. They know also, from the nature of the earth layers, that this whole area was covered by the sea during a part of the Ice Age and later reëmerged. During this submergence it is quite likely that their rims were washed down from an originally greater height, and that other changes took place in them.

But through all these changes enough of their original form has persisted to make this unique great family of shallow craters one of the greatest geological riddles of the earth.

Profs. Melton and Schriever thought up all the answers to this riddle they could think of, likely or otherwise, and then tried to see which one would best fit the conditions as they found them. Origin by volcanic action, by persistent northwest winds, by eddying swirls in the sea, by several other causes, were all discarded because they failed to explain one or more of the features of the "bays." But the idea that a comet consisting of a large number of great rock or iron masses had swept across the Carolinas held up better than any other, and until they can find some really serious flaw in it they rest on the provisional conclusion that the "bays" were formed in this way.

A Colder Earth

WE SPEAK of the earth as being terrifically old. It might be better to think of this mighty Mother as perennially, even millennially young. For half a billion years or more ago, in the remote geological time called pre-Cambrian, earth conditions were not essentially different from what they are now. Contrary notions, formerly widely entertained even in scientific circles, are having to give way, Prof. J. J. Sederholm of the University of Helsingfors, Finland, has declared.

As compared with Cambrian and pre-Cambrian times, the most recent of the great ice ages, the Pleistocene, was no more than yesterday. Yet because of its very nearness to our own period (for we may even be living in a mere interval in the Pleistocene) new developments in its story are of especial interest to us human beings.

With a thermometer in the depths of a Wisconsin copper mine as their "calendar of prehistory," two geologists have estimated that the last ice age withdrew from northern Wisconsin twenty to thirty thousand years ago. The scientists, Drs. W. O. Hotchkiss, president of Michigan College of Mining and Technology, and L. R. Ingersoll, of the University of Wisconsin, told how they obtained their data and made calculations. The new figure is much less than the estimated period since the Niagara Falls region was free of a continental glacier. It is greater than the seven or eight thousand years European geologists have determined from studies of layers of sediment as the time since the retreat of the last ice sheet from parts of Norway and Sweden. But it does agree roughly, as geological time is approximated, with the dates set for the retreat of the last great ice sheet from Europe and North America.

The temperature measurements, which were made at levels 500 feet apart to a depth of one mile, also indicate that the melting of the ice "was followed, perhaps after several thousand years, by a period distinctly warmer than the present, which was succeeded in turn by one slightly cooler and lasting until rather recent times." Only the average temperature of the ground varied in this manner, it was pointed out, while the average air temperature could have been different. The calculations depend on the assumption, which geologists consider reasonable, that the last ice sheet covered the site of the measurements for about fifty thousand years. In this time it would have cooled the ground to the same temperature throughout the mile depth in which measurements were taken.

Strange Animals

EVEN MORE FASCINATING than the story of the formation, age, and shiftings of the rocks themselves is the story of the life that swarmed and struggled on the face of the earth in past ages. Recent research has brought to light many dramatic tales, in which the protagonists range from tiny sea creatures to lumbering dinosaurs, from humble plants to ferocious saber-tooth cats. Among them also are the oldest and strangest of the more immediate zoölogical cousins of men.

California fossil beds of Eocene time, 55 million years old, have yielded the remains of two hitherto unknown genera of lemuroid animals, creatures resembling monkeys but lower in the scale of life. The finds were described by Prof. Chester Stock of the California Institute of Technology. One of them constitutes the newest representative of the primate family known from America. No representatives of this lemuroid group had hitherto been described from California; all previously known specimens being from the intermontane basins of the Rocky Mountain region.

Little animals of the same group lived also in what are

now the Badlands of South Dakota 35 million years ago, or some such matter. Broken fragments of the skull and jaws of such a creature, found last summer by geologists of the Scott Fund Expedition of Princeton University, had their identity established by Prof. Glenn L. Jepsen. The animals belonged to the primate sub-family Plasiadapidæ, and lived during Oligocene time, which is well back toward the beginning of the Age of Mammals. The fossils are the first of their kind and age to be found in North America, and the skull is stated to be the most perfect representative of its zoölogical group yet discovered anywhere.

A further discovery of outstanding importance made by the Scott Fund Expedition was a prehistoric alligator skeleton in a fine state of preservation. Dr. Jepsen also announced the discovery of a second location for dinosaur eggs in North America, situated in the Big Horn Basin, Wyoming.

The activities of the expedition were conducted for the most part in the titanothere beds of the Badlands of South Dakota. Most previous collectors have confined their efforts to seeking specimens of the enormous rhinoceros-like animal for which these beds are named; the Princeton group was thus able to collect more than a ton of smaller specimens which had been overlooked. Included in the material were bones of rats, rabbits, carnivores, and an extinct animal related to the opossum, as well as specimens of the saber-tooth cat and giant pig.

Our Dwindling Inheritance Increases

MAN'S RELATIONS to Earth are not confined to terror at her natural destructiveness, understanding of and defense against it, and curious pryings into the story of her past. Earth has gifts for Man, if he knows how to seek and find them.

Oil and gas will have increasing use as energy sources in the United States, and by 1950 they will account for nearly half of the expanded fuel requirements of the nation. A forecast of the relationship between coal and petroleum in the future and a survey of future energy requirements was presented by Prof. W. Spencer Hutchinson of the Massachusetts Institute of Technology and August J. Breitenstein, Ashland, Pa., engineer.

In 1950 it is estimated that 499,500,000 tons of coal will be used compared with 517,018,000 tons in 1930. The situation is reversed for petroleum, with 1,419,000,000 barrel consumption predicted for 1950, and 868,484,000 barrels consumed in 1930.

Total energy per capita demanded in the United States showed a consistent growth, and it increased at a faster rate than the population. Chief sources of energy today are the mineral fuels, coal and petroleum, which between them account for more than 90 per cent of the demand, with water power supplying only 10 per cent. A marked change has occurred in the relative proportion of energy obtained from coal and oil. Only 30 years ago 91 per cent of the country's horsepower came from coal, and only 4 per cent from oil and natural gas, but in 1930, horsepower from coal had dropped to 60 per cent, while the proportion furnished by oil and gas had risen to 31 per cent. By 1950 it is estimated that coal will furnish only 46 per cent of the country's power, while 45 per cent will come from oil and gas and 8 per cent from water power.

Consumption of coal in this country reached its zenith in 1917, with 6.08 tons per capita. From this year the decline was rapid. It was only 4.2 tons in 1930, and they forecast but 4.16 in 1950.

Other findings of the study by Prof. Hutchinson and Mr. Breitenstein are:

Whereas in 1930 the effective energy supply in the United States, expressed in trillions of British Thermal Units, was 9,031, it will have risen to 14,500 by 1950. In 1930, the energy supply per capita, expressed in millions of British Thermal Units, was 73, while in 1950 it is expected to be 94. Whereas bituminous and anthracite coal accounted for 60.3 per cent of the total energy derived in 1930, it will account for only 46.6 per cent in 1950. Petroleum and its natural products, including also natural gas and natural gas gasoline, will show a marked rise. Accounting for only 31.6 per cent of the total energy derived in 1930, they will account for 45.3 per cent in 1950. Water power will account for exactly the same percentage of the total energy derived in 1950 as in 1930, namely, 8.1, although the energy applied by hydropower will be greater than in 1930.

Petroleum, now one of the principal wealths of the world, was originally garbage—offal from the endless complex banquet of the sea, that not even the bacteria in the bottom slime would eat.

This un-pretty picture of the origin of "black gold" was reported by Dr. Parker D. Trask of the U. S. Geological Survey. Dr. Trask and his associates have for a number of years been conducting an exhaustive study of both modern and ancient sea-bottom deposits, seeking for further knowledge of how petroleum was formed in the first place, so that seekers after oil may have a better idea of what kinds of geological formations are likely to yield paying results to their expensive drillings. They found that fine-grained beds contain more organic matter than coarse-grained: clay more than silt, silt more than sand. They learned, as was to be expected, that where the sea bottom is rolling and irregular, richer deposits are to be found in the hollows than on the submarine hilltops or slopes. They found, above all, that the dead bodies of the myriad sea plants that escaped eating by fishes and other marine animals were not left as raw materials for oil-making until even the bacteria of the bottom slime had taken from them such materials as they wanted for themselves.

This bottom bacterial action seems to be of the highest importance in the formation of the stuffs that eventually become petroleum. Crude plant materials, and such fishes and other animal carcasses as settle to the bottom, have relatively high nitrogenous and carbohydrate contents, which are unsuitable for working over into oil. The food requirements of the bacteria seem to be especially aimed at these non-oil-producing food materials, thereby leaving the organic débris in better condition for the oil-making processes themselves.

Oil-making seems to be an exceedingly slow job. It is not going on in the sediments now forming on the ocean bottom, but it is in progress in sediments laid down on the sea bottoms of geological yesterdays. The steps are not known with anything like satisfactory certainty, but there seems to be no doubt that great increase in sedimentary thickness, with resulting pressure and heat, squeeze and fry out the material that eventually becomes petroleum. It then seeps along migration paths through sandy strata, and collects in pools where impervious rock layers bar its further wanderings.

Earth Exhausted?

THE POSSIBLE EXHAUSTION of iron and steel of the present age of metals forebodes no evil for civilizations-to-come, in the picture of the future drawn by Prof. Colin G. Fink of Columbia University, inventor and authority on electrochemistry. For the next age will be that of aluminum, Prof. Fink predicted. And aluminum is the most abundant common metal in the earth's crust, being even more common than much-used iron, which it is expected to supplant for many purposes.

"The keynote of the coming new era will be the large number of new products and devices," Prof. Fink declared. "Among the metals the one metal to enter the widest variety of new fields will be aluminum—aluminum for railway equipment, aluminum for roofs and buildings, for food containers, for transmission, for airplanes, for tank cars, pipe lines, fencing, etc. Finally we should mention the new aluminum plate, superior to tin plate in many respects, developed at the electro-chemical laboratories at Columbia.

"Whereas the supply of raw material for many of our metals is comparatively limited in years, the supply of bauxite or aluminum ore is almost limitless. Thus, for example, whereas copper at the 1929 rate of consumption will last but forty or fifty years, the aluminum ore reserves will satisfy our demands for many hundred years."

In the relative abundance of the common metals in the earth's crust, taking the parts by weight, aluminum leads with 80,000, iron is second with 50,000, while copper is seventh with only twenty, Prof. Fink pointed out. He said that for every pound of copper in the earth's crust there are 4,000 pounds of aluminum.

Minerals and War

UNEVEN DISTRIBUTION of minerals essential to modern civilization threatens the peace of the world, Prof. Richard M. Field, Princeton geologist, gave warning.

Until the geographical location of important metals, coal, oil, nitrates, phosphates, and potash is seriously considered from an international point of view, Prof. Field predicted, there never can be a reasonable amity among nations, no matter what other factors may affect international affairs. U. S. government statistics show that 28 minerals constitute more than 70 per cent of the gross value of the mineral raw materials of commerce. English-speaking people in the United States and the British Empire have, Prof. Field said, "by one means or another gradually acquired the absolute or partial control of two thirds of the essential mineral resources of the world."

The Japanese situation is the present outstanding problem in mineral resources. Japan has barely enough copper and zinc for domestic consumption, with an inadequate supply of iron, chromium, and manganese. She is entirely dependent on outside sources for practically all other mineral supplies.

Italy, another first-class power, is in about the same position as Japan, except that she has no control over petroleum and coal and is a little better off as to iron and lead. Both Japan and Italy are in a worse position than Great Britain would be if she were divorced from the British Empire. Spain is described by Prof. Field as "a nation that is not making the most of her natural resources." This country, he predicted, may become a source of trouble in the international affairs of Europe. With the exception of certain ferro-alloys and petroleum, Spain has adequate deposits of the important mineral resources and an excess of copper, iron, lead, manganese, and mercury for export.

Germany has inadequate supplies of metallic minerals but excesses of coal and potash. France is only a little better off than Germany, Prof. Field said, with more aluminum and iron than she needs but no petroleum. France also has great phosphate deposits available in Morocco. The United States has all she needs within her own sovereign territory with the exception of the ferro-alloys.

Mineral ores, ranging from those of aluminum to those of vanadium, play an important part in this modern industrial world. The nation or area of the world that is lacking in a particular kind of mineral raw material is at a great disadvantage and dependent upon other nations or areas.

Where and under what nationalistic control are the world's minerals produced? As Prof. C. K. Leith of the University of Wisconsin summarizes:

Aluminum—More than half the world's alumium ore, bauxite, is produced in Europe, the rest by United States, British Guiana, and Surinam, with production of the metal about equally divided between Europe and North America. North American interests control about half of the mining and refining.

Chromite—Africa is the mining center for chromite, the ore of chromium, two thirds of the world supply of which is used in the United States largely for alloying steel.

Copper—Half of the world's copper industry is located in the United States, with the next important region, Chile, Canada, and south-central Africa. Control lies in American, British, and Belgian hands, with American control of 83 per cent of the refinery production.

Iron and steel—the bulk of the world's iron and steel industry is concentrated in western Europe and the United States, where it is either owned completely, or nearly so, by domestic capital.

Lead—Although widely scattered over the world, one-third of the lead industry is located in the United States, with Mexico, Australia, and Canada ranking next.

Manganese ore—Russia in 1929 produced a third of the world's manganese ore, and world control is split between Britain, Russia, Brazil, and America.

Mercury—The liquid metal comes principally from Spain and Italy, the United States producing 17 tons in 1929, or 15 per cent of the world supply.

Molybdenum—The United States dominates the situation, producing 94 per cent.

Nickel—Canada is the nickel nation, producing 90 per cent.

Nitrates—Chile is the only commercial source of natural nitrates, but synthetic nitrates from the air have broken this monopoly.

Petroleum—The world's oil industry is concentrated principally in the United States, secondarily in Russia and in northern South America.

American capital controlled 70 per cent of the world production in 1930.

Potash—World production is concentrated in Germany and France, but there are deposits of vast potential productivity in the United States and Morocco.

Silver—Production is restricted largely to North and South America, especially Mexico and the United States.

Sulfur—United States with 85 per cent and Italy with 11 per cent of the world's production dominate.

Tin—Mining is concentrated in the Malay States, Bolivia, and the Netherlands East Indies, with British interests dominating.

Tungsten—China supplies half and Burma one fifth of the world's total.

Vanadium—Two thirds of the production is consumed in the United States, largely for steel alloying, but Peru with 60 per cent, Southwest Africa with 20 per cent, and the United States with 17 per cent are the producers.

Zinc—This industry is centered largely in the United States, with 40 per cent production, and Mexico, Australia, Germany, and Poland each furnish 10 per cent.

CHAPTER 10
EXPLORING UPWARDS

MANY AND VARIED are the instruments with which man has pushed ever upward and made subject to his knowledge the mysterious regions of air above all familiar clouds, above the winds, into the realm where the midday sky is dark and where every sound produced would be strangely faint and feeble.

The airplane soars aloft and brings down daily records on which predictions of the weather are based. Sealed spheres of modern metals carry men aloft to regions never visited before. Unmanned balloons carry registering instruments yet higher and bring down records of nature's secrets as yet beyond the direct reach of our own experience. And higher still one gleans knowledge of the elements by watching the movement of strange clouds so far above the surface of the globe that they gleam at night with the sun's reflected light, by observing the trails of meteors sometimes left after their momentary flash across the sky, and studying the auroras—most distant of all visible phenomena in the earth's atmosphere.

Yet higher than the meteor's trail and even much of the aurora's splendor, are sent the impulses of the radio, and they, too, bring back their message of structure in the heights beyond the reach of man but already within his understanding.

Most interesting of these means for probing the depths of the stratosphere because it gives first-hand experience of conditions there, yet rarely because of our inability, until recently, to construct the adequate and costly equipment, is the method of manned flights in the so-called stratosphere balloons.

In a metal sphere, built as a submarine is built, to with-

stand tremendous pressures without allowing the slightest
crevice to appear, men have stowed themselves with their
scientific instruments, ballast, and their personal necessities
for the space voyage. Then, as the heat of the sun expanded the gas in the huge balloon above their heads, they
have been carried far above the clouds to that region where
the temperature changes but little with change of height
known as the stratosphere.

Although the stratosphere balloonist will tell you that
the dangers of such a flight are nothing as compared with
that of the pedestrian crossing the street at a busy inter-
section, still the perils of a space voyage are well recognized by all who have planned or taken part in them. Each
is given careful consideration, and every precaution humanly
possible is taken to avoid or minimize the danger.

Of prime importance is the providing of air for the lungs
of the flyers. The density of the air at the altitudes attained
by the stratosphere flights is less than 10 per cent of standard, and the pressure only about 2 inches as compared with
a sea-level pressure of 30 inches. Above the base of the
stratosphere, about 7 miles up, temperatures in middle latitudes are nearly constant with height at an average value of
about 67 degrees below zero on the Fahrenheit scale.

The first safety provision was then to insure that the
stratosphere gondola should be airtight and pressure proof.
Soap bubbles were used as frail instruments in the first pre-
cautionary tests of the *Century of Progress* metal sphere.

Breathing Aloft

WHEN THE GONDOLA was completed at Akron, the pressure inside the sphere was pumped up to 20 pounds to the
square inch, and the outside was then painted over with a
solution such as that used by children for bubble-blowing.
A tiny soap bubble betrayed the presence of each of the
tiniest leaks through which the precious supply of oxygen
might seep away.

The most difficult points to seal are around the hatches
or openings in the upper half of the sphere. Two doors are
used for each opening, one pressed in from the outside

against a rubber gasket and the other forced outward from the inside. This pressure is exerted by an ingenious screw that draws the doors together at their centers.

Submarine experts joined with aëronautic experts in making the "hull" of the first American stratosphere balloon, for the problem of resisting abnormal pressures is much the same for both types of vessel, although the ship of the sky has the pressure applied from within rather than from without.

In the submarine and stratosphere types of vessel, it is necessary to carry along the atmosphere to be breathed by the crew. Upon this problem, also, aid was secured from the navy's experts on submarine air conditioning. A specially devised apparatus was constructed for air conditioning in the stratosphere flight. It weighed only about 4.8 pounds but was capable of keeping the air in good breathing condition for two men for twenty-four hours. Oxygen was carried for two purposes, for breathing and for maintaining the pressure constant within the ball. Regardless of the diminishing pressures outside as the ship traveled skyward, the pressure within the sphere was maintained steadily at six tenths of an atmosphere, or about what it is at the top of a moderately high mountain or about 13,000 feet above sea level. Provision was also made in the American "stratostat" to reduce the moisture content of the air. This again had a twofold purpose, the comfort and health of the flyers and the prevention of frost formation on the inside of the shell. Little bags of drying agents were placed in the window openings to keep Jack Frost from painting obscuring patterns on the quartz and glass.

The second great peril of the space voyager is that of storm. Frost and freezing rain to weight the ship, boisterous winds to buffet it, downward vertical currents to dash it to the earth, and lightning to strike the hydrogen with deadly fire. These are the dangers presented by the weather. And since man can do nothing about the weather, these dangers are to be avoided only by careful forecasting and patient waiting until all conditions are favorable.

This always means delay and repeated delay until the nerves of promoters are frayed and the courage of the pilots doubted by the skeptical. Wind and weather differ from height to height just as they vary from point to point on the earth's surface. The flyer who is traveling cross-country can to a certain extent choose his weather by varying his altitude, selecting favorable winds and dodging fogs and rains and lightning discharges. But the flyer whose course lies straight up must take whatever comes. And seldom indeed does every successive height present a pleasing prospect.

The fact that the place of landing is determined by conditions entirely beyond the pilot's control and only partially within his powers of prediction, presents the stratosphere balloonist with his third great danger. When a balloon takes off for a flight into the stratosphere, no man knows exactly where it will come to earth. It may be in the jungle wilds miles from food or other succor. It may be in a city's busy thoroughfares. Or it may be on the ocean's desolate expanse.

The steering of a balloon is quite a different matter from the guiding of an airplane or dirigible. The balloon must travel wherever the currents of air carry it. The only means within the power of the pilot for guiding his stratosphere craft is to select a time when weather reports indicate that the currents are in general in a direction in which he wishes to go. This again means waiting and waiting with the patience that a scientist must have.

Lieut. Commdr. T. G. W. Settle and Major C. L. Fordney, the first American stratospherists, awaited westerly currents of moderate velocity that bore them almost due east from Akron and landed them in the marshy ground of the New Jersey cranberry bogs. Here was soft wet ground suitable for landing—the gondola is prepared for water landing even better than for ground—yet no houses, men, or even cattle were in the way to be injured. An ideal landing place, with the wading ashore a disagreeable but unhazardous task.

The Soviet flyers in the *U. S. S. R.* George Prokofiev, Ernest Birnbaum, and Konstantin Godunov, were more fortunate in having wind currents which carried them only 72 miles from their starting point. It is said to have remained visible to observers in Moscow as a tiny speck in the sky throughout the entire ascent and descent.

The ill-fated *Osoaviakhim*, or *Sirius* as she was known from her radio call letters, was carried several hundred kilometers to the village where the fatal crash occurred.

The pilots of the *Explorer*, who made the gallant attempt for the National Geographic Society and the U. S. Army, chose northwest winds which carried them out of the woods onto safer plains.

By far the greatest peril of the stratospherist is the terrific speed of the descent. It is not the soaring to unknown heights that the flyer fears, it is the abrupt return to the hard, resistant earth.

The stratosphere balloonist makes his ascent with the rising sun. Starting with a bag only partly filled with hydrogen gas, he awaits the warming rays of the sun to heat and expand the gas, gradually lifting him up and up. At noon, with the sun most nearly overhead, the ceiling is reached. Then as the sun descends, the gas contracts and the balloon begins her thrilling downward trip. It is then that ballast must be discarded, and discarded with all possible speed. The first American carried a ton of lead dust for this purpose. They were prepared to follow this with a hundred pounds of other ballast, if necessary.

Each scientific instrument was equipped with its own little parachute so that it might be sent down "on its own" in case its weight became a burden. Even the men themselves were prepared to jump. This did not become necessary.

Each extra ounce of burden carries the ship with that much greater force toward the earth. So it was that the *Osoaviakhim*, her flyers exultant over their success, entered the lower levels of the atmosphere. Here the air was filled with fog, and the temperature was at the freezing point. The *Sirius* call, "all is well," was followed by a message stating that visibility was so poor that the flyers could not determine their position.

These are the conditions in which frost forms, and frost forming on the gondola meant an increasing weight at a moment when each particle of added weight increased the danger. Perhaps the flyers were not prepared to jump. Per-

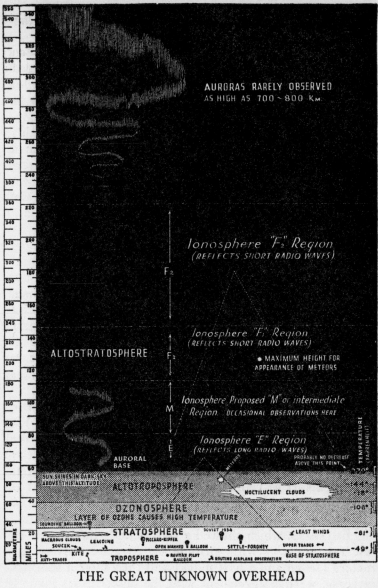

THE GREAT UNKNOWN OVERHEAD

FIGURE 4

A GRAPHIC representation showing everything that science has discovered
to a height of 350 miles.

113

haps they were unable to open the hatches. Perhaps there was no time.

The gondola hit the earth with such force that residents of the vicinity reported an explosion. Men, gondola, and the scientific records achieved in this record flight were all lost. Only a fragment of barograph tape indicated that they had climbed to heights never reached by man before.

Not gathered frost, but a disastrous tear in the fabric, brought to earth the *Explorer* with Capt. William E. Kepner, Capt. Albert W. Stevens, and Lieut. O. A. Anderson.

Scientists need weeks and months to evaluate the data collected by the recent stratosphere ascents. Most interesting are the cosmic ray observations.

Measuring Cosmic Rays

IN THE SPRING of 1922, direct measurements of cosmic rays were made at extremely high altitudes. Then Dr. Robert A. Millikan and Dr. I. S. Bowen sent up sounding balloons from Kelly Field, Texas, to almost twice the heights that had previously been attained for cosmic ray measurements. They reached an altitude of 15.6 kilometers, or nearly ten miles.

In 1932, such measurements were made up to nearly seventeen miles above the earth's surface. Prof. E. Regener, of the Physical Institute of the Technical High School, Stuttgart, Germany, sent up his cosmic ray detector attached to two rubber balloons and protected against the cold by a sort of cellophane "hothouse," which caught the sun's rays and kept the instrument inside well above the freezing point.

His results, which showed a considerable increase of cosmic ray intensity with altitude up to about twelve kilometers (seven and a half miles) and thereafter a less rapid increase, were in agreement with the observations made on the Piccard flights and were checked also, and more closely, by the observers in the *U. S. S. R.* The Regener as well as the Millikan observations were made with an electrometer.

In the Piccard flight, a difference was found between the

action of the ionization chamber, one of the instruments for detecting cosmic rays, and the Geiger counter used for the same purpose. The relative indications of the counter increased at a greater rate than those of the ionization chamber, as the balloon soared upward. In the highest altitudes reached, the activity of the counter was three times that of the ionization chamber.

Both instruments were carried by the American stratospherists Settle and Fordney on their flight, and also an ionization chamber shielded by an external layer of lead shot. They were self-recording and gave satisfactory records, confirming in Dr. A. H. Compton's opinion the assumption that the cosmic rays are charged particles not radiation like super gamma rays or X-rays.

Because of the great size of this American balloon, it was possible to carry in the gondola cosmic ray meters whose weight would have been prohibitive for smaller balloons. The heavier instruments gave higher orders of precision than those used in earlier balloon experiments. The cosmic ray counter designed by Dr. Compton and Dr. R. J. Stephenson was surrounded by 200 pounds of fine lead shot. The shot added weight, but it served to avoid complications in interpreting the measurements. Dr. Millikan's counter also had greater precision than was previously possible with lighter devices.

It had also been planned to measure the direction of the cosmic rays, but the observers were foiled in this attempt by an unexpected circumstance. The gondola spun around so rapidly at the heights that any such observations were rendered completely out of the question. This difficulty was overcome in the *Explorer,* but the records were damaged.

Regarding the color of the sky in the rarefied regions of the stratosphere, there is not such good agreement. The Belgian and the Russian flyers reported a deep purple sky which might be expected on theoretical grounds. The first American flight reported, however, no tinge of purple or violet in the stratosphere's sky.

Their visual observations, checked by the use of a spectroscope. showed that the sky had instead a peculiar yellow and green. Close to the horizon was a layer of white due to clouds far below. This shaded into a steel blue, and then into a saffron yellow, this color apparently born of light scattered from distant cirrus clouds of the high altitudes and traveling a long way through the atmosphere. Overhead the color shaded rapidly through green to a deep blue. The skylight at 90 degrees from the sun was found to vibrate entirely in one plane, that is, to be completely polarized, and not split up as it is in the denser regions of the atmosphere near the earth where dust is abundant.

Radio broadcast of the signals from the stratostats demonstrated that short-wave signals can be transmitted from these great altitudes to the earth with great clearness and freedom from static. The very short wavelength of 19.7 meters was used by the American flyers for sending down reports of their adventure to those waiting below. The reception was excellent, as it was also from the unfortunate *Osoaviakhim*.

Meteorologists have learned comparatively little from these new ascents, for their instruments had already been sent much further up into the stratosphere than human beings have been able to go. The routine flights of instrument-carrying balloons extend to heights of about 12 miles, or as high as the American stratospherists ventured. On numerous occasions, they have reached even greater altitudes. The American record for these sounding balloons was set at Avalon, Calif., in 1913, when an altitude of 33 kilometers, or 20 miles was reached. Yet this is not the highest altitude claimed. The record belongs to a German balloon which rose from Hamburg to an altitude of 35.9 kilometers, or 22 miles. If these two records are correct, they surely represent the largest heights that can be expected by this means, for there are theoretical reasons for doubting whether balloons can rise much beyond 30 kilometers (19 miles).

Clouds Tell Tales

ASIDE FROM THESE instrument-carrying balloons, many other devices are used by the meteorologist to learn what is going on aloft. Clouds are as important to the meteorologist as to the poet or the painter. They commonly sail above the earth at all levels from the low rain clouds that almost hug the surface to the wispy "mares' tails" or cirrus clouds that graze the base of the stratosphere something like 7 miles above. The experienced observer needs only his eyes and his watch to learn from the drifting of the clouds the wind direction and speed at the levels where they occur.

A simple instrument aids him in this. The nephoscope, as it is called, consists chiefly of a black mirror, mounted in a circular frame marked off in degrees. From the distance the cloud image on the mirror moves in a given time, and from the cloud height, the wind velocity is readily calculated. Also the wind direction at the cloud level is accurately determined.

On the occasions when the sky fails to provide clouds at the desired heights, the meteorologist sends up pilot balloons somewhat like the ones children pursue in the parks on summer days, uncolored ones for a blue sky, red or black ones to show up against clouds.

They are inflated with a certain amount of hydrogen, carefully weighed and then set loose. Nature, in one of her most gracious moods, has provided that a balloon of this type, inflated to a definite "lift," will rise at a nearly constant rate. Since the rate is already known to the observer, a watch is the only instrument needed to tell him the altitude of the balloon. A type of surveying instrument, known as the theodolite, gives him the necessary data from which to compute the cross-country distance covered, and thus the wind direction and velocity at selected altitudes until the balloon is a tiny speck fading from the sight.

Another method which was used during the World War for securing the same information in upper wind levels is the sending up of a bomb or shell which bursts at a predetermined height. The drift of the smoke clouds is then observed. Sometimes a balloon is sent up with a number of bombs which burst at different heights. The rate of travel of the balloon and its direction are determined by the sound as it is received on the ground below.

For knowledge of the winds which may stir at heights

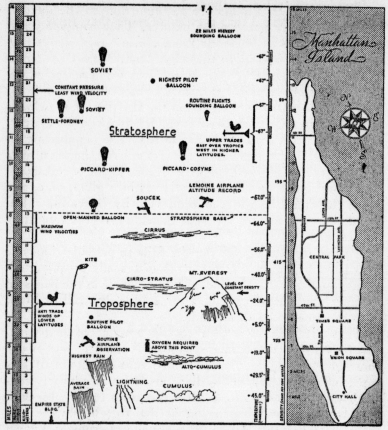

THE FIRST SIXTEEN MILES UPWARD

FIGURE 5

THROUGH troposphere to stratosphere, man has risen to discover new facts for science.

above the limits of balloons and shells—something like 22 miles—the weather man depends upon the drifting trails of meteors rocketing across the night sky, auroras, and the rare, bright, noctilucent clouds. The latter are clouds of material, perhaps spewed up from earth by the violence of volcanic eruptions to heights far above the ordinary clouds. So lofty are they, that they reflect at night the sun's bright glow, and shine with its light as does the moon. From this fact they get their name of noctilucent.

Photographs taken of these clouds from stations a known distance apart reveal that they shine more than forty miles above the surface of the earth.

How did they get there? The very presence of a cloud at such a height above the surface of the waters of the earth speaks to the physicist of the composition of the air over which they float. From their existence Dr. W. J. Humphreys, authority on meteorological physics of the U. S. Weather Bureau, has reasoned that above the stratosphere, where temperatures are constant and there is consequently no up-and-down movement of the air, there must be another troposphere or region of convection.

Heat in the air at such heights can be caused by a layer of ozone, an allotropic form of oxygen; and such an ozone layer is now assumed by physicists to exist about 35 to 60 kilometers above the earth (22 to 37 miles). Here the temperature is probably something like that on the Desert of Sahara on a summer afternoon, probably about 108 degrees Fahrenheit. This area is known as the ozonosphere.

Above the hot layer, there is again a cooling of the air and a consequent upward movement of the heated air and downward swirl of the cooler, forming an upper troposphere to which Dr. Humphreys has given the name "altotroposphere."

Eventually, of course, this cooling is continued to the point where the amount of heat lost by radiation is exactly equal to that gained by absorption and the result is an everlasting *status quo*—an upper stratosphere, or "altostratosphere." The base of the altostratosphere lies about 90 kilometers overhead (or 56 miles), Dr. Humphreys has calculated. At that point the temperature must be about 270 degrees below zero Fahrenheit, only 105 degrees Centigrade or 189 degrees Fahrenheit, above absolute zero.

Above the distant region where noctilucent clouds float in isolated beauty there is another region of atmosphere, or rather series of regions, of greatest importance in the conduct of man's present-day affairs. It is the structure of the atmosphere in these farthest heights that makes possible that modern necessity of communication, the radio.

The S O S of the ship in peril on the sea, the messages with which far-away adventurers at the ends of the world keep in reassuring touch with those at home, and the globe-encircling signals of radio amateurs and professionals are all made possible by reflection from an ionized layer, consisting of electrified particles, many, many miles above the tallest transmitting tower.

Radio Sounds the Heights

THE EXISTENCE of this radio roof of the world, known as the Kennelly-Heaviside layer because of the two men whose independent theories first called attention to it, was demonstrated in 1925.

When a transmitting station sends out a series of radio signals, the energy goes in two ways which may be described as the ground wave and the sky wave. The ground wave travels along the surface of the earth, gradually becoming less powerful as it spreads out over a greater area and as energy is absorbed from it. The absorption of energy is greater for short waves than for long waves, but at broadcasting frequencies, the ground wave is seldom potent for a range greater than about 60 to 90 miles. For very short wavelengths the range is only a matter of a few miles.

Meanwhile, the sky wave travels upward until it reaches the ionized layer of the atmosphere and then is reflected back in much the same manner that light is reflected from a mirror. A receiving station located only a short distance from the transmitting station will pick up the signal first from the ground wave, and then after an interval as an "echo" from the sky wave.

It is the length of the time interval between the ground-wave signal and its echo from the sky that gives a clue as to the height of the ionized layer. Assuming that the radio wave travels with the speed of light, physicists have computed the "virtual height" of the ionized layer. This "virtual height" is somewhat greater than the actual height, because it is known that the radio wave does not actually travel quite as fast as light, but is slowed slightly.

From the "virtual height," however, it is possible to compute the actual path of the wave with a fair degree of accuracy.

Another clue to the height of the ionized layer is given by the variations in the strength of signals received at a station within range of the ground wave. When the echo, or sky wave, returns to the receiving station within such a time that its phase coincides with that of the ground wave, it serves to strengthen the signal received. When, however, the phases of the two component waves are opposed, the resulting interference causes the signal to be weakened. These two conditions alternate as the frequency of the transmitted wave is varied, and the increase of frequency required to change the relative phases by 180 degrees can be used to estimate the layer height. Other methods have been devised for measuring the height of the ionized layer and all serve to confirm the results of these two methods.

One of the first results of the measurements of the height of the layer was the discovery that the Kennelly-Heaviside layer is not a single ionized area, but two—one about twice the height of the other. The upper layer, sometimes called the Appleton layer from its discoverer, the British physicist, Prof. E. V. Appleton, has a much greater ionization density than the lower layer and serves to reflect short radio waves that penetrate through the lower region.

Three layers are now recognized by scientists in the United States: one known as the "E" layer, at a height of about 65 to 75 miles, then the "F_1" layer, at 115 to 140 miles, and finally the "F_2" layer, which extends from about 150 miles overhead to an unknown height perhaps 220 miles above us.

In still another region between the "E" and the "F_1," or about 80 to 110 miles up, evidence has been found from which some scientists assume still another layer, which they have called the "intermediate" or "M" layer. Profs. E. V. Appleton and J. A. Ratcliffe, British scientists, believe this region to be more heavily ionized and consequently more prominent than the "E" region in the early morning and the late evening. Higher layers "G" and "H" have also been suggested.

Whether radio waves will be reflected by the lower "E" layer, or whether they will penetrate it and continue up to some greater height and be reflected by one or another of the higher layers, depends upon the frequency or wavelength of the impulse. The greater the frequency or the smaller the wavelength, the higher will the radio impulse penetrate into the ionosphere, and the longer will be the time interval before the echo returns.

The maximum frequency which will be reflected by the lower layers, called the critical frequency for that layer, varies also with the time of day and other factors.

While physicists are engaged so actively in determining the structure of the ionosphere and its effect on affairs of the earth's surface, they are not neglecting the study of the source of the ionization. Ultraviolet light from the sun is undisputed as the chief producer of the ionization, but thunderstorms and the "runaway electron" accelerated by the electric field of the thundercloud, the cosmic ray, and other factors have influences of as yet undetermined importance on the ionic density and also on the layer heights.

In the solution of these and kindred problems, the geophysicist and the physicist have an opportunity to repay their debt to the radio engineer for his invaluable aid in probing the secrets of the upper air.

CHAPTER 11
GEOGRAPHIC ADVENTURING

We sometimes wonder whether it is not going to be rather dull for people born with the discovery complex a hundred years or so hence. What outlet of energy will they find for their restless feet and inquiring minds?

Even now, the only continent left to be explored in quantity, so to speak, is Antarctica. South America has jungles, to be sure, not yet penetrated by explorers and reduced to the tame estate of known and mapped land. There are stretches of Arabian desert and Mongolian plain that are waiting for discovery by people capable of telling the world about such places. ("Natives" who may live in these undiscovered lands rarely know how to discover themselves, and so they miss all the fame.) Every continent has features that the explorer can work on. But the big, dramatic adventures of discovery are nearly all appropriated. Even the mountains and valleys under the sea, and conditions of the upper air are being explored.

The only hope for future generations of discoverers lies in unexpected tricks of fate. The airplane has prolonged the possibilities of geographic discovery, for flying across a continent for the first time is discovering it from a new angle with many important implications; but such speculations are remote and fanciful. One fact is, however, clear: the chances of being a great historic figure in geography are not very bright for future generations.

The three main prizes for geographic discovery fame that are most discussed today are these: to be the first to stand on top of the world's highest mountain; to explore the great unknown areas of South Polar land, and to fly across it, from sea to sea; and to explore the vast unknown areas of ocean floor and intermediate depths. The years 1933 and 1934 saw determined attacks started in both these fields, as well as other expeditions of scientific importance.

Mount Everest Ho!

FOURTEEN PICKED MOUNTAINEERS set out to scale the forbidding heights of Mount Everest, hoping to succeed where previous climbers always failed. The expedition set new records, but not the coveted record of complete success. Meanwhile the first attempt to fly over the crags and peaks of Everest was initiated. The first flight succeeded.

Both the Mount Everest expeditions were British. This conquest of a great mountain is a deed that British explorers, because of empire prestige in the East, have taken to their hearts. In announcing plans for the flight over Everest, Lord Clydesdale was quoted as saying:

"Americans have flown over the North Pole and the South Pole. The Pacific Ocean has been crossed by air, and the Atlantic has been frequently flown in recent years. There is only one original flight worth while: that is the flight over Mount Everest, which stands out as the only significant part of the world not conquered by aviators."

April 3, 1933, was the day of the historic flight. The Houston Everest Expedition (named in honor of its sponsor, Lady Houston) had established its base at Purnea. There had been a full year's planning for a dash that would take three hours, if all went well. The two big biplanes waiting at the Lalbalu airdrome were a Houston-Westland and a Westland-Wallace. Each was equipped with a Bristol Pegasus S 111 9-cylinder high altitude supercharged radial engine. The line-up for the flight was: in one plane, Lord Clydesdale, pilot, and Col. L. V. S. Blacker, observer; in the other, Flight-Lieut. D. F. McIntyre, pilot, and S. R. Bonnett, observer. To Everest and back was 320 miles.

The three main purposes of the expedition as set forth by the leader, Air Commodore P. F. M. Fellowes, were:

"To fly over and photograph Mount Everest, to survey the immediate surroundings of the mountain, and to prove that the highest mountain in the world is not an insurmountable barrier to air transport."

The flight itself was a thrilling triumph of man over antagonistic nature. Everest is never friendly, beautiful and alluring though it may be. On a day selected as favorable, the flyers were met by the hurricane winds that are always swirling in treacherous currents round Everest. They fought back, and forced their planes to the tip of the highest peak, 29,141 feet aloft, clearing it by fully 100 feet, and circling over it for fifteen minutes. The bitter coldness of the air was at the rate of 45 degrees below zero Centigrade and never higher than 30 below in the cockpits. The ice plume that floats several miles long from the tip of Everest proved to be a maelstrom of crackling ice that sent a barrage of rattling shot into the cockpits. The flyers were bundled in heated clothing and warmed goggles. But heated in such circumstances is a comparative term. Col. Blacker's oxygen mask became a solid mass of ice. The cameras were equipped with heated films, lenses, shutters, and plates. But in Col. Blacker's report of his picture-making in *First Over Everest,* the book of the flight by the expedition members, he tells vividly of his struggle to expose plates and to lift the heavy cinema camera now and again to run off fifty feet or so of film.

So chilled was the metal of the plane that hatchway fastenings were stiff.

"I struggled with them," he writes, "the effort making me pant for breath, and I squeezed my mask onto my face to get all the oxygen possible."

Even wind, cold, and ice are not all the weapons that the mountain can summon. A dust curtain ordinarily hangs over the region to a height of 5,000 or 6,000 feet. On the flight day it rose to 19,000, shutting off the terrain that the cameramen were so anxious to map by vertical photography. On this one point Everest won the day. The victory, however, was temporary, for the flyers (A. L. Fisher replacing Bonnett) returned April 19th and shot two strips of the coveted vertical pictures.

The main trophies of the two flights are the pictures. Men will never climb Everest from the south, and therefore mapping from that side could best be achieved by making photographs from the air and overlapping them to form a complete mosaic map, worked out exactly to scale. The picture map thus formed reveals two unknown glaciers, a high altitude lake, and many other new details of the region. Oblique photographs, which supplement the vertical shots, show the highest tip of the world to be a fairyland of even greater beauty and majesty than had been realized.

The experiences of the flyers have yielded considerable other information of value. On the second flight, for example, Flight-Lieut. McIntyre wore over his face only a mask he made himself, leaving eyes and upper part of the face uncovered. Suffering no ill effects, he demonstrated that human eyes and skin can withstand the cold of high altitude flying, a point on which the contrary view had prevailed. The equipment chosen for the flights proved adequate, only two minor mishaps being experienced. Future projects for air surveying of mountainous country will be benefited by records of the Everest flight.

The expedition that tried to climb to the top had a much harder time. Led by Hugh Ruttledge, the party pushed its way up, establishing camp after camp at higher levels. On May 29th, camp six was set up, after a struggle against storms, at a height of 27,400 feet, and next day the dash—if painfully slow ascent can be so called—was being made for the top. P. Wyn-Harris and Laurence R. Wager began the endurance climb. Men who have tried to scale the heights of Everest tell vividly of their feelings in the ordeal. Throats are parched by thin air. Hearts pound mercilessly. Stupidity presses on mind and body so that any exertion seems too much to ask. Taking one step forward is such effort that a dozen breaths must be drawn before another step. Yet the climbers must still push their dragging bodies to a higher, more perilous point. In 1924, Mallory and

Irvine disappeared in the mists apparently only 600 feet from the top and were never seen again. Wyn-Harris and Wager were more fortunate. When they could no longer pull themselves farther up on sloping rocks covered with loose, fresh snow, they retraced their steps through the blizzard to the camp. On June 1st, F. S. Smythe set out alone to try for the top. He reached the same point as the others, about 28,100 feet on the western wall, when he found the rocks ahead unclimbable in the slippery, fresh snow. His was the ironic situation of having ample time to reach the summit, and strength left for the climb, only to be defeated by one of Everest's "demons"—snow.

There may be few dashes on Everest in the future. The Dalai Lama, who died late in 1933, informed the British government that he could allow no more climbing expeditions on the mountain. Everest is holy in the eyes of Tibet's Buddhists, and they have always been reluctant to see foreigners invade the refuge of the "Mother Goddess of the Mountain Snows." Mishaps to expedition parties have always been attributed by the local inhabitants to demons of the mountain. The worst summer in twenty years, as Tibetans reckoned, followed the 1933 expeditions, and the Tibetan explanation of that was: the gods are angry; we must be careful. A brave and forbidden ascent was attempted in May, 1934, by a lone Briton, Maurice Wilson, who, disguised as a Tibetan, eluded border guards and left his three porters at 21,000 feet to make a heroic dash toward Everest's peak. He never returned.

Antarctica Adventures

THE ANTARCTIC was the goal of two widely heralded expeditions in 1933. A brave start on the venture of flying across the unknown continent—if continent it is—was made by Lincoln Ellsworth and Bernt Balchen. It was the aim of the Ellsworth Transantarctic Flight Expedition to fly from the Ross Sea to the Weddell Sea, then turn the plane without stopping and fly back, a round trip of 2,900 miles. This would be the longest non-stop polar flight yet attempted, and with the exception of about 300 miles of the route it would cover a region of the world never seen by man. All along the way, a clocklike camera was to map the terrain, automatically snapping an exposure every ten seconds. From the records might be definitely learned, for one thing, whether this portion of the Antarctic deserves the name of continent or whether it is several islands welded together in enormous masses of ice.

But the flight was never made. The *Polar Star,* a powerful low-wing Northrop Delta monoplane especially built for polar conditions and long cruising radius, arrived at the Ross Sea safely. But while the plane rested on the ice at the Bay of Whales, the shelf suddenly broke up, and the skis of the plane slipped through a crack in the ice. After hours of hard work the crippled plane was rescued, but the damage was too serious to be repaired on shipboard. The flyers were forced to turn back, postponing their venture to another year.

The second Byrd Antarctic Expedition sailed from Boston in September, 1933, for a long stay in the most inhospitable land in the world. Two ships carried the men and tons of equipment down to Little America. The extraordinary range of supplies needed for a year or more of life in the barren Antarctic is well known from the record of the first Byrd expedition. Interesting equipment added for the second expedition included tractors and an autogyro.

It was to be very largely an aëronautical expedition, Admiral Byrd said before he sailed. He planned to fly into the uncharted areas of the far interior, and expected "ten times as much flying" as on the first trip. Exploration of Marie Byrd Land, which the Admiral discovered and named for his wife, was one goal of the expedition. And with the exploration was to be continued the large program of scientific researches that the first expedition began.

On Marie Byrd Land, for example, there are lofty mountains with rocky tips sticking up through the ice. Such peaks are prime clues to whatever land is under the ice blanket. By struggling with winds and cold, a geologist can manage to gather a few treasured rock samples from the exposed points. Then by comparing the kinds of rock collected in other parts of the Antarctic, he can gain an idea of how the mountains are related in history and structure.

It is not yet known whether the mountains of Antarctica are an extension of ranges on South America, Africa, and Australia. If the mountains do prove to be sections of long chains now broken down in part and covered by the intervening ocean, it will indicate that long ago in earth history a certain amount of migration of life was possible from the South Polar land to these continents and vice versa. Biologists think this must have happened, for otherwise they can only wonder how the ancestors of Australian kangaroos, wombats, and other pouch-carrying animals managed to reach Australia from South America, where the marsupials presumably had their origin. At present, so little is known about the far-off times in Antarctica that Dr. Isaiah Bowman, director of the American Geographical Society, of New York, once said: "Finding a fossil marsupial in Antarctica would excite science almost as much as a message from Mars." That the South Polar region was once much warmer is sure, because coal beds outcrop in the mountain peaks, indicating that 150 million years ago the weather was mild enough for trees and plants to live and die and decay and be packed down to form coal. Today there are only two flowering plants in the Antarctic—both of them scrawny stunted things.

Almost every science has errands it would like done in the Antarctic. Physicists are eager to have records taken of the cosmic rays. As far as such researches have gone, they have shown that rays from outer space gain in intensity as higher latitudes are reached. The polar regions may yield data to help settle the problem of whether the cosmic rays are electrons.

Geologists want to know: How thick is the ice sheet and is it shrinking? The South Pole is 10,000 feet above sea level, but a German geologist, Prof. W. Meinardus, has expressed the view that the most of the Pole's loftiness is ice, and that the land below may rise only 2,000 feet above sea level. If he is right, the ice sheet is an indicator of so vast a store of cold that it is easy to see why the Antarctic's main product is weather, bad weather at that. No one knows yet how directly the United States and Europe may be affected by the storms and cold waves that are manufactured in the far South. One of the most practical researches of the Byrd expedition is to gather records in the hope of finding the rules that govern the output of Antarctica's weather factory. William Haines, of the U. S. Weather Bureau, has accompanied both expeditions to make meteorological studies.

Scientists will be studying the records of the expedition long after its return, and many of the important accomplishments are not transmitted daily by radio but will return in the notebooks and journals written in Antarctica.

Only a close examination of an Antarctic map shows what great portions of the outline are expressed in dotted lines. The Pacific quadrant has a large share of the dotted lines. Starting from the edge of the ice pack at two different points 900 miles apart, Admiral Byrd flew his seaplane southward across the ice fringe to hunt the continental borders. Snow, fog, and poor visibility handicapped the flights, but he covered 150 miles before turning back with the report that he had sighted only sea-borne ice, no trace of the coast. The flights are believed to subtract 200,000 square miles of unknown land from the Antarctica map, adding them to the Pacific Ocean.

Once in Fifty Years

ASIDE FROM great adventures of discovery, there is much important geographic work going on all over the world. An International Polar Year has been achieved, and its results are being compiled. That in itself is an event of major interest. Thirty-three countries joined in the agreement to push explorations for a Second International Polar Year, August, 1932, to August, 1933. Fifty years ago, a First Polar Year was launched, in the first effort to combine forces of the world for the Herculean task of studying Polar phenomena.

CHAPTER 12
DOING SOMETHING ABOUT THE WEATHER

Hot enough for you today? The weather has been an unfailing topic of talk ever since the times when Noah prophesied rain and his skeptic neighbors wouldn't believe him.

It is an unfailing topic of talk because it gets home to every one of us, most personally and intimately. Concern for your comfort at the moment, for your health tomorrow, for the state of your pocketbook if the coming cold wave compels you to order more coal or furnace oil—these hit home immediately to every citizen. And to many, changes in weather bring even acuter problems than these, for they may have major effects on all kinds of business. The aviator must consider his chances of snow or sleet, the orchard owner must decide whether or not he shall "heat all outdoors" to hold killing frost at arm's length, the shipper with perishable goods in transit must make up his mind whether to let them go ahead or put them into a warm roundhouse. Every cold wave, hot spell, high wind, dust storm, drought, or long rain compels millions upon millions of dollars' worth of business decisions. Small wonder then that we all talk about the weather, and that the Weather Bureau is one of the most indispensable (though at the same time most be-cussed) of all government organizations.

But despite occasional grumbling to the contrary a recent statistical check-up shows that four fifths of the Weather Bureau forecasts are correct.

New Deal for Weather

Nobody grudged, then, when the news broke that plans had been drawn to make the Bureau even more effective than it is as an agency for the scientific study of the weather and for its reliable forecasting.

The project for the Weather Bureau's New Deal was developed by a committee of the Science Advisory Board, an organization called into being by executive order of President Roosevelt last summer, and working under the auspices of the National Academy of Sciences and the National Research Council.

Chief among the Board's recommendations was that the Weather Bureau, together with the aërological services of the army and navy, adopt the so-called air-mass analysis method of studying the weather, to supplement (not supplant) the standard methods now in use.

Air-mass analysis is an effort to get at the causes of the familiar procession of "highs" and "lows" that march across today's weather maps. It looks upon these fluctuations of atmospheric pressure as symptoms or tangible effects of grand-scale dynamic forces at work in the earth's thick blanket of air. It sees the atmosphere as the battle-ground of a ceaseless push and tug between great mountainous moving bulks of air, chilled by polar cold on one side, heated by tropical suns on the other, meeting and clashing and throwing off storms and tempests, rains and droughts, fair weather and foul, as the dust and swirl of conflict between mighty genii of old. It makes of the weather a cosmic drama. Weather maps will thus take on something of the appearance of battle maps.

The idea of anything so fluid and apparently continuous as the air being separable into distinct masses that can come into conflict with each other like opposing armies is a bit difficult to grasp at first. You can understand it more readily, perhaps, if you are a good enough swimmer to get along under water when strong waves are in motion. You will remember how such waves seize and push you about, even though you cannot see their boundaries. Dynamic air masses may be thought of as waves, of super-tidal-wave proportions, moving in air rather than in water.

Another simple way of visualizing the air-mass concept is to dash a quart or so of water, tinted with a few drops of red ink or laundry bluing, lengthwise into a partly filled bathtub. You will see the moving mass of water plow through the stationary mass almost as though it were a solid projectile, before it slows down and spreads out and mingles with it when its force of movement is played out.

You may even see, if you watch closely enough, little unevennesses, swirls and eddies, along the front where the two masses of water meet and push each other. These are the small-scale analogues of the high- and low-pressure areas that are the basic data of the present-day weather-forecasting methods, and which show up as the familiar nests of concentric circles or ellipses on the weather maps.

Of course, a moving air mass that comes into conflict with other air masses does not originate outside the atmosphere like the quart of colored water you threw into the bathtub. That was rather an oversimplification of the picture, for diagrammatic purposes. As the weather is actually bred, the air over some special area of the earth, say the ice of Greenland or the hot sand and rock of Nevada, hangs steady until it is loaded with cold or heat, or in some way achieves an "energy gradient" with respect to the air of neighboring regions, and then it begins to migrate. Whereupon some more weather gets started.

The contact between two meeting air masses, the "interface" where the conflicting play of differing energies takes place, is known to aërologists as a "front" (that battle-map analogy again!). Since the earth's atmosphere is several miles deep (that is, that part of it affected by "weather" as we think of it), such a "front" is not a line but a surface, ranging from a flat wedge shape to a more or less vertical wall. Sometimes the front between air masses really is nearly vertical; more often it slopes one way or another, and one air mass will run under the other and lift it up, like the toe of a slipper running under a rug, or a plowshare under the sod.

It becomes obvious, then, that the air-mass analysis method of weather study cannot be content with sitting on the ground. It has to get up into the air, to study oncoming weather changes for what they are: events taking place in three dimensions. For this, weather men must get themselves wings. Fortunately, wings are available through the army, the navy, and the Department of Commerce service for civil aviation, so the Board recommended "that the whole system of recording and reporting meteorological data in aid of forecasting be consolidated under the Weather Bureau, except for the activities necessary to the army and the navy."

Cycles in Weather

THE WEATHER SCIENTIST'S perennial hope for methods that will enable him to make dependable forecasts for whole seasons or even for whole cycles of years is moving a little closer toward realization. A leader in this field, Dr. Charles G. Abbot, secretary of the Smithsonian Institution, has described successful long-range weather forecasting based on the mathematical study of the 23-year sunspot cycle. During many years of study of variations in solar radiation, Dr. Abbot discovered a correlation between these variations and the number of sunspots, as the spot cycles wax and wane. The study was complicated and made highly difficult by the fact that there are a number of these cycles, of varying length, which overlap and often partially hide each other. Finally he perceived that all the periodicities in solar radiation are nearly submultiples of 276 months or 23 years. These submultiples are obtained by dividing 276 by 3, 4, 6, 8, 11, 13, 15, 18, 25, 34, and 39. He thereupon conceived the idea that the tedious method of determining periodicities individually might be omitted, and their combined effect might be found by discussion of a 23-year cycle.

"The method is fortunately even more useful for forecasting precipitation than for temperature," Dr. Abbot stated. "Its inexactness is believed to be due to the difficulty of forecasting irregularities in the appearance of sunspots, and allowing for their effects upon the phases of the component periodicities of variation."

Encouraged by his success, Dr. Abbot ventured a forecast of weather in Central India for the years 1942 to 1948. Basing his opinion on a well-known, clear-cut cyclic correlation there, he stated that subnormal precipitation is probable for that region during the six years mentioned.

If Polar Ice Should Melt

ALTHOUGH they usually prefer to stick to definitely ascertainable facts and to cautious and relatively short-range forecastings, weather scientists do sometimes permit themselves the luxury of a little "speculative meteorology." Prof. W. J. Humphreys of the U. S. Weather Bureau has ventured a Wellsian look into a remoter though not at all impossible future.

What would happen, he asked, if the earth's polar ice caps should melt? If the mysterious southern continent where Byrd and Ellsworth struggle with endless glaciers should become bare of all glaciers? If Greenland's icy mountains should become as Patagonia's land?

The idea is not as impossible as it sounds. It is not normal for the earth to have its both ends frozen solid; it seems so merely because it has been so during all of man's recollected history. Speaking in terms of geologic ages, it is the usual, the normal thing, for the earth to be ice-free. Ice ages, such as the one in whose twilight we moderns are living, have been the exception rather than the rule in the long history of the earth. There have been only three such periods of really major importance: the Pleistocene Age, which began a million years ago, more or less, and is still in process of liquidation; an Ice Age not long after the close of the Coal Age, perhaps a quarter of a billion years ago: and finally one near the dawn of all well-recorded life on earth, that misty period known as the Cambrian, vaguely from half a billion to two thirds of a billion years back. During the rest of the time the climate at the poles was at least temperate; some geologists used to believe it was outright tropical.

The existence of permanently refrigerated spots on the earth has a decided influence on the behavior of the earth's blanketing ocean of air. The migrations of chilled air masses toward the south, their encounters with warmed air masses from the tropics migrating toward the north, and the ebb and flow of battle that ensues when such masses of air encounter each other, make up a large part of the story of the weather, especially in those regions of intemperate climatic contrasts and changes which we have ineptly called the temperate zones.

The first and most important change a disappearance of the Arctic and Antarctic ice regions would accomplish, Prof. Humphreys said, would be the removal of the present type of climatic contrasts in these middle latitudes. The sun would still shine on the tropics and subtropics, to be sure, warming the air, making it less dense, and inviting cooler air from elsewhere to slide under and lift it up. Moisture-laden warm air from over the oceans would migrate over the lands that are now the tropical rain belts and monsoon regions, leaving them still lands of heavy rain. The tropics, he thinks, would be relatively little changed, except perhaps that their present tropical characteristics might be intensified.

But in the lands of the mid-latitudes, especially in the Northern Hemisphere (where the greater area of such lands lies), a startling and not at all favorable change in climate would occur. At present, the great grain lands that feed the world—Canada and the United States, Russia and China, and in the Southern Hemisphere Australia and Argentina—owe their fruitfulness to the rain- and snow-yielding storms that result from the encounter of moisture-laden warm air from lower latitudes with chill, moisture-condensing air moving down from the regions of perpetual cold. Our crops are born of these stormy marriages of the genii of the air.

Remove the northern partners, or weaken them appreciably, and the rains will dwindle or even cease altogether. This is the fate in store for the great grain belts as they now exist: they will become first thin-grassed lands fit only for marginal herds of sheep and goats, then even that scant vegetational cover will disappear—its end hastened, perhaps, by desperate overgrazing carried on by starving nomad shepherds. Then will Iowa and Nebraska, Manitoba and Saskatchewan, become extensions of a Great American Desert stretching southward to the borders of

SETTLE-FORDNEY STRATOSPHERE BALLOON

THE Settle-Fordney stratosphere balloon, ready to leave on the morning of November 20, 1933. The flight resulted in a world's record of 61,243 feet or more than eleven and one half miles above the earth. A Soviet army balloon subsequently attained an altitude of 67,585 feet. The record for an airplane, made about the same time by an Italian flier, is about 47,500 feet.

RECORDING WIND AND COLD

THESE two pictures (above and above right) show how weather observations are taken at one of Uncle Sam's most important weather stations, atop Mt. Washington. In the one above a pilot balloon has just been released to measure wind velocity. In the other, temperature is being taken. Wind velocity has registered as high as 186 miles per hour on the mountain. That is super-hurricane strength. Temperatures far below zero have also been registered. With a wind velocity of 98 and a temperature of 25 below zero, Mt. Washington weather has been found to have a cooling ratio equal to the minus 60 degree temperatures of the Antarctic. And all within a few miles of Boston.

STRATOSPHERE BALLOON

THIS IS the apparatus that rises into the stratosphere, sending temperature and pressure information back to earth by radio. When in flight, the parachute and the meteorograph extend about seventy-five feet below the balloon, and the balloon is blown up much larger than is shown in the picture. Such balloons have risen higher into the stratosphere than has man.

AIR THRILLS

Army airmen Kepner, Stevens, and Anderson are wondering just how long their stratosphere balloon *Explorer* will hold together, just before the precipitate ending of the July 28, 1934, flight. Left, ring of Nebraska dust caused by impact of gondola. Still in the air are the parachutes of two of the fliers. Between the parachutes are white specks of balloon fabric floating to earth. Epic photographs made by Master Sergeant Gilbert from an accompanying Army plane piloted by Lieut. J. F. Phillips, copyrighted by The National Geographic Society.

the Mexican tropics, empty and arid as the Sahara is now, the soil burned dry of its fertility by the summer suns and blown into towering dust storms by occasional winds. But for the most part even these winds will be lacking, for the wind-engendering cold air from the north will fail. It will be a land of stagnant death. And the great grain lands of central Europe and Asia will share its fate.

What will the peoples of the earth do when the old, long-relied-on corn lands fail them? The first and most obvious answer is, "go north." There will be folk-migrations of vast extent, compared with which those that preceded the Fall of Rome were but picnic excursions. If we are no more civilized than we are now when this irresistible *Drang nach Norden* begins to make itself felt, if the nations possessing northern lands refuse to admit the hordes of new immigrants who will clamor for admittance and passage to the new frontier, there will unquestionably be terrific wars, and in the trail of those wars famine and pestilence.

Nations possessing broad lands in the North may well be justified in denying their gates to hard-pressed folk from the increasingly desert South. For the lands of the North will not suffice to support as large a population as will by that time swarm in the grain-belt lands of the world. On the ordinary Mercator-projection map these great Northern lands—Alaska, northern Canada, Greenland, Siberia—loom huge. But look at a globe, or at a map that spreads and distorts the Northern areas less, and you will at once see that their area, even if all were fertile, is not equal to that of the temperate-zone lands of the present day.

Moreover, much of this Northern land will be unsuited for human support even when the ice does finally melt off. A great deal of what is now forest in northeastern Canada stands on almost bare rock, with the roots of the trees holding precariously in a few inches of raw humus and half-decayed leaves and moss—"duff," the foresters call it. Such lands must forever remain forest, to be of even minor usefulness to mankind.

Bald rock, also, will probably be the whole inheritance of the nations when the ice sheets over Greenland and Antarctica melt away. Much of the rock underlying the forests of Canada was left stark and bare when the great twin ice sheets of northeastern North America slowly retreated a hundred thousand years ago; any soil they may once have had had been cleared away as with a plane by the plowing fronts of the ice lobes. It is highly improbable that any appreciable part of the sub-ice surfaces of Greenland and Antarctica today are in any better case. They may some day be useful for airplane fields, and miners may exploit them for coal and minerals, but it is beyond human imagination to think of plowing them and planting corn.

But supposing peace to come among the nations (or their fragments) after the great wars of Arctica and Antarctica, and supposing the relics of their populations spared by the sword, famine, and pestilence to be settled down in a wearied peace. Would the broad lands for which they fought be there to receive them?

Not in anything like their present form. For the ice caps of the polar regions now contain, locked up away from circulation in rivers and oceans, enough water to raise the world's sea level about 150 feet. This is enough to make a material reduction in the coastal land areas of the world. Much of our Atlantic and Gulf coastal areas, including the greater part of Florida and a deep embayment up the Mississippi valley, would be thus flooded. The greater part of Holland would disappear, and a goodly share of Belgium, as well as wide stretches of the North Sea coasts of both Britain and Germany. Denmark would be reduced to a mere collection of tiny islands. The Baltic "succession states"—Finland, Lithuania, and the rest—would have to cede stretches of their sea fronts to the hungry sea. Every harbor in the world would be rendered useless, and new ones created.

But all these changes would be of little moment after all, for all these countries, or at least the great hinterlands that support them, would be producing nothing to ship; so what would be the use of harbors, or the importance of lost coastal lands?

But the Arctic Ocean would be demanding its acres, too, and there the rub would hurt worse. For most of the lands that slope towards the Arctic fall off very flatly and gradually as long, level grasslands becoming sea swamps and then sea. Up this sea plain, and spreading out from the banks of the rivers that meander through it, the sea will spread its hundred-and-fifty feet of added elevation, and the lands for which the nations may fight their last Armageddon will be sadly curtailed by the time they are won.

There are other changes that might well challenge our thought: whether the southland trees that will migrate northward to replace the present spruces and willows will be able to take hold in such poor soil; whether any survivors at all will be left of the present interesting Arctic and Antarctica fauna, such as caribou, musk ox, sea elephant, and penguins; how well or how ill the human inhabitants will take to an environment of temperate, perhaps even warm-temperate climate, rather stagnant, accompanied by the present long polar day in summer and by the correspondingly long polar night in winter; a score of other questions.

CHAPTER 13
THE CHEMICAL REVOLUTION

NECESSITY, the old adage tells us, is the mother of invention. If that is the case, then economic depression such as America and the world have been experiencing must be a stern and exacting stepmother, demanding ever quicker and more efficient performance from the youngling entrusted to her not too tender care.

But invention in America, and particularly chemical invention, has had no need to hang its head before its hard-featured, cold-eyed foster parent. Chemical invention stepped out and showed what it could do when times are tough. Research chemists and chemical manufacturers vied in making old processes more economical or evolving them into processes essentially new and better. They met public demand for thrift or have tempted it through attractive novelty.

So many and so varied were the things thus developed that a full description of all of them, with the stories of the romance of research behind each product, would fill a thickish book. The recital of just a few of the high-lights, chosen at random from a dozen scattered fields of science, will have to suffice.

"Vinyl" was one of the most eye-catching of the many new or little-familiar words that were flashed upon the public view during Chemical Invention's months of hard-times effort. It has all the earmarks of a specially coined trade name: it is brief, easily pronounced, presents an unfamiliar yet not disagreeable combination of letters, and starts with a good attention-catching initial: V. The name was invented by a chemist who wanted a designation for a compound of carbon and hydrogen.

Rubber from Chemicals

VINYL remained more or less a laboratory curiosity for many years, though chemist after chemist added bits of knowledge about its behavior and properties from time to time. It leaped into public attention most dramatically in 1931, while the depression was yet comparatively young, through its use by Prof. J. A. Nieuwland of Notre Dame University, and a group of research chemists of the great Du Pont works in Delaware, in their quest for that modern equivalent of the ancient alchemists' "philosophers' stone" —synthetic rubber.

The researches of Dr. Nieuwland made vinyl acetylene, a compound in which the old familiar automobile headlight gas of pre-electric days figured prominently, available on a large scale at a comparatively low price, and the eager research team at the Du Pont works did the rest. They produced a stuff now known by the trade name of DuPrene, which has many of the properties of rubber, though it is not rubber and varies from it in some respects. In some ways, especially in its resistance to solution by hot oils and greases, it stands out ahead of rubber, and in spite of its very much higher price is replacing rubber for certain special uses.

Vinyl was also developed by other industrial firms. The Carbide and Carbon Chemicals Corporation went in heavily for what are known as the vinyl resins—compounds of vinyl with other chemicals that bid for a place in the sun against such older materials as hard rubber, celluloid, and bakelite. The great versatility of the vinyl resins was strikingly demonstrated in a house which the Carbide and Carbon Chemicals Corporation erected. Here nearly everything in a home so modern and so beautiful as to be the desire of every bride and the despair of every bridegroom, was made of various compounds and modifications of vinyl.

Other synthetic plastics were developed in Germany and the U. S. S. R., using as raw materials such cheap and endlessly abundant stuffs as coal, lignite, and peat.

Another notable high light of recent chemical invention was the development of a kind of leather that never needs to have a brushful of blacking put on it. This was evolved in the laboratories of the Mellon Institute in Pittsburgh, by a young man named Robert H. Geister. The conventional vici method of treating leather is followed to a certain point, when the skin is impregnated with filling agents in a new manner. This supports and lubricates the fibers, tending to prevent their breaking down under wear and causing the leather to lose shape. When shoes of the new leather are worn, the warmth of the feet gradually and continuously works the impregnating materials to the surface. Only a slight brushing will then give them a good polish. The new leather can be made in all colors, and it is claimed to be practically scuff-proof, soft and pliable, yet shape-holding, durable, and water-resistant.

Chemistry Aids Repeal

WHEN WHISKY became once more a legal object of scientific research, it received the careful attention of chemists, who made extensive investigations into that necessary but as yet little understood process known as aging, with a view to making more scientific and rational the various processes of artificial or quick aging, as yet in many instances based on guesswork or rule of thumb.

The chemists started their research, as scientists always should, with a question: What happens to whisky when it lies barreled for years in warehouses? New things, they found, slowly come into existence in it, that are not present when it flows from the still as raw spirits. They are various acids and substances called esters, which combine to give the mature liquor its tang and "fruitiness."

At first the acids form faster, then the esters catch up with them, so that by the end of four years these two classes of flavoring materials are in equilibrium. The much-prized oiliness of some whiskies is due to substances that come out of the charred container, not out of the liquor itself.

All these events that take place in the leisurely years of aging are chemical processes, and like other chemical processes may be speeded up, once we understand what they are. Various chemical processes are accelerated by the use of oxygen, of ultraviolet rays, of electrolysis and catalysts, or substances like finely divided metal sponge that hasten chemical changes without being themselves changed. All these methods are now being tried in efforts to speed up the ripening of whisky. Sometimes they are used on the natural liquor itself, sometimes after the flavoring substances have been mixed into it.

One very practical chemical problem, which has been with the human race doubtless since Stone Age times, is the oxidative tendencies of oils and fats—in other words, their tendency to turn rancid. Spoilage of butter and cooking fats, of olive and nut and palm oils, has for centuries been a bane to housewives as well as to manufacturers and merchants. Promising steps toward the solution of this problem have been made by chemists of the U. S. Department of Agriculture. Two principal "leads" have been followed: the addition of various chemicals to the products to slow down the rate of spoiling, and their protection from factors that tend to speed up that ill process. In the first category, the use of maleic acid (a natural ingredient of apple juice) and of some of the phenols, or carbolic-acid relatives, has been found to be beneficial. In the second, it was discovered that certain wavelengths of light promote rancidity, so that wrapping the products in paper or other containers colored to exclude those particular rays would slow down the process materially.

Death to Insects

PROMINENT among the up-and-coming chemical candidates for popular recognition is rotenone, the latest addition scientists have made to their arsenal of munitions to be used against the innumerable insect enemies of our crops, gardens, orchards, forests, animals, clothing, houses, and everything that is ours. It is already in fairly wide use, and promises to offer keen competition with some of the old familiar insect poisons, especially with the various compounds of arsenic.

Not all insects are susceptible to rotenone, but to those it can kill it is extremely deadly. Tests have shown it to be fifteen times as toxic as nicotin spray to aphids when used as a contact poison, and thirty times as toxic as acid lead arsenate when tried as an internal poison on caterpillars.

Chemistry has brought many revolutions to wood-using industries in the South: in lumber and its by-products, in the tremendous development of rayon manufacture, in turpentine, rosin, and other naval stores, in the gleaning of dollars from land holding nothing but stumps. The latest contribution of chemistry to potential industrial development in Dixie is a direct challenge to a wood use hitherto traditionally confined to the North: the making of print paper. Under the guidance of an industrial chemist, Dr. Charles H. Herty, a good grade of white print paper was experimentally produced on a fairly large scale from Southern pine, long despaired of as a paper-pulp source because of its high content of resins and other troublesome substances.

The depression, which gave the impetus to so much of chemical development in this country, was responsible also for the expansion into a great socio-industrial experiment of what had once been planned merely as emergency chemical plants. At the same time, it completely transformed the use to which these chemical plants are to be put.

Food for Plants

DURING the World War, the great Muscle Shoals dam on the Tennessee River was brought into being primarily to supply a huge manufacturing development for the fixation of atmospheric nitrogen into chemicals, to be made into explosives for use at the front and also into fertilizers to increase the productivity of American farms, so that the fighters might be fed. The war ended, and the Muscle Shoals nitrate establishment was therefore of relatively little use for its original purpose, and became an economic white elephant and a political bone of contention.

Came the New Deal. Senator Norris' dream of the use of Muscle Shoals dam primarily for the development of electric power for general distribution was suddenly realized, and rapidly expanded far beyond its original magnitude, to become the nucleus of a planned industrial and agricultural development for the whole Tennessee Valley region.

In the meantime, there stood the nitrate development, still a white elephant. But the soil in the Tennessee Valley, and elsewhere in the country as well, needed other fertilizer elements, especially phosphates. In the Tennessee Valley region there are great deposits of crude phosphate minerals. Additional construction was put in hand, and July 1, 1934, was set as the date for the first production on the new manufacturing schedule. At the same time, the emergency character of the plants is remembered: they are capable of re-conversion into nitrogen fixation establishments on short notice should any national emergency demand it.

Chemical revolutions are sometimes born naturally, able from the start to make their own way; sometimes they receive deliberate fostering care for political, social, or military reasons. In the latter class, perhaps, belongs the nationally promoted enterprise for the production of oil fuel from coal in Great Britain—which may, in its turn, have economic repercussions in foreign lands as well as in the oil-producing members of the British Commonwealth of Nations. This chemical revolution is aimed at peace-time benefits as well as war-time security, for although in time of war Great Britain's lack of oil would be a serious handicap, unless something can be done to restore her coal mines to full production, a large bloc of the population of the British Isles can be counted permanent corps in the armies of unemployed.

Another excellent example of the influence economics has, or may have, over a chemical revolution is afforded in the strong effort to obtain legislation on a national scale to promote, by one means or another, the use of alcohol made from surplus grain as an admixture in motor fuel. Somewhat more radical is the proposal advanced by a Czech engineer, K. Cuker, to use a motor fuel composed of alcohol, naphthalene, and sugar.

Any use of alcohol as a motor fuel is conditioned upon getting it free of water. Ordinary commercial "pure

alcohol" contains 10 or 15 per cent of water and is not
suited for fuel use, especially if mixed with the hydrophobic
petroleum derivatives. It just won't mix with them. Various
new processes make it commercially practicable to dehydrate
alcohol completely, mostly by passing it through water-
thirsty but alcohol-spurning chemicals. A long-neglected but
now newly recognized drying agent of this sort is common
gypsum, or calcium sulfate, rendered "soluble-anhydrous"
by a process described by Prof. W. A. Hammond of
Antioch College and Prof. J. R. Withrow of Ohio State
University.

The successful mining of sulfur under water was reported as an outstanding chemical achievement. This credit
for the practical application of the so-called Frasch process
to vast deposits of sulfur under lakes and swamps in
Louisiana goes to Lawrence O'Donnell, chemical engineer,
and his associates. Bravely begun during the depression, the
project had to overcome economic as well as chemical engineering problems. The yields of sulfur have far exceeded
the expectations of the engineers in charge of development
and operation. Whereas a plant was built with the expectation of turning out perhaps 300 long tons per day, it has
reached a production of 1,400 tons and regularly produces
1,200. The mining is carried out by sinking a shaft 700 feet
below the bottom of a lake where a stratum of sulfur 200
feet thick lies. Pipes leading to the plant on the shore are
sunk, and the sulfur, liquefied by superheated water, is
forced out by means of compressed air. To date 200,000
tons of sulfur of 99.92 per cent purity have been taken
from the wells.

Riches from the Sea

A NEW MANUFACTURING PLANT established by the Dow
Chemical Company near Wilmington, N. C., daily pumps
through itself a literal river of salt sea water, drawing it
from the ocean and discharging it again into the Cape Fear
River. More than a third of a billion pounds of water is
sucked in daily by its monster pumps and comes tumbling
out of its discharge gates. What happens to it on the way

through explains why this sober industrial chemical company has done such an apparently fantastic thing.

For the sea water is made to yield 15,000 pounds of bromine every day, by first acidifying it and then introducing the cheaper element chlorine. The chlorine has a more powerful attraction for the elements that are united with the bromine in the sea water, forces a chemical divorce, and leaves the bromine free to come out of solution, when it is captured and prepared for market. The entire bromine product of the new plant is used in the process of preparing "ethyl-gas" motor fuels.

The Dow Chemical Company also developed a process through which one third of our whole requirements for iodine can be satisfied by extracting that important element from oil well brines, hitherto simply an expensive nuisance to the petroleum industry. Another development was an acid solution sold under the trade name Dowell; sent down the shafts of nearly spent oil wells, it renews their youth and greatly increases their yield.

Chemical industries are often frowned upon as belonging to the hazardous trades. But chemistry can cure its own ills, remove its own hazards. Thus, the cyanide bath now widely used for copper plating of steel can be replaced by a new non-poisonous electroplating solution developed by Dr. Colin G. Fink and Chaak Y. Wong of Columbia University. A complex copper salt, chemically known as disodium diaquodioxalatocupriate, is used in the new bath, along with sodium sulfate and boric acid. The new method will be available for use in large automatic plating installations where strip steel, standard steel parts, etc., are coated with copper as the first step to other coatings. A satisfactory copper deposit is obtained in only one minute with a low electrical current density with the new "oxalato" bath.

Sounds can cause chemical changes of many different kinds if only the sounds are intense enough. This was reported in America by Dr. Earl W. Flosdorf and Dr. Leslie A. Chambers of the University of Pennsylvania School of Medicine, and in Europe by Prof. A. Szent-Györgi of Szeged University, Hungary. Most of the sounds used were shrill as well as intense, but one type of apparatus produced a sound of only moderately high pitch, two octaves above middle C of the piano. The sounds, projected into liquid media, coagulated proteins, broke down ethyl acetate to produce acetic acid, cracked vegetable oils with the generation of acetylene gas, and to a slight extent decomposed starch to produce glucose.

A spectacular demonstration was the apparent soft-boiling of an egg subjected to the effects of the intense sound for a few minutes, without any raising of the temperature. All the changes take place quickly, some of them in a fraction of a second, so that the nature of the action causing them is an interesting problem to chemists. Drs. Flosdorf and Chambers believe them to be due to a momentary kinetic, or speeding-up, effect on the molecules involved, affecting them in much the same manner as heating.

The first indication that sound or sound-like vibrations could effect chemical and biological changes was obtained by Prof. R. W. Wood of the Johns Hopkins University, and Alfred L. Loomis, working at the latter's private laboratory at Tuxedo Park, N. Y. The vibrations they used were far above audible pitch, in what is called the "super-sonic" range. The pioneers in the discovery that audible sounds could have similar effects were Prof. O. B. Williams of the University of Texas and Prof. Newton Gaines of Texas Christian University.

With all these accomplished advances there are also hints of possible future advances just as great. At a meeting of the American Chemical Society in Cleveland, Dr. Niewland, the pioneer of DuPrene development, quietly read a paper announcing his discovery that a solution in wood alcohol of the chemical compound boron fluoride gives as powerfully acid a reaction as that of sulfuric acid itself. He offered no suggestions for practical application of this discovery, and the fact still lies unused, just as vinyl was unused until he and his colleagues in the industrial field got to work on it. But it may become a highly important fact in applied chemistry some day.

Similarly, Prof. O. F. Stafford of the University of Oregon announced that a familiar enough but hitherto little investigated chemical, acetamide, will dissolve more different substances than any other solvent known. This property seems to be tied up with the chemical similarity of various parts of acetamide's structure to other compounds. What this new approach to the alchemist's dream of a "universal solvent" may mean practically is not yet known; but since all life processes occur in solutions, and also since many important industries are dependent upon solubility relationships, Prof. Stafford's discovery will probably turn out to be scientifically significant and industrially useful, once the curiosity and ingenuity of chemists have had time to be applied to it.

CHAPTER 14
TRANSPORT GOES MODERN

A IR CONSCIOUSNESS" in a new sense has invaded the world of transport. The new meaning of the well-worn phrase does not refer to acceptance of aviation as a popular medium of travel.

The current air consciousness has come to designers of automobiles and railway trains. These engineers have become practically aware of the fact that air has weight, that a 28-inch cube of air, for example, tips the scales at one pound. This bit of factual information is not new, but until recently it had not been reckoned with in the design of vehicles.

Air is like a wrestler. Its weight is an advantage with which it opposes the motion of vehicles through it. But, like the wrestler, air also has weaknesses which can be successfully attacked.

The automobile, more than thirty years after its introduction, is becoming a thorough creation of engineering and research, designed scientifically to be the best possible vehicle for highway transportation. Proponents of this new era of automotive transportation see success coming to their teaching. These missionary engineers have a very effective way of presenting their theme to the great mass of individuals who, of course, believe that the present automobile is the acme of technical perfection and could scarcely be improved.

"If we started out today to design a fast automobile," declared a prominent engineer, "and were not handicapped by precedent and fashion, our new automobile would not look like, act, or be mechanically arranged like present automobiles. Every automotive engineer who has kept abreast of developments along automotive lines—automobile, aëronautic, submarine, racing—will concur in this statement, radical as it may seem."

When the automobile was originally designed, it was a slow-moving vehicle, the next step forward from the horse and wagon. At that time, when the style and general arrangement of the car were established, there may have been reason for simulating in appearance and general arrangement the horse-drawn runabout or milk wagon. Reliability and speed were then conspicuous by their absence, and consideration of aërodynamic design, which is tremendously important to high-speed travel through air, would have been far-fetched and ridiculous.

The Penalty of Speed

THIS CONSIDERATION of aërodynamic design has become most disturbing to the creators of automobiles. It made itself felt just a few years ago, when cars began to dash along the highways at cross-country touring speeds of 40 miles per hour and faster, for that is about the speed at which interference offered by air becomes a major portion of the resistance to be overcome by a moving automobile.

This wind resistance increases approximately in accord with the square of the speed, so that at higher speeds it is much larger than the mechanical rolling and friction resistances which increase approximately in direct proportion to the speed.

Tests reveal that a conventional sedan, with an air drag of 48 pounds at 30 miles per hour, has to exert a force of 84 pounds to overcome air resistance at 40 miles per hour, 132 pounds at 50 miles per hour, 180 pounds at 60 miles, 228 pounds at 70 miles, 300 pounds at 80 miles, and 360 pounds at 90 miles.

Aërodynamic research is not new. It helped the Wright brothers fly the first heavier-than-air craft and has continued to improve both airplanes and airships. By use of properly streamlined hulls, the submarine designer shapes his underwater vessels to travel faster, and the chief difference between moving through the air and under water is a difference in density of the fluids, water being about 100 times as heavy as air.

Direct measurement of the air resistance of an automobile on the road under actual driving conditions was made by Prof. W. E. Lay of the University of Michigan. He built a "floating" body and mounted it delicately on ball bearings so that slight air pressure would shove it back. This force was restrained only by a piano wire and measured by a draw bar dynamometer in the rear of the car. The shape tested was not that of an automobile. It was a rectangular box in shape, with rounded edges and corners, made over steel tubing frame covered with airplane fabric, doped to keep it taut. These methods of getting wind resistance obviously require that the vehicle being tested move through the air.

In most aërodynamic research for streamlining the situation is reversed. The air moves and the auto stays still. The vehicle or a model is put in a wind tunnel and air is blown at it at high speeds. Some corrections are necessary because the ground is lacking and because models are used. In general, results are more satisfactory than the more natural methods. Gustave Eiffel, builder of the famous Paris Eiffel tower, twenty years ago tested models of automobiles, locomotives, and railway coaches in wind tunnels.

Odd facts emerged from wind-tunnel and other air-resistance tests. An early discovery was that the conventional sedan is more efficient aërodynamically when run backward than when run forward. The British Admiralty turned to fast-swimming fish for information that might aid in designing airships. The tunny, salmon grilse, Greenland shark, and blue whale were investigated. It was found that nature's aquatic streamlining was most efficient in the shark and whale, and their shape, somewhat modified, was used in one experimental streamlined automobile.

Streamlines Victorious

STREAMLINED AUTOMOBILES built experimentally date from the early days of the automobile, although the advantages of streamlining are only now being accented in the designs and advertising offered the buying public. Two decades ago an Italian automobile with blunt nose and short pointed rear was manufactured, and about a decade ago a German engineer built a more conventional streamlined vehicle. A number of truly streamlined automobiles have been built in recent years by Sir Dennistoun Burney, British airship designer, and Walter T. Fishleigh, American builder of the "tear-drop" car. The engine is at the rear in the latest designs of these automobiles, making the streamlining possible and giving easier vision, more passenger space, and more riding comfort from low center of gravity due to seats swung between the axles.

No automobile approaching streamline perfection has been put on the assembly line. However, by rounding off the corners, bulging the nose, and flattening the tail of the old familiar automobile, some real headway has been made in conquering air resistance and in introducing the public to streamlining.

The automobile, of Model 1933, consumes 30 per cent less power in overcoming air resistance than its predecessor in 1928, it was shown by wind tunnel measurement on models by R. H. Heald of the U. S. Bureau of Standards. But the air resistance of the 1933 car is more than twice that of a completely streamlined car of the same frontal area.

The aërodynamic characteristics of six small-scale replicas, ranging from one quarter to one fifteenth natural size, were studied in the wind tunnel at air speeds from 13 to 70 miles per hour. These six models were a 1922 sedan, a 1922 touring car, a light sedan of 1928, and of 1933, and two models of the autos of tomorrow. The 1933 model was a composite model and not an exact duplicate of any actual make. It was equipped with disk wheels, exposed bumpers, fenders, headlights, and spare tire. One model of the auto of the future differed from it in having the windshield inclined at a 45-degree angle, the top rounded front and rear, and a general smoothing of lines. The other model of the future presents a radical departure in design; the whole upper is rounded, blunt in front, and tapered to the rear so that it resembles a section from a thick airplane wing. The wheels of this car are enclosed in the body.

Mr. Heald measured the resistance offered by these models to air currents of known velocity, and from these data he obtained the so-called drag coefficients which express the aërodynamic efficiency of the model. These coefficients ranged from 0.0017 for the 1922 sedan, 0.0018 for the 1928 sedan, 0.0014 for the 1933 sedan to 0.0005 for the car of the future.

The significance of these figures can be more readily appreciated when these drag coefficients are converted into horsepower consumption for an actual automobile. At a speed of 60 miles per hour air resistance devours: 27 horsepower for the 1922 sedan, 33 horsepower for the touring car of the same period, 26 horsepower for the 1928 sedan, 18 horsepower for the 1933 sedan, and 8 and 6 horsepower for the two streamlined models. The slight improvement of the 1928 model over those for 1922 is due, not to any improvement in aërodynamic design, but to a reduction in frontal area, and to a lesser extent this is true also of the 1933 car as compared to the 1928 model.

The few "ultra" 1934 models better the economy of the typical 1933 car. But even they are not fully streamlined. Engineers feel that advantage cannot be made of streamlining until the engine is put in the rear. From the point of view of the manufacturer who, to sell, must build to please the public, this is a very radical change. Since 60-miles-an-hour touring is a reality, it is only logical that this speed, and the higher speeds that will soon be reached, be achieved with economy.

The Passing of the Iron Horse

STREAMLINING THREATENS the orthodox order of railroad transportation just as it is bringing technical revolution for the highway vehicle. Perhaps the most radical change will come to the "iron horse." Its iron is already giving way to aluminum. Gasoline and fuel oil in internal combustion engines and electricity in motors may replace coal and steam. Speed by rail will more nearly approach speed by air.

A pioneer in railway design is the Union Pacific's blunt-nosed aluminum bullet of the rails, completed by the Pullman Company early in 1934. It resembles a huge airplane fuselage on wheels. From his cab at the very top of the rounded nose of the train, the engineer has a view before and on either side of him. Behind him the tubular, aluminum alloy construction that forms the car bodies ends, over 200 feet away, in a graceful, almost fin-like tail. The weight of the complete three-car train is about 85 tons, approximately the weight of one conventional Pullman sleeping car. One truck supports the adjoining ends of two cars and there are only four trucks for the three cars.

The train is powered by a 600-horsepower distillate-burning engine to reach a maximum speed of 110 miles per hour and to cruise at 90 miles per hour. The internal combustion engine is directly connected to a generator which produces electricity that drives two traction motors mounted on the axles of the front truck. The fuel tanks have sufficient capacity for a 1,200-mile run. Steam locomotives usually carry coal for a run of about 100 miles. The entire power plant weighs about 20 tons in contrast with the 316-ton weight of the conventional 7,000-type passenger locomotive.

There is not a break in the wind-tunnel-determined lines of this train. Sealed windows are flush with the outer surface, doors close like those of an airplane, vestibules are completely covered, and trucks are shrouded so that only a few inches of wheels show where they meet the rails.

The Burlington *Zephyr*, a lightweight 100-mile per hour stainless steel streamlined 3-car train, is the first rail car to be powered with a Diesel engine. Built in Philadelphia by the Edward G. Budd Manufacturing Co., it is 197 feet long, weighs only 95 tons, and due to articulated cars, the sixteen wheels of four trucks support the whole train of three cars. There is ample mail, express, and baggage space, and 76 passengers are seated in air-conditioned comfort and served meals from an electrical buffet-grill. Electricity actually turns the wheels of this train, but the electricity is produced by a generator driven by an eight-cylinder 660 horsepower two-cycle Diesel engine using heavy oil as fuel, which allows considerable economy of operation.

Economy of operation, light weight, rapid acceleration and deceleration, rather than straightaway speed achieved by streamlining, are the features of another new breed of train put in service by the Texas and Pacific Railway on a 490-mile daily run. Making frequent stops, this two-car train maintains a schedule speed of 50 miles per hour and makes a top speed of 75 miles per hour. It is said to operate at twice the speed and half the cost of the steam train that it replaced. Its light weight of little more than 50 tons is achieved by spot-welded, seamless steel construction. The passenger car is mounted on sixteen pneumatic, rubber-tired wheels, a French creation. The power plant consists of two 240-horsepower gasoline engines coupled to generators that feed four 85-horsepower electric motors, two mounted on each truck of the forward car.

The dean of American lightweight, high speed, internal combustion-engined trains is the Clark Autotram, which saw extensive service on the Michigan Central out of Battle Creek, Mich. A one-car unit, air conditioned and made of aluminum alloy, it carries 42 passengers on frequent-stop, short-haul service. The Autotram's 16-cylinder engine, under a hood on the front of the car, is capable of driving it from 100 to 110 miles per hour. Cruising speed is from 85 to 90 miles per hour. The rear of the autotram tapers to a sharp "V" shape. Mechanical drive and steel-rimmed, rubber-cushioned wheels are distinctive features.

Ideas imported from automotive and airplane design were used in the building of the one-car "railplane" by William B. Stout, automobile and airplane designer. This lightweight, well streamlined 50-passenger car is powered by two standard motor-bus gasoline engines to cruise at 60 miles per hour. Its fuel consumption at mile-a-minute speed is a gallon of gasoline every six miles. A standard power plant now in production was used in order to keep costs down. To be accessible and to be kept away from the body so that passengers would get no vibrations, the entire power plant mechanism was mounted below the car on the forward truck, the engines being located outside the truck beyond the wheels.

The "railplane" weighs 26,000 pounds complete, is 60 feet long, and has a top speed of 90 miles per hour. Both ends of the car are rounded off, and retractable steps reduce wind drag. Sidewise as well as endwise streamlining has been embodied into the design to take care of crosswinds when the car is in operation.

The revolution in transport has had a focus in Europe. Germany's rail zeppelin, fanned along by a gasoline-engine-powered propeller, in 1931 traveled between Berlin and Hamburg at a 105 miles per hour average. In France, J. H. Michelin, of tire fame, shod the motor bus with a tire that operated on rails. It was used by the Budd Company, which in 1932 built America's first pneumatic-tired rail coach for the Reading Railway, and later the Texas and Pacific Company train. The flying *Hamburger,* a Diesel-electric, two car, 94 miles per hour unit, has succeeded the rail zeppelin in Germany. In France, a rail car driven by an 800-horsepower engine is said to be capable of a speed of 125 miles per hour with 80 passengers.

Thus the railroads fashion and test fleet, lithe rail craft to compete with the low travel cost of the automobile and the speed of the airplane. As a result of this modernization, the familiar railroad train with its puffing locomotive may gradually disappear from the landscape, taking with it smoke, cinders, slow schedules, and the heroic traditions of steam railroading.

Electricity is creeping over some of the great rail transportation arteries of the nation, doing its share in banishing steam. The Pennsylvania Railroad has nearly completed the electrification of its important rail link between New York and Washington.

Queen of the Seas

UPON THE SEAS, there will soon be in commercial service the largest vessel in the world, one that outstrips the *Leviathan* and the *Majestic* by wide margins. She is France's *Normandie,* launched in the fall of 1932.

The *Normandie* has an overall length of 1,027 feet, 963 feet between perpendiculars, and will be rated at approximately 75,000 gross tons. The *Leviathan's* registered tonnage is approximately 60,000, more than the *Majestic's* 56,000 but her length between perpendiculars is only 907 feet, 6 inches, compared with 915 feet, 5 inches, for the *Majestic*. The *Normandie's* breadth of 119 feet, 6 inches accounts chiefly for her greater tonnage. The vessel is a little more than 19 feet wider than either the *Leviathan* or the *Majestic*.

Only the British liner *R-534* on which, because of economic conditions, construction was suspended for many months, will rival the *Normandie*.

In addition to excessive size, the *Normandie* will contain the largest electric motors ever built. Rated at 40,000 horsepower each, the new motors will give the vessel a total horsepower of 160,000; but even then she will not be the most powerful ship. The U. S. S. airplane carriers *Saratoga* and *Lexington* bear this title with 180,000 horsepower plants in each. Each contains 8 motors rated at 22,500 horsepower, connected in pairs to 4 propelling shafts. The turbo-electric machinery has been designed for a service speed of 30 knots to enable the *Normandie* to cross the Atlantic from Havre to New York by way of Plymouth under all conditions in less than five days.

On highway, on rails, and on sea, the progress of transportation continues. We travel faster and more frequently from place to place on the surface of the earth. The world becomes smaller, and our lives can contain more accomplishment and enjoyment.

CHAPTER 15
COMMUNICATION, NEW MODEL

TELEVISION, for more years than prosperity, has been "just around the corner." Following the flowering and fruiting of sound broadcasting, there were high hopes for the similar entry of sight broadcasting into our homes. Several systems of transmission of scenes and motion pictures by wire and radio were brought to the point of experimental demonstration. A dozen or so television broadcasting stations went "on the air" with sight and sound. While there was a wave of amateur interest, while a few purchased and enjoyed the novelty of commercial television sets, the perfection was not such as to hold the audiences. As the depression progressed, the brave, pioneering television stations were engulfed one by one until television was practically off the radio waves and relegated to the laboratories whence it sprang.

For a decade during the commercialization of broadcasting there had been under development a modern version of the electric eye, a method of television that is so different and promising in its principles that it may become the instrument that will bring television around its corner. Dr. V. K. Zworykin, who first researched in the Westinghouse laboratories and then in the Camden laboratories of the RCA Victor Company, is the inventor of the iconoscope, as the pick-up or sending instrument is called, and the kinescope, as the receiving tube is named.

The iconoscope (literally "image observer") is the closest artificial imitation of the human eye yet devised. It has no scanning disk or other moving parts. The only thing about it that moves is a thin stream of electrons, a cathode ray, played back and forth across a sensitive artificial "retina" by changes in a magnetic field.

The "seeing" end of the instrument is within a vacuum tube and consists of a flat plate, representing the retina or sensitive inner surface of the eye. On this, as on a photographic plate, the scene to be "televised" is focused by a lens system exterior to the tube. This retinal plate contains many thousands of tiny silver globules, each turned into a minute photoelectric cell by chemical treatment with the element caesium. On a 4 by 5-inch plate such as used there are 3 million of these little photocells.

The trick of this non-living "electrical eye" apparatus is that it has persistence of vision similar to that of the human eye. It is an electrical latent image mechanism that stores electrically the information given it by the projected optical image. It can reproduce its electrically stored information when it is desired. Older television systems were instantaneous in their action and could use only the light of instant of scanning.

Iconoscope and Kinescope

A SIMPLE ELECTRICAL EXPERIMENT illustrates the principle behind the iconoscope. A condenser is connected in series with a photocell. The photocell is illuminated. The light on the photocell is converted into electricity which flows and charges the condenser. The condenser is made to discharge by flashing upon it a beam of electrons shot from a cathode tube.

The screen in the iconoscope is a thin sheet of mica coated on the back side with a continuous metal layer. On its front is the mosaic of small isolated photo-sensitive globules. Dr. Zworykin makes this mosaic very simply by evaporating a thin film of silver upon the mica, then breaking it into separate particles by heat and sensitizing the silver with the element caesium. The globules "soak up" the light converted into electricity when an image is projected by lenses upon the screen. Each photo-sensitive globule gets a positive electrical charge in proportion to the amount of light that falls upon it.

The screen is scanned regularly by the electron beam that releases these charges, and this produces changes in the electrical capacity of the metal layer on the other side of the mica. By attaching an amplifying system to that metal layer, there can be drawn off from the system a fluctuating current that is an electrical representation of the light picture on the screen.

At the receiving or reproducing end of the Zworykin television system, the transmitting current is fed into a kinescope or cathode ray receiving tube in which there is created a stream of electrons, which varies in strength with the fluctuations in the current. Pulled by a set of electro-magnets corresponding to those in the iconoscope, the electron stream plays rapidly back and forth across a screen, which fluoresces or shines when the electrons bombard it strongly, is dark when they do not. Thus the original scene is reconstructed.

Iconoscope and kinescope may bring the realization of practical television. The sensitivity of the iconoscope is approximately equal to that of photographic film operating at the speed of a motion-picture camera. It can therefore televise any scene of which movies can be taken. The resolution or detail possible is extraordinarily high. It is better than that of a newspaper halftone with its 60 dots to the inch. The television pictures can be light-painted in from 250 to 500 lines, compared with a fifth to a tenth that number which was the limit of earlier television systems. The whole system is electrical without a single mechanically moving part, and that simplifies and speeds its action.

In one respect the iconoscope is superior to the human eye. It can see ultraviolet and infrared radiations which are invisible to the human eye. Combined with the extraordinary amplification possible, this will make Dr. Zworykin's apparatus a powerful aid to science. Television microscopes and television telescopes are possibilities.

A super-microscope seeing by television would be able to convert into electricity light beyond the range of human eyes and then the electricity could be amplified hundreds and even thousands of times. This electricity, converted into visible light, would allow the scientist to see with great brilliance radiations that are invisible in the actual scene under the microscope. It might even be possible to view a microscopic scene many miles away by transmitting by tele-phone wire or radio the electrical current representing the light.

The light-gathering devices of the Zworykin iconoscope may be used in the construction of an electronic telescope that will allow astronomers to view faint nebulæ and stars whose light is too feeble to be seen or recorded satisfac-torily on photographic plates. The heavens might be viewed by television as they would appear if our eyes could see light of a very limited range. The great 200-inch reflecting telescope now building may even be dwarfed for some pur-poses by an electronic telescope that would be able to col-lect more light and then multiply it many fold.

Micro-rays of Marconi

WHEN IT DOES COME, television is expected to use short radio waves, for there is room in the high frequency or short wave portion of the radio spectrum that was despised up until a few years ago. The proper transmission of tele-vision requires much more breadth of frequency band than sound broadcasting. When the waves become short, there are many new, unused channels available. Between 10 meters and 5 meters there are 1,000 channels three times as wide as existing broadcast channels, and an additional 8,000 channels exist between 5 meters and one meter, each 30 kilocycles wide, free from static, fading, and interfer-ence by distant stations.

The great Marconi has said:

"There is a great vista opening up in the micro-ray region. The tiny waves are not limited to optical dis-tance, and I stake my reputation on it—micro-waves are not affected by static."

Guglielmo Marconi again confounded the prophets. He proved that ultra-short radio waves are able to pass through mountains and even curve around the surfaces of the earth to receiving stations far below the horizon.

History repeats. For in 1901 Prof. H. M. Poincaré, distinguished French mathematician, predicted that communication with electrical waves would be limited to about 165 miles. In that same year Marconi demonstrated that electrical waves could be sent and received across the Atlantic Ocean.

Modern theories had predicted that the ultra-short waves would act like light waves from a searchlight and would not be detectable beyond the horizon. Messages were sent from the inventor's yacht to an experimental station 94 miles away in inland Italy, more than three times the predicted distance.

The explanation for this property of the waves to bend about the earth and to curve around objects is not known. Theorists have attacked the problem by treating the radio waves as light waves and have extended the diffraction theory which explains the microscopic bending of light around corners to the ultra-short radio waves, but without marked success. Nevertheless, a vast new communication field opens.

Marconi's new waves are only two feet long as compared to the ordinary radio waves of about 900 feet. Their most distinctive feature is that they are almost like light waves and can be focused upon a receiver, thus allowing private communication. It is thought that they cannot be reflected back from the ionized layers of the upper atmosphere, which act as huge reflectors to ordinary radio waves. A beam of the ultra-short waves directed upwards would pass through this region which is about 200 miles above the earth, and would shoot off into interplanetary space.

Marconi and investigators in this country and abroad are using the ultra-short waves much like a searchlight. Since the waves are not much longer than light waves, they may be focused and projected by parabolic reflectors and antennæ similar to a section of an automobile headlight. These "quasi-optical" waves are thus not adapted to long-distance communication but may readily be developed for private communication between stations where wire telegraphy or telephony is impracticable.

In contrast to long radio waves, the ultra-short waves have the advantages of being efficiently projected in small directive beams, requiring minute amounts of power, of not being affected by atmospheric disturbances, and of allowing secrecy of communication.

The renewed interest in these short waves has brought the question of allocation of wavelengths to various types of broadcasting. In the earlier days of radio the commercial broadcasting stations received the then popular band of wavelengths from about 200 meters to 500 meters. The amateur radio experimenters were given the then impractical short-wave band from 5 meters to 100 meters. But time has shown that the latter band is extremely valuable, and it has been encroached upon by the police, air transport lines, and governmental services. The congestion that has arisen may be relieved by the growing use of the ultrashort waves from about 5 meters down to 5 centimeters or about 2 inches. Below this minimum wavelength the waves are too greatly absorbed by the atmosphere to be valuable for communication purposes.

Although the spread in wavelength of these quasi-optical waves is very small, the frequency range is enormous. Carrier waves of commercial broadcasters have a range of frequency from 500 kilocycles to 1,500 kilocycles, and as each station needs about 10 kilocycles for a channel there are only 100 frequency bands available. The ultrashort waves have a frequency range of from 60,000 kilocycles to 6 million kilocycles. Thus there would be room for 594,000 channels if each station would still require a 10-kilocycle band.

The new shorter waves have already replaced optical or light signaling between coastal stations and between forts along a frontier. They will be found advantageous in many cases where the erection and maintenance of an ordinary short-distance telephone or cable circuit is difficult or too expensive.

Already micro-rays are being pressed into practical use. Early in 1934 there was inaugurated across the Channel between the British airport of Lympne and the French airport of St. Inglevert a radio link that operates on a shorter wavelength than any other commercial services in the world. Teleprinters and two-way telephone service function on wavelengths in the neighborhood of 17.5 centimeters, and the distance between the two stations is 56 kilometers (35 miles). Police-patrol cars are now using the ultra-short radio waves to combat the criminals in Eastchester, N. Y., and Bayonne, N. J. For the first time in history officers on patrol in motorcars are able to carry on two-way conversations with their headquarters' "desk." The radio waves used are only a few feet long (about 40,000 kilocycles).

Music with Perspective

FOR THE HIGHEST QUALITY of electrical reproduction of music and sound, we must turn to telephone wires capable of carrying as broad a band of frequencies as are fed into the microphones.

So far has the electrical communication art progressed that it is possible to pick up the music of a symphonic orchestra playing in one city and reproduce it in another with a fidelity, depth, and spatial effect that creates the illusion of the orchestra's presence behind the curtain of an empty stage. Auditory perspective, coupled with tone and volume control, has made technically and artistically successful the wire transmission of symphonic music.

Three loud speakers on a Washington stage empty of human beings but bathed in colorful light, three telephone lines running to three microphones in Philadelphia where the Philadelphia Symphony Orchestra played, Leopold Stokowski in the Washington hall whirling electrical control knobs instead of wielding a baton, telephone engineers alert in operating the electrical circuits. These were the ingredients of the most advanced development of musical reproduction that was demonstrated in a Philadelphia-Washington concert for the National Academy of Sciences in the spring of 1933. It was the result of two years of scientific research conducted by American Telephone and Telegraph Company engineers with the collaboration of Director Stokowski.

Three loud speakers at left, right, and center of the empty stage, each connected with a similarly placed microphone on the remote stage of the actual performers, give perspective to the music and sounds. Musicians could tell just where the violins or horns were placed. People moved across the distant stage, and the audience of the empty stage "followed" them about the empty stage by using their ears.

A wide range of nine musical octaves, from three below middle C to nearly six above, was utilized for the first time in electrical transmission of music. This corresponds to all frequencies from about 35 cycles per second to about 16,000 cycles per second. Radio by federal regulation is limited to a band of 5,000 cycles per second. When experimentally the high and low frequencies are chopped off by electrical filters, the damage to the tone and overtone qualities is readily apparent. Each of the three telephone wires carried the full range of frequencies, and the frequency channels utilized therefor roughly totaled nine times those of the most perfect radio transmission.

In loudness range, the orchestra or other sound being transmitted can be varied from an output equivalent to a millionth of a watt to a sustained hundred watts and even a kilowatt at momentary peaks without distortion. The sound can be raised from the rustle of leaves to beyond that of a roaring airplane engine.

Talking Around the World

As THE TELEPHONE offers its aid to musical art, it continues to improve its primary service of making it possible for anyone to talk to anyone else anywhere else.

Not a decade has passed since the first commercial telephone circuit between Europe and North America was put in operation. Yet it is possible to talk around the world. There are 66 intercontinental telephone circuits totaling 250,000 miles in length. All of them are radio circuits, all but one operating on short waves. But plans have already been made to supplement the important route between Europe and North America with a telephone cable. Wire instead of wireless links between the continents promise to be important in the future.

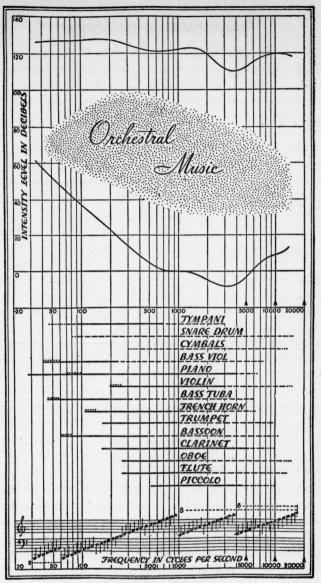

THE RANGES OF MUSIC

FIGURE 6

THE dotted area shows the portion of the total auditory range of sounds that one uses in listening to orchestral music in a concert hall. Below are shown the frequency ranges of many of the component instruments. The dashed and dotted lines at the right show the additional frequencies or "harmonics" audible to 30 per cent and 60 per cent of the auditors. Some of the dotted lines at the left overlap the solid lines, indicating that only 60 per cent of the auditors can hear some of the lower notes which some instruments are supposed to produce. The intensity scale is represented in decibels above a zero level of one ten-thousand-million-millionth of a watt per square centimeter in a plane free wave.

Courtesy Bell Telephone Laboratories.

At present the following ocean-bound areas can communicate directly with each other: North America and Europe, North America and South America. North America and Eastern Asia, Europe and South America, Europe and Eastern Asia, Europe and Australia and Java, North America and Hawaii, Eastern Asia and Java.

As the earth is girdled with telephone talk and blanketed with radio music, as radio makes ready to have eyes as well as ears, there comes evidence that a strange radio impulse is coming to earth from the vicinity of the very heart of the Milky Way.

Hisses of the Cosmos

THIS MYSTERIOUS Milky Way static or cosmic "hiss" was discovered by Karl G. Jansky, of Bell Telephone Laboratories, while working with an extremely sensitive receiving set at Holmdel, N. J. Disentangling this particular kind of static from other sorts that are heard in radio sets, Mr. Jansky noted that the hiss was always a little stronger coming from one direction than from all other directions, and that this direction of maximum static hiss was continually rotating around the horizon, approximately once a day.

Mr. Jansky made many observations, attempting to check the idea that the hiss had something to do with the sun's position and the earth's daily motion. He discovered that the direction of the hiss progressed slightly in position in the sky with each day. For a year he gathered observations daily, without making any announcement. Apparently the hiss was not following the sun, but something that gained on the sun four minutes a day or a whole rotation of the heavens in a year. This is exactly what the stars do, as every amateur astronomer or star-gazer knows. The cosmic static was therefore seemingly hitched to a given place in the heavens or the Milky Way. It is a stream of radio impulses coming from some fixed point outside the solar system in the great aggregation of stars known as the Milky Way, in which our sun is a mere minor star.

Mr. Jansky's radio was short-wave, tuned to 14.6 meters

or 20,600 kilocycles, but he feels sure that these interstellar static impulses will be found all up and down the
radio spectrum, probably increasing with frequency in the
high-frequency or short-wave portions.

The point from which the Milky Way static comes is very
near the location of the center of our Milky Way galaxy
as determined by Dr. Harlow Shapley, director of Harvard
College Observatory. The point is where the plane in which
the earth revolves around the sun crosses the center of the
Milky Way. It is also the position toward which the solar
system is moving with respect to the stars. The astronomical coördinates of the newly discovered radio waves are
right ascension 18 hours and a declination of about minus
or south 20 degrees. If you want to see where this is in the
heavens, look at the Milky Way between the constellations
of Sagittarius and Ophiuchus.

What generates the cosmic hiss is as yet unknown, just
as the origin of the cosmic ray is unknown after many
years of research. The center of the Milky Way is computed to be some forty thousand light years from the solar
system, and the power of a generating station, measured in
earthly terms, would be prodigious, perhaps millions upon
millions of times as powerful as any broadcasting station
on earth.

Perhaps the cosmic hiss is the by-product of some widespread galactic happening, such as transmutation of mass
into light, a mighty murmur of atoms disturbed. Mystics
may see in the Milky Way static messages from intelligent
beings on unseen planets of remote stars, but scientists will
not support this view. There has been presented another
problem for the future of science to solve.

CHAPTER 16
WINGING FORWARD

THOUSANDS of airplanes, in this fourth decade after Kitty Hawk, thunder applause to the Wrights, those bicycle makers who with daring Yankee ingenuity and experimentation did what was "impossible" yesterday and commonplace today.

More impressive than staged tributes, more important than the opening of museums that preserve the relics and the details of the birth and growth of the airplane, are the utilitarian and cultural uses of the airplane in our civilization today. As mails, passengers, and freight are whisked through the air, over mountains and seas, consuming in hours distances that formerly wasted days and weeks of human time, we should accept this as evidence that other dreams of science and engineering may be materialized.

Pessimists among us may lament that the airplane, like other scientific inventions, may be used for warfare's destruction or for disquieting competition with more established ways of doing things. That is one of the incidental prices of progress of any sort and not an argument for the stifling of research and experimentation.

Orville Wright, the first man to fly an airplane, must wish that his brother Wilbur, an untimely victim of typhoid fever which since has been conquered by medical and sanitary science, could be with him in the years of full fruition to see the triumphal pageant of aviation. The practice and science of aviation today utilizes the energy and intelligence of thousands of followers of the Wrights, yet the world is grateful for the continued quiet interest and stimulation of that great pioneer, Orville Wright, in a science and art now too wide-flung for any one human being to follow in its millions of details. His inconspicuous, almost shy, participation in the important planning of Uncle Sam's

National Advisory Committee for Aëronautics research, his other unpublicized aids to present aëronautical activities, are evidence that a father is proud of his precocious child.

Speed from Research

SPEED IS the prime factor in making the airplane useful for commerce and for national defense. Research in laboratories has made possible remarkable progress in speed and efficiency of airplanes. In a brief year increases of 40 to 60 per cent were achieved in the speed of multi-engined airplanes, even though the engine power was not increased a single horsepower. A normal 125 miles per hour cruising speed became 200 miles per hour. The effect was striking, telescoping air transport schedules and saving hours of time and dollars of money.

This major advance was made possible largely through the researches of the National Advisory Committee for Aëronautics, the federal government's independent agency for aëronautic development with laboratories at Langley Field, Va.

In calling attention to the recent improvement in military and civil airplanes, President Roosevelt has stated that the principal underlying cause has been

"the efficient functioning of the National Advisory Committee for Aëronautics in coördinating and planning for the research needs of aviation, civil and military, and in conducting the necessary fundamental scientific researches to serve the needs of all agencies."

"I concur," President Roosevelt wrote, in sending the N. A. C. A. report to Congress, "in the Committee's opinion that the continuous prosecution of fundamental research in aëronautics is essential to the national defense and to the future of air transportation upon a sound economic basis."

The great increases in speed and efficiency which opened a new era in the development of both military and commercial aircraft arose as a result of these factors:

1. Research on engine location and cowling. The results of the cowling research of the N. A. C. A. were published in 1928. The results of the engine location research were issued confidentially to the army, navy, and industry in 1930, and were kept confidential until 1932, when the first American airplanes embodying the principles had been designed and actually constructed.

2. Reliable retractable landing gears were developed by the army, navy, and industry.

3. Increased horsepower was obtained with same size weight of engines, by development of increased revolutions per minute, higher compression ratio, improved fuels, and improved cylinder cooling.

4. Satisfactory controllable-pitch propellers were developed.

5. New and more efficient wing sections were developed by the N. A. C. A.

6. Improved streamlining and use of wing flaps were introduced, with the assistance of N. A. C. A. researches.

While the conventional airplane undergoes refinement and becomes more efficient, eyes of aëronautical engineers are turned toward the future. Just as the airplane of World War days seems strange and crude alongside the latest air transport liner, so the airplane of today may seem very old-fashioned when compared with the prevailing type of heavier-than-air aircraft of 1940.

The airliners and fighting aircraft of the future may not have the appearance of today's conventional airplanes. They may even be descended from cousins of the present airplanes rather than in the direct line of descent.

In recent years a strange sort of flying craft, nicknamed the "windmill," has been seen in our skies. This is the autogyro, product of the genius and persistence of Juan de la Cierva, the Spanish inventor. The American version of the autogyro was produced by Harold F. Pitcairn and it has been flown rather extensively. This rotating-wing aircraft and machines like it may well be the aircraft of the future, although at present its American factory is closed.

Wings That Rotate

IT IS PREDICTED that flying machines with rotating wings will be superior to the conventional airplane as soon as their possibilities for high speed are practically developed. John B. Wheatley, aëronautical engineer of the N. A. C. A., has analyzed the potential qualities of various aircraft types. The autogyro and the gyroplane are the two types of rotating-wing aircraft which, according to Mr. Wheatley's analysis, have the possibilities of becoming superior to the conventional type of fixed wing airplane now widely used. The reason for the pronounced possibility of the autogyro and the gyroplane is the inherent ability of their rotors or moving wings to attain their maximum liftdrag ratio at any desired forward speed. The novel cyclogyro, with the paddle-wheel wings, is rated by Mr. Wheatley as being approximately equal in merit to the airplane, while the helicopter is definitely inferior.

The autogyro is the best known of all rotating-wing aircraft. The gyroplane is sponsored by E. Burke Wilford of Philadelphia. The autogyro and the gyroplane present a very similar appearance, with blades that rotate freely under the action of air forces about a vertical axis, replacing to a large extent the conventional wing of the airplane. The aërodynamic principles of the autogyro and gyroplane are practically identical, and their differences are largely structural.

Low-speed control in the autogyro and the gyroplane is superior to that of the airplane, Mr. Wheatley's study showed. The reliability is equivalent to that of an airplane. Emergency landings will be easier. The low-speed performance is superior to that of an airplane. Airplane high speeds will probably be exceeded. The control system is as simple and easy to use as that of the airplane. First cost will be slightly higher, but maintenance and operating costs will be equivalent to those of the airplane. Mr. Wheatley believes that the rotating-wing type of machine is likely to be used by the private flyer and the unskilled pilot because of the increased safety and the smaller landing field required for it. Almost all the hazards encountered in flying an airplane are connected with the phenomenon of a gradual weakening of control as the flying speed approaches its minimum. As minimum speeds range from 50 to 75 miles per hour, an undesirable premium is placed upon piloting technic during landings and take-offs. A rotating-wing aircraft suffers very slightly from these handicaps because the relative velocity of the lifting surfaces to the air is independent of the translatory velocity of the machine and is always large, so that the angle of attack of the lifting surfaces is well below "the burble point," where they lose the ability to lift. Rotating-wing aircraft allow low-speed flight and lessen the piloting skill required for emergency landings and take-offs. They make the pilot more independent of meteorological conditions, because at low speed a shorter visibility is required for the same degree of safety.

The gyroplane has been flown, and models have been subjected to intensive wind-tunnel research by the N. A. C. A. The cyclogyro is of such recent origin that it has not yet been demonstrated at full scale. It consists of a fuselage of conventional form, supported in the air by power-driven paddle-wheel wings, one on each side, rotating about the lateral axis. The paddle-wheel rotors perform the functions of both the wings and the propeller of the conventional airplane.

The airplane is nearly synonymous with speed. Yet the ordinary automobile of today is capable of as much speed as the fastest airplane of 1910, when the world's speed record was 66.20 miles per hour. The cruising speed of modern transport airliners is about equal to the 194.51 miles per hour, which was the airplane world's record in 1920. The speed record made by Francesco Agello, the Italian pilot, on April 10, 1933, is 423.82 miles per hour, over 7 miles per minute. The question is: How fast will it be possible in future years to push an airplane through the air?

Experiments in wind tunnels where air streams of high velocity can be sent over models that can be built for a few dollars provide some preliminary answers. An engineer of the N. A. C. A., John Stack, has performed some experiments and made some computations. He considers a hypothetical airplane that is not beyond the limits of possibility. Taking one of the best wing-fuselage combinations found as a result of tests in the N. A. C. A. variable density wind tunnel, he made the model proportioned so that the full-scale airplane it represents would have a fuselage large enough to contain a 2,300-horsepower engine. Protuberances and excrescences of any sort that would cause the slightest surface irregularity would be absent, because at very high speeds even a very small projection will cause power-using drag. The landing gear would be completely retractable, or the airplane would be catapulted and landed on water with the aid of suitable retractable hydrodynamic surfaces. The pilot would look through a transparent fuselage section or see by means of a system of mirrors. The engine would be completely enclosed and cooled by skin-type radiators.

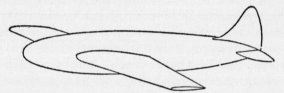

HYPOTHETICAL HIGH-SPEED AIRPLANE

FIGURE 7

As visualized by John Stack, National Advisory Committee for Aëronautics engineer, this airplane should travel about 9 miles per minute, or 540 miles per hour. Its wing span is only 29 feet, and its fuselage diameter is 40 inches.

With such a craft a speed of some 544 miles per hour might be attained. At high airplane speeds the effect of the compressibility of the air enters into limiting the performances of the airplane, and the air cannot be considered incompressible, as it can when the speeds are low. When the speed increases to above 500 miles an hour the effect of the air's compressibility begins to be strongly felt, and finally the effect of adding just a mile or two per hour to the speed requires an impossibly large increase in horsepower. If an airplane such as visualized by Mr. Stack adds another 100 miles per hour to the world's record speed,

the daring pilot will be traveling at a rate relatively close
to the speed of sound itself, which is about 740 miles per
hour. And once a craft is driven through the air at between
500 and 600 miles per hour, aëronautic science will, from
the physics of the case, be content to rest on its laurels.
Serious plans to push airplane speed records to higher
velocities are, however, likely to be few, since the costs are
great and the returns are glory and not profits.

Cheaper Airplanes

SINCE AUTOMOBILES have become such a usual form of personal transportation, the development of the private airplane to be used like an automobile has been considered a
logical development. Why are not airplanes available at
about the cost of a low-priced automobile? This question
was asked concretely by Eugene L. Vidal, director of
aëronautics in the Roosevelt administration, when he said
that what this country needs is a good $700 airplane. The
suggestion raised enthusiasm among many who hope some
day to have an extra $700. Many engineers felt that a
satisfactory private airplane could not be produced and
sold for the price suggested. But a questionnaire circulated
by the Department of Commerce to over 18,000 pilots,
students, mechanics, and others, indicated that over half of
them would buy a small two-seat low wing monoplane if it
could be produced for about $700. Some federal public
works funds were made available to get the project under
way, and the outcome may be increased use of cheaper airplanes for pleasure and business.

Better and Safer Airways

GIVEN AIRPLANES and pilots, there must be skyways over
which they can fly safely and with a high degree of reliability under all sorts of conditions. The airways have been
lighted, and emergency landing fields have been established
and maintained by the government as a part of its widespread service to the public. In clear weather airplanes may
fly by night over lighted airways with minimum of risk.

When by day or night fog and mist obscure the light beacons and landmarks and shroud the landing fields, airplanes are grounded and helpless.

Radio and science have now solved the problem of blind flying and blind landings. As soon as airways and airplanes are equipped with the necessary devices, the mail will go through regardless of the weather, no matter how low the ceiling. Two little pointers, kept crossed over one tiny spot on an airplane instrument board, make possible "happy landings" that are directed by radio when the unseeing pilot and plane are plowing through darkness and fog.

This latest development in radio aids to aëronautic navigation has completed the chain of devices that now make blind flying practical. With eyes flashing over this little dial and pointers, the pilot can swoop down out of fog and complete darkness with mathematical precision until the wheels of his airplane scrape the solid earth of the airport's runway.

Many of our present pilots can remember all too clearly the days when the only thing that helped a pilot fly from one primitive field to another was his own ingenuity and resourcefulness. Night flying was then a gamble with death.

The first step in applying radio to the guidance of airplanes was when radio beacons were set up at intervals along the airways. Simple receiving sets in the airplanes picked up these signals that gave the pilot a point-to-point method of establishing his position. This allowed him to get through short distances of bad weather as long as he could still see his general landmarks and runways.

Scientists at the Bureau of Standards next concentrated on better methods of guiding the pilot so that the possibility of becoming lost would be very small. A radio device for direction finding was developed that allowed the pilot either to see or to hear his way along an approximately straight line between two airports.

Directional waves broadcast from airports are now picked up in modern airplanes on two vibrating reeds. When the vibrating lines are equal in length the airplane is on its course, a deviation from the true course increasing the deflection of one reed and decreasing the other. Distance indicators actuated by radio waves tell the pilot the distance to and from various stations.

The Bureau of Standards then developed a new transmission-line antenna, called the TL antenna, which sends out highly accurate directional guiding radio waves. Waves from the older loop antennas were subject to a variable rotational effect, particularly at night, due to the action of the ionized layers of the upper atmosphere on the horizontal components of the broadcast wave. The TL system gets around this difficulty.

Thus the airways were clear for night flying as long as the runways at the airports were visible. Taking off in absolute darkness was a stunt that a pilot would do if necessary, but landing without seeing the ground was considered an impossibility.

Many schemes were proposed that were based on the idea that a meter which would show the height of the plane with great accuracy would allow the pilot to sink slowly to a "pancake" landing after he had been guided to the edge of the field by the directional beacons.

Endeavors were made to put the familiar echo to work. Using the principle of the sonic depth finder developed to sound the ocean, an instrument was devised which shot a sound wave down to the ground from the plane and measured the time taken for it to be reflected back. This gave a measure of the altitude. But this scheme had obvious disadvantages, such as lack of directional guidance. Something had to be added. Since 1928 scientists from the Bureau of Standards have been working at College Park, Maryland, to solve this problem of finding a simple and effective radio system that would ensure foolproof landings under conditions of no visibility. Success came through the use of a new radio apparatus developed by this group of scientists. It was given its first installation at the Newark, N. J., Municipal Airport after the tests at College Park.

The system depends upon three elements in order to inform the pilot of his position in three dimensions: height above the ground, direction to right and left, and distance from the runway. These elements are provided by the runway localizing beacon, marker beacons, and the landing beams. The runway localizing beacon informs the pilot of his directional position with respect to the airport and guides the plane over the runway. The low-power sending apparatus for this beacon, which is similar to the large inter-airport directional beacons, transmits two radio waves to the pilot from two small directional antennæ. These radio waves carry two different sounds or frequencies spreading out from the transmitter like a figure 8. In the top and bottom circles of the 8 a 65-cycle note is broadcast, and in the quadrants not occupied by the circles an 87-cycle note is preponderant. There are thus four lines spreading out from the center of the figure along which the two different kinds of signals are equally strong.

An instrument on the pilot's instrument board shows him whether the plane is proceeding along a line of equal signal strength. The volume of the signal is automatically con-.trolled so that the pilot does not have to tune or control the instrument in any way. This directional indicator is the vertical pointer on the small dial that is the key instrument for all blind landing. The pilot simply guides his plane either to the left or right until this pointer stands straight up. Then he is directed along one of those four lines that stick out from the imaginary figure eight. That line is the line of the runway.

The marker beacons tell the pilot how far he is away from the runway. A meter on the instrument board reads this directly up to distances as great as five miles. The needle of this instrument moves across a scale because the receiving set picks up more and more energy as the plane draws closer to the field. As a final step in this distance-indication scheme two signals are sent out by two marker beacons. The pilot hears the first of these through his head phones when he is 2,000 feet from the edge of the airport, and the second when he crosses the boundary. Thus the marker beacons tell him how far he has to go before landing.

The radio landing beam is the most important part of the scheme, because it keeps the plane on a mathematical curve in a vertical plane which tapers to a perfect three-point landing on the runway. The radio wave from the sending station located at the far end of the field spreads out from that point over a horizontal section shaped like a piece of pie. This high-frequency beam is tilted up from the earth's surface at an angle of 80 degrees.

The airplane receiving set picks up this energy and influences the horizontal needle of the master instrument. Airplanes do not fly directly down the beam, but follow a curved path underneath it. This curvature of the plane's path diminishes as the plane approaches the ground so that the path of flight is the line along which the receiver picks up a constantly intense signal from the sending station. There is a balance between the loss of intensity in gliding below the beam and the increase in intensity in approaching the transmitter. The pilot simply keeps that horizontal needle pointing directly across the face of the master instrument and glides down to a perfect landing.

Over a hundred landings have been made with the pilot completely blinded by a hood pulled over the top of the cockpit. In dense fog over Newark airport, and with all air traffic at a standstill, successful demonstration flights were made. Col. Charles A. Lindbergh was one of the expert pilots who tested the apparatus by making blind landings, and he called it the greatest single achievement in aviation history.

Due to curtailment of federal funds for further development and research, progress in the applying of this radio blind-landing device to the nation's airways does not promise to be rapid. Science has conquered the darkness and the fog for the aviator, and when aviation is ready to equip airplanes and airways with the simple apparatus necessary, safe blind flying and "happy landings" on fog-hidden fields will become one of the everyday wonders.

CHAPTER 17
THE SCIENCES OF LIFE

AMERICAN ACHIEVEMENT in the field of biology has been given world recognition by the award of the Nobel Prize in Medicine and Physiology to Prof. Thomas Hunt Morgan of the California Institute of Technology, leading geneticist and originator of the gene theory of heredity.

The gene is to the student of heredity what the atom is to the physicist. No one has ever seen a gene, as no one has ever looked upon an atom, although attempts have been made to demonstrate to human senses these tiny carriers of heredity by microscopic and photographic means. Dr. Morgan developed his theory in the same way that Einstein evolved the famous physical theory of relativity —through mathematics and the use of numerical data. But he obtained his numerical data from an enormous number of experiments.

The minute single sperm and egg cells, from the mating of which the new individual results, have within them smaller units known as chromosomes. The number of chromosomes is greater in some kinds of plants and animals than in others; for man it is forty-eight. The chromosomes are so tiny that all the chromosomes in the original cells of all the inhabitants of the earth could be contained in a teacup. This chromosome, or biological "molecule," is now believed to be made up of a row of genes which are conceived of as being like beads on a string, held together by some chemical attraction, perhaps—normally in the same order for the same species of creatures. The genes control the development of the individual, and they are distinguished by their effect on certain characteristics such as eye color, hair texture, skin color, and so on.

Dr. Morgan based his theory on the observed fact that

certain genes, when inherited together from one parent, are associated also in the offspring. The frequency of these associations varies. Some groups come out together much oftener than others. These variations in "linkage frequencies" were accounted for by Dr. Morgan by a change of partners between parts of the paired chromosomes, the more distant pairs changing more often, and the closer ones clinging longer. These variations enabled Dr. Morgan actually to make maps showing the order or location of genes in the chromosomes.

Dr. Morgan's historic experiments were performed with the ordinary tiny fruit fly, familiar to housewives and fruit dealers through its fondness for hovering about bananas and other fruits. It is particularly useful to the geneticist because it produces new generations so quickly.

Gene, How Small?

EFFORTS have often been made to obtain indirect measurements of a gene's dimensions, just as physicists use indirect means for measuring the sizes or masses of molecules, atoms, electrons, and other invisible particles with which they work. The latest of such caliperings of the gene established its maximum volume as one quintillionth of a cubic centimeter. This is just about the space that fifteen protein molecules, one of the largest of the organic chemical aggregations, could crowd into. This determination was announced by Drs. John W. Gowen and E. H. Gay of the Rockefeller Institute for Medical Research.

The two scientists based their discovery of the gene's size upon the discovery made several years ago that X-rays will smash into genes and change the bodily characteristics that they transmit. They worked with the same sort of fruit flies used by Dr. Morgan. X-rays were used to bring about the changes in genes that are known as mutations. The magnitude of the average gene was found by dividing the amount of chromatin, or material in the chromosome, by the number of genes estimated by the mutations observed. The total number of genes in any one cell was shown to be not less than 14,380. This corresponded to a largest gene size expressed numerically in cubic centimeters as one-tenth multiplied by itself eighteen times. In attempting to visualize this extremely small volume, one quintillionth of a cubic centimeter, it may be helpful to remember that a centimeter is a little more than a third of an inch.

While the manipulators of the gene were thus searching for the still elusive mode of operation by which it causes evolutionary changes, a geneticist of more mathematical bent was endeavoring to make the course of evolution a measurable and predictable thing. Results achieved in this direction were demonstrated at a meeting of the National Academy of Sciences, by Dr. Harry H. Laughlin of the department of genetics of the Carnegie Institution of Washington, located at Cold Spring Harbor, N. Y.

Dr. Laughlin's method takes cognizance of hereditary differences hitherto considered too small to be bothered with, and by charting the direction of their development with great exactitude will enable scientists to foretell, on the basis of measurements of a few generations, the present trend of evolution at the close of a great many generations. Since the application of the Mendelian principles to the science of genetics, students of that subject have been interested quite largely in characters determined by single genes or hereditary units, or at most by a small number of genes. But some of the hereditary traits of greatest practical and social importance, like running ability in thoroughbred horses or height in men, have defied analysis into separate genes. They are probably due to the interaction of thousands of genes, and only their new results, as they show themselves in departures in offspring from average conditions in parental stocks, can be measured.

Dr. Laughlin's method takes such a departure from a parental average—say an increase of a fraction of an inch in height of offspring over height in parents—and maps its course through several generations. On the same graph he traces another line, representing the thing with which comparison is to be made. Neither line is straight, but in both a tendency or direction can be traced. The two lines tend to converge, and the point where they intersect represents the culmination of the evolutionary development of that particular character—the genetic mean. This is the present evolutionary goal.

One line of development to which Dr. Laughlin applied his method had the advantage of being all finished and done with, so that he could make his prediction and then look to see whether it had been fulfilled. It had to do with the skull length in titanotheres, monstrous beasts that ran their course during some fifteen million years early in the Age of Mammals. These animals have been studied in great detail by Dr. Henry Fairfield Osborn, honorary president of the American Museum of Natural History. They started with skulls less than a foot long, and before they became extinct they had skulls about a yard in length. According to Dr. Laughlin's charting, they could have become even bigger-headed, if other conditions had not cut them off before the tendency of their skulls to grow had completely worked itself out.

The old problem of the inheritability of acquired characters was brought under new attack in Germany. When the male white mouse is poisoned with alcohol or certain plant toxins, such as ricin (found in the castor bean plant), the sex cells are affected in a specific way. A true mutation, that is transmitted as a functional change in the animal's descendants, is caused. These observations were reported by Dr. Agnes Bluhm of the Kaiser Wilhelm Institute of Biology, Berlin. The change shows itself in the offspring in the fact that there is a greater mortality in their litters. If, however, the children of an alcoholized male are mated among themselves, the mortality rate is less in the grandchildren and may disappear entirely in the great-grandchildren. This fact would seem to indicate that the alcohol had simply a harmful effect which was wiped out in two generations and had not produced a really hereditary characteristic.

Dr. Bluhm stated her belief, however, that a distinct mutation is produced in the sex chromosomes of the male, which in interbreeding is obscured by the fact that in the fertilization of an egg by the affected sperm cell there is produced in the egg an antagonistic substance, something after the manner of a toxin-antitoxin reaction. The reason for this belief is based on the results of cross fertilization. When a male of the alcoholized strain is mated with a normal female, the mortality in the young is always greater than when a female of the alcoholized strain is mated with a normal male. When the male mouse was poisoned or immunized by gradually increasing doses of ricin, his immediate progeny showed hypersensitivity to small doses of ricin. Like the alcohol effect, this physiological reaction tended to disappear in the successive generations, but its existence in the male cell could be brought out by cross fertilization. That the effect was specific for the ricin and not simply a general weakening or injury was demonstrated by testing the progeny with other poisons, snake venom, for example, or abrin.

Eyes of Babies

THE TRADITION that all babies' eyes are blue at birth has been shattered. Taught by physicians, physiologists, and geneticists for many years, this "fact" was proved a fallacy by the simple means of actually examining under good illumination the eyes of nearly five hundred new-born infants in the hospital of the Johns Hopkins University. Dr. W. C. Beasley, instructor of psychology at the university, made the examinations.

Not only were other colors than blue found in the new-born babies' eyes, but brown was found in 79.5 per cent of the white infants' eyes and 99.3 per cent of the Negroes'. Many eyes held several colors. Yellowish and reddish browns were seen, and greens, violet, gray, and lavender, as well as flecks and streaks of as many as 187 different hues. Only 28 of the 455 infants examined had plain blue eyes.

But there is a reason for the tradition that all white infants have blue eyes. For the eyes at birth have a clouded appearance, due perhaps to lack of clearness in the fluid between the front of the iris and the cornea. This cloudiness acts as a veil to hide the true colors of the eye from the casual observer. The resulting appearance is a murky look which could well be described as dark blue or gray.

If you look at the young baby's eyes closely, however, with bright illumination and some optical aid such as that afforded by a reading glass or pocket microscope, you will be rewarded by seeing the real eye color shine through. And you will probably notice many things about the eyes that you have never seen before. You may see streaks radiating from the center like the spokes of a wheel. Or you may find a ragged patch, either large or small, surrounding the pupil. Or a narrow ring around the pupil. Or all sorts of flecks, spots, and streaks. Altogether 200 different combinations of these patterns were found to be possible in human eyes.

Babies in Bottles

BABY RABBITS, developed from eggs that were fertilized outside the mother's body and brought to birth in the body of a second mother rabbit, were produced in the Harvard University laboratory of general physiology by Prof. Gregory Pincus and E. V. Enzmann. These little rabbits, "fathered" in a glass flask by sperm extracted from a male rabbit, may be looked upon as the first actual approach to "ectogenesis," or "babies born in a bottle," about which scientists with a romantic bent, like J. B. S. Haldane, have been dreaming for years—though it is admittedly still a long way from realization for human beings.

Each of the two litters of "ectofertilized" rabbits which Prof. Pincus and Mr. Enzmann have succeeded in obtaining may in a sense be said to have had three fathers and two mothers, for in each case three male and two female rabbits were required for the process. In the strict biological sense, of course, the real mothers were the females that supplied the ova and the real fathers were the males that supplied the sperm; the others would rate more as auxiliary or foster parents.

To produce their "ectofertilized" rabbits, the Harvard scientists first mated a female rabbit with a male which had been rendered incapable of producing sex cells by a simple surgical operation. The mating act stimulated the liberation of the ova from the ovaries, or female sex cells, which, however, still remained unfertilized. Then the ova were removed from the mother rabbit's body and placed in a suitable fluid in a glass vessel. Sperm from a normal male rabbit was added, and allowed to remain with the ova until each one had received the fertilizing male cell. Certain changes observable under the microscope indicated to the watchers that this process had taken place.

In the meantime, the "foster-mother" rabbit had been prepared for her rôle by being mated with another male incapable of producing functional sex cells. Into her maternal tissues, thus stimulated to activity, the ova of the other rabbit, fertilized in a glass vessel with the sperm of a male she had never seen, were introduced. They developed, and in due time the young rabbits were brought forth.

In order to have a check on the correctness of their technique and to make sure that the second mother rabbit's own ova were not chance-fertilized by stray sperm cells, rabbits of different breeds were used throughout, so that the coat color of the young ones would indicate their actual parentage. This was in both cases indubitably traceable to the ova and sperm cells in the glass vessel.

The way for the experiments of the two Harvard physiologists was prepared by the work of earlier research men, to whom their communication gives due credit. That fertilized egg cells could be transplanted from the body of the mother animal into the body of another female, where they would then go through normal development, had been demonstrated as early as 1905 by an English physiologist, W. Heape, and his results had been confirmed in 1922 by a German group, A. H. Biedl, H. Peters, and R. Hofstätler. Prof. Pincus had obtained similar results in 1930, but his effort to carry the process one step further had not then succeeded.

Dr. A. J. Waterman of Brooklyn College removed young rabbit embryos in extremely early stages of development from the bodies of their mothers and planted them upon suitably prepared artificial media. This artificial food material was not even from rabbits, but partly from chickens and partly from rats. The young embryos lived for several days, and advanced several stages in their bodily development.

Drs. J. S. Nicholas and D. Rudnick of Yale University transplanted rat embryos of from five to twelve days' development onto the embryonic membranes in incubating eggs, thus making the developing chicks, even before hatching, a sort of foster parents of the alien animals. The younger the rat embryos, the poorer the success of the grafts, but enough of the older ones "took hold" to make the experiment a success. Notable in these grafts was the normally rapid development of the nervous system.

Dr. Margaret R. Murray of Columbia University made tissue cultures of rat skull bones taken from embryos in the fourteenth to sixteenth days of prenatal development. In the rat, the hardening of these bones usually begins with the seventeenth day. This ossification occurred in the bones growing in the laboratory glassware just as though they had still been attached to their original embryo bodies within the body of the mother.

Babies born in glass flasks in the laboratory, instead of being brought forth by human mothers in the age-old painful way, have been a dream of modern biological romancers, just as the "homunculus," or synthetic little human being, was one of the dreams of old-time alchemists. In a little book called *Daedalus, or Science and the Future,* published ten years ago, J. B. S. Haldane prophesied the "birth" of the first ectogenetic baby in 1951. But even with these recent successes before them, scientists are hardly inclined to expect, in so near a future, that particular type of "blessed event."

Tough Turtle Hearts

While one group of physiologists were thus demonstrating the ability of animals in extremely early life stages to live and grow under unusual conditions, others made equally astonishing demonstrations of single organs from full-grown animals to survive conditions even more unusual. They proved, among other things, that you can't make it too cold for a turtle's heart. E. Alfred Wolfe and

Richard A. Torgesen of the University of Pittsburgh reported their experiments with the tough hearts of these sluggish reptiles. As is well known, the heart of a turtle will keep on beating for hours after its owner has been killed and the organ itself removed from its body. Such excised hearts were immersed in liquid air, at a temperature of 192 degrees Centigrade below freezing, for 3, 5, 7, and 10 minutes respectively. Then they were placed in a cold physiological solution and allowed to thaw out gradually. The hearts resumed their beats within a few minutes. At first the beats were irregular and slow, but within a few minutes more they were pulsing regularly, though somewhat more slowly than other turtle hearts that had not been given such a drastic chilling. As all the hearts gradually slowed down during a three-hour period, it was noted that the ones given the longest freezing became "tired" first. Hearts exposed to freezing for more than ten minutes did not resume their beating at all.

Plant tissues, as well as animal organs, proved their capacity of survival. Dr. P. R. White kept thousands of growing root tips alive and increasing rapidly for over a year, without any attachment to their parent plants, and fed only from an artificial liquid medium, at the Rockefeller Institute for Medical Research, New York.

What appears to be in many respects the "best" lower animal brain ever studied was exhaustively examined at the Smithsonian Institution by Dr. C. J. Connolly, of the psychology department of the Catholic University of America. The brain studied by Dr. Connolly is that of a three-year-old mountain gorilla, which died in the National Zoölogical Park in Washington, D. C. It was turned over to the Catholic University psychologist because he has made a specialty of comparative cerebral anatomy.

The brain of this little gorilla, who weighed only forty pounds at his prime, was larger than the brains of many adult gorillas which have been studied, and indeed is one of the largest great-ape brains on record, in spite of its late owner's extreme youth. It is the first brain of a mountain gorilla ever studied in detail; all other gorilla brains which have been examined were those of the coast gorilla subspecies. The baby gorilla's brain weighed 466.6 grams, a little over a pound. The average weight of the brains of six adult female coast gorillas reported by Dr. Connolly was 379.3 grams, about three quarters of a pound. The average brain weight of three young male coast gorillas, comparable in age to this young mountain specimen, was only 318.3 grams.

If the gorilla's brain grows at the same rate as that of a human being, this baby mountain gorilla, had he lived, would eventually have had a brain weighing more than 600 grams. The lightest normal human brain weighs about 1,100 grams. If the assumption of an eventual 600-gram adult brain-weight for the male mountain gorilla is correct, this represents substantially more than half the human brain weight; and hitherto apes have been allowed less than half.

Tough Germs

WHEN IT COMES to standing up under the vicissitudes of life or withstanding various harmful conditions in the environment, germs that grow slowly can "take it" better than their faster-growing relatives. On the other hand, many germs can be "toughened" by forcing them to grow more slowly.

Experiments with one common variety of bacteria which showed this relation between rate of growth and hardiness were reported by Dr. James M. Sherman and George M. Cameron of Cornell University. Those species of bacteria and other higher organisms which have been able to adapt themselves to life under conditions unfit for most organisms are the slow-growing ones, it seems.

What Dr. Sherman and Mr. Cameron proved true for bacteria, two of their Cornell colleagues demonstrated for higher organisms also. Full feeding means shorter life. If you would have many days upon the earth, be abstemious. This would seem to be the conclusion to be drawn from experiments on laboratory animals, reported by Dr. Clive M. McCay and Miss Mary F. Crowell. They used 106 rats in their research. They divided the animals into approximately equal groups. All were fed diets qualitatively complete. "Two groups were retarded in growth by inadequate calories only, while the third group matured rapidly with ample calories," the experimenters reported. "This experiment is in progress and in its fourth year, but the results are conclusive in showing that the animals that mature slowly have a much greater life span than the rapidly growing ones. This extension of the life span by means of retarded growth indicates that the potential life span for a given species is much longer than has been anticipated. Furthermore, these data suggest that the longer life span of the female may be related to the slower growth rate of the female sex as the animal approaches maturity."

Not only "the colonel's lady an' Judy O'Grady are sisters under their skins," but plants and animals of the most diverse kinds share a wide physiological kinship. Evidence to this effect was produced by Prof. A. Butenandt and Prof. H. Jakoby of the University of Göttingen, when they obtained a substance chemically identical with a female sex hormone, theelin, hitherto obtained mainly from animal sources. Sex hormones like theelin are spread throughout the whole animal kingdom from the highest down to the lowest single-celled organisms. Similarly acting substances are also found in plants. It has been known for some time that the plant hormones could stimulate sexual activity in animals and that the animal hormones affected the plant's development, stimulating ripening and blossoming. The reason for this, it appears from the work of Prof. Butenandt and Jakoby, is that the sex-stimulating hormone in both plants and animals is the same substance. While their investigation was restricted to palm nuts, it is probable that the sex hormone of all plants is the same.

Speed Secrets

BIOLOGICAL SCIENCE, like any other science, steps ahead most decisively and boldly when new techniques are made available for the examination of life phenomena that are too small, or too rapid, or too subtle for ordinary naked-eye observation.

One of the most promising things turned to the aid of biology during recent months is the ultra-high-speed motion-picture camera of Dr. H. E. Edgerton and K. J. Germeshausen of the Massachusetts Institute of Technology. Devised originally to record purely mechanical happenings in the fast-moving rotors of electric generators and similar machines, it has been seized upon by the students of the life sciences to record the equally rapid events of such things as the flight of an insect or the fall of a cat. When a cat falls upside down and lights right side up, it takes her less than a quarter of a second to make the turn and be ready to land on all fours. She turns over in less than two feet of drop, front feet first, then her hind feet, swinging her rigidly held tail as a balancing pole.

The machine used is simpler than the conventional motion-picture camera because it has no shutter and no device to start and stop the film every time a fresh "frame" is exposed. The intermittent lighting necessary for making movies is supplied by a special lamp that can be turned on and off again thousands of times a second, each flash registering a picture. The result is a slow-motion film that makes the ordinary kind seen in news reels seem to gallop by comparison.

Effects of Alcohol

Dr. CARL C. SPEIDEL, of the University of Virginia, made use of a new technique for nerve-growth study in an effort toward the solution of an old and much-vexed question which has lately had a great revival of interest due to the repeal of prohibition legislation. Little or no perceptible harm, he found, is done to the nerves by mild, daily drinking of alcoholic beverages, but permanent damage is done by the alcohol consumed on a "spree." These facts, observed on frog tadpoles, are nevertheless applicable to man.

The question of just what happens to the nerves during alcoholic intoxication is important because of the fact that the mental processes, the coördinating mechanism, the senses and control of muscles and movements, which are all known to be affected by alcohol, are intimately related to the proper functioning of the nerve cells.

Dr. Speidel found that in very dilute alcohol, less than five-tenths of 1 per cent, tadpoles may live indefinitely with little or no indication of any special nerve irritation. In much stronger alcohol solutions, more than 3 per cent, death usually ensues within an hour or two. Alcohol solutions in the neighborhood of 2 per cent brought on marked changes in the nerves, such as marked swelling, undulating movements of the myelin sheath, appearance of vacuoles, or spaces between the myelin sheath and the enclosed nerve axis, followed by gradual separation of these structures, and an assumption of an irregular wavy course by the nerve axis. In strong alcoholic intoxication, the myelin sheath separates from the nerve axis. According to one theory, the surface of junction of the myelin sheath and the nerve axis plays the chief rôle in conducting nervous impulses. If this is true, Dr. Speidel's observation that the sheath separates from the axis under strong alcoholic intoxication explains why a drunken man cannot walk or talk straight and is more or less insensible to pain. The structural changes brought about in the nerve fibers are not specific to alcohol but are due to the irritation it produces and can be brought about by other irritants. The complete degeneration of the myelin sheath segments by strong alcoholic intoxication is permanent, but the slight irritative changes from mild daily intoxication of brief duration are quickly repaired, Dr. Speidel found. New sprout growth and new formation and growth of myelin segments may take place on fibers subjected to such irritation.

Coral Islands

THE "LITTLE CORAL WORKERS" celebrated in the old-time moralistic nursery verses have been getting more credit than they deserve as builders of islands. So it would appear, at least, from data offered by Dr. Marshall A. Howe, assistant director of the New York Botanical Garden. Plants, not coral animals, do the lion's share of the work in building up so-called coral islands and atolls, Dr. Howe indicated. He cited one detailed study made on a South Sea island, where two kinds of lime-secreting seaweed occupied first and second places, respectively, as limestone builders, with third place going to a group of one-celled animals known as the foraminifera, and the corals coming in fourth. He backed this up with similar observations elsewhere, including a semi-enforced study of the richness of lime-secreting bottom vegetation made by himself once when becalmed for two days out of sight of land, in a small boat on the Bahama Banks. Dr. Howe did not deny the claims of the coral animals to a considerable part in reef and island formation, and to a dominance in some places, such as the Great Barrier Reef of northeastern Australia. But he is convinced that in the formation of many, if not most, of the so-called coral reefs or islands, lime-secreting plants—the algæ—have contributed more than have the corals.

CHAPTER 18
OUR NATURAL ENEMIES

IN BIBLICAL TIMES, the yearning dream of peaceful security common to mankind of all lands and times was summed up in the phrase "under his own vine and fig tree." And the ultimate enemies were they who threatened fruit and shade.

In our own land and time these enemies have been recognized as being much less in size but more numerous and much more potent for harm than Philistines or Egyptians or Assyrians. They are those who overcame even the Egyptians—the locusts. They are those who caused the Assyrian host to be "melted like snow in the glance of the Lord"—the microscopic germs of disease. Only these latter attack not only man but his vine and his fig tree.

In our own land the fig tree has been replaced, at least for purposes of shade, by many other kinds of trees. But probably none is more characteristic of the American scene than the native American elm. The great elm under whose shade George Washington received the commission of command over the armies of the Revolution has been focused on every school child's imagination; and indeed the tree itself stood, until its recent reluctant death, on the common of Cambridge, Massachusetts. Any really formidable foe of the American elm is thereby a foe to the American sense of tranquillity and peace.

America has recently been reinvaded by such a foe— coming, ironically enough, from France, the land that helped Washington's Americans in their struggle for liberty, and bearing (though unjustly) the name of that land that sheltered the Pilgrim Fathers when they first fled from oppression in their home country. The so-called Dutch elm disease, a most destructive fungous infection of all elm species save only one exotic elm from the Orient, has broken through our defenses again, and is entrenched in the land where Washington campaigned for freedom—the terrain around New York, especially on the New Jersey side.

Once before, the Dutch elm disease had been discovered in America—in 1930, when a few trees in Ohio developed its symptoms. These were at once ruthlessly destroyed, and it was hoped that the invasion was at an end, though the Department of Agriculture scouts did not relax their vigilance.

But when the new attack came, it did not develop where it was being watched for. The enemy had already effected a landing and had established itself before its presence was suspected. During the 1933 summer, infected trees were found scattered among the elms of a 150 square mile area in Essex, Hudson, and Passaic counties of New Jersey. Later, other trees were found on the New York side. In 1934 trees were succumbing at the rate of 200 a day, and over 3,000 trees in the New York City region had been killed early in the summer. The seriousness of the situation can hardly be exaggerated, Department of Agriculture experts declared. The elm is one of the most valuable shade trees in New Jersey and adjoining states. If the disease should spread to New England, it would menace the most important shade tree of that area. Destruction of diseased trees is recommended as the only safe procedure. Not enough is known about the life history of the fungus to allow any other method.

Dutch elm disease is caused by a fungus that invades the growing tissues of the tree, sapping its life and at last turning the leaves prematurely yellow or brown. Under the bark its marks look like a kind of cryptic writing, whence its scientific name *Graphium ulmi*. The fungus is carried from diseased to healthy trees by two species of small beetles, at least one of which is now firmly established in the eastern part of this country, even where the disease is not present. The insects, tunneling under the bark, unwittingly carry the fungus right where it will do the most mischief.

Conclusive evidence that Dutch elm disease came in as a

stowaway in elm logs shipped from Europe for use in the production of veneered furniture was obtained by scientists of the U. S. Department of Agriculture, coöperating with other federal and state agencies. As a result of the information they acquired during the summer, it was possible to draw up quarantine regulations permitting the continued importation of the logs, after rendering them incapable of starting new foci of the disease. Importers coöperated willingly, once the danger to American shade trees was pointed out.

The logs in which the beetles have been detected, in at least three American ports of entry, are special "burl" logs, grown so as to provide a highly ornamental grain similar to curly maple. Although most of them apparently come from France, the logs are for some reason known to the furniture trade as "Carpathian elm." The import trade in these logs is not large, relatively speaking, and apparently only about a dozen veneer plants in the country handle them.

Dutch elm disease plays no favorites. Apparently no species of elm tree is immune from this deadly fungus. All American species of elm on which the infection has been given a chance, whether by natural infection or deliberate experiment, have proven highly susceptible. One species only, the Chinese elm, has an apparent immunity. But this immunity is only apparent, for when the tree is inoculated with the fungus it develops the characteristic brown markings in its young wood, although the leaves do not die and fall off as they do in other species. This permits the Chinese elm to harbor the disease and yet live; but it makes it a "carrier," just as there are human beings who harbor typhoid and other disease germs with no harm to themselves but with great danger to their neighbors.

Tree lovers everywhere are called upon by the U. S. Department of Agriculture to examine their elms for any signs of the disease. Watch for wilting or yellow or brown leaves accompanied by brown streaks in the young wood. When such cases are found, cut pieces of the infected twigs as big as a lead pencil and send them to the Dutch Elm Disease Laboratory, Morristown, N. J. There are other diseases with the same symptoms, and the cause of the trouble cannot be definitely diagnosed till the specimens have been cultured.

It is not often that a fungous disease of tree or crop plant succeeds in invading our shores so conspicuously as did the Dutch elm disease. The defense lines thrown up by the U. S. Department of Agriculture are now for the most part too tight and too strong for any such insinuating foe to get by.

C. C. C.

AMONG the most encouraging drives instituted to combat fungi, bacteria, and viruses that man cannot see even with a microscope was that by the army of previously jobless men, the Civilian Conservation Corps, who fought the blister rust disease of white pine in the great forests of the Northwest, and in the lesser Eastern areas where there is any white pine left.

Blister-rust control was the major job of 35 conservation camps in northern Idaho, where vast acreages of Western white pine are threatened. Seven thousand young Conservation Corps workers were distributed through the heart of the best white pine country in and adjoining the Coeur d'Alene, St. Joe, and Clearwater National Forests, working on government, state, and private lands. Control work was also done in the Lake States and in the Northeast, on national, state, and private forest lands, and to some extent in portions of the national forests in Pennsylvania, Virginia, West Virginia, and eastern Tennessee. The work on the national forests was directed jointly by the U. S. Forest Service and the blister rust control division of the Bureau of Plant Industry. The boys found blister-rust control hard, monotonous work. It involved constant struggling through thick brush and down timber on steep slopes in the hot sun, but they rapidly became seasoned to the job and turned out some excellent work, according to U. S. Forest Service officials.

The disease is controlled by the eradication of currant and gooseberry bushes of the genus *Ribes,* which form the alternate hosts for the blister-rust fungus and spread the disease to the pines. Control work was done both by hand pulling and by the use of chemicals. It was necessary to cover every foot of ground to find all the wild currant bushes.

But if the most conspicuous fungus foe of our plants was a foreign invader, the most prominent insect enemy that has troubled us recently is a native. For the Years of the Locust are upon us again. Grasshoppers were bad in the grainlands of the Northwest in the summers of 1934 and 1933, and the summer before that, and the summer before that; and they give evil promise of continuing into summers yet to come.

Years of the Locusts

OUR WESTERN GRASSHOPPERS are real locusts, not the same exactly as the Biblical ones, but close cousins, nevertheless. There are four species of them, that make most of the trouble in the wheat belt. The one known as the "lesser migratory grasshopper," offspring of the "Rocky Mountain grasshopper" of pioneer days, has become the worst pest.

By a curious inadvertence of popular naming, we have given the locust's ill repute and terror to two relatively harmless insects, for the dog-day "locust" and the seventeen-year "locust" are not locusts at all, but cicadas.

Scientists long ago learned how to fight our grasshopper locusts with considerable effectiveness, by scattering baits of arsenic-poisoned bran in the way of the creeping hordes of young insects before they take to their wings. The state of Minnesota has reduced the depredations of the pest to minor proportions during the present locust cycle by using this method of warfare, but the less wealthy states to the west, the Dakotas and Montana, have not had the money for bran or arsenic or man-hire, so they have been caught in a vicious and ever widening spiral of the devouring pests. If they cannot find money to carry on the war, only a cold, wet spring or some other combination of natural factors unfavorable to the locusts can save them. Whenever the mild winter passes into an unusually early, warm spring, there is grave danger that the locusts will hatch and begin crawling before the poison-spreading armies can take the field against them. When that happens, no one can even guess at the consequences.

American fighters against grasshoppers will regret that we have no plant such as was reported from Central America. While looking for ways of utilizing natural plant and other enemies to combat the locust plague, Guillermo Gandara, formerly of the Mexican Ministry of Agriculture, discovered a weed which is really an automatic trap for these destructive insects. In the Republic of San Salvador, Sr. Gandara found a plant whose stems were thickly covered with young locusts in the hopper stage. The insects would not scatter even when he shook the plant, and he found that the reason was that they were trapped. The weed has three-sided stalks whose edges bristle with hook-like hairs. In the daytime the plant catches locusts and other insects which wander into its way, and at night armies of carnivorous ants arrive to eat up the prisoners, climbing the smooth sides of the stems. In the morning the plant is clean once more, ready to work again, and so it is an automatic trap. Sr. Gandara believes the weed might well be planted in fences about fields in areas subject to locust plagues. The plant, which sometimes grows as much as five feet high, has purple flowers when it blooms, trifoliate leaves, and seeds in a pod. It has been identified as of the genus *Meibomia,* but as a species, Sr. Gandara finds it new, proposing to call it *Meibomia trigona.*

Insect Regiments

GRASSHOPPERS, however, though the most conspicuous and perhaps the most destructive of insect pests during recent campaigns, were by no means the only insect regiments that took the field against man. Chinch bugs, among the most troublesome of the foreigners in our more southerly grain fields, made themselves especially obnoxious by reason of opportunities afforded through heat and drought at just the right time—from their own point of view. A thriving season for chinch bugs of course means more chinch bugs to begin the following season, so Bureau of Entomology workers have issued suggestions for the continued fight against them. Farmers are cautioned against risking barley, millet, or oats in infested fields, for these grains are especially susceptible to chinch-bug attack, Dr. W. H. Larrimer of the Bureau of Entomology states. Rye and wheat are less liable to their attacks. Planting soy beans with corn is recommended, because the broad leaves of the beans shade the ground and discourage the bugs from laying eggs there. Fall plowing, and especially the destruction of clumps of grass, destroy their winter quarters. Chemical warfare, with creosote and coal tar, is effective against this creeping enemy horde. If nothing better is immediately available when they start to migrate, a dusty furrow will bring them to at least a partial halt.

One of the necessary things in any kind of warfare is to study your enemy's movements and learn the concentration and distribution of his forces. For this it is important to be able to identify particular units of his troops when you see them. This principle has been applied against that very pestiferous enemy, the mosquito, by scientists of the Bureau of Entomology. If therefore you see pink mosquitoes (or blue ones), don't jump to the conclusion that the repeal of Prohibition has had a reducing effect on the old familiar pink elephants. The insects' pinkness (or azureousness) will mean only that they have been marked by an inquiring entomologist, who wants to know how long they live, where they go to lay their eggs, how far they can migrate, or other intimate details of their lives of evil, to the end that he may reduce the slap-and-scratch batting average of your community—and perhaps its incidence of malaria as well. The new method of giving mosquitoes distinctive and conspicuous colorings consists in spraying them with an exceedingly fine mist of either methylene blue or eosine, the latter a strongly pink dye. The spray must be very fine, to avoid drowning the insects at once; but if the nozzle is properly adjusted the mosquitoes dry off in a few minutes and fly away—marked for life. How long one of these fragile structures of wings, legs, and biting apparatus can survive the threats and buffetings of this rough world was vividly shown by a tinted mosquito in the Columbia River region. This veteran was still on the job 104 days after its blue baptism. Some of its companions of the same spray bath were found at a distance of four or five miles.

Man's insect enemies are not content with chewing up his crops. They attack "his ox and his ass, his manservant and his maidservant," and their impudent jaws and suckers and stings spare not even the aristocratic skin of the boss himself. And while man commonly fortifies himself behind screens or mosquito netting, he is not always so thoughtful of his poor beasts, as the latter sometimes find out to their sorrow. For example, a furious attack by a mosquito horde near Miami, Florida, resulted in the death of at least 173 head of livestock and poultry. While blood loss was an important factor, death may have been due to the injection of a toxin by the mosquitoes as well as to loss of blood. Few of the reports of fatal attacks on man and animals by mosquitoes have been verified, but a check of the losses in this instance was made by T. E. McNeel of the U. S. Bureau of Entomology.

The foregoing are only a few fleeting glimpses into the great panorama of the strife between man and the insects, during the recent past. The war is endless, and waged on a thousand fronts. Many scientists are quite frankly pessimistic about man's ability to win in the end.

Nevertheless, the dark view may not be justified, however useful it may be for recruiting purposes. For in all wars we know of, the progressive, the adaptable, the fighters with new ideas, have been the winners in the end. And insects haven't had a new idea in ages. They are the world's arch-conservatives. They have hardly shown a change during all the time that man, and back of him all his mammalian ancestry down to the humblest, have been evolving and conquering for themselves a place in the sun. Insects have the advantage of numbers, persistence, toughness; but man thinks and plans. Compared with the insects he not only has the stature of a Goliath but the wits of a David.

CHAPTER 19
RESTORING THE FACE OF NATURE

To RESTORE the face of nature" was one of the pledges made by President Roosevelt at the beginning of his administration. Nature demanded it, the technical knowledge was at hand to accomplish it, and there was good reason to think that the American public would back up such a program.

For many years the popular conscience responded mostly to the two items of self-accusation that we had wasted our forests with ax and fire, and that we had killed off much of our wild game. The more or less immediate response was the establishing of the Forest Service, charged with the administration of what was left of woodlands in the public domain, and with efforts to recreate destroyed forests on both public and private lands so far as possible. A second response was a parallel effort to preserve and restore wild animal and bird life through hunting restrictions, the establishment of game sanctuaries, and the execution of international treaties for the protection of migrating wildfowl.

From these beginnings, through a generation of public agitation and scientific investigation, a full catalog of our national sins against ourselves has been drawn up. Some of the later items in it now loom as more formidable menaces than do the destruction of our trees and the killing of the animals and birds that lived among them.

Most notable among these newer items has been the recognition of the seriousness of erosion, the washing away of the soil itself on which all forests, grazing lands, and farms alike depend. The soil is a humble thing, and damage to it, even outrageous damage, does not strike the casual beholder vividly and dramatically as does the vanishing of a forest before the ruthless axes and saws of lumberers or in the roaring red breath of a forest fire. But if the ruin of soil is more insidious, it is also more irrevocable: a forest will return in mere centuries, but thoroughly ruined soil is not brought back in anything short of millennia.

Exploiting the Soil

MAN'S EXPLOITATION of the soil, to gain a living therefrom, has passed through three phases. Primitive man was a hunter and a gatherer of wild roots and fruits. Surviving primitive peoples still follow this mode of life. This first phase yields little in the way of food and clothing, and hence will support only sparse populations. But it disturbs the soil little or not at all; primitive man lives "in balance" with nature, as other wild animals do.

The second phase of man's exploitation of the soil was the domestication of certain animals and their herding on natural pasture lands. Man left the forest edges, where hunting is best, and took to the open grasslands. The herdsman's mode of life is necessarily nomadic: when the cattle or sheep have eaten the grass thin, he must move on; when the tribe and its herds have grown too large, a separation must take place. Such a crisis in the affairs of a nomadic tribe is told dramatically in the thirtieth and thirty-first chapters of the Book of Genesis, in the account of the separation of Isaac and his wives and his flocks from the household of his father-in-law Laban.

The third and final phase in the winning of a living from the land came when man learned to domesticate plants as well as animals. Cultivating certain grasses (for all grains are grasses) and eating their seeds directly, instead of pasturing his flocks on wild grasses and living on their milk and flesh, enabled and even necessitated the establishment of permanent fields and hence permanent abodes near by. With agriculture came larger populations, and civilization—which means a dwelling in cities.

As man passed from one phase of advancing culture to the next, he did not discard the earlier phase, but continued to practise it on the lands less suited to the later and higher one. Thus, in our own time and country, we find farmers growing corn on their best land, leaving the second best in permanent grass for pasture, and going hunting on the brushy hilltops or in the wooded river bottoms. Or, on the grander scale, we find the great corn lands of the continent in its broad central valley, its historic "cow country" on the grasslands of the Great Plains, and the rugged mountains to east and west still yielding game and lumber —"wild crops"—on the old, original, primitive basis.

The difficulty which civilized man in a well-settled land encounters is twofold: he overcuts the forest and overhunts the wild beasts, overgrazes the range lands, and finally, he overtills the fertile soil. All three of these over-uses mean that he must strip the soil of its natural protecting cover of vegetation: he must expose his mother, the Earth, naked to the contumely of the elements. And she takes revenge upon him by becoming lean and furrowed and unfruitful. Excessive erosion is Earth's resentful answer to overexploitation.

Erosion, to most of us, means the cutting of deep, fast-washing gullies into the soil, its degeneration into "badlands." But the real harm of erosion is usually done before the gullying stage is reached, in what is known as sheet erosion. This consists in the washing away of the top layers of the soil, in which the most valuable mineral nutrients and humus constituents are concentrated. A field after really damaging sheet erosion may look no different —but the farmer finds out the difference in diminishing crops or increased fertilizer costs for a maintained yield. The gullying develops out of the sheet erosion, first as shallow furrows, which grow deeper and wider, finally cutting whole fields away, into deep, wasting ravines.

Another phase of erosion which has not received the attention it really should get is the wind erosion that has become increasingly common and damaging during the recent droughty years, especially in the West. The terrific dust storm of the spring of 1934 in the Middle West, parts of which even beclouded the sky over New York City, was the most sensational recent example of this type of destruction. Such storms affect much of the winter wheat areas, and to some extent the overgrazed range lands, during winters when the usual protecting snow blanket is lacking. Then the dry high winds whirl the topsoil into the air, exposing the roots of the plants and killing a large part of the crop. The looted topsoil flies eastward, sometimes for hundreds of miles, to descend as choking dust storms, so that the wind-blown soil is accursed both in its going and in its coming. The dust storm of 1934 piled this soil so high in some places that snow plows had to be used to clear the roads.

Start of Erosion

EROSION, whether by water or by wind, may be started in a number of different ways, but basically all forms of it trace back to the same cause: the stripping away of the natural vegetation, which removes the mat of roots binding the soil together and the canopy of leaves (whether prairie grass or forest trees) that shield the surface from the loosening impact of falling rain or the rush of drying and lifting wind. Burning or clean logging-off of a "closed" stand of timber can thus expose the soil, and so can the famished, root-close cropping of sheep on rangeland overloaded with stock. But the largest cause of erosion, and the cause of the most damaging erosion in that it affects the best lands, is agriculture itself, especially the cultivation of annual crops in which the soil must be kept constantly loose by hoeing or plowing, as with corn and cotton. Our most profitable agriculture is in a state of constant paradoxical dilemma: the cleaner and more weedless the farmer keeps his fields, the more likely he is to lose the best part of them through erosion.

As early as 1929 a National Committee on Soil Erosion, appointed by the U. S. Department of Agriculture, made its first report in which erosion was clearly recognized as a national menace. East, Southeast, South, and Southwest were the regions most afflicted; but even the choicest cornlands of southern Iowa, northern Missouri, and equally favored farm areas, were not found untouched by the spreading plague of land waste. Spectacularly summed by a soil expert of the Department of Agriculture, the picture

of 500,000,000 tons of the best topsoil wastefully and use-
lessly muddying the Mississippi and its tributaries every
year was presented to the American people, not to mention
the tragic seaward voyages down many other rivers of the
cream of farmlands and pastures. Forty tons of soil from
a single acre of land washed out by a single rainstorm was
another dramatic sample figure, more comprehensible in
terms of loss to individual farmers. The evil existed; it
was increasing; it must be checked and remedies applied.

The creation of work-relief agencies, especially the
Civilian Conservation Corps, the Public Works Administration, and the Civil Works Administration, offered an
unprecedented reservoir of labor which could be used in
part in the battle against erosion. The appropriate agencies,
working in close coöperation, moved into the field very
rapidly. Although the campaign will take many years—will,
indeed, never be completed—decisive beginnings have already been made.

Defense against erosion takes two general lines, to meet
the two principal phases of erosion.

Gullying or lateral erosion is met by counter attack in
the gullies themselves. To keep them from cutting deeper,
and to prevent them from eating out sidewise and under-
mining large blocks of loose soil to crumble and wash away
in their steep, rain-time torrents, dams are thrown across
them at close intervals. These slow down the rush of the
water and thereby prevent the increase in the steepness of
the slope. They also fill up with silt, thus becoming series
of terraces; eventually, perhaps, they are buried completely, establishing a new and gentler slope in the gullies.

Thousands of these check dams have been built in gullies all over the country, by workers in all the emergency
labor armies: C.C.C., C.W.A., P.W.A., as well as by
the older established federal, state, and local agencies and
by individual farmers themselves. The half-hearted and
losing fight against gullying, carried on with insufficient
labor and material, has taken the effective aggressive for
the first time. The dams have been built of whatever material the terrain afforded or the value of the eroding land
justified: all the way from expensive concrete and matched

masonry to loose rubble, logs, and even the humble stake-and-brush barrier—which is often more effective than it looks.

Supplementing the dams, which form the first emergency defense against the merciless tooth of flowing water, soft but insatiable, are means for holding the sliding sides of the gullies. Most efficient of these are the roots of living plants; the field armies against the ravages of rain, suddenly recognized as potential enemy as well as friend, have set millions of cuttings of such trees as willow and black locust, which take hold quickly and bind the soil firmly with fast-spreading mats of rope-like roots. In between the bodies of these taller fighters the lesser infantry of the plant kingdom thrust themselves: tough grasses, legumes, sorghums, and other thick-growing crop plants are used. Together the heterogeneous phalanx holds the precariously conquered slope.

At the top, the problem is simpler though much more extensive. To stop sheet erosion in some regions, all that must be done is to restore the natural mantle of vegetation. This can be done completely—in time—in forest, brush, and grazing lands. The process can be speeded by the planting of trees and the sowing of grass. Such plantings have been made at increasing rates during the current campaign, and even more rapid progress in this part of the restoration of the face of nature is hoped for in the future. The restoration of natural vegetation, of course, implies also the cessation of its destruction through overgrazing, ruthless lumbering, and, above all, fire.

So nearly complete a conquest of surface erosion cannot be hoped for on the lands where it is the greatest and costliest menace. Corn and cotton, wheat, oats, and garden vegetables, must continue to demand freedom from weeds and loose tilth of the soil, which means a continual drain of surface layers in the run-off of all rains. Even the great commercial orchards and vineyards are conducted on a clean-cultivation basis, which of course means more surface erosion. We must make up our minds to pay for our bread and cotton with the loss of part of the most valuable inch of our farm soil.

But the toll need not be paid so recklessly as we have been paying it; there is no need to cut holes in the corners of our pockets. Even clean-cultivated fields on sloping lands can have their surface erosion materially reduced by terracing, which gives a series of flat planes for the cultivation of the crops, interspersed with steep "risers" which must be supported with sod or other soil binders, or even with walls. The vine growers on the canyon sides of the Rhine and the Moselle, the subjects of the old Andean Incas, the rice cultivators on Japanese, Philippine, and East Indian mountain sides, even the prehistoric "lychet" farmers of the New Stone Age on the steep hill lands of England, have all been successful practitioners of terrace farming.

Allied to terracing, but making less demands on hand labor in an age of machine farming, are the practices of contour furrowing and of strip-cropping cultivation. Both have been coming into use for a number of years, though agrarian conservatism has resisted their introduction, sometimes, where they were most needed. The ability to plow a straight furrow has long been a traditional test of farming skill; it is common to see hillside lands laid out in furrows as intolerantly straight and disregardful of slope as an ancient Roman road. Every such furrow becomes, somewhere in its course, a steep channel, inviting rain- or thaw-water to charge down it in a little torrent—of course taking its soil tax with it. The remedy is simple: to keep the furrows all on the same level on the hillside, like contour lines on a topographic map. Such furrows catch and conserve the water; they serve as long, narrow reservoirs instead of flumes. And more important still, they do not encourage surface erosion, deepening into gullies.

Strip-crop cultivation is a modification of the terracing idea. In essence, it consists of planting the plowed crops on the flat parts of the field, and on the slopes, preferably running on contour lines around the hill, alternate concentric strips of crops, like sorghum or millet, that develop tight, soil-holding mats of roots.

An indirect attack on the erosion problem comes from the project to induce farmers on poverty-bound stony hillsides, such as those in certain parts of the southern Appalachians, to give up their land before it all washes out from under their feet, and to resettle themselves on smaller but more productive farms in the richer-soiled valleys. Any removals of this kind will, of course, have to be made with the full consent of the families concerned and after careful study of all factors in the situation; for the government would not want to risk the unhappy results that might come from too hasty action. Submarginal farms thus acquired will be planted to trees, or if the soil is too poor to support forest it will be allowed to revert to brush. In either case the erosion will be checked.

Erosion, modern soil scientists point out, has been one of the heavy factors in the "freezing" of Chinese civilization, once the foremost in the world. Every Chinese looked out for his own farm and chopped down trees where he pleased without benefit of advice or hindrance from an enlightened government. The deforested, overfarmed hillsides wore into the worst badland gullies in the world, with nothing to prevent spring thaws and early summer rains from pouring down upon the plains as the world's most terrible floods. The leaders of the war on the Erosion front believe that Americans are capable of more than the Chinese degree of coöperation, and that they will act to escape a Chinese fate.

The terrible land hunger of our pioneer forebears led to the wasting of our forests, the overcultivation of our corn lands and the stripping of the grass from the Western range, bringing upon all three land types the curse of erosion, which we have lived to inherit in our day. The descendants of the settlers on this land inherited impoverished acres. They have left it, disillusioned and broke, or they have hung on, equally disillusioned and impoverished, simply because they had nowhere else to go.

Saving Wild Life

BUT THE HUMAN VICTIMS of the land speculator's greed were not the only ones, nor even the first. As the destruction of the forest, and the plowing of the prairie, had driven to extinction, or near it, such native upland animals as bison, pronghorn, elk, wild turkey, and passenger pigeon, so the draining of lake and marshland carried the menace of a similar fate to ducks, geese, and many other swimming and wading birds, as well as to shoals of fishes. Sportsmen and nature lovers united in protest, and their organizations strove to obtain protective legislation, as well as to save what fragments they could, either by private purchase or public enactment, of the natural feeding and breeding grounds of our native water life. But theirs seemed a losing fight, as lake after lake was sucked dry by the thirsty ditches of the "land developers."

To these conservators of lowland life the news that a great deal of our land would have to be taken out of cultivation and restored to some semblance of its original state came as a most welcome word. They know that at anything except undependable boom-time agricultural prices, the type of land they were most interested in would yield greater returns in game than in any cultivated crop, so they suggested its retirement along with the upland "submarginal" acreages.

The setup within the Administration has been most favorable, for not only the President but his two departmental heads most directly interested officially—Secretary of Agriculture Wallace and Secretary of the Interior Ickes—had long been strong supporters of the wild life conservation movement.

Early in 1934 a special non-official committee appointed to investigate practical possibilities made its report to Secretary Wallace. The report covered not only the question of protection and restoration of migratory waterfowl of the lowlands, but also upland game, song, insectivorous and ornamental birds, and mammals. Projects for the purchase of about five million acres and the rehabilitation and administration of these lands were submitted for immediate consideration, with the suggestion that a much larger acreage might be utilized upon further study. Some 400 projects were submitted, distributed over all the states of the Union. More than three fourths of the areas recommended were for the preservation and increase of migratory wildfowl, but the other types of wild life were all remembered in the remaining projects. Research in all aspects of wild life was recognized as imperative from the outset, and suitable areas for this purpose were provided for. The research called for is of the kind intended to yield data both for the better scientific understanding of wild animal life and for the use of that understanding in the practical matters of its protection, management, and utilization.

The costs of setting up the New Deal for American wild life were estimated as ranging from as much as fifty million dollars for a thoroughly good job to a minimum of a little less than half that sum. Funds for that purpose, the committee noted, were available in already existing appropriations subject to the direction of the President. Further funds, the committee suggested, could be obtained from two principal sources: a Federal "Duck Stamp" to be affixed to every hunting license, and a small tax to be levied on every box of shotgun ammunition. This would be supplemented by the proceeds of game and fur cropping, which of course could not be estimated in advance. But in any case, the restoration of at least a part of the American birthright in wild bird and mammal life can be made largely, perhaps wholly, a self-sustaining enterprise.

Prominent in President Roosevelt's effort to "restore the face of nature," though less novel, is the endeavor to bring the nation's forest resources into order and to provide for their conservation and rational use in the future.

Saving Forests

FOREST RESOURCE CONSERVATION as a popular movement was already at least a generation old when the new Administration went into action. Foresters and economists had become acutely aware of our dwindling woodland resources during the last years of the nineteenth century, and the necessity for doing something about it had been effectively propagandized into the popular will at the beginning of the twentieth, especially under the leadership of Theodore Roosevelt and Gifford Pinchot.

Accordingly, when the new President cast about for some wholesome occupation which might absorb a large part of the drifting population of jobless young men, it was only natural that the many needs of our forests, long known but hitherto unattended to for lack of men and material, should cry out, "Here emergency can meet emergency and the two cancel each other." So the Civilian Conservation Corps (C.C.C.) was rapidly recruited and sent into the woods. The thousands of youths worked at all kinds of things that must be done to make timberland productive: planting, thinning, clearing snags and slash, building roads and trails, cutting fire lines, checking soil erosion, fighting insect pests and fungous diseases. Some units of the C.C.C., to be sure, worked in unforested country at other tasks, but the major effort of this emergency work army was expended in the forests. When winter came, those parts of the C.C.C. that had been employed in the colder parts of the country were transferred south, and the work went on.

But an organization like the C.C.C. must be regarded for what it is: frankly an emergency measure, doing the tasks that its hands find to do, but not even pretending to make basic contributions toward solving the real forest problems. Forest policies and their permanent execution require different handling.

So far as the publicly owned forest lands, national and state, were concerned, the U. S. Forest Service and the several state forestry departments have for some years been carrying forward conservation campaigns. Without pretending that all problems of public forest management had been solved, the claim could none the less be fairly established that substantial progress in the right direction was being made. Further, it could hardly be denied that some of the difficulties of public forest administration were at least in part due to the methods pursued by private individuals in forest lands, in timber and wood products industries, and in such intimately contacting enterprises as stock grazing and farming.

To bring some order out of this situation, a conference of the lumber and timber products industries was called, under the chairmanship of Secretary of Agriculture Wallace. This conference brought together representatives of the U. S. Forest Service and other agencies charged with the care of forest lands, several groups of professional foresters, the U. S. Chamber of Commerce, and the lumber and timber, pulp and paper, and naval stores industries. Forestry, all agreed, must be taken out of the class of extractive industries and placed in the class of sustained industries, where the very nature of a growing tree obviously indicates it should belong.

The end sought, though statable in a single simple phrase, "sustained yield," is not so simply attained. Many problems, some inherent in the nature of forests, some economic, some involving the human equation, must be solved and their answers reconciled. The report undertook to do this, at least in outline, in such a way as to include even the individual farmers' timber lots, as well as the huge holdings of private lumber companies and the great state and National forests.

The recommendations of the conference were contained in no less than forty-six sections, beginning with the combating of fire, insects, diseases, and other natural forces of destruction, and carrying through to suggested sources of funds for the prosecution of new lines of research in the forests. Outstanding suggestions include: consolidation of administration of publicly owned forests, elimination of unnecessary competition in marketing between public and private forests, vigorous pursuit of the present policy of adding to public forests by purchase of new lands, adjustment of tax burdens on private forest lands to encourage rational rather than forced marketing, federal organization of credits, increased protection against fire, etc., establishment of sound lumber specifications, increased appropriations for administration, education, and research.

While most of this program is quite frankly commercial in its aims, if it operates successfully it cannot help but be a powerful aid in the general program of restoring the face of nature. Not only those who hope to see cash returns for private or public exchequers, but also those who are interested in forests for rest and recreation, hunting and fishing, protection of watersheds and beautification of the landscape, will seek success for the coöperative effort pledged by public and private agencies concerned in the new effort in American forestry.

The preservation of productive lands against the waste of erosion, and the return of the less profitable acres to something like their original wild condition, are not the only man-made aids to nature's complexion that have been devised in recent years. Although no more swamps are being dried at present, the desert is still being watered. Great irrigation works are being pushed more actively than ever, particularly at Boulder Dam on the Colorado.

This involves an admitted paradox. It seems illogical to many that the government should be paying farmers to keep out of cultivation lands already well developed, as well as buying up large tracts of low productivity to be restored to their primeval condition as forest or swamp, and at the same time should be bringing into cultivation these irrigated areas of exceedingly high potential productivity. The illogic is only superficially apparent. It is good sense, even in a land embarrassed with a surplus of agricultural products, to enable a man to produce his crops on good soil with less expense and labor, rather than sentence him to remain on poor soil, struggling to make a worse living.

New Crops

EVEN MORE IMPORTANT, however, is the government's search for noncompetitive crops which such areas can produce. The problem can be solved, the scientists are confident, because of the unique character of the climate of the prospective new farming area. The great bulk of American farm lands are in regions of humid climate, depending on rainfall for their water supply, and not having the hot sun and dry desert air of the Southwest. Their crop possibilities are already well realized, and while the Southwest irrigated country can compete with some of them, the moist-climate areas cannot compete with the irrigated Southwest in producing the crops to which that region is best adapted.

An irrigated land with hot sun and dry air must look to such countries as Egypt and Mesopotamia, the first homes of farming, for agricultural suggestions. And this is just what the Department of Agriculture scientists are doing.

One of the staple crops of the Boulder Dam area will probably be Egyptian cotton, especially the American-bred Pima variety of Egyptian cotton, and a new Pima-Sakel hybrid suitable for making sewing thread. These cottons are not competitors with the varieties grown from Texas to Georgia. They are special, long-fibered cottons, used mainly for tire fabric, sewing thread, fine lisle hosiery, and certain other special kinds of clothing. The American market absorbs all the Egyptian-type cotton that can be grown in the Southwest at present, and sends to Egypt for thousands of bales more. It is expected that much of this present import requirement can be met by extending Egyptian cotton culture into the new irrigated lands as they become available. Other possibilities of the area are dates and Smyrna-type figs. These three crops are well-tested possibilities for Southwestern irrigated agriculture.

There are other crops that can possibly be handled in the Boulder Dam area, which either are not now cultivated at all in this country, or at most only in a minor way. Such are the pistache, the most expensive nut imported into this country, the ephedra shrub, which has suddenly become an important medicinal plant, and the South American wax palms that yield carnauba wax, used in varnishes and in shoe polish.

Before any of these can be recommended to settlers on the new lands, they must be tested out in the region, their possibilities realized, and adaptations made to overcome difficulties of cultivation and handling. For this reason it seems desirable that the Department of Agriculture scientists should go now into this unirrigated desert region, make limited test plantings irrigated with water from deep wells, and arrange a planned agriculture for the country in advance of its settlement.

CHAPTER 20
NEW IDEAS ON EVOLUTION

DEPRESSIONS, BUT DEPRESSIONS in the history of human evolution, have been the world's great spur to progress. Successive hard times have been the evolutionary sieves, sorting the fit from the unfit.

Such, at least, is the novel theory propounded by Dr. Carey Croneis of the University of Chicago, who looked back over the earth's immensely long geologic history and saw in it the same moral that the more thoughtful historians and economists have been finding in the story of our own briefer, more rapid pulse of financial booms and slumps. Resolutely he declared that through the millions of centuries, hard times have been good times, and good times really bad times in disguise. Geologic history has repeated itself over and over in an ever ascending spiral; a cosmic depression has scourged the planet, eliminating inflated stocks, trimming the chastened survivors to the bone, and sending them forth fitter, more alert, more able to take advantage of the returning better times. But the better times have betrayed those who trusted them too much, luring them into overdevelopment and too optimistic expansion, so that when the next crash came—as come it always did—down they went in their turn, and the cycle repeated itself.

"Even the continents have had their ups and downs," Dr. Croneis stated. "And of course their areas have changed remarkably throughout the past. They have presented bold, swashbuckling outlines when they stood high, but they have made sorry, attenuated showings during their periods of depression. Old Mother Earth has indeed suffered many vicissitudes. Her facial expres-

n is one of great mobility. Although the changes are
ordinarily too slight to be noted by the casual observer,
the geologist knows that during the long geologic past
her face has been wrinkled where now it is smooth, and
unmarked where now it is deeply furrowed. As amanu-
enses to the 'Old Lady' the geologists also know that she
still entertains young ideas. She has surreptitiously lifted
her face time and again. But the parable from the past
is more clearly understood and more definitely encouraging when we remember that the earth has not only risen
above her earlier depressions, but she has generally risen
higher, rejuvenated and youthful after each succeeding
deluge. . . .

"If all geologic time is taken as 2,000,000,000 years and
is represented on a clock dial as one hour, then 33
minutes of that hour elapse before the age of inverte-
brate animals is well under way. Even the beginning of
the age of reptiles and the dominance of the dinosaurs
occur only nine minutes before the minute hand reaches
twelve. More surprising still is the fact that mammals,
the dominant life of the present, have been the ruling
animals of only the last paltry two and a half minutes
of the hour.

"And man, commonly thought to have been present for
1,000,000 to 2,000,000 years, has only occupied the
center of the stage a breathless two or three split
seconds. In fact, man is such a newcomer that he has
existed only while our geological clock has been striking
the hour.

"But in spite of the fact that 'depressions' occurred long
before the advent of life, it is the effect of 'hard times'
upon the organisms which particularly concerns man,
the rankest of the untried *nouveaux riches* among the
animals, many of which for ages have lived in intimate
association with man's relatively new acquaintance, Im-
mortal Depression."

Through all of these ages of recurring depressions, the
curve of life pursued an upward spiral, as Dr. Croneis saw

it. However, it was not the smooth, optimistic, unbroken rise pictured in a day when evolution as a popular idea was a new thing under the sun. Dr. Croneis admitted setbacks as well as advances; the curve is ragged, though still always upward trending. In times of stress, he said, the weak organisms have died out, but the strong have always emerged from the troughs of trouble more powerful than ever. Modified to fit the changing environment, they have been ready to take advantage of the return of "good times."

When Dr. Croneis spoke of a "strong" organism, he did not at all mean bulky in muscle, but strong in the balance of a fit body and an alert mind. If the world's recurring geologic hard times have been consistently ruthless toward any one tendency, it has been toward the piling up of huge bulk without intelligence governing it. One need only mention the dinosaurs, out of a dozen possible examples.

When or how life began on earth is a riddle which science is still unable to answer. The oldest rocks that contain fossils at all, known as the Cambrian, show that at that remote point in time (roughly half a billion years) animal life was already amazingly diversified. All the principal groups except the backboned animals were represented, and even these showed some hints of beginnings. It would not be too rash to say, therefore, that the known fossil record accounts for only the last half of life's long story on this planet; though admittedly it is this second half that is the most dramatic and exciting, and the nearer you come to the present the faster the action becomes.

In the lack of fossil records, then, we cannot say what catastrophic depressions preceded the Cambrian, the first stage we know anything about. From the tortured shapes of some of the earlier rocks, we can guess that they were numerous enough and severe enough. For the present the rest remains shrouded in mist.

But from the Cambrian on, through all the Paleozoic, or Elder Age of Animals, the response of life to the challenge of calamity is written large, time after time.

First Families

IN THE EARLY SEAS, the aristocracy were the trilobites, creatures related to crabs and lobsters, resembling in general appearance their diminutive remote cousins the many-legged "pillbugs" you find under boards and in damp cellars.

> "Incredible as it may seem," said Dr. Croneis, "they were the first families then; and in their time there was no living thing to dispute their prominence, at least in the matter of intelligence. Nevertheless, in their own life history they tell the old but ever recurrent story of the survival of the simple and the destruction of the specialized. The ornate members of the group (for even the intelligent have never completely resisted the urge of megalomania), like overexpanded individuals, families or industries, flourished in times of plenty, but they became extinct long before their lowly, generalized, and conservative cousins had departed from the scene."

At last, however, times got too hard even for the fittest of the trilobites; or more likely a newer aristocracy, driven into more efficient living by the spur of tight times, eliminated them. At any rate, several geological depressions later, the race of fishes ruled the world, and were facing another period of crisis, with their water supply dwindling and their pools becoming so stagnant that gill-breathing was becoming nearly impossible.

This was one of the Big Moments of the history of animal life. Dr. Croneis pictured it briefly:

> "A few ganoid types, with the true spirit of pioneers, used their fringed fins to crawl painfully from the desiccating ancestral pools to other less stagnant ones. These first air-breathing, partially land-living vertebrates not only gave rise to the amphibians (relatives of frogs and salamanders)—they originated a Paleozoic parable to the effect that, then as now, animals or industries which, instead of bowing to hard times, use what resources

they have to meet the changing situations are likely to be rewarded handsomely with the return of prosperity."

These fish that came ashore because they had to, and liked it, ruled the world when the land consisted largely of endless warm swamps rich with coal-forming vegetation and a-hum with giant insects for the new rulers to eat. But the Coal Age, an apparently boundless era of easy pickings, crashed into a terrific period of cold and drought.

This particular geologic depression ended not merely a chapter but a whole volume. The Paleozoic was closed, and the Mesozoic, the Middle Ages of geologic history, came on.

When hard times hit the world of the amphibians, some of them, more enterprising than the rest, were stimulated into developing more active bodies, armored with scales, fit to withstand the droughtier air and to scramble more ably for the living that was now harder to get. They were like the energetic tribal chieftains of the ancient world at the breakup of the Roman Empire, who founded the first feudal aristocracies. Their descendants, bigger and more heavily armored, became the real barons of the geological Middle Ages, the dinosaurs. Thus an entirely new ruling group arose out of the depression, and when prosperity came again they were its masters.

But they learned nothing from the experiences of their ruined predecessors.

"The Mesozoic reptiles were megalomaniacs of the most confirmed sort," said Dr. Croneis. "They were the masters of all the important habitats. The dinosaurs ruled the land, marine reptiles invaded and conquered the sea, and the 'flying dragons' or pterodactyls were lords of the air.

"But scurrying underfoot of the giant dinosaurs were a few mouse-like primitive mammals. They were subservient indeed to the gigantic masters of the moment, who, as is characteristic of the great (and especially the near-great), probably were totally unaware of the mammals' presence. But these small creatures, like some

apparently insignificant individuals and many un-
promising infant industries, had great potentialities.
They proved their mettle at the close of the Mesozoic,
when the earth went through one of her really great
depressions.

"This was, indeed, a time of revolution and of the
'reddest' sort, for the reptiles, like Russian royalists,
were nearly blotted out, and they have never again been
particularly dominant. But the small mammals weath-
ered the hard times successfully. Out of their crude beginnings have come the greatly diversified and ruling
mammalian types of today.

"They were one group which was not overexpanded at
the time when opportune depression hit them. In effect,
they sold the market short and made their fortunes in
the steady decline of reptilian values. The roots of that
great modern spreading tree of mammalian types were
firmly anchored in the very depression which was too
drastic for the optimistic dinosaurs who, to the final
crash, continued bullish on 'Brawn not Brains, Inc.' "

So far Dr. Croneis. He did not tell the final tale, that of
man. For man also was born of a depression, one of the
greatest of depressions of more recent geologic time, the
Pleistocene Ice Age. Human beings may have existed on
the earth before the glaciers came, burdening the land over
half Europe and North America and chilling the rest far
down toward the tropics, but if they did we have no very
conclusive evidence of it. Such pre-glacial men, if they
existed at all, lived in days of ease and didn't have to hustle
for a living. So, in all likelihood, they would have been con-
tented to remain very much like their zoölogical cousins,
the apes, clever and entertaining up to a certain point, but
dull beyond that, and quite irresponsible and improvident.

The glaciers changed all that. By the time the Ice Age
was half over we have plenty of evidence that man was on
the job, looking out for Number One and Family in first-
class order. He had learned to keep warm in spite of the
glaciers, by taking to caves or building wickiups on the
riverbanks where he fished, and by wearing clothing made

of animal skins. He had invented improved tools and weapons of stone, which no ape ever did or thought of. He had made the most important discovery of all human history, lowbrow though he was: he had learned the use of fire.

All honor to *Homo Neanderthalensis!* Certainly he was no beauty, and decidedly not as handsome as his artist cousin of Cro-Magnon, who came along later and supplanted him. He had a queer-shaped head, with a queer-shaped brain inside. But such talents as he had he used in a tough spot, and he had the gumption to found the fortunes of the whole human race, right in the middle of the world's worst depression!

But we are ahead of our story. Aside from what he may have been intellectually, when the remote ancestor of this fire-inventing, depression-conquering being dropped from his ancient arboreal home and landed literally on his feet, he was beyond much question a strange-looking creature. But just what he looked like nobody now knows—and in the opinion of Gerritt S. Miller, Jr., of the U. S. National Museum, nobody is entitled to more than a tentative guess. Quite certainly, he holds, neither gorilla, nor chimpanzee, nor orang-utan, nor any other great ape of their size and kind, was ever ancestor to man. Mr. Miller presented this idea before the scientific world in three technical articles. This dictum, in flat contradiction to the orthodox Darwinian thesis still stoutly adhered to by very many zoölogists and anthropologists, calls for an equally stout defense.

Man as a Giant

MR. MILLER was willing to offer it. The great apes, he said, are giants of their tribe, too big to become ancestors of man, who is also a giant but of a radically different type. Giants, he explained further, have never been shown to have begotten anything but creatures of their own kind; or at most they have become ancestors to other giants very much like themselves. Citing an evolutionary chain with fewer missing links than there are in man's, he called attention to the fact that present-day elephants are descendants of other elephants of types now extinct, but they do not trace any part of their ancestry back to the mastodons, giant beasts like elephants but distinct from them, and having no modern descendants. Other lines of big animals whose evolutionary history is well established show the same thing: giants do not beget other kinds of giants. The great apes are too big to be our grandsires.

However, Mr. Miller asked that it be distinctly understood that in repudiating the great apes as ancestors he was not denying man's kinship to other mammals. He had not turned anti-evolutionist. He held, and still holds, that man's relations, "according to the flesh," are to be sought among the primates, or lemur-monkey-ape order of animals, where evolutionists of all colors of opinion have always placed them; where, indeed, the great Linnæus, who was not an evolutionist, classified man himself. But he would seek man's direct ancestry among smaller extinct creatures in this order rather than among the limited group of great apes, highly specialized along different lines from those of his own development.

The idea that man is a giant may come as a surprise, but if we take a look through the monkey house in the zoo, or through a reasonably complete zoölogy book, we see at once that it is so. The great bulk of the hundreds of primate species—monkeys, apes, and kindred animals—are much smaller than we are. They are of sizes that range, as Mr. Miller put it, "between that of squirrels to that of bird dogs, of a dozen or two that are somewhat larger, and of four whose great bulk makes them wholly exceptional—gorilla, orang, chimpanzee, and man."

And even among these four "giants" of his miscellaneous kinship, man takes foremost rank in at least one respect: He is the tallest. Six-footers are not uncommon among men, and seven-, or even eight-footers, though rare, are not unknown. Six-footers among the great apes must be excessively rare. There have been some monsters reported among them, but authentically recorded specimens of gorillas and orang-utans all fall short of a tall man's height.

This is mainly because of their relatively short bandy legs, for their bodies are long and often terrifically bulky. One well-measured gorilla five feet seven and one-half inches tall weighed 360 pounds, and not nearly as large a proportion of his weight went into legs as would be the case in a man.

One thing that has undoubtedly helped in getting apes a reputation for being taller than they are is their relatively enormous arm length. Former heavyweight champion Jack Dempsey was sometimes called a "gorilla" by sports writers because he had a 74-inch reach, yet a real gorilla 5½ inches shorter than he is had a reach of 97 inches! An ape like this, with its legs imperfectly seen in the underbrush but waving its great arms in the air, would undoubtedly add several cubits to its stature in the mind of an awed and imaginative traveler.

But regardless of which of the big primates can claim the honor of being the biggest, it is undoubtedly true that we are all giants together, and that the organ-grinder's monkey, not much larger than an ordinary cat, comes closer to being an "average" specimen of the great mammalian order to which we all belong.

In excluding the great apes from man's ancestry, Mr. Miller made it specifically clear that he did not mean all the anthropoids, or man-like apes. From his exception he excused the gibbons, which are small anthropoids of southeastern Asia and the East Indies. These are most obviously not giants, for the average weight of grown-up animals is only about ten pounds—just the weight of a big new-born human baby.

Yet even so, Mr. Miller emphatically disclaimed any implication that gibbons are ancestral to human beings. The existing and known fossil gibbons are highly specialized tree dwellers, with enormously elongate arms and hooklike hands and relatively short legs. Man is specialized in exactly the opposite direction, with all the work of getting about delegated to his long, ground-adapted lower limbs and his arms only moderately developed. So the gibbon as we know him could hardly have been ancestral to man on this one count alone.

The whole point is, Mr. Miller said, that we simply do not have enough fossil material as yet to build any kind of a reasonably solid bridge between man and any specific line of primates. All the factual evidence points backward to some such connection, but it does not point definitely enough to justify us in saying just where that connection was, or when it existed.

The Part Males Play

ALTHOUGH we may not be able to trace man's descent with certainty, it seems fairly clear that man, in the sense of the male sex only, has been an important factor in determining the forms assumed by any developing society whether among humans or among those animals which he patronizingly calls "lower." This is the idea expounded by Prof. William Morton Wheeler of Harvard University. Beyond peradventure, males are the world's worst nuisances. They are always showing off, always demanding attention, and always disrupting the best-laid plans. They begin when they're small boys by walking on their hands to catch the attention of the new little girl with yellow curls. They continue by bickering and bloodying each other's noses. They keep it up as they grow older by competing furiously for such things as golf cups or gold coins, and by ripping the world to pieces with useless wars. No doubt of it, the male is a nuisance.

As directed long ago, Dr. Wheeler went to the ant to learn wisdom. He studied her ways, and the ways of her relatives the wasps and bees, and the ways of those other social insects the termites, which are often called ants although they are not.

These two great groups of insects, the ant-bee-wasp fold and the termites, have developed the most perfect societies in the world. There are never any internal wars, never any duels, never even an interesting barroom fight (though they do have their bootleggers!)—never any of the noisy upsetting behavior we have come to look upon as natural to males among ourselves and our backboned kin, down through apes and dogs to turtles and fish, with a side branch to accommodate gamecocks and even male canaries. There isn't any ego in a beehive or a termite nest. Rugged individualism just doesn't exist for ants and wasps. The individual is simply a functional part of the group. "Assert yourself!" is clean outside the whole behavior pattern of the social insects.

Why? How do these swarming small creatures, these meek who may in the end inherit the earth which we messy giants apparently don't know how to use properly anyway —how do they manage to get along without the least trace of internal friction? The answer, says Dr. Wheeler, lies in the fact that all the orders of social insects have solved the Problem of the Male. The sex that rules the roost among the backboned animals, especially the mammals and birds, is practically nonexistent as a social force among the bees, ants, and wasps; and in the other great order of social insects, the termites, the males have been as completely "socialized" as their meek sisters. No aggressive sex, no fights. It is all very simple.

But if you eliminate the males, how do you keep the group alive? Used as we are to the biological processes among ourselves and the other familiar larger animals, in which male coöperation is necessary for the production of every individual, that question looks like a poser.

But the social insects do not find it so. They have simply made reproduction a specialized job—one of the many things they carry on at a high level of efficiency by assigning it along with other functions in the astonishing division of labor they somehow manage to carry out without any bosses. They have given the job of egg-laying to one female (or at most a very few) in the group, and that one female needs but one mate. So one male is enough, biologically, for an insect city of many thousands of individuals. He exerts no other influence in the affairs of the termitarium.

But if the lone male in a termite colony is reduced to a position compared with which that of the Prince Albert, Victoria's consort, was a veritable czarism, the rôle of the male among the bees is even more drastically reduced. The male termite at least stays alive and is a real husband to his queen. The male bee mates but once with the young queen who deigns to accept him on her marriage flight—and that very act seals his doom. For part of his vital organs are thereby torn out: his marriage is hymeneal hara-kiri, no less.

The mated queen flies back to her hive to assume the duties of motherhood. She lives in the dark, laying endless series of eggs in the brood cells the workers prepare for her. How, from that single fatal wedding, is she able to keep up her tremendous fertility?

The answer to that riddle had to await the researches of many generations of puzzled entomologists and practical bee keepers. But it was finally learned that the queen bee has in her body a special container in which the entire stock of male sex cells from her long-dead mate are stored. The queen is able to release them at will, to fertilize the eggs she lays. She must release them, for if she lays un-fertilized eggs they hatch only into useless males—drones. This is the ultimate and completest solution of the Problem of the Male—the essential parts of him, biologically speaking, are stored in the female's body, and the rest, the living individual, is ruthlessly mangled, discarded, and left to die.

As compared with these almost perfectly smooth-running, female-controlled societies among the insects, the turbulent groups among male-dominated higher vertebrates cut a sorry figure, if we take completeness of socialization for a criterion of high biological development. Said Dr. Wheeler:

"The male has now become so dominant in our modern patriarchal societies that we might regard them as male societies in contradistinction to the female societies of the bees and ants and lower mammals and the bisexual societies of the termites. Moreover, many of the mani-festations of this dominance show quite clearly that a portion of the human males have never been completely socialized. Throughout the ages the aggressiveness, curi-osity, unstable intelligence, contentiousness, and other asocial and antisocial tendencies which the male has in-herited from his anthropoid ancestors have kept society in a constant turmoil. Indeed, our histories seem to be little more than the elaborately recorded misbehavior of males."

Yet this boiling of the social kettle kept up by the irrepressibly troublesome male is not a net social loss, Dr. Wheeler indicated in closing his discussion. Wastefully, perhaps, but no less effectively, this constant unrest makes for progress. Ants, bees, wasps, and termites have been as they are for fifty or sixty million years—absolute communisms world without end amen. In far less than that time the mammals have arisen, evolved their diverse forms, seized dominance of the world, and finally produced the most restless, most troublesome, most pugnacious, and most intelligent animal the world has ever seen—Man.

So Dr. Wheeler ended by admitting that the

"restlessly questing intellect, driven by the dominance of the mammalian male, furnishes the necessary stimulus to progress in human societies. Female societies, like those of the ants and bees, lower mammals, the matriarchal human clans and bisexual societies like those of the termites are indeed harmonious, but stationary and incapable of further development."

CHAPTER 21
THE FIGHT AGAINST DISEASE

NEARLY HALF THE PLAGUES of the world can be controlled. Scientists working in laboratories and at bedsides have learned the way fourteen out of the thirty-two or so major diseases are caused and spread. They have forged powerful enough weapons so that some of the world's worst plagues could be practically wiped out. That they have not been is because the bulk of mankind lags behind these leaders in making practical application of the knowledge at hand. Part of the lag is for lack of economic as well as intellectual and moral resources.

Mothers need no longer watch in helpless anguish while a choking gray membrane fills small throats and smothers the last spark of life. One prick of a shiny steel needle, one dose of toxoid from a glass syringe, protects a child from diphtheria. A scratch on the arm insures him against the danger and inevitable disfigurement of smallpox.

Chalked up on the credit side of the scientific ledger are vaccination against smallpox; antitoxin, toxin-antitoxin, and, now, one-dose toxoid for diphtheria; vaccines that protect men from typhoid fever and even yellow fever; antilockjaw serum; vitamins to prevent or cure scurvy, rickets, and pellagra; and sanitary knowledge to keep foods and water supplies germ-free.

On the debit side there still remain such plagues as infantile paralysis, encephalitis, influenza. In the winter of 1932–33, this last disease was again epidemic in America. The cases were mild and deaths were few. So far as knowing what exactly caused the disease or how to check it, however, man was no farther ahead than in the dark days of 1918, when the disease in most virulent form raged throughout the world.

Progress in the fight against infantile paralysis, or poliomyelitis, to call it by its scientific name, is being made. Most of the little sufferers can now be saved from the deformities and crippling effects of the disease. Physicians have found that nearly nine tenths of the affected muscles in cases of infantile paralysis can be restored to normal within two years by proper care and exercise. Treatment must be started early to prevent the weakened muscles from stretching. Best results are obtained with muscles classed as "good' at the start of treatment. About two thirds of muscles classed as only "fair" may be restored to normal, while more than half of those classed as "poor" become normal. A new medical term, poliotherapist, has been coined to describe the persons who are trained to give this muscle treatment under the physician's directions.

Much of the muscle reëducation in these cases is done with the patient in the water. An important center for this type of treatment is the foundation at Warm Springs, Georgia. This was founded by President Franklin D. Roosevelt in order to give other poliomyelitis sufferers the benefits which he gained from rest and treatment there.

Much hope was felt for the benefit to be derived by early treatment of the disease with convalescent serum. Experience during the last few years has somewhat dashed this hope, showing the value of the treatment to be rather dubious.

Evidence indicating that the disease enters the body through the nose and attacks the nervous system directly has been accumulating as a result of investigations by Dr. Simon Flexner of the Rockefeller Institute for Medical Research, Dr. Harold K. Faber of San Francisco, Dr. Maurice Brodie of New York, and others.

At the fall meeting of the National Academy of Sciences in 1933, Dr. Flexner reported that he finds that exposed endings of the nerves of smell, situated in the delicate membrane lining the nose, are the gateway by which the virus of the disease may enter the system. The nerve trunks to the brain, nerve connections in it, and nerves returning to the body surface are the paths the invasion follows. So long as it stays with nerve tissue, the disease virus is to a large degree isolated from the blood and lymph, so that protective substances formed in the body or introduced into it cannot reach it effectually and it is free to continue its malignant work.

Dr. Flexner made his studies exclusively on rhesus monkeys, in which he produced the disease by introducing into their noses a suspension in salt solution of the spinal cord of a paralyzed monkey. But he extended the significance of his findings, stating:

> "While this communication relates specifically to poliomyelitis, it applies in principle to still other infectious and inflammatory diseases of the brain and spinal cord."

Sleeping Sickness

ANOTHER of these epidemic nervous diseases of virus origin, encephalitis, popularly known as "sleeping sickness," caused much concern in the late summer and fall of 1933. An outbreak, said to be the worst in the history of the United States for this disease, occurred in St. Louis and surrounding country, extending to Kansas City.

The scientific disease fighters of the country met this new challenge in characteristic fashion. With all the knowledge and skill at their command, they sought to check the epidemic and to remedy the disease in the persons it had attacked. At the same time, they turned the disaster into an opportunity to increase their knowledge of the disease.

It was not only the size of the outbreak that aroused attention. It was the desire to learn more about this disease, which is a comparative newcomer among disease plagues, and also the fact that in the St. Louis epidemic the disease seemed to be taking a new form.

In the first place, the outbreak came in high summer, whereas previous outbreaks have occurred in winter or early spring. It attacked middle-aged and old persons for the most part; formerly the young have been the chief victims. Furthermore, the symptoms by which a physician may recognize the disease showed some important differences from those of the previously recorded cases.

Disturbances of the motor functions of the eyes were

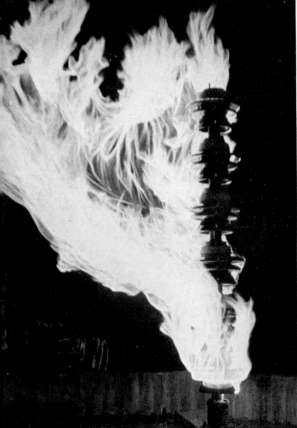

LIGHTNING

When lightning strikes, two discharges take place. The first endures only a few millionths of a second, looks like a white, pasty substance dripping over the insulators, and cannot be seen. The second lasts from one fifth to one half a second, is more beautiful and elaborate, and can be blown into striking designs. This is what the eye sees. The photograph shows the second discharge of an artificial bolt of lightning.

C. Edward Magnusson

ELECTRIC SPARKS

Of what is an electric spark made? This brilliant whirligig design, known as a Lichtenberg figure, partly answers that question. Such discoveries help engineers determine what happens when lightning strikes a high voltage transmission line. The upper black dot is the positive terminal, the lower the negative one. The picture is about "life-size."

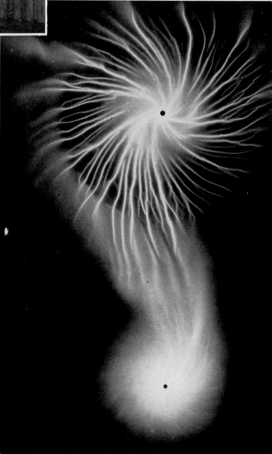

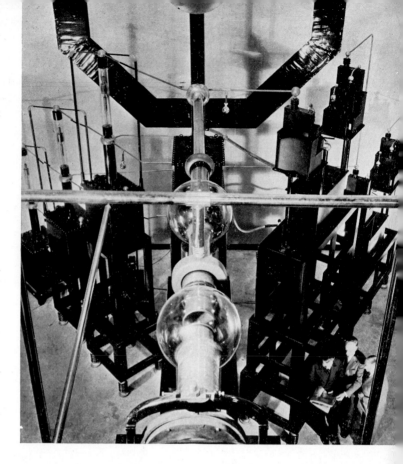

CANCER WEAPON

THE mightiest weapon yet to enter the war against cancer is the giant 800,000 volt X-ray tube at Mercy Hospital, Chicago. On a current of one one hundredth of an ampere it emits radiation equal to an amount of radium worth $75,000,000. It is the largest X-ray tube in the world. Elaborate safeguards protect the operators from the tube's rays. The patient is seen and spoken to through a periscope and if the door to the treatment room is accidentally opened, the X-ray is automatically cut off.

SPECTRUM OF A METEOR

ONLY a few bright lines, yet a high prize for science. It is the spectrum of a meteor, believed to be the first ever purposely obtained. Examination of this Harvard Observatory photograph will tell scientists what elements were burned during the swift flight of annihilation through the earth's upper atmosphere.

NE YEAR PLUS

AN EXAMPLE of what modern training can do. Johnny was an adept at roller skating soon after his first birthday. He also climbed steep inclines, scaled ladders, and in general manifested a desire to "try anything once." His twin brother, who was not accorded the special training given Johnny, was healthy and happy, but still comparatively helpless at one year of age, just like any normal baby.

MERCURY BOILER DRUM

MERCURY, instead of the water that is ordinarily used, is vaporized within this porcupine-like boiler drum to turn a great 20,000-kilowatt turbine at Schenectady, N. Y. Seven such boilers are installed in the new power plant, requiring 270,000 pounds of mercury, or almost 90 per cent of a year's ordinary consumption in the United States.

very rare instead of common. There was a more uniform involvement of the meninges or membranes enveloping the brain and spinal cord, with corresponding increase in the number of cells in the spinal fluid. The picture the patients presented was that of a general feverish disturbance, often with gastro-intestinal symptoms; evidences of brain involvement such as an apathetic or immobile facial expression; usually sleepiness, stupor, coma, or delirium; usually a moderately stiff neck with headache, which was often the first and most pronounced symptom, and other pains, as of the abdomen or legs; tremor and catatonic semi-rigidity were common in the more severe cases. The fever stage was more definite and regular than usually observed in encephalitis, but sometimes the temperature became normal within a very few days. The patients who recovered apparently were restored to good health, and so far there is no evidence of the distressing physical or mental changes which follow in a high percentage of usual attacks of encephalitis.

The outbreak appeared to be most like that centering on the southern side of the Inland Sea in Japan in 1924, which was then considered atypical.

From the St. Louis epidemic scientists obtained definite evidence that the disease is caused by a virus. This had been suspected but never before proved. One of the first bits of evidence appeared early in September when Dr. Margaret G. Smith, of the Washington University School of Medicine in St. Louis, found "inclusion bodies" in the kidneys of some of the patients that had died of the disease. These are small specialized particles that appear within the cells of persons or animals afflicted with diseases caused by filterable viruses and are regarded as more or less indicative of such diseases.

Another big step toward the conquest of this disease was the successful transmission of the disease to monkeys and later to mice. Since the days of Koch and Pasteur, scientists have known that once a human disease can be established in laboratory animals, they can proceed more quickly with their efforts to study the disease.

While so far no curative or preventive serum has been developed, scientists working at Washington University in St. Louis, the National Institute of Health of the U. S. Public Health Service in Washington, and at the Rockefeller Institute for Medical Research in New York City, discovered that encephalitis patients develop in their blood substances known as immune bodies which give resistance to the disease. This discovery was made as a result of the success in establishing the disease in mice. Material from the brains of encephalitis victims in the St. Louis epidemic produced the disease in the mice. Serum from the blood of other St. Louis encephalitis patients protected the mice from such injections, giving them resistance to the disease.

A dramatic incident of the study of this encephalitis outbreak was the use of convict-volunteers to clear up a disputed point. Mosquitoes had been unusually prevalent in St. Louis and surrounding country during the late summer, and it was thought by many physicians and lay persons that these insects had played the chief rôle in the spread of the disease.

Following the precedent established by Walter Reed in the study of yellow fever, the scientists in charge of the encephalitis investigations decided to test the theory by letting mosquitoes bite encephalitis patients and then feed on healthy men who had not been exposed to the disease. If the previously healthy men developed encephalitis, it would be proof that mosquitoes could transmit the disease, although it did not mean necessarily that they had been the carriers in this outbreak. Convicts were chosen because the scientist could be sure that these men had not already been infected by chance contact with an encephalitis patient.

Volunteers were called for at the state penitentiaries of Mississippi and Virginia. The men who took part in the test received their freedom in return for taking their chance of disease and death in order to advance scientific knowledge. Since none of these men developed encephalitis, the experiments so far show that mosquitoes do not carry the disease from man to man. Evidence that they may play the carrier rôle in a similar disease of horses had previously been obtained by Major R. A. Kelser of the U. S. Army Medical School. This had been an additional argument in favor of the mosquito vector theory.

Following closely on the mosquito experiments came the suggestion that encephalitis may actually be virus influenza of the brain and nervous system. This theory, advanced by Dr. Earl B. McKinley, dean of George Washington University School of Medicine, has so far not been either proved or disproved.

Yellow Fever

WHILE THIS MASS ATTACK was being made against encephalitis, which is a comparative newcomer among the disease plagues of the world, medical scientists were continuing their fight against other, more familiar foes. Among these was yellow fever.

When Walter Reed and his co-workers proved the rôle of the mosquito in carrying the disease, it seemed as if this plague had been conquered. So it had, for those of us who live in regions where mosquito extermination is practicable. But the disease has continued to take its toll among missionaries, government officials, and others whose business takes them into the heart of the tropics where the yellow fever mosquito still holds sway. Particularly hard hit have been the scientists who have continued to study the disease in remote regions of the world. Protection for these groups was at last achieved when Drs. W. A. Sawyer, S. F. Kitchen, and W. Lloyd of the Rockefeller Foundation, working at the Rockefeller Institute in New York City, developed a serum-vaccine that gives immunity from the disease. Recent examination of those who were first given the vaccine now shows that it confers immunity lasting at least two years. Efforts are being centered on making the injections less difficult and less costly in human blood, but so far it is not yet practical as a means of protecting whole populations against yellow fever.

Quarantine regulations and mosquito extermination had already relegated yellow fever to the group of diseases that constitute a plague only in the tropics. Medical scientists have recently found, however, that other diseases they have classed as plagues of the more or less remote tropics are becoming important disease problems of the temperate regions since improved transportation has made tropical countries less remote.

Disease of Bad Plumbing

IN MID-AUGUST of 1933 two cases of amebic dysentery or amebiasis, always considered a distinctly tropical disease,

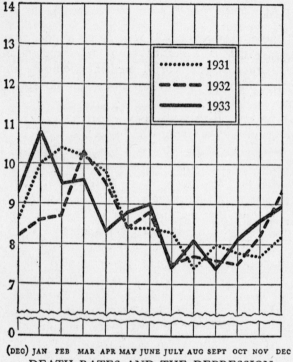

(DEO) JAN FEB MAR APR MAY JUNE JULY AUG SEPT OCT NOV DEC
DEATH RATES AND THE DEPRESSION

FIGURE 8

THE figure as plotted by the Metropolitan Life Insurance Company shows the death rate, per 1,000 population, from all causes. The depression years brought no major change in mortality percentages in the United States.

were reported to the Chicago Board of Health. An immediate investigation was started, and it was found, first, that both patients had eaten in the same hotel, and second, that some diarrheal cases had occurred in the same hotel.

including two more cases of amebiasis. The following day a temporary laboratory was set up on the premises and excreta from all food handlers were collected and examined by trained technicians experienced in diagnosing amebiasis.

This disease is caused not by a bacillus or virus but by a small, one-celled organism known as an ameba. There are many amebæ, but the one causing the disease is the Endamoeba hystolytica. Other kinds of dysentery are caused by bacilli. The amebæ are spread by contaminated water or foods that are eaten raw or by healthy carriers who handle food. Cooking kills the organisms. Once they have invaded the digestive tract, they burrow into the lining of the intestines and form cysts there. The irritation they cause in the intestines gives rise to the symptoms of the disease. Generally the cases are chronic rather than acute. After recovery, the patients may still have amebæ encysted in the intestinal walls, and some of the cysts, which are the infective stage of the organism's life cycle, will be excreted from time to time. If the carrier does not know that he is harboring and excreting amebæ or is careless in matters of personal hygiene he is apt to contaminate food or water and thus spread the disease.

Food handlers were therefore suspected as being the source of the cases reported in Chicago. Out of 364 of these examined at the hotel where the first cases had occurred, 11 carriers of the amebæ and 15 cases of the disease were found. The infected food handlers were excluded from the kitchens, and stringent sanitary regulations were put into effect with unusual measures of sanitary supervision designed to check further spread of the disease among the guests of the hotel. A laboratory was maintained in the hotel, and food handlers were examined regularly and were closely supervised in the kitchens. The latter were cleaned and freshly painted in order to emphasize, in the minds of the employees, the need for cleanliness.

At this time it was believed that the outbreak was strictly food-borne, and with all these precautions no alarm was felt that it would spread any further. Nevertheless, in order to bring the matter to the attention of health officers, a report was made to the American Public Health Association at its annual convention in October. As a result, it was found that a number of cases of amebiasis had occurred in other parts of the country, all or nearly all of them in persons who had visited the Chicago Fair during the summer. Among the patients were a number of prominent persons whose illness was given considerable publicity.

Unfortunately, not all the cases were recognized as amebiasis. Some patients were operated on for appendicitis or other abdominal conditions, with fatal results in several cases. This was due to the fact that amebiasis had always been considered a tropical disease, and physicians practising in the North did not consider the possibility of its occurring among their patients, none of whom had recently been in the tropics or subtropics. Because of this, the U. S. Public Health Service early in November sent out a warning to health officers and physicians throughout the country to be on the lookout for cases of amebic dysentery.

Meanwhile, the Chicago Board of Health had continued its examinations of employees of the hotel and of a neighboring hotel where cases of the disease had also occurred. When several cases of the disease among non-foodhandling employees of the two hotels and new carriers who had not been infested at the first examination were found, further investigation was ordered, and a special committee of sanitary engineers and epidemiologists was appointed to study the situation.

Their investigation revealed that contaminated water had probably been the source of the outbreak. In one of the hotels, on July 2d, two sewer pipes had broken under the ice-storage room, permitting sewage to flood areas where food and ice were stored, prepared, and handled, and also where 345 food handlers worked. Many of these ate their meals in the basement in the quarters which were flooded.

In the other hotel, water and sewage had penetrated into the ice-handling area during a heavy rain on June 29th. Connections were found in one hotel between water and waste pipes through which contamination of the water supply of portions of both hotels might have occurred.

It was also found that the sanitary sewer pipes, installed many years ago, were badly corroded, so that a five-cent kitchen fork could be pushed through the main pipe. There were many leaks, and in a number of places wooden plugs had been used to stop holes. Unfortunately, the sanitary sewer which carried nearly two thirds of the load of one hotel passed directly over a tank in which drinking water was refrigerated for the dining rooms and the floors. The cover of this tank was not watertight.

The danger of disease being spread by contaminated water has long been recognized by health officers and sanitary engineers, and nearly every city and state has laws forbidding the existence of cross-connections in plumbing which permit sewage or contaminated water supplies to mix with supplies of water for domestic use. Nevertheless, it is apparent that such cross-connections do exist in many of these hotels and buildings and in many communities besides Chicago. Where they do exist, they are a constant menace to the health of human beings.

The total number of cases of amebiasis in this outbreak will probably never be known. Up to January 24, 1934, 721 cases had been reported from 206 cities, all of them apparently originating from the Chicago source. There were 14 deaths from amebiasis in Chicago. In addition, 1,049 carriers of the disease were discovered in that city.

Cancer Unconquered

ANOTHER UNCONQUERED PLAGUE still remaining on the debit side of the scientific ledger is that old and very important disease, cancer. Despite the many wild-goose chases that scientists have made after the cause and means of curing it, very little is actually known as to its cause, and surgery or radiation treatment or a combination of the two are still the only means of producing anything like "cures." Radiation treatment has advanced to the point where scientists at the Mercy Hospital in Chicago are using an 800,000 volt X-ray machine to send into the body bigger doses than ever before, in the hope of reaching and destroying deep-lying tumors. Installed early in 1933, this giant weapon against the disease seems to be making some headway, and patients treated with it have been gratifyingly free from radiation sickness and skin burns. The tube was built by Dr. W. D. Coolidge at the General Electric Company research laboratories in Schenectady and is used under the direction of Dr. Henry Schmitz, director and guiding spirit of the Mercy Hospital Institute of Radiation Therapy.

Laboratory investigations into cancer continue, and bit by bit new and important knowledge of the disease is gained, such as the discovery of a powerful reducing substance in malignant tissue. This substance, called "reducytin" by its discoverer, Dr. Leslie J. Harris of the Nutritional Laboratory, Cambridge, England, is significant because abnormality of reducing action is one of the most important characteristics of cancer tissue.

Other English investigators added to the knowledge of cancer the important discovery that the cancer-producing substance in coal tar is a previously unknown compound of hydrogen and carbon, 1.2 benzpyrene. The scientists who made this discovery, Drs. J. W. Cook, I. Hieger, and C. L. Hewett, of the Cancer Hospital Research Institute in London, also synthesized the substance in their laboratories and found the synthetic compound as effective as material isolated from pitch in producing cancer of the skin in mice. Working with Prof. E. C. Dodds of the Courtauld Institute of Biochemistry, Dr. Cook found that this and another, related compound of great cancer-producing power also have the ability of certain hormones to awaken sexual desire in animals.

A substance that checks the growth of certain types of cancerous tumors has recently been found by Dr. James B. Murphy of the Rockefeller Institute for Medical Research in New York City. Dr. Murphy found the tumor-inhibiting substance in the tumors themselves, while in placental tissues and embryo skin he found another tumor-inhibitor which may be the same as the one found in the tumors themselves or may be a different substance capable of producing a similar result.

A discovery that points to a means of avoiding cancer was made as the result of twelve years of research by Drs. M. R. Curtis, W. F. Dunning, and F. D. Bullock, of

Columbia University's Institute of Cancer Research. These men found that liability to cancer is not carried in the germ cells that carry other hereditary traits. The cancer change is in a body cell and is due to some sort of irritant. The change is known technically as a somatic mutation. Commenting on the discovery, Dr. Francis Carter Wood, director of the Institute, said:

"This is an extremely hopeful discovery, for it means that while long life is one factor in having cancer, as was shown long ago from the life insurance records, the only other is the amount of irritation, so that if irritation can be avoided a person is not likely to develop the disease."

In their fight against disease, medical scientists have never been unmindful of the fact that the body puts up a good fight itself, aided not by any medicines or treatment but by certain defensive forces of its own. As a result of such a fight, the body often acquires more or less lasting resistance to a disease, as in the case of typhoid fever. This resistance to disease goes by the scientific name of immunity and has been extensively studied in recent years by investigators in many different research centers.

A method of measuring the degree of immunity acquired by different tissues of the body has been reported by Prof. Reuben L. Kahn of the University of Michigan. Prof. Kahn found that when an animal is given immunity from a disease, its skin and other tissues acquire protective properties, as well as the blood. He pointed out that if it is possible to learn the extent of immunity of all the tissues of an animal, medical scientists will be able to fight germ diseases more successfully than at present. Prof. Kahn's studies showed that when an animal is immunized, its body tissues acquire a new property: namely, the capacity to detect and anchor or combine with the immunizing substance whenever they come in contact with it. The protective nature of this change is evident, since by combining with the substance against which the animal is immune, the tissues prevent its diffusion or spread throughout the body.

For these studies Prof. Kahn received the $1,000 prize award of the Association.

Another investigator, Dr. Valy Menkin of Harvard University Medical School, has reported that he finds the extent to which disease germs can invade the body depends on the amount of inflammation they cause at the site of their entry.

By injecting a dye into the body at a place where bacteria had previously been injected, Dr. Menkin found that staphylococci, the organisms that are found in boils, limit the extent of their invasion to a very small area. They do this by causing a rapid inflammation which results in mechanical obstruction of the draining lymphatics, the avenues by which the disease germs, or other foreign matter, might continue their invasion of the body.

The pneumococcus and the fearsome streptococcus, on the other hand, do not cause such rapid obstruction of these

MAJOR DISEASE PLAGUES OF THE WORLD
FIGURE 9

Controllable	*Uncontrollable*
Scientists know enough of how these are caused and spread and of how to prevent and treat them, so that they could be almost wiped out if this knowledge were put into practice	Scientists do not yet know enough about cause, spread, treatment, or means of preventing these diseases to consider them controllable or "conquered."
smallpox (prevention only; no specific treatment)	cancer
diphtheria	pneumonia
yellow fever	bubonic plague
malaria	cholera
typhoid fever	measles
scurvy	leprosy
beriberi	encephalitis
pellagra	influenza
rickets	infantile paralysis (poliomyelitis)
hookworm disease	typhus fever
rabies (antirabic serum effective only if given before disease has developed; no specific treatment)	meningococcus meningitis
	gonorrhea
	tuberculosis
tetanus (antitetanus serum effective only if given before disease has developed; no specific treatment)	arthritis
	scarlet fever
	Rocky Mountain spotted fever (all forms)
tularemia	undulant fever
syphilis	psittacosis

avenues. In the case of the streptococcus, Dr. Menkin found the avenues are open for as long as two days. This gives the disease germs a chance to get far in their invasion of the body and probably accounts for the serious effects on the whole system of infection with these organisms.

In the old days, disease plagues of all kinds were particularly fierce during hard times. Consequently modern fighters of these plagues have watched anxiously for the reappearance of old, partly vanquished plagues or the development of new ones during the years of the economic depression that started in 1929. The signs have all been remarkably reassuring, but the medical scientists have continued to warn against a feeling of overconfidence. Diseases due to malnutrition may develop slowly and may not become apparent for many years. Communicable diseases like smallpox, typhoid fever, and cholera are only held in leash by the constant vigilance of quarantine and sanitary officers and other health department officials. Medical and health authorities agree that economy in these directions is dangerous. The defensive forces, consisting chiefly of efficient health departments and adequate food, especially for children, must be kept up or much of the benefits of scientific medicine, gained through a century of study and struggle against disease, will be lost.

WHO'S WHO—FOR VITAMINS
FIGURE 10
A

Identified by Prof. E. V. McCollum and by Prof. L. B. Mendel and T. B. Osborne in 1913.

Fat-soluble; not yet obtained in pure crystalline form.

Formed in the liver from carotene, the yellow coloring matter of plants such as carrots, spinach, etc. Is mainly stored in the liver, hence is found in liver oil of cod and other fish. Both the vitamin and carotene are found in butter, egg yolk, and cheese, but the principal coloring of egg yolk is another yellow pigment, xanthophyll. The vitamin itself is probably colorless, and fish-liver oils which are exceptionally rich in it are not yellow.

Necessary, like all essential food factors, for growth. Especially important for the health of epithelial tissues. These include the skin and mucous surfaces and the secretory glands. Deprivation of vitamin A injures the mucous surfaces and facilitates the development of infections. The eyes are especially susceptible to injury from A deficiency. Ophthalmia (xerophthalmia) may result.

Chemical formula proposed by Dr. P. Karrer in 1933 is probably $C_{20}H_{30}O$.

B₁

Discovered in 1896 by Dr. C. Eijkman. Studied by Dr. C. Grijns, 1901. A crude crystalline preparation obtained by Dr. C. Funk in 1911, who, on account of its basic properties, named it "vitamine" from which this whole group of food factors get their name; other crystalline preparations obtained by B. C. P. Jansen and W. F. Donath in 1926, and subsequently by Dr. A. Seidell, by Dr. A. Windaus and by others. Their tests were all curative for pigeons made polyneuritic by feeding polished rice. The chemical formulæ based on analyses are different in the case of each preparation. It is improbable that entirely pure crystals have been secured. According to Windaus this vitamin contains sulfur. Water soluble B was discovered independently by Prof. E. V. McCollum in 1915, who first showed its necessity for growth and as a normal dietary component.

Water soluble.

Found especially abundantly in the germ or embryo of cereals and in yeast. It is, however, widely distributed in relative abundance in such foods as tomatoes, whole cereals, peas, beans, tubers and roots.

Deprivation of B₁ results in injury to the nervous system, producing beriberi, widely prevalent among polished-rice-eating peoples.

B₂

Discovered by Prof. E. V. McCollum in 1925. Multiple nature of vitamin B indicated by Drs. A. D. Emmett and G. O. Luros in 1920. B₂ was definitely proved to be separate from B₁ by Drs. M. I. Smith and E. G. Hendrick in 1926. Drs. Joseph Goldberger, G. A. Wheller, R. D. Lillie, and L. M. Rogers in 1926 reported a pellagra-preventive factor, P-P, which they afterwards identified as B₂ in English nomenclature, or vitamin G in America. Probably isolated by Drs. R. Kuhn, H. Rudy, and T. Wagner-Jauregg in 1933.

Proposed chemical formula is $C_{17}H_{20}N_4O_6$.

Is found especially abundantly in yeast, wheat germ, milk, eggs, lean meat, liver, and many vegetables.

Is generally believed to be a dietary factor preventing pellagra.

B₃, B₄, B₅

These additional fractions of vitamin B have been suggested but their nature and relations are still uncertain.

C

In 1907 Drs. A. Holst and T. Frölich produced scurvy in guinea pigs by feeding experiments. That this disease was due to lack of vitamin C was demonstrated by Drs. B. Cohen and L. B. Mendel in 1918. Vitamin C was identified as hexuronic acid (having the chemical formula, $C_6H_8O_6$) and isolated by Drs. W. A. Waugh and G. C. King in 1932 and immediately after by Drs. J. L. Svirbely and A. Szent-Gyorgyi. The substance was first obtained in crystalline form by Szent-Gyorgyi. It was named ascorbic acid by Dr. W. N. Haworth in 1933, who suggested a formula for it in the same year, as did Dr. P. Karrer. Altogether five suggestions have been made as to its exact chemical structure (structural formulæ). There is much evidence in support of the view that ascorbic acid is not a hexuronic acid but another type of acid derived from a sugar of the glucose family but not glucose itself.

Synthesized in the form of l-ascorbic acid in 1933 by Drs. T. Reichstein, A Grüssner, and R. Oppenauer, and by Dr. Haworth and associates.

Is relatively abundant in fresh fruits and vegetables and green leaves;

occurs in extraordinary amounts in paprika. It is said that more than a pound of the pure vitamin (ascorbic acid) has been prepared from that source.

Prevents scurvy.

Water soluble.

D

Curative value of cod-liver oil for experimental rickets in pups first demonstrated by Prof. E. Mellanby in 1919. He suggested that this effect was due to an excessive abundance of vitamin A, but in 1922 Prof. E. V. McCollum and co-workers demonstrated the existence of a new fat-soluble vitamin governing calcification of bones, namely, vitamin D.

Through the studies of Drs. J. Raczynski, A. F. Hess, C. Rosenheim, and T. A. Webster, and A. Windaus, by 1928 it was shown that the mother substance or precursor of vitamin D is ergosterol. This parent substance is now made in large quantities every year. Irradiation with ultraviolet rays converts ergosterol into the vitamin.

Isolated in crystalline form by Drs. E. H. Reerrink and A. van Wijk in 1929; in 1932 by Drs. R. B. Bourdillon and T. A. Webster and by Dr. A. Windaus and associates.

It is especially abundant in fish-liver oils and is now sold in large quantities under the trade name of viosterol, which is ergosterol activated with ultraviolet rays. Ergosterol or a closely related substance is found almost universally distributed in natural foods. Therefore these become antirachitic when irradiated.

Promotes normal bone growth, prevents rickets and osteomalacia.

E

Discovered in relation to the female by Drs. H. M. Evans and K. S. Bishop in 1922; in relation to the male by Dr. K. E. Mason in 1925.

Found in wheat germ and lettuce and certain other green vegetables.

Essential to reproduction though not more so than vitamin A. Lack of A causes sterility through interference with ovulation. Lack of E causes sterility in the female through failure of normal development of the fetus in the womb; in the male by causing degeneration of the testes.

CHAPTER 22
SPEAKING OF GLANDS

INTO THE WITCHES' CALDRONS of old went many a bit of liver, of spleen, and of other animal glands. Out of the caldrons came mysterious brews to endow a man with surpassing courage, strength, and wisdom, or a woman with grace and beauty to charm a lover.

Into the modern chemists' flasks go ground-up bits of animal glands, and out of them come extracts stranger and more potent than ever dreamed of by witches of old: modern magic to speed up growth and save a child from being a dwarf; modern potions to stimulate sex functions, to make a man drink more water, to increase his tolerance for sugar or to decrease it, to quicken or slow the tempo at which he lives.

The mystery of the glands intrigued the earliest students of the human body. Long before the dawn of scientific medicine, glandular tissue was prescribed for various conditions and ailments. Scientific methods have now replaced the groping empiricism of the ancient healers, and facts about the glands have replaced fanciful ideas.

While the earliest scientists busied themselves about the functions of the large, so to speak obvious glands of the body, such as the liver, pancreas, gastric, and salivary glands, it is the group of small inconspicuous glands without ducts which in recent years have occupied the center of the stage. They have been found to be of the greatest importance in regulating the machinery of the body. Having no ducts, their secretions are emptied into the blood or lymph. They have been designated therefore as glands of internal secretion, or endocrine glands, and the branch of medicine that deals with them goes under the special name of endocrinology. With increased knowledge, interest in this subject has grown with a mighty crescendo till at the present time endocrine research is going on at a furious pace all over the world, and with breath-taking results.

Among the first wonder-working potions to come out of the chemists' flasks were adrenalin, life-saving aid in emergencies; thyroxin, extracted from the pace-setting, U-shaped gland in the neck; and insulin, boon to the diabetic. Search for an elixir of youth, for an antidote to lost virility, long centered on the sex glands, and it was Brown-Séquard's interest in this phase of gland study that in 1889 stimulated modern interest in endocrinology. To-day, however, the pituitary gland is coming in for most of the attention in the centers for biological and physiological research.

Driver Gland

MODERN SCIENTISTS have found that the pituitary is in the driver's seat, and that this bit of tissue, the size of a hazelnut kernel or a large old-fashioned pill, hanging from the base of the brain, is closely related to all the other ductless glands and to the sympathetic nerves, and through them exercises its influence over the body. To one eminent scientist this gland seems to be a modern Aladdin's lamp, with the reputed ability to produce more miracles than the original Aladdin ever dreamed of.

For example, six children and one young man of eighteen years, doomed to be dwarfs, were rescued from this sorry fate by one group of modern Aladdins. These were three physicians who specialized in the study and treatment of the endocrine glands.

The young people ranged in age from seven to eighteen years. They were from about two inches to more than a foot shorter than the shortest height normal for children of their ages. One seven-year-old girl was only one inch taller than her three-year-old sister. Examinations showed that the growth deficiency was due to deficient functioning of the pituitary gland. Some of the patients also showed signs of deficient thyroid gland activity.

The patients grew from 1 to 2.7 inches when under the

care of the modern Aladdins. The young patients had all been under observation for several months prior to treatment, during which time six of them did not grow at all, while one grew half an inch. Similar results are being obtained with small patients elsewhere.

The medical scientists were able to stimulate the growth of these young people, not by any lamp-rubbing, but by

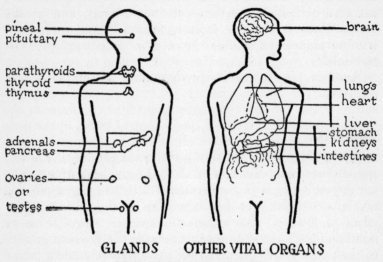

GLANDS   OTHER VITAL ORGANS
LOCATING THE GLANDS

FIGURE 11

THESE diagrams show the position in the body of the glands of internal secretion and some of the more commonly known vital organs.

administration of a growth "potion" obtained from the front or anterior part of the pituitary gland. The "potion" came out of a laboratory where chemists had been putting bits of the gland into their flasks and treating them with various reagents until they obtained an extract of the growth-stimulating principle of the modern Aladdin's lamp. That such a principle is present in the gland was first realized when scientists found that giants and dwarfs had abnormal pituitary glands. During the active stage of gigantism, that is, while the giant is still growing, overgrowth or tumor of the front lobe of the pituitary is found.

The gland presents the opposite picture of undersize or atrophy in dwarfs.

Discovery of the growth-controlling function of the pituitary gland was followed by discoveries of some of its other functions. By "chemical dissection" of the gland, to use a term coined by Dr. J. B. Collip of McGill University, Montreal, one of the most active investigators of the pituitary, scientists have obtained six anterior pituitary extracts, each having a different and striking effect on the body. Whether each of these circulates in the blood as a true hormone, or glandular secretion, has not yet been determined.

Another pituitary miracle may turn out to be a new treatment for Graves' disease, or exophthalmic goiter, resulting from the discovery of the pituitary's effect on the thyroid gland. The latter is the U-shaped gland in the neck which regulates the metabolism or energy conversions constantly going on in the body. Overactivity of the gland speeds the metabolism to a dangerously high rate, from which result excessive nervousness, disturbed digestion, and accelerated heartbeat. Underactivity produces the reverse effect of lowered metabolism and general sluggishness of mind and body. In children this retards the physical growth to the point of dwarfism and the mental development to the level of idiocy. From the pituitary gland scientists have very recently isolated a principle which brings about overactivity of the thyroid, with consequent elevated metabolic rate, and the familiar protruding eyes and enlarged gland or goiter. Dr. Collip and his associates obtained an extract so potent that one cubic centimeter, or about twenty drops, produced exophthalmic goiter in 200 guinea pigs.

While they were working with this extract, striving to get a chemically pure substance or even the hormone itself, if it is a hormone, they made another surprising discovery. After continued injections of the thyroid-stimulating pituitary extract, the metabolic rate in experimental animals drops, eventually becoming much lower than normal. The animals apparently develop resistance or immunity to the extract. When blood from these animals was injected into normal animals, or into animals whose pituitary glands had been removed, the thyroid-stimulating principle had no effect.

Animals that had become resistant to the thyroid-stimulating pituitary hormone, however, responded to a dose of dried thyroid gland with the rise in metabolic rate characteristic of an increase of thyroid substance in the body. This indicates that the resistant substance in the blood acts between the thyroid gland and the pituitary gland, checking the effect of the latter on the former, and not between the thyroid gland and the other body tissues.

Present treatment of Graves' disease is directed toward inhibiting the effect of the thyroid gland on the tissues by surgical removal of part or all of the gland. The indications are that future treatment may be directed toward checking the thyroid-stimulating hormone of the pituitary with serum from resistant animals. Of course, much more investigation will be needed before anything like practical application in humans can be attempted. Meanwhile, further investigations along these lines are being made by Dr. Collip and his associates.

The Pituitary and Diabetes

ANOTHER DRAMATIC DEVELOPMENT of the anterior pituitary story is the relation between this gland and the body's use of sugar. Dr. B. A. Houssay of Buenos Aires showed that the death which usually occurs soon after the pancreas is removed can be either prevented or averted for a long time, if the pituitary gland is removed at the same time as the pancreas. The latter organ is the one that contains the insulin-producing islands of Langerhans. When this organ does not produce enough insulin, diabetes follows.

Now Dr. Herbert M. Evans and his associates, working at the University of California, have found that a true diabetes can be produced in dogs merely by giving them a certain extract of the pituitary gland. This, together with the work of Houssay and other scientists, seems to establish the fact that there is a relation between the pituitary gland and the body's use of sugar. Dr. Evans and associates are now at work on the task of distinguishing this possible new hormone, the diabetogenic hormone, from the others of the pituitary gland.

The relation between diabetes and the pituitary gland has been observed and investigated by many other scientists, among them Dr. Harvey Cushing at the Harvard Medical School and Drs. B. O. Barnes, J. F. Regan, and W. O. Nelson, working in the laboratory of Prof. A. J. Carlson at the University of Chicago. On the basis of these investigations, one very modern Aladdin, Dr. James H. Hutton of Chicago, has been rubbing the pituitary lamp, figuratively speaking, to relieve diabetes. In a series of cases, he found X-ray treatment of the pituitary and adrenal glands improved the patients' condition and enabled him to reduce the amount of insulin they had been taking. This type of treatment, however, is still regarded as experimental. The diabetic must continue to rely on insulin, diet, and exercise to control his disease, while Dr. Hutton's method is subjected to further trial.

Another new pituitary hormone apparently presides over the vitally important cortex of the adrenal glands. Without this part of the adrenal gland, or cortin, the hormone it produces, life cannot go on. When the pituitary, by a very delicate operation, is removed from its protected location in the center of the head, the cortex of the adrenal gland wastes away. A certain extract of the pituitary gland, however, restores to normal the adrenal cortex that had atrophied upon removal of the pituitary. If the research of the future shows this pituitary extract to be distinct from all the other pituitary hormones, it will be the new adrenalotropic hormone of the pituitary, although the relation of this pituitary-adrenal situation to the adrenal cortical hormone essential for life is not yet clear.

There are at least two other hormones produced by the anterior pituitary. One of these, the lactogenic, influences the secretion of milk by the mammary glands. The other is a sex hormone, or it may be that there are several pituitary sex hormones. Reports of this gland's effect on the sex organs are being made at a bewildering rate. Grafts of the gland or doses of its sex hormone bring about sexual maturity in immature animals, and in senile animals they cause an increase in the size of the atrophied sex organs, renewal of sex function, and restoration of the erotic impulse.

These six or more hormones are all produced by the anterior pituitary; but the "Aladdin's lamp of the head" has a hind lobe, the posterior, which also secretes one or more important hormones. Early investigations of the pituitary centered in this part of the gland. In 1898 Dr. William H. Howell, of the Johns Hopkins University, discovered that an extract of this part of the gland has a special physiologic action. This extract causes a marked rise in blood pressure by stimulating the heart muscle and the smooth muscle cells in the walls of the blood vessels. It also exerts a stimulating influence on all smooth muscles throughout the body. The smooth muscles are the involuntary muscles, such as those of the digestive tract, uterus, heart and blood vessels.

In recent years so much of interest has been discovered in regard to the functions of the anterior lobe that the importance of the posterior lobe has been rather overlooked. Dr. Harvey Cushing, formerly of Harvard Medical School and now at Yale University School of Medicine, has lately called renewed attention to its significance. In his opinion, this hind part of the gland is fully as important as the front part. His studies show that the secretions of the posterior lobe produce changes in the body just as profound as the anterior pituitary hormones. The posterior pituitary hormone, pituitrin, exerts its influence through one set of nerves (parasympathetic) somewhat as epinephrine, or adrenalin, hormone of the adrenal glands lying above the kidneys, acts through another set of nerves (sympathetic) to effect its mobilization of the body's forces to meet emergencies.

Glands and Emotions

THE ADRENAL GLANDS discharge relatively large amounts of hormone under emotional stimuli, such as rage or fear. The same emotional stimuli may cause a discharge of posterior pituitary hormone. The excess adrenalin discharged as a result of strong emotion causes the heart to pump more quickly and forcefully (increased blood pressure); the liver to release its store of sugar (glycogen) for additional fuel for the body; the air passages to dilate, permitting freer breathing; and the blood vessels of the skin and abdominal organs to contract, thus increasing the amount of blood available to the muscles and nerves which must meet the emergency. If extra pituitrin is discharged in response to emotional stimuli, it affects the same parts of the body as epinephrine, but in a different way. Blood vessels of skin and muscles are apparently not contracted by pituitrin, but enlarged to carry a larger supply of blood. The heart pumps more forcefully, as under the influence of adrenalin, but not more quickly, as with adrenalin. The activity of the digestive organs is stimulated rather than checked.

Evidence that pituitrin discharged under emotional stimulus may act in this way has only recently been found. Ordinary injections of even large amounts of the posterior pituitary principle produce an effect similar to injections of adrenalin. Dr. Cushing has found, however, that pituitrin produces an entirely different effect according to where it is injected into the body. When injected under the skin, into the muscles, or into a vein, it produces the familiar adrenalin-like effect. When it is injected directly into the ventricles of the brain, it produces entirely different results, namely flushing and sweating and reverse action of the digestive tract with retching and vomiting. It seems likely that when the hormone is discharged spontaneously from the gland in response to emotional stimulus it acts through the nerve centers in the brain, with the same results as when it is injected into the ventricles of the brain. The question of when and how and with what results the posterior or hind lobe of the pituitary discharges its hormone has not yet been conclusively settled. Enough has been learned of the possibilities, however, to justify Dr. Cushing's contention that this is an important and fruitful field for further scientific investigation.

Latest research on the posterior lobe of the gland suggests that here may at last be found a means of controlling those conditions characterized by high blood pressure—

that common and troublesome modern complaint. Dr. Cushing thinks that some of these disorders may be due to overactivity of the posterior lobe which secretes a blood-pressure-raising hormone. Removal of this part of the gland is always followed by a fall in blood pressure, he has observed. Possibly discovery by the biochemists of a hormone to counteract an excess of the blood-pressure-raising pituitary hormone may prove to be the solution of the problem.

Other attributes of this part of the gland recently discovered are its influence on the body's use of fat, sugar, and water. Finally, this gland is now known to have an effect on pigment cells in the skin of animals, including man. Darkening of the skin is a characteristic of the disorder brought on by an overactive pituitary, while persons suffering from too little pituitary secretion have a veritable "peaches and cream" complexion.

The pituitary, as befits its position of master gland of the body, has been getting the lion's share of scientists' attention in the last few years, but it has been by no means the only subject of endocrine research. Four grain-of-wheat-sized glands in the neck, adjacent to the thyroid and hence called the parathyroids, have furnished material for another exciting chapter of endocrinology. Because they are so insignificant-looking and so closely attached to the thyroid, sometimes buried in it, medical scientists used to think the parathyroids were just part of the thyroid. But when they were removed with the thyroid gland in operations to relieve Graves' disease and goiter, dire things happened to the luckless patients. Muscular cramps and convulsions seized them, and they died a death not unlike the horrible death of lockjaw or tetanus. From this similarity the condition got its name of parathyroid tetany. This condition results when the parathyroids are removed or when through injury or disease they fail to produce enough of the hormone by which they exert their influence on the body.

Normally this influence is directed toward stimulating or regulating proper bone development. Parathyroid hormone, or parathormone, as it is called, calcium or lime salts, and vitamin D are the triad which scientists have found necessary for proper bone formation and growth. Rickets and parathyroid tetany have become familiar to scientists because of the symptoms that arise when there is lack of any of the three factors.

The Man Who Shrank

NOT SO FAMILIAR, until the last year or two, was the picture of the opposite condition, hyperparathyroidism. Through the rare courage and coöperation of a victim of this disease, Captain Charles Martell, medical scientists now have complete knowledge of the symptoms and signs and chemical findings in this rare condition. They even have reason to believe that it is not such a rare malady as has been supposed. Best of all, their newly won knowledge has given them a means of remedying the condition if it is recognized early enough.

The valiant young captain's story belongs in the annals of medical heroism. He was a master mariner in the merchant marine, and when only twenty-two years old he was navigating transports through the war zone. He was a powerfully built, healthy man of six feet one—until he began to have rheumatic pains in his legs and back, and actually to shrink in size. His neck grew shorter and fatter, so that he had to buy larger sized collars, and his mates began to tease him because of his pigeon breast. His muscles grew weaker, he stumbled often, fell over a chair and broke his arm. He persisted in his duties at sea even after pain and muscle weakness made it difficult for him to climb stairs and ladders, until abdominal pain and vomiting forced him to seek medical aid. Because of the rheumatic pains, his ailment was diagnosed as arthritis and for one year he was treated for that condition but failed to improve. In fact, he was losing ground all the time, and losing inches from his stature. Eventually he lost a full foot. At the end of the year's treatment he stumbled over a chair and fractured both bones of his left forearm. An X-ray picture taken at that time showed that his bones were less dense than normal, which suggested that he was suffering from the bone disease, osteomalacia. His broken arm had to stay in a cast for nine months before the bones knit. During the two years he suffered two additional fractures of his arms.

For four months at a time he lay stretched on a frame, trying to regain some of the lost inches. The stretching apparently added half an inch to his height, bringing it up to five feet nine inches while he was lying in bed. However, when he was measured after standing erect for half an hour, his height was only five feet six inches. Then he wore a supporting body brace.

At this time his neck had shortened, his head was sinking, and his lower jaw had become deformed, protruding forward so that his teeth were out of alignment. X-ray pictures showed that the bone disease now involved all the bones in his body. He was put on diets containing large amounts of foods rich in the bone-building elements, calcium and phosphorus. Medicines containing these minerals, and in addition cod-liver oil, thyroid extracts, adrenalin, light rays, quartz-lamp treatment, and milk irradiated to increase its vitamin D content were tried. But he showed no improvement, and almost all the time he was in the hospital he suffered from weakness and nearly constant pain in his bones and joints.

After it became evident that he was suffering from a disease of the bones, he was transferred to Bellevue Hospital, where scientists of the Russell Sage Institute of Pathology, Drs. R. R. Hannon, E. Shorr, W. S. McClellan, and E. F. DuBois, began investigations of the chemistry of his body. They observed changes in his blood chemistry and excretions similar to those previously observed in dogs when an active parathyroid gland extract was administered. This suggested to Dr. DuBois that the captain was probably ill because of an excessive secretion of his parathyroid glands. When the Institute, a part of Cornell University, closed its laboratories for the summer, Captain Martell was sent to Massachusetts General Hospital in Boston, where Harvard Medical School scientists, Drs. Joseph C. Aub, Walter Bauer, Fuller Albright, and Charles L. Short, continued the investigations. They confirmed the findings observed by Dr. DuBois and his co-workers.

What had happened to weaken the young captain's bones so that they could no longer support the weight of his body but bent under the load until they were deformed? Medical scientists consider bone an active tissue, like skin and muscle, that is constantly being built up and broken down. Bone diseases, such as rickets and osteomalacia, are conditions in which the building-up process is faulty. The new tissues, instead of being normal bone, are deficient in lime salts. Lime or calcium is one of the elements that give bones their hardness.

This condition may result from several causes. Malnutrition and lack of certain dietary factors such as vitamin D and calcium is one cause, resulting in rickets in children. Another cause is repeated bearing and nursing of children which may divert the calcium from the mother's system to her child's, leaving her with diseased and weakened bones. A third cause is disturbance of the glands of internal secretion, particularly the parathyroid glands.

Much of this knowledge about bone diseases and their causes was gained from investigations and experiments on dogs, guinea pigs, and other laboratory animals. Captain Martell did not hesitate to join the ranks of experimental animals, letting the doctors treat him, operate on him, and make test after test. When they wanted to stop after four operations, he threatened to leave the hospital and find another where the proposed operations would be carried out. He fought his rare disease as he would pilot a disabled ship through a stormy sea, insisting that the doctors carry on their investigations, not so much to save himself as to add to medical knowledge.

But the dogs and guinea pigs and other non-human laboratory animals had done their part, too. Working with them, Dr. Collip had extracted the potent hormone of the parathyroid gland which he called parathormone. Parathormone, he found, relieved the agonizing cramps and convulsions of parathyroid tetany and saved the lives of animals after their parathyroids had been removed. Of course, if every scrap of parathyroid was cut out, doses of parathormone had to be repeated indefinitely to keep the animals alive.

Dr. Collip then gave doses of parathormone to normal animals. Bone deformities, weakness of muscles, finally of the whole body, and brittleness of bones were among the symptoms that followed. Tests of blood and excretions indicated that more calcium was being lost than was being taken in by the animal. Consequently, the new bone tissue being formed lacked the necessary lime salts to harden it, and the bones became thinner because lime salts were being excreted at so rapid a rate.

Tests and observations of Captain Martell showed that he had the same symptoms as these laboratory animals that were getting excessive amounts of parathormone. For a short time the Boston physicians gave Captain Martell parathormone. The effect was to increase the severity of his pain and other symptoms.

By this time, Dr. Bauer and his associates were convinced that their patient was suffering from overactive parathyroid glands, probably as the result of a parathyroid tumor. So they decided to remove by surgical operation the parathyroid tumor, if they should find one. At the first two operations one parathyroid gland was removed from each side. Examination of these glands showed them to be entirely normal. So two more operations were performed, the surgeon searching the right and left sides of the thyroid for a possible tumor, and even removing one lobe of this gland. There was no improvement in Captain Martell's condition as a result of these operations, and by this time his physicians thought he had stood enough. With undaunted valor the young captain insisted that they go on. At his request three more operations were performed. At the fifth the surgeons searched the upper left neck region, and at the sixth the upper right neck region.

Finally, at the seventh operation, the surgeons explored the upper middle part of the chest in front, known medically as the anterior mediastinum. There they found a parathyroid tumor and removed it. So far as known, this is the first parathyroid tumor found in this location and successfully removed.

It was too late to save the brave captain. He lost his last fight, dying at the age of thirty-six. But the knowledge gained through his rare courage has already enabled the physicians to find a similar tumor in a similar location in another patient. This patient had previously undergone two unsuccessful operations.

"Had it not been for our experience with Captain Charles Martell," Dr. Bauer commented, "this patient might have gone along for some years longer without the tumor being removed."

Cortin, the Life Fluid

ANOTHER WONDER-WORKING POTION which has recently come out of the chemists' flasks is cortin, produced by adrenal gland cortex. This is the outer portion or rind of the adrenal glands; the inner portion, called the medulla, is the part that produces adrenalin. Life cannot go on without the adrenal cortex. Occasionally the cortex becomes diseased and fails to produce enough of its hormone. Until the recent discovery of the cortical hormone, there was no hope for patients suffering from this condition, which is known as Addison's disease. Their skin turned a peculiar bronze color, they grew thin and anemic and gradually wasted away. Cortin has been their life-saver, as insulin has been the life-saver of diabetic patients. Like insulin in most cases, cortin must be given regularly to keep the patient alive and healthy. This is known as replacement treatment, the doses of cortin being given to replace that which normally is produced in the individual's own body.

All these new facts do not tell the entire story of the ductless glands. The dramatic discovery of insulin has often been related, and the achievements in treatment of thyroid disorder, particularly exophthalmic goiter, are also well known. Other parts of the story cannot be written until after much more research has been carried out by medical scientists. These modern Aladdins, who do not think of themselves at all as wonder workers, will not be content until they have gained complete knowledge of the structure, function, and relation of all the ductless glands and in addition are able to correct and eventually to prevent disease and abnormalities resulting from endocrine disturbances.

GLANDS AND THEIR HORMONES*
FIGURE 12

GLANDS	HORMONES
Pituitary—"Master Gland." Hangs from brain in hollow of protecting bone in center of head.	*Hind Lobe* (Posterior). Pituitrin Pitocin Pitressin Antidiuretic Probably one or two more other hormones. *Front Lobe* (Anterior). Growth-stimulating; one or more sex-stimulating. Diabetogenic ⎫ Probable but not Thyrotropic ⎬ yet completely ac- Lactogenic ⎪ cepted. Adrenalotropic ⎭
Thyroid—"Pace Setter." U-shaped gland in front of neck.	Thyroxine.
Adrenals (suprarenals). 2 cocked-hat-shaped glands, 1 atop each kidney.	*Medulla* (inner part). Epinephrine (adrenalin). *Cortex* (outer part or rind). Cortin. Probably a sex-stimulating hormone. Probably a lactation hormone. Probably a blood-pressure-raising hormone.
Parathyroids. 4 grain-of-wheat-sized glands attached to the thyroid.	Parathormone.
Pineal—"Seat of the Soul," according to Descartes. Cone-shaped gland in the head.	Possibly secretes a hormone regulating bodily development and onset of puberty.
Thymus. Located in the chest.	Function unknown; enlarged thymus in a child known to be dangerous, but if detected may be successfully treated.
Pancreas.	*Islands of Langerhans*. Insulin. Vagotropic hormone.

*See also Figure 11.

Ovaries.   *Graafian follicles.*
                                              Theelin.
                                              Corpora lutea.
                                              Progestin.
                                              Relaxin.

Testes.   Androtin.
                                              Inhibin (probably).

Placenta.   Emmenin.

Stomach.   Gastrin.

Small intestines.   Secretin.
                                              Cholecystokinin.

TABLE OF HORMONES
FIGURE 13
INSULIN.

 Secreted by the islands of Langerhans in the pancreas.

 Controls the body's use of carbohydrates (sugar and starches) in foods; lack of insulin results in diabetes, which may be relieved by regular, measured doses of the hormone; too much insulin causes convulsions and results in a newly observed disease known as the "hungry disease" (because excessive hunger is a prominent symptom) and also as hyperinsulinism, relieved by increasing the carbohydrate content of the diet and also by surgical removal of part of the pancreas.

 Discovered in 1921 by Dr. F. G. Banting and C. H. Best working in the laboratory of Prof. J. J. R. Macleod at the University of Toronto; preparation and refinement of an extract for practical use accomplished with aid of Dr. J. B. Collip, now professor of biochemistry at McGill University.

 Isolated in pure crystalline form by Dr. J. J. Abel, Johns Hopkins University, 1927.

CORTIN.

 Secreted by the cortex of the adrenal or suprarenal glands.

 Necessary to life; relieves symptoms of Addison's disease and prolongs lives of patients, but must be continued throughout the patient's life; said to control the body's utilization of sugar, to maintain the normal circulating volume of fluid in the blood vessels, to be necessary for the proper functioning of all body tissues, to help the body utilize vitamins C and B_1, and to play a rôle in disease resistance.

 Discovered in 1930 by three groups of investigators at different laboratories: Prof. Frank A. Hartmann of Buffalo; Professors J. M. Rogoff and G. N. Stewart of Cleveland; and Prof. W. W. Swingle and Dr. J. J. Pfiffner of Princeton.

 Isolated in very potent, possibly pure, crystalline form in 1932–1933 by Drs. A. Grollman and W. M. Firor, Johns Hopkins University.

EPINEPHRINE (adrenalin).

 Secreted by the medulla of the adrenal or suprarenal glands.

Slows and strengthens the heartbeat and increases blood pressure; increases output of sugar in kidney excretion; in times of stress, in fear, anger, or pain, acts through the sympathetic nervous system to mobilize the physiologic forces of the body to meet the emergency; increases output of blood sugar from liver, raises content of sugar in blood with consequent loss of sugar through kidneys.

Discovered by Dr. George Oliver and Sir Edward Sharpey-Schafer, University College, London, in 1894; extracted by Prof. John J. Abel, in 1898, isolated in crystalline form by Dr. T. B. Aldrich and simultaneously by the Japanese investigator, Jokichi Takamine, in 1902.

Synthesized by Dr. Franz Stolz, Germany, 1903–1904, and by Dr. H. D. Dakin, England, 1905.

Chemical name is dihydroxymethylaminoethylolbenzene; chemical formula is $C_9H_{13}O_3N$.

THYROXINE.

Secreted by the thyroid gland.

Regulates the processes of oxidation in the body; deficiency of thyroxine slows the body and mind, resulting in myxedema in adults, cretinism and idiocy in infants, also in one type of dwarfism; excess thyroxine increases speed of vital activity, resulting in exophthalmic goiter or Graves' disease.

Discovered and isolated by Dr. E. C. Kendall, Mayo Clinic, in 1916.

Synthesized by Dr. C. R. Harington, University of London, in 1926.

Chemically it is a tetra-iodo substituted derivative of the p-hydroxyphenyl ether of tyrosine; formula is $C_{15}H_{11}O_4NI_4$.

PARATHORMONE.

Secreted by the parathyroid glands.

Regulates calcium metabolism and thus influences bone development; deficiency of this hormone results in the convulsive condition known as tetany; excess results in faulty bone formation with softening of the bones and resulting deformities, the condition being known as hyperparathyroidism or osteitis fibrosa cystica.

Discovered in 1923 and 1924 independently and almost simultaneously by Dr. J. B. Collip, Dr. A. M. Hanson, Faribault, Minn., and Dr. Louis Berman of New York.

PITUITRIN.

Secreted by the hind or posterior lobe of the pituitary gland.

Causes contraction of smooth muscle tissues, including the heart, thus increasing blood pressure, intestinal motor functions and uterine contractions; plays a rôle in determining color of skin and in regulation of fat, carbohydrate, and water metabolism; some of these effects are probably due to other pituitary hormones than pituitrin.

Discovered by Dr. George Oliver and Sir Edward Sharpey-Schafer in 1895.

GROWTH HORMONE.

Secreted by front or anterior lobe of pituitary gland.

Discovered by Dr. Herbert M. Evans, University of California, in 1921.

Stimulates growth.

PROLAN (sex hormone).
Secreted by front or anterior lobe of pituitary gland.
Discovered by Prof. Philip E. Smith and Prof. E. T. Engle, College of Physicians and Surgeons, New York, and, almost simultaneously, by Drs. B. Zondek and S. Ascheim of Germany in 1927; presence of such a hormone suggested by work of Dr. C. Foà of Italy about 1900 and Drs. H. M. Evans and J. A. Long of the University of California in 1921.
Probably two and maybe more sex hormones from this gland; one of them, Prolan A, believed to cause the ovary to produce theelin; Prolan B believed to stimulate production of progestin by ovaries previously affected by Prolan A, but the duality of A and B is still unsettled; Prolan also has stimulating effect on the male sex glands.

THYROTROPIC.
Secreted by anterior pituitary.
Presence suggested by early investigators; extracted by Dr. J. B. Collip and associates in 1933.
Causes hyperthyroidism and exophthalmic goiter.

DIABETOGENIC.
Secreted by anterior lobe of pituitary.
Discovered by a number of workers in 1932–1933 (see Chapter 22); first suggested by Dr. B. A. Houssay of Buenos Aires.
Influences carbohydrate metabolism; can produce diabetes in normal dogs or prevent it in dogs whose pancreas has been removed.

PROLACTIN (lactogenic).
Secreted by anterior lobe of pituitary.
Discovered by Dr. Oscar Riddle, Carnegie Institution at Cold Spring Harbor, N. Y., in 1932.
Stimulates milk secretion.

ADRENALOTROPIC.
Secreted by anterior lobe of pituitary.
Discovered by Prof. Philip E. Smith.
Stimulates cortex of adrenal glands.

ANDROTIN.
Secreted by the male sex glands (testes).
Extracted from the sex glands of bulls by Profs. Carl R. Moore and F. C. Koch, University of Chicago, in 1927.
Isolated in pure form by Dr. Adolf Butenandt, University of Göttingen, in 1929.
Essential to the normal development of both primary and secondary sex characteristics.
Chemical formula $C_{16}H_{28}O_2$.

THEELIN.
Produced by graafian follicles of the ovaries; also, perhaps, by the placenta.
Discovered in follicular fluid by Drs. Edgar Allen and Edward A. Doisy at Washington University, St. Louis, in 1923.

Obtained in pure crystalline form by Dr. Doisy and associates at St. Louis University in 1929.

Maintains normal sexual rhythm; essential to formation of secondary female characteristics.

Chemical formula is $C_{18}H_{22}O_2$.

PROGESTIN.
Produced by ovaries (corpora lutea).

First extracted by Prof. George W. Corner, Rochester University, in 1930.

Besides secondary sex-stimulating rôle, prepares the uterus for reception of the fertilized egg cell and pregnancy.

RELAXIN.
Produced by ovaries (corpora lutea).

Discovered by Prof. F. L. Hisaw, of the University of Wisconsin, in 1929–1930.

Said to promote relaxation of the pelvic ligaments as a preparation for childbirth.

EMMENIN.
Produced by the placenta.

Discovered by Dr. J. B. Collip in 1931.

Stimulates the activity of the ovaries.

SYMPATHIN.
Secreted at endings of sympathetic nerves in involuntary muscles (may be two hormones instead of one).

Discovered by Prof. Walter B. Cannon, Harvard University, in 1931.

Produces effects very similar to epinephrine.

SECRETIN.
Produced in the intestines by the action of acid on prosecretin.

Discovered by Sir William Bayliss and Dr. E. H. Starling of London in 1907.

Stimulates the pancreas to produce its digestive juices.

CHOLECYSTOKININ ("gall bladder mover").
Produced by the intestines.

Discovered by Dr. A. C. Ivy, Northwestern University, in 1928.

Causes contraction of the gall bladder.

GASTRIN.
Produced by the stomach.

Discovered by Dr. J. S. Edkins of London in 1906.

Stimulates the production of gastric juice (the stomach's digestive juice).

CHAPTER 23
DRIVING OUT THE DEVILS

Possessed of the devil." That is the way many primitive people have thought—and still think—of disease. In the Stone Age, medicine men cured the ill, or tried to, by driving out the devils.

When our own civilization developed an art and a science of medicine, this idea was dropped, so far as physical disease was concerned. The idea has prevailed much longer, however, with regard to disease of the mind. Up to very nearly modern times a person so afflicted was considered bewitched, lunatic, crazed. When his fellows found they could not drive out the devil or evil spirit that had upset his poor mind, they were content to feed and shelter him and restrain him from harming himself or others. Unfortunately, the victim was sometimes confused with the evil spirit, and the generally ignorant persons in charge of him were more concerned with punishing the evil behavior than with caring for the victim.

The first change toward the modern attitude came in 1798, when Pinel humanely and dramatically struck the chains off the poor wretches in the Paris asylum for the insane. Soon after, disordered minds became the subject of scientific study. Then, gradually, the idea of disordered minds—insanity—gave way in the thoughts of a few inspired physicians to the idea of sick minds and mental disease. That was the beginning of a new branch of science, psychiatry, and of efforts to cure mental disease. The even more inspired idea of preventing it did not come until the beginning of the twentieth century, when Clifford W. Beers wrote:

"A most important function of the Society for Mental Hygiene will be the waging of an educative war against the prevailing ignorance regarding conditions and modes of living which tend to produce mental disorders. This commonsense prophylaxis—or work of prevention—will, in time, bring under control the now increasing population of our hospitals and asylums."

This remarkable man had wandered for three years in the dark world of the insane and had emerged with a healthy mind and an inspired vision of help for his fellow wanderers. His vision was first expressed in a powerful autobiographic tract and scientific memoir, *A Mind That Found Itself*. It soon after took even more practical form when a group of men gathered at a house in New Haven and launched the drive to awaken humanity to the fact that the insane are mentally ill and not possessed of the devil. It has grown since then into a national and international mental hygiene movement. The term, mental hygiene, was suggested by Dr. Adolf Meyer of the Johns Hopkins Medical School and Hospital.

In 1933 the leaders of the movement—a far larger group than in 1908—gathered in the same New Haven house, now the Faculty Club of Yale University, to celebrate the twenty-fifth anniversary of the beginnings of mental hygiene. They found much cause for pride in the achievements of the quarter century.

Asylums have been turned into hospitals. The mentally ill are treated not as criminals to be punished, but as unfortunate sufferers from a disease no more disgraceful than is influenza. The light of scientific treatment is finding its way into one of the dark corners of our unfolding civilization. The mental hygiene movement, with its accent upon prevention and humane, medical treatment, has spread to a long list of nations, ranging from Argentina to the Union of South Africa. An international committee on mental hygiene has been formed to hold international congresses from time to time.

In spite of all this growth, and in spite of some 700-odd psychiatric and child-guidance clinics now functioning in the United States alone, much remains to be done.

One fifth of all the beds in state mental disease hospitals

in the United States are filled by a single mental disease, schizophrenia. This mental ailment has been likened to a dream state, but it differs from normal dreams mostly in that upon awakening from sleep the dream is not dismissed and the activities of the dream are largely carried out rather than merely visualized. The cost of this one mental disease has been put at no less than $1,000,000 daily, and some estimate it at $2,000,000 daily. This includes the cost of caring for the patients in institutions or at home and the loss of their removal from productive pursuits.

Schizophrenia, though a big problem, is only one of many awaiting solution by physicians and others who are fighting mental and nervous diseases.

Preventive and educational measures are the twentieth-century weapons with which modern medicine men are trying to foil the devils that cause mental and nervous diseases. Some other modern weapons, used to drive out the evil spirits once they have gained control of the mind, seem as fantastic as those used by the witch doctors and medicine men of old. For instance, mosquito glands have become one of the aids used to rout the devilish spirochete of syphilis when it invades the brain and causes the mental disease known as paresis. The glands happen to be a convenient way in which to transport the parasites that cause malaria, and a good bout of malaria has been found very effective in the treatment of paresis.

Malaria Fights Mental Ill

THE MALARIA TREATMENT for paresis was discovered almost accidentally by a Viennese scientist, Wagner von Jauregg. He was awarded the 1927 Nobel Prize for this discovery. It happened that in a Vienna hospital some patients suffering from paresis also were attacked by malaria. When they recovered from their malarial attack, their mental condition seemed much improved. Amazed, Prof. von Jauregg investigated. He tried injecting blood from malaria patients into the veins or muscles of other patients suffering with paresis. The same thing occurred. After recovering from malaria, about one third of these

patients showed marked mental improvement and were
later able to return to their homes and go to work. Prof.
von Jauregg reasoned that the high temperature caused by
the malaria killed the spirochetes that cause syphilis and
that were producing the mental disorder, paresis, in patients
who had had syphilis for a long time. In 1920, when he
was reasonably sure that this could not be an accident, he
published his findings.

Immediately scientists all over the world began injecting
blood from malaria patients into their paretics, with generally gratifying results. Since the fever was the agent that
produced the desired results, other methods of inducing
high fever in paresis patients were tried, among them short
radio waves. The malaria method continued to be the favorite, but presented one rather serious drawback. This was
the fact that the blood of malaria patients might contain
the causative organisms of other diseases besides malaria.
These were transmitted to the paresis patients along with
the malaria, sometimes with fatal results. To avoid this
danger, scientists of the U. S. Public Health Service and
of the Ministry of Health in London decided to let the
mosquitoes, in which the malaria parasite spends part of its
life cycle, do the job of infecting the paresis patients with
malaria. They knew that this was the way people acquired

LIFE HISTORY OF MALARIAL PARASITE IN MAN AND IN
MOSQUITO

FIGURE 14

IN the first picture (above left), an infected mosquito has bitten a man,
and the parasites, called sporozoites, enter the blood, making their way
into the red corpuscles. They mature, and then the sexless parasite begins
to divide, forming spores which finally break out of the old corpuscle and
enter a new one, starting the cycle over again. This takes two days. The
man, being infected, is now bitten by an uninfected mosquito, and the
malarial parasite passes into the mosquito's stomach with the human

malaria naturally. They were gratified to find that the mosquito acts as a sort of filter for other disease germs. No matter what might be picked up with the malaria parasites in the blood the mosquito has sucked, it is only the malaria that is transmitted when the insect bites its next victim.

Once this point was established, the U. S. Public Health Service set one of its entomological experts, Dr. Bruce Mayne, at the job of breeding the anopheles mosquito, which is the malaria-carrying one, and letting it suck blood from malaria patients in a Southern hospital where there is always a plentiful supply of these patients. The infected mosquitoes were then sent to hospitals in the North and West, where there is no natural source of malaria for treating paresis. This was rather expensive, since a medically trained attendant had to go along to see that the mosquitoes reached their destination safely, that they did not escape into the community to start a malaria epidemic, and that they performed their task of infecting paresis patients with curative malaria. There was a heavy loss to be borne with every shipment, since nearly two thirds of the insects in each lot were either dead or too feeble to bite when they reached their destination. Nor was there any way of knowing definitely whether or not the individual mosquito was

LIFE HISTORY OF MALARIAL PARASITE IN MAN AND IN
MOSQUITO—2

blood (opposite right). Next day fertilization takes place and the fertilized cell, called the ookinete, burrows through the mosquito's stomach wall. The ookinete (above left) forms a cyst under the stomach wall lining and begins to divide and form sporozoites. Meanwhile the cyst enlarges. Finally the sporozoites escape from it and migrate to the mosquito's salivary gland. From fertilization to invasion of this gland takes five days or more. In the gland (above right) the malarial parasites wait until the mosquito again bites, when the cycle is repeated.

actually infected. It might have failed to catch any malaria parasites with the blood it sucked from the malaria patient, and the paresis patient, consequently, had to be bitten by several mosquitoes. Fortunately, the paresis patients do not seem to mind this. However, Dr. Mayne figured that it was costing the government $200 per mosquito to get the insect bred, infected with malaria, and transported to the paresis patient outside the malaria belt.

Trying to find an easier, more economical way of using mosquitoes to transmit malaria, he recalled that when the mosquito bites, it deposits on its victim's skin a bit of saliva which contains the malaria parasites. This gave him the idea of trying to give the paresis patient malaria by injecting into his veins the salivary glands of a malaria-carrying mosquito. The results were entirely satisfactory; the paresis patient gets his dose of curative malaria; Dr. Mayne can be sure that each gland shipped will be useful in producing malaria; and the cost is much reduced, since the glands are packed in a thermos bottle, to keep them at the desired temperature, and sent by mail.

Paresis, which is an end-result of syphilis, is a familiar old evil spirit that has inhabited men's minds and caused untold anguish for very many years. The fight to cast it out has largely been carried on by modern medicine men, but medicine men of the very earliest days tried to drive out another devil which we know under the name of epilepsy. This name is given to a condition characterized by recurrent fits and attacks of unconsciousness, although medicine men believe that the fits and unconscious spells are due to various fundamental causes and are not all one disease.

Epilepsy and the Tapeworm

A VERY RECENT DISCOVERY is that some cases diagnosed as true epilepsy are actually cases of infestation with tapeworm larvæ. Apparently convincing proof of this was presented to the Royal Society of Tropical Medicine, in December, 1933, by Col. W. P. MacArthur, professor of tropical medicine at the Royal Army Medical College and consulting physician to the British Army. The epileptic seizures are due to invasion of the brain by the eggs of the tapeworm (which form small, cyst-like masses called cysticerci), and particularly to the degeneration of these parasites after they have died, Col. MacArthur explained. He has found as many as two hundred cysticerci in some brains.

Investigating the occurrence of epilepsy among soldiers, he found over sixty definite cases of infestation with cysticerci. Twenty such cases have been diagnosed in London hospitals during 1933. Six of eight soldiers recently invalided from India and victims of cysticercosis had been certified as cases of "true epilepsy." These cases of cysticercosis, which is the medical name for the condition, have no symptoms to distinguish them from ordinary epilepsy. Cases of cysticercosis had been wrongly diagnosed as acute mania, melancholia, delusional insanity, dementia, brain tumors, and the nervous disease, disseminated sclerosis. Col. MacArthur believes that in England many persons in civil life who have been stigmatized as hereditarily insane are suffering from cysticercosis acquired during residence abroad.

Another condition which appears to be epilepsy has recently been traced to tumor of the pancreas with increased production of insulin and consequently greatly decreased amount of sugar in the blood. This condition, called hyperinsulinism, is practically the opposite of diabetes. As a result of the lack of sugar, the patients suffer from convulsions which are often mistaken for epilepsy, and from mental confusion resembling that of alcoholic intoxication. Removal of the pancreatic tumor has relieved the condition. In one case it was necessary to remove nearly seven eighths of the pancreas with the tumor. This is said to be the first time so large a portion of the pancreas has ever been removed as a curative measure. The operation was performed by Dr. Evarts Graham, a St. Louis surgeon. The patient was a year-old infant who had had repeated epileptic-like convulsions and whose mental development was retarded. One week after the operation the amount of sugar in the blood had returned to normal and remained so, and the convulsions stopped.

Many other causes of epilepsy have been suggested, both psychological and physical. A recent study of complete histories of 1,000 epileptics indicates that while the disease itself is not inherited, vulnerability to it may be. Present methods of treating the condition are largely dietetic. Many authorities find that epileptics get along better and with fewer convulsive attacks when they eat relatively large amounts of fat and very little carbohydrates, that is, sugar and starchy foods.

The importance of the amount of water in the body in this condition has also been investigated by modern medicine men, although ever since the time of Hippocrates a "moist" brain has been associated with epilepsy. Dr. Temple Fay of Philadelphia believes that the abnormally large amount of fluid found over the cortex of the brains of epileptics at post-mortem examination increases the pressure and that this causes the convulsions. When the pressure is relieved by operation, the convulsions cease, he and other physicians have observed.

Another modern medicine man, Dr. Irvine McQuarrie of the University of Minnesota School of Medicine, believes that the cause of epilepsy may be faulty structure of the brain cells, which appears to let some of the important mineral, potassium, leak out or to let other substances enter when much water is drunk.

When epileptic patients are kept from drinking much water, many of them do not have convulsions, Dr. McQuarrie found, and they excrete much more sodium and chlorine than potassium. When under certain conditions these patients are allowed to drink large amounts of water, so that some of it is stored in the body cells, the reverse is true. The patients have epileptic convulsions, and at least twenty-four hours before these start, the amount of potassium in the urine may be found to be very much increased. This, Dr. McQuarrie thinks, indicates a "leak" of potassium from somewhere in the body, probably from the brain cells.

The convulsions, which occur when water is stored in the epileptic's body, without storage at the same time of a certain amount of mineral matter, are due to dilution of the body fluids surrounding the cells, Dr. McQuarrie suggested. When just enough common salt (sodium chloride) is added to the diet to keep the extra water from diluting the body fluids, the convulsion tends to be prevented.

Psychoanalysis

A STRICTLY MODERN METHOD of driving out the devils of mental and nervous diseases, although first promulgated over thirty years ago, is psychoanalysis. This method has been the subject of much discussion by both scientists and laymen. Scientific opinion has differed sharply on it, although it has now become an accepted method of handling certain types of disease. A careful and unbiased evaluation of it was reported by two New York physicians, Drs. Leo Kessel and Harold Thomas Hyman.

"Despite our receptive attitude toward psychoanalysis as a form of therapy, in twelve years we have seen only a handful of patients who have benefited from their experiences," they declared in their statement to the American Medical Association in November, 1933.

Of 33 patients, 16 were classified as failures. This group included all the patients suffering from mental disease, as distinguished from nervous disease, and all patients over the age of forty at the time of the analysis. Seventeen of the patients, slightly over half, were helped. In five the cure was considered specific. In the other cases, the results were good but not startling, and in some cases were due to modified circumstances in the patient's life.

The New York physicians considered as a specific and successful result the patient who, as a result of his character portrayal, so rebuilt his personality as to be able to live in harmony in his peculiar and particular surroundings; in addition, the result must have been obtainable only by psychoanalysis. They considered the analysis unsuccessful if the patient continued to have symptoms after it, if he discontinued the analysis, or if he was compelled to alter his way of life as a confession of inability to make an adjustment.

Among the limitations which they list for the method

are the facts that few physicians are at present qualified to practise it; the method takes so much time that each physician can only treat a very few cases each year, and the expense of the treatment is prohibitive for most patients. Disappointing also appears to be the fact that the method offers least help in cases of actual mental disease, drug addiction, and alcoholism, where the need is greatest.

However, Drs. Kessel and Hyman believe that the Freudian school offers the only intelligent approach toward the successful management of many psychiatric problems, and that it has influenced widely the physician's manner of thinking and approach to many of the problems met in everyday practice.

The task of driving out the devils appears to be enormous and difficult. Lay persons are not qualified to handle the job, and even physicians feel, for the most part, that they need several years of special training before they are competent to care for patients requiring treatment for complex disorders of the mind and nervous system. The way has been shown toward humane treatment of the insane and toward prevention of mental and nervous disease. The cry now is for better trained psychiatrists, and more of them, to guide the preventive efforts and to care for the unavoidable cases of mental sickness.

CHAPTER 24
RACE BETTERMENT

THE IDEA OF COMPULSORY STERILIZATION of the unfit of an entire nation astounded many people when Hitler's law for Germany was first proposed and again when it was actually enacted. Yet in parts of the United States and other countries eugenic sterilization is an accomplished fact.

This has come about as part of the growing movement for race betterment. The movement was started by a group of forward-looking persons who considered the enormous improvement in races of plants and animals other than man that resulted from discovery of the laws of heredity and their intelligent application. These people saw no reason why similar methods should not be adopted for the improvement of the human race. The support of many others has been won to the cause by the burdensome and ever growing problem of caring for the unfit members of society.

In a wide sense, race betterment is furthered by education, by disease prevention, and by improvement of the health and living conditions of the people. More specifically it could be accomplished by scientific breeding of men, as of other animals. Since it is almost impossible to make human beings improve their breed, leaders in the movement for race betterment have attacked the problem from the negative angle of breeding out the undesirable elements of the race by means of eugenic sterilization. This, ostensibly, is the reason for Hitler's adoption of compulsory sterilization of the unfit in Nazi Germany. It is the reason why more than half the states in this country, twenty-eight, to be exact, and several foreign countries now have eugenic sterilization laws on their statute books.

The subject has been heatedly and protractedly dis-

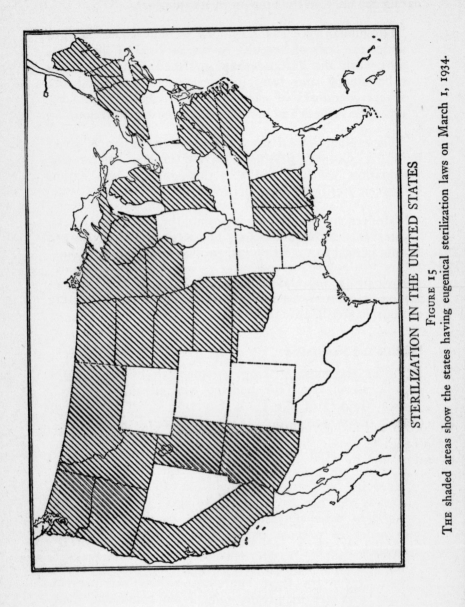

STERILIZATION IN THE UNITED STATES

FIGURE 15

THE shaded areas show the states having eugenical sterilization laws on March 1, 1934.

cussed. Eugenic sterilization is an aid to nature in eliminating the unfit, in the opinion of its sponsors.

"The human race has developed through countless ages under the laws of heredity by the survival of the fittest. The weak and defective have perished. Only the physically strong and mentally alert could withstand the severe conditions of early life, reach maturity and become the fathers and mothers of the next generation."

This explanation of the need for sterilization is given by E. S. Gosney, president of the Human Betterment Foundation, which is active in the fight for legalization of eugenic sterilization in this country.

"Modern civilization, human sympathy, and charity have intervened in Nature's plan. The weak and defective are now nursed to maturity and produce their kind."

Such protection and encouragement of the unfit is misguided humanitarianism, Mr. Gosney and other supporters of eugenic sterilization contend.

The Law and Sterilization

PERHAPS the most striking argument in favor of legal eugenic sterilization for humans was advanced by Mr. Justice Holmes of the U. S. Supreme Court in handing down a decision upholding the Virginia sterilization law.

"We have seen more than once that the public welfare may call upon the best citizens for their lives," he said. "It would be strange if it could not call upon those who already sap the strength of the state for these lesser sacrifices, often not felt to be such by those concerned, in order to prevent our being swamped with incompetence. It is better for all the world, if instead of waiting to execute degenerate offspring for crime, or to let them starve for their imbecility, society can prevent those who are manifestly unfit from continuing their kind."

"Three generations of imbeciles are enough," he commented, referring to the fact that the case had been appealed by a feeble-minded inmate of a state institution, daughter of a feeble-minded woman and mother of an illegitimate, feeble-minded child, but who objected to being sterilized.

On the other hand, eugenic sterilization is opposed as being unscientific and unfair. One group of its opponents question whether society or the state is justified in depriving the individual of his or her right to bear children. Another group, appealing less to emotion and more to reason, question whether enough is known of the laws of heredity to justify eugenic sterilization.

Eugenics is a young science, Dr. J. H. Landman pointed out at the recent meeting of the American Society of Zoölogists. Dr. Landman is instructor in history in the College of the City of New York. His interest in the matter, aroused by legal aspects of eugenic sterilization, led him to investigate the eugenic, social, and therapeutic value of this kind of legislation.

"Much that is myth, fable, or postulate passes for scientific fact," he declared. "The scant scientific eugenic knowledge has been prostituted to justify ancestor worship, race superiority, snobbery, class distinction, intellectual aristocracy, and race prejudice.

"It is this meager genuinely scientific knowledge of eugenics that constitutes justification for compulsory human sterilization."

While Dr. Landman merely raises the question of whether eugenic sterilization is justified, opponents of the measure take a more definite stand. Not enough is known about heredity for anyone to say surely that a child of given parentage will positively be so diseased or defective as to become a burden to himself and society, they contend. In this connection another argument is raised. Medical science and the healing art have made remarkable progress and, it is hoped, will go even further in the conquest of disease. Consequently, it is going too far to say that neither the "unfit" parents nor their child can ever be cured of disease or defect and made "fit."

A third argument is that it may prevent the birth of a genius or of some great benefactor to humanity. This is based on the fact that some geniuses and benefactors have come from stock which the eugenicists would have labeled as "unfit." Still another argument against eugenic sterilization is that unscrupulous persons in authority in penal, reform, and mental disease institutions may use it unfairly.

Methods of Sterilization

WHILE THE WISDOM of eugenic sterilization is still under discussion, the actual method of achieving it has been worked out and fairly well standardized by medical scientists.

Sterilization for eugenic purposes, or for medical reasons when the health of the individual seems to require it, is a simple surgical procedure. For women it is an abdominal operation called salpingectomy and is practically equivalent to an easy operation for "chronic" appendicitis in relative simplicity and speed.

"It is a major operation involving two weeks or more in the hospital, but the risk to life is negligible; one California surgeon has performed more than five hundred without a fatality or single serious complication," states one authority.

Vasectomy, the operation for sterilization in men, can be performed in the surgeon's office in five or ten minutes. It is practically bloodless. In state hospitals the patient is generally kept in bed for a day or two to prevent complications. When the operation is done in private practice, the patient usually walks away to his work and does not lose any time.

Sterilization by modern methods does not involve the removal of any glands or organs and does not affect the individual in any way except to prevent his or her having any children. Vasectomy and salpingectomy are not the

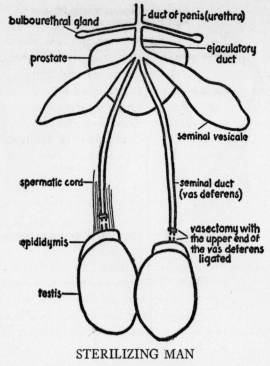

bulbourethral gland

duct of penis (urethra)

prostate

ejaculatory duct

seminal vesicale

spermatic cord

seminal duct (vas deferens)

epididymis

vasectomy with the upper end of the vas deferens ligated

testis

STERILIZING MAN

FIGURE 16

THE diagram shows the important morphological parts of man's genital apparatus. It also shows the more usual type of vasectomy or male sterilization, i.e., the ligation of the severed seminal ducts leading from the testes.

From *Human Sterilization*, by J. H. Landman. © *The Macmillan Company.*

same as castration. They do not change the appearance of the patient or alter his emotional state; neither do they bring on or hasten the changes incident to physiological aging which occur naturally. Salpingectomy consists in tying and cutting the Fallopian tubes or oviducts down which the ova or egg cells pass into the uterus. Vasectomy consists in similarly closing the tubes that carry the spermatozoa from the glands where they are secreted.

To understand the operation, it must be remembered that the reproductive organs have two functions: one is to produce the germ cells, the ova and spermatozoa; the other is to produce hormones which diffuse through the body and

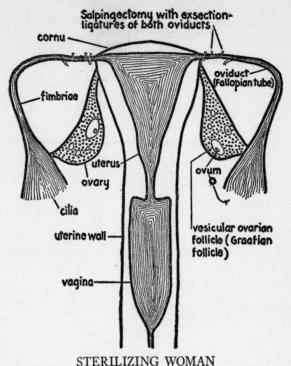

Salpingectomy with exsection-
ligatures of both oviducts

cornu

oviduct
(Fallopian tube)

fimbriae

uterus
ovary

ovum

cilia

uterine wall

vesicular ovarian
follicle (Graafian
follicle)

vagina

STERILIZING WOMAN
FIGURE 17

THE diagram shows the more important morphological parts of woman's
genital organs. It also shows the more usual type of salpingectomy, or
female sterilization, i.e., the ligation of the oviducts.

From *Human Sterilization*, by J. H. Landman. © *The Macmillan Company.*

maintain youth and vigor. The sterilization operation prevents the union of the germ cells from which offspring
develop, but in no way interferes with the secretion of the
hormones.

X-rays and radium have been tried as agents of sterilization, but present several disadvantages. The dosage is
doubtful, and the results may be only temporary, or if permanent may be equivalent to castration, since the radiation
may destroy the hormone-producing part of the glands.

Neither vasectomy nor salpingectomy is infallible. Occasionally sealed channels have reopened, either because the
walls failed to adhere to close the passage, or because the

stitches, taken to hold the cut ends until they adhered, had themselves cut through the tissues, leaving a tiny opening. The success of either operation may be determined by relatively simple tests.

Other methods of sterilization, particularly for women, have been tried, and according to one authority there is need for further experimentation in this field to find a better method than salpingectomy, which is a serious and comparatively painful operation. Injections of sex hormones have been tried as a means of temporary sterilization, but sterilization for eugenic purposes is generally intended to be permanent.

Sterilization Laws

SPONSORS of the eugenic sterilization movement in this country are working to increase the number of statutes providing for it until it includes the full roster of states. Furthermore, some of the states not now on the list formerly had such laws, but for various reasons, chiefly because of ineffectual or unconstitutional provisions, these have been repealed.

Outside of this country and Germany, Denmark, the Canton of Vaud in Switzerland, and the Canadian province of Alberta have eugenic sterilization laws. Movements in this direction have been started in England, Western Australia, Norway, Sweden, and Finland.

Up to January 1st of last year, sterilization operations had been performed on 16,066 persons in the United States. The first eugenic human sterilization bill in the United States was introduced in the Michigan Legislature in 1897. An act providing for such sterilization was passed by the Pennsylvania Legislature in 1905 but was vetoed. Indiana's sterilization law is the oldest, having been passed in 1907. California and Connecticut followed two years later. Vermont and Oklahoma are the states most recently enacting such laws, both in 1931.

The state laws differ greatly in details, but in general they provide that inmates of state and sometimes of county institutions for the insane, feeble-minded, and epileptic are to be sterilized on the recommendation of the superintendent when approved by a board of physicians. The board must have examined the patient and his history and be convinced (1) that the patient is unlikely to recover from the condition for which he is in the institution and consequently will never be able to provide or care for any children he may have; and (2) that the disease from which the patient suffers is likely to appear in his children, if any. Further, some states provide that persons not inmates of institutions but wishing to be sterilized for eugenic, health, or economic reasons, and who cannot afford to have this done privately, may have it done free of charge at some state institution after giving written consent. In some states the sterilization of inmates may be performed only with the consent of the inmate or his legal guardian. In others the inmate or his guardian or nearest kin is given the right to appeal to the courts. According to some of the laws, sterilization is to be performed only on inmates of state institutions, including reformatories and prisons, before parole or release. Sterilization is also allowed in some states either with or without the consent of the individual, when the medical board believes it will benefit the individual's health. At least five states prohibit unauthorized sterilization operations except as a medical necessity; for example, if a woman's health might be impaired or her life endangered by having children.

CHAPTER 25
STUDYING HUMAN BEHAVIOR

No ONE HAS SEEN A MIND. No one knows exactly what a mind may be. Many psychologists, indeed, have come to doubt that the human mind is a proper object of scientific inquiry. No one has ever observed a brain while it is alive and functioning in human thought. Yet its nature, and the natural laws governing its behavior, are of paramount importance in erecting social structures and avoiding social calamities such as the great depression. The psychologist attempting to study man's mind is in something of the predicament of the physicist who essays the study of electricity. These scientists cannot see or hear or feel the materials of their research, but must reach conclusions through the indirect but instructive method of observing the resulting behavior.

What of man's behavior is instinctive—automatic response controlled by his hereditary nature? And what is the result of his training and environment? This is an old controversy: nature *vs.* nurture. New evidence has been found to indicate the extreme importance of early training in infancy.

What is the original equipment of senses with which we comprehend the world? No one knows just how his own particular universe appears to the new-born infant, but recent researches indicate that it does not greet him in the form of the "great booming, buzzing confusion" conceived by psychologists a few decades ago. Infants can see objects about them from the moment of birth, although just how they view them is not yet known. They can also distinguish sounds and perfumes.

New light has been thrown on the theories of hearing— that perplexing question of how sound waves of varying

284

frequencies reach the brain and are interpreted as tones of different pitches.

The psychoanalytic school of psychology has had a great influence in stimulating the study of the early training of children because of the emphasis placed by this theory on the importance of early impressions and emotional experiences. If the conflicts and mental ailments and blemishes of adult life can be traced to an origin in some injury to the growing personality of the baby, then how important the first few pre-school years become from the standpoint of mental hygiene and healthful development!

From another point of view, the behaviorist leads to the same emphasis on pre-school education. The native endowment of the child is of minimum importance, according to the behaviorist, who has demonstrated that much of the equipment of the individual previously considered to be "instinctive" or hereditary is actually the result of learning in very early life or perhaps even before birth.

A child has no instinctive fear of wild or other animals, they tell us. He is by nature frightened by loud and sudden noises. If a dog appears, barking loudly, the child then learns fear of dogs or perhaps of all four-footed animals. This process is termed "conditioning."

It is only a little over a decade since Dr. John B. Watson, father of behaviorism, in researches conducted with the many newly arrived infants at the Johns Hopkins Hospital, found that the original, truly instinctive fears are not more than two: fear of loud noises, and fear of sudden loss of support or of dropping through space.

A successor of his, studying infants at the same university, Dr. W. C. Beasley, has narrowed this brief list even more by eliminating the fear of loss of support. This fear must be acquired, too, it seems. For the youngest infants do not show any sign of fright at dropping, provided they receive no rough handling in the process, but come volplaning down on a soft pillow which is stopped without jar at the end of the drop. On the contrary they enjoy the sensation as children of a flying age should.

By the time the six-year-old applies for admission to school to "begin" his education, he already has acquired an

AGES OF MAN—INFANCY
Figure 18

Chronological Age	Mental Age	Developmental Age	Motor Age	Anatomical Age (Provisional) (Ossification in hand and foot) Centers for		Psychotic Age: Parallel Behavior, Infants and Mental Patients (Level of retrogression of mental patients)
				Boys	Girls	
2 months	Regards mother's face with deep interest—Makes several different vocalizations—Eyes follow moving person—Watches dangling ring.	Makes facial response to close approach of adult.	Lifts chest when prone—makes arm thrusts.	Capitatum (wrist bone)	Capitatum (wrist bone)	Absence of contact with others — Motionless — Continual soiling—Drooling—No use of, or any understanding of, words. Psychotic age, 3 months. Diagnosis: Schizophrenia (simple).
4 months	Examines adult's mouth movements in speaking — Shows displeasure when ring is taken away.	Smiles definitely at another infant—Laughs aloud — Responds by crows to adults' play—Plays in simple manner with rattle—Splashes in bath.	Reaches for dangling objects — Holds head steady when carried—Lifts head and shoulders from position on back—Sits when supported.	Tibia distal (lower end shin bone, leg)	Tibia distal (lower end shin bone, leg)	
6 months	Turns head toward ringing bell—Vocalizes several well-defined syllables—Listens to speech attentively—At table, will handle and scratch it—Can hold 1 object each hand briefly.	Plays with rattle—Plays with ring—Crows or coos actively—Enjoys manipulation of objects —Smiles responsively at adults—Shows recognition of familiars.	Takes real grasp of spoon—Can seize a cube —Fingers coördinate—Sits momentarily without support.	Fibula distal (lower end splint bone, leg)	Radius distal (lower end outer bone forearm)	Indifference to other people—Grimacing—Mannerisms—Repetition of words and movements —Solitary play. Psychotic age: 6 months. Diagnosis: Schizophrenia (hebephrenic).

286

8 months	Bangs vigorously on table—Looks for dropped toy—Engages in genuine game with toy.	Gives voice to recognition—Responds to frolic play—Pats or smiles at image in mirror.	Raises self to sitting position.	Radius distal (lower end outer bone, forearm)	Third finger 1st phalanx (bone nearest palm in middle finger)	Periodic rage—Rigid immobility—Repetition of words and movements of others—Unintelligible babbling—Hurting of self. Psychotic age: 12 months Diagnosis: Schizophrenia, catatonic excitement or catatonic stupor.
10 months	Responds to request "Give me the spoon" by moving it but tightening hold — Imitates sounds—Can hold 2 objects.	Makes advances toward another infant—Dangles ring by string in play—Plays "peek-a-boo."	Pulls up to standing position—Can pick up small object with finger and thumb.	Third finger, 1st phalanx (bone nearest palm in middle finger)	II Metacarpal (bone of palm in line of index finger)	
12 months	Can play with 2 objects, banging them together—Says 4 words—Uses jargon—Can hold 3 objects — Uses spoon — Helps in dressing.	Repeats performance laughed at—Uses string to pull ring—Waves "Bye-Bye."	Stands alone — Walks alone—Builds tower of two blocks.	Great toe 2nd phalanx (bone under nail)	III Metacarpal (bone of palm in line of middle finger)	
14 months	Uses sentence of 2 words—Names picture—Repeats things said.		Walks on street—Walks backward.	II Metacarpal (bone of palm in line of index finger)	V Metacarpal (bone of palm in line of little finger)	Hatred of parents for punishment or deprivations—Sulking—Negativism—Resentment of control of actions by others—Limited sociability—Egoism. Psychotic age: 15 months. Diagnosis: Schizophrenia (paranoid).
16 months	Piles up 7 or 8 blocks—Can give full name—Helps to put away belongings.		Goes up and down stairs alone—Tries to stand on one foot.	III Metacarpal (bone of palm in line of middle finger)	I Metacarpal (bone of palm in line of thumb)	

AGES OF MAN—INFANCY (*Continued*)

Chronological Age	Mental Age	Developmental Age	Motor Age	Anatomical Age (Provisional) (Ossification in hand and foot) Centers for		Psychotic Age: Parallel Behavior Infants and Mental Patients (Level of retrogression of mental patients)
				Boys	Girls	
18 months	Understands forbidding—Looks behind mirror for reflection—Uses tool to pull object within reach—Says 5 or more words—Points to nose, eyes, or hair.	Turns pages of book—Looks at pictures.	Can hold something while walking alone—Climbs on stool—Can stand on one foot.	V Metacarpal (bone of palm in line of little finger)	I Metatarsal (bone of sole in line of great toe)	Dogmatism—Resentment of control—Fearful of injury by others.
2 years	Obeys simple commands—Understands 2 prepositions—Names 3 of 5 objects—Points to 5 objects on card—Uses words in combination—Creases paper in imitation—Vocabulary, 272 words.	Places blocks in row to make train—Individual play — Interested in other children, but does not play with them—Plays with mimicry—Tells experiences—Plays catch, kiddie car, sand.	Runs—Piles tower of six blocks—Imitates vertical or horizontal strokes—Can guide a kiddie car around objects—Walks up and down steps touching wall.	I Metatarsal (bone of sole in line of great toe)	II Metatarsal (bone of sole in line of second toe)	Psychotic age: 21 months. Diagnosis: Paranoid and delusional states.
3 years	Can copy a circle in 3 trials—Knows 5 prepositions — Names key, penny, knife, watch, pencil—Repeats 6 to 7 syllables—Vocabulary, 896 words.	Question-asking age.	Can cut with scissors successfully — Can hit nail with hammer—Can button front buttons—Can wash himself—Walks up and down steps not touching wall.	III Metatarsal (bone of sole in line of middle toe)	V Metatarsal (bone of sole in line of little toe)	Pressure of activity—Distractibility—Egotism—Irritability—Destructiveness—Personification of inanimate objects and lower animals—Docility—Indecision—Apprehension of punishment.

				Boys	Girls	
4 years	Can copy a cross, square—Counts 4 pennies—Repeats 4 digits—Vocabulary, 1,540 words.	Plays in groups of four or five.	Can manage all buttons—Can bounce a ball—Likes to walk, run, jump, climb—Goes up steps alternating feet, no support.	Angularity of bases Metacarpals II-V (ends, adjoining wrist, of bones in palm)	Medial (ulnar) extension of ossification in distal epiphysis radius (end, adjoining wrist, of outer bone forearm)	Psychotic age: 30 months, 2½ years. Diagnosis: Delirious and confusional mania. Delirious and confusional depression.
5 years	Can draw imitatively a triangle and a prism—Names 4 colors—Gives age—Vocabulary, 2,072 words.	Ring around a rosy—Farmer in the dell—Plays coöperatively with other children.	Can lace shoes—Can hop, skip, jump down steps—Turns somersaults—Goes down steps, alternating feet, no support.	Boat-shaped outline distal epiphysis radius (end, adjoining wrist, of outer bone forearm)	Same as boys	

AGES OF MAN—CHILDHOOD

FIGURE 19

CHRONOLOGICAL AGE	MENTAL AGE	DEVELOPMENTAL AGE		ANATOMICAL AGE (Provisional) Contour of bony outlines in ossifying epiphyses (cartilaginous bone ends)	
		Boys	Girls	Boys	Girls
6 years	Knows right from left—Counts 13 pennies—Can name nickel, penny, quarter, dime—Repeats 16 to 18 syllables—Vocabulary, 2,562 words.	Plays house, Indians, school, etc.—Likes tag, scooters—Enjoys simple nature stories — 81% play with girls.	Plays house, dolls, ring games — Likes cutting out with scissors, looking at pictures—Enjoys simple nature stories.	Angular outline of epiphyses for metacarpals II-V (bones of palm except thumb)	Same as boys.
8 years	Can count backwards 20 to 1—Can give similarities between common objects—Defines otherwise than by giving use — Vocabulary, 3,600 words.	Still interested in dramatic games, house, Indians, school, etc. — Plays hide-and-seek, etc. —Growing self-assertion —End of Santa Claus—Begins to like reading—73% play with girls.	Plays house, dolls, cutting out, pictures—Likes hide-and-seek, jacks, drawing, swinging, sliding—Reads fairy tales.	Bases metacarpals II-V quite angular (bones of palm except thumb)	Boat-like contour on distal epiphysis of radius (lower end outer bone forearm) has sharply angulated lateral outline and almost covers end of shaft.
10 years	Can detect absurdities—Can name 60 words in 3 minutes—Repeats 6 digits or 20 syllables—Vocabulary, 5,400 words.	Beginning of interest in team games and clubs—Beginning of gangs—Loss of interest in girls —Likes stories of invention, biography — Meccanno—64% play with girls.	Beginning of interest in love stories, like stories of home and school—Last of keen interest in jumping rope and cutting out—Drawing.	Boat-like contour on distal epiphysis of radius (lower end outer bone forearm) has sharply angulated lateral outline and almost covers end of shaft.	Vertical ridges on sides of epiphyses of metacarpals II-V (bones of palm) plainly visible

12 years	Can define abstract terms like pity, justice—Can interpret fables—Repeats 5 digits reversed—Interprets pictures (tells their story, not just description)—Vocabulary, 7,200 words.	Team games popular—Clubs—Period of restless activity—Avoids girls—Likes adventure books, electric trains, mecanno—Only 20% play with girls.	Avoids boys — Likes dancing with girls, and zesthetic (fancy) dancing—Enjoys girls' books—Movies—Loses interest in dolls.	Vertical ridges on sides of epiphyses of metacarpals II-V (bones of palm) plainly visible	Sharp recurved outlines on distal epiphysis of radius (lower end outer bone of forearm)
14 years	Can give difference between a president and a king—Arithmetical reasoning—Repeats 7 digits—Vocabulary, 9,000 words.	Beginning of social interest in other sex—Interest in clothes begins—Waning interest in adventure stories—Reads about mechanics and inventions—Plays football—70% play with girls.	Interest in boys begins—Awakening of great interest in dress—Ball-room dancing—Definite ideas about vocation—Likes team games—Reads adult fiction, much sentimental fiction—Shows lack of self-consciousness with elders.	Sharp recurved outlines on distal epiphysis of radius (lower end outer bone of forearm)	All epiphyses of phalanges (fingers) united. Epiphyses of metacarpals (bones of palm) uniting
16 years	Can give difference between abstract terms like ignorance and stupidity—Repeats 6 digits reversed or 28 syllables—Adult intelligence—Vocabulary, 11,700 words.	Increase of social interest in other sex—Adult reading—Adult recreation—64% play with girls.	Loss of interest in outdoor games — Adult reading, especially sentimental fiction—Adult recreation.	Union with shafts of epiphyses of all terminal phalanges hand (bones under nails)	Distal epiphyses of radius and ulna (bones of forearm) uniting

These tables (Figures 18 and 19) are based on the results of scientific investigation showing what the average child can do at different ages. In many cases the results are provisional and they should not be considered as standardized instruments for measuring. By way of explanation of the Anatomical Age Scale, it should be pointed out that much of what is hard bone in adults is soft cartilage in the young, and therefore the age at which the centers of ossification in the bone first appear, and the age at which the epiphyses, or cartilage disks at the ends of certain bones, complete their attachment to the main shaft of the bone, have been found to be very significant in indicating physical development. Credit for the material in these two tables is particularly given to Dr. Lewis M. Terman and Dr. Charlotte Buhler for the Mental Age Scale; to Dr. Paul H. Furfey for the Developmental Age Scale; to Drs. Mary M. Shirley, L. Dewey Anderson, and Magda Skalet Skeel for the Motor Age Scale; to Dr. T. Wingate Todd, Dr. C. C. Francis, H. V. Morley, and P. P. Werle for the Anatomical Age Scale; to Dr. George E. Gardner for the Psychotic Age Scale, and to Dr. Arnold Gesell.

enormously complex equipment of conditioned responses, habits, and skills added to his inherited mental wealth. Partly through the instruction of his parents and associates, but largely through accident, he is by the age of six already pretty well educated or modified by experience.

In recognition of this finding, the school age is being pushed nearer and nearer to the cradle days. The kindergarten of a few years ago is being superseded by the nursery school where infants of two years or even younger are "conditioned" along approved lines. Many have been organized by the Federal Emergency Relief Administration to give employment and at the same time to place the benefits of these schools within the reach of those who cannot afford to pay for the advantage.

But just how great an advantage is correct early training to the child? the psychologist asks. What happens to the child who is deprived of it? Is he irreparably harmed by this neglect, or do nature and heredity proceed quietly with his development in spite of, or regardless of, the early influences of school and home?

The Remarkable Twins

NOTABLE, IN PROVIDING a partial answer to this vital question, is the experiment to which Johnny and Jimmy, twin infant sons of a New York taxi driver, have contributed. One of these boys, Johnny, who is now only a two-year-old, has been given special training and exercises from the time he was but twenty days old. The other was left undisturbed in his crib to follow the usual routine of the unhandled modern infant. Dr. Myrtle B. McGraw, of the Normal Child Development Clinic of Babies Hospital, conducted the training and is responsible for the interesting results of the experiment.

In some matters, she found, Nature takes her own course and cannot be hurried or diverted. Both babies learned to sit alone, to reach for their toys, and to stand erect at very nearly the same time. In fact, their development along these lines was surprisingly parallel, although the question of whether they are identical twins is in doubt.

The primitive reflexes—that mysterious equipment of

response to certain situations that infants seem to have as a sort of hold-over from their ape-like ancestors—appeared and disappeared at the same time in both children, and in this they resembled every normal infant who comes into this world. When a young infant has his hands placed on a rod, they will automatically and involuntarily close over it so firmly that he will hold his own weight for a considerable time. If he is lying on a bed and the bed is suddenly roughly jarred, his arms will fly up in a circular movement as though he were trying to embrace something. This latter reflex is strangely reminiscent of the baby monkey clinging to the mother lest he fall from his lofty tree-top nursery.

But these reflexes are soon lost, and training has no effect whatever on their course.

In motor skills, however, the differences between trained Johnny and untrained Jimmy are amazing. Johnny at the age of eighteen months could already roller skate, making turns, and coasting with poise and pleasure. He could swim under water. He could dive. He could walk up a slide tipped at the dizzy angle of sixty-one degrees, the angle produced by raising one end of a board six feet long on a support five feet high—an incline as nearly straight up as anything less sure-footed than a cat could hope to navigate. Jimmy would not even attempt these feats.

Of particular import to those interested in the character development of children is the amazing difference in personality between these two youngsters. It seems to be this subtle difference in personality that accounts for their divergent achievements. For Jimmy obviously has adequate motor and mental equipment for doing many of the performances of which Johnny is capable. What he lacks is the confidence that comes from meeting obstacles and mastering them.

Jimmy looks at the steep slant of the slide, hesitates, and turns away.

Johnny walks right up.

Jimmy, sitting at the top of the tall stool, holds out his arms with a winsome smile for some adult to help him down.

Johnny wiggles over onto his tummy, digs toes into the side of the stool, and kicks off.

"He has such confidence in himself and the world that after a few trials he will attempt anything he is directed to do," Dr. McGraw has said of Johnny.

Nevertheless, it is Jimmy, the winsome, cuddlesome, quiet boy, who is the favorite in the home. It would seem that the virtues ordinarily admired by adults and encouraged by them in the young are not those born of successful contact with life and adventure.

Dr. McGraw began her experiment with the twins when they were but twenty days old, but other psychologists have attempted to solve the riddle of the child mind from almost the very moment at which the young human breathes his first in this world, undaunted by the difficulties of contact with that mind.

In a way, the mysteries of the human mind are most impenetrable when hidden behind the velvet depths of the new-born infant's eyes. The baby does not speak our language, and we are at a loss to read his. His response to all situations is either a general, undifferentiated activity of legs and arms and trunk and lungs, or a placid repose which soon becomes slumber.

Out of the Minds of Babes

STILL, IF THE NEW-BORN is parsimonious with information about himself, at least he does not give false testimony. Human words too often serve only to conceal thought. Some are therefore seeking to read or interpret the principal means of expression of the infant, that is, activity. Devices are attached to the bed of the child which will record the generalized, all-over movement of the infant in proportion to its intensity. Or motion picture apparatus is made ready to snap a picture of it. Then, with the patience of a modern Job, the psychologist awaits the moment when the infant is sleeping quietly. This means that nothing already present in the environment is disturbing him.

Now the new element is introduced into the situation.

Perhaps it is the lovely (to adults) odor of violet or the disagreeable one of asafœtida. If then activity results, it is apparent that the child responds to that particular odor in that particular concentration.

The new-born does respond to odors, and the greater the concentration of odor, the greater the activity. Moreover, the little one only a scant three hours old responds just as well as his elder of ten days. Individual differences have been observed, but no noticeable age, sex, or race differences.

It was in the laboratories of Ohio State University that Dorothy R. Disher, working under the direction of Dr. F. C. Dockeray, discovered that the new-born can respond to the fragrance of flowers surrounding his mother's bed as well as to the less agreeable odors of the hospital.

Different odors, she found, vary in their capacity for evoking activity, but the infants showed no signs of being pleased with some and rejecting others. That may have been because likes and dislikes are not inborn but acquired, or it may mean merely that the infant cannot express his tastes.

Using a similar technique at the Iowa Child Welfare Research Station, LaBerta Weiss discovered that the new-born is able to distinguish different degrees of illumination or of sound. That he can tell moderately bright illumination from dim, and noises of low intensity from noisier ones, is demonstrated by his greater activity during the dimmer illuminations and less intense noises.

Scientific backing for the age-old custom of singing the baby to sleep was obtained by Dr. Karl C. Pratt at the Central State Teachers College, Mt. Pleasant, Mich., who observed that noise produces activity but that musical notes are quieting. But more interesting, because at variance with what had been taught for generations, is the discovery that the new-born can see.

Not blind, like the new-born kitten, but aware of all the many beauties of form and color and light and shade. Not the unresponsive lump of mere potentialities that has been pictured by psychologists of the past. An interesting observer of the world, already gaining experience, already learning, already subject to change by his environment, whether for better or worse; this is the 1934 picture given us of the new-born.

The fact that babies only three brief hours old can see objects and turn their heads to follow their movement with the eyes was demonstrated at Johns Hopkins University by Dr. W. C. Beasley. By means of a specially constructed projector and viewing screen, he has been able to obtain the first quantitative measurements on brightness discrimination, visual acuity, and accommodation in the new-born. By using special lighting to brightly illuminate the infant's eyes without injury or annoyance to the baby, and with the aid of a specially designed telescope for enlarging the eye, Dr. Beasley found out many things new to science.

The protective device nature provides for shielding the eye from painful intensities of light—a reflex contraction of the iris—is totally absent in many new-borns. Some are able to fixate both eyes on a single object, but others are not. It is this lack of ability to fix both eyes on a given point that gives to some young babies that cross-eyed or cock-eyed look.

Another ability concerning which Dr. Beasley has accumulated new information is the power of the lens in each eye to adjust itself to the changing distances of an object from the eyes of the infant. Unless these lenses, one in each eye, are in focus for the object viewed, the impression which the person gets is one of a blurred object.

The experiments show that new-born infants have very good vision at close range, but do not follow objects which are from sixteen to twenty-five inches away from their eyes. The optical systems of their eyes, which include a shorter optic axis and a thicker crystalline lens (shorter focal length) than that of the older child or adult, are adapted for near vision only.

Brain Action

NEW PROGRESS has been made toward understanding the action of the nerves in carrying impulses to and from the brain. When a stimulus such as a sound is regularly increased in intensity, the perceived intensity does not increase continuously but in small steps. The length of these steps constitutes the differential threshold; it is the smallest difference in the sound that can be perceived or noticed. Each new step may have a new quality and may produce a different kind of reaction. Research by Prof. H. Piéron, of the College of France, has led him to the conclusion that each of these steps up in perceived intensity represents the calling into action of an additional neuron, or nerve cell. The impulses characteristic of the neuron, are true "neuroquanta" analogous to the quanta of physical energy, Prof. Piéron believes, and it takes at least two neuroquanta to set in action a neuron in a cortical center of the brain.

Anatomists have also contributed information regarding the physical development of the brain and its bearing on the development of intelligence in the growing child. Researches conducted at the Western Reserve University by Drs. Y. T. Loo and T. Wingate Todd indicate that although it takes the human body about 20 years to reach its adult size, the brain matures in from four to six years, depending upon whether the child is well or poorly nurtured.

Thus the youngster who enters the first grade at school has a brain of adult size and development. Some parts of his brain were fully developed long before that time. The parts of the cerebrum which govern vision and hearing are fully grown and developed by the end of the first year. The area where memories are stored, and the area devoted to learning, grow vigorously from soon after birth but make their greatest changes before the child is two. The area utilized in attention and concentration, on the other hand, makes its most vigorous progress between two and six years.

This does not mean, however, that the child's intelligence ceases to develop at this early age. Intelligence, as measured by psychological tests, continues to grow for about the same length of time that the body continues to develop. It ceases growth usually by the age of eighteen, or at any rate in the early twenties.

By a more indirect route, the psychologist has also been

studying the brain. Certain errors made consistently by your different senses have served as clues for the research of Dr. George Kreezer, which he carried on at Berlin and at Cornell University. Just as the modern criminologist can examine microscopically the hair of an individual and reveal his identity, so this psychologist has analyzed these eccentricities of the senses to reveal the organization of the brain behind them.

Your senses play you certain tricks so consistently that they are well known to the psychologist who knows them as "time errors" and "space errors."

If you see a light of a certain intensity, and again, a few seconds later, see a light of exactly the same intensity, you will probably judge the second light to be slightly brighter than the first. This is a time error.

If you see a light a little to your left and then another of exactly the same intensity a little to your right, you will judge the left light to be brighter. This is a space error. Some persons—and they may be those with a tendency to left-handedness—are exceptions to this rule; they consistently judge the right light to be the brighter.

The errors do not all come from the eyes, however. If you hear a tone at your left and then another of exactly the same intensity at your right, you will judge the right tone to be louder—you will, that is, if you are one who judged the left light to be brighter. If you are one who sees the right light as brighter, you will hear the left tone as louder. Thus there appears to be some relation between these space errors of sight and hearing, but the relation is a negative one. The errors of hearing are consistent with, although opposite to, errors of vision. Yet each type of signal comes to the brain through separate sense organs and over separate networks of the brain's telegraph wires, the nerves.

These perception errors are not due to differences in the sense organs. Neither are they a matter of the nervous pathways to your brain. That has been established. They depend upon the brain itself. They indicate that a certain organization must exist in the brain which in some respects at least conforms to the space-time organization of the material world outside the self, and helps us to account for our perception of that world. For some reason as yet unknown, but due to the organization of the brain, left and right, sooner and later, here and there, give us different sense experiences.

The senses are another fertile field of research for the psychologist, for it is only through the contact with the world and with other individuals, obtained through the avenues of the senses, that mental life is made possible.

Sounds and Hearing

MUCH OF THE RECENT RESEARCH on the senses has been centered on the perplexing problem of how we hear. The deep rumble of the bass drum, the beautiful notes of a singer's voice, the high tones of the violin, the shrill shriek of a siren, and the almost inaudible squeak of insects all reach your ears as sound waves of various lengths and intensities. How are they differentiated by your hearing mechanism? How does your brain recognize them for the very different sounds that they are?

One theory that has been held in the past is that parts of the membrane of the ear are tuned to a certain frequency; that when the ear receives a sound of a particular frequency, a part of the membrane corresponding to that frequency would pick up the vibration in much the same manner that a string on a piano will sound when you stand before it and hum a tone. A nerve fiber attached to that part of the membrane would then conduct the impulse to the brain.

A second theory (the telephone frequency theory) presupposes that the auditory nerve fibers are capable of carrying impulses of all audible frequencies. The experience of physiologists in measuring the frequencies carried by other human nerve fibers makes this supposition very doubtful indeed.

Sounds are audible when the frequencies are as great as 20,000 a second. Yet it does not seem likely that any nerve fiber can respond to frequencies much greater than 1,000 a second. Nerve fibers must have a resting period after each impulse is carried; this rest or refractory period precludes the possibility of such rapid response.

A modification of the theory was therefore suggested in 1929 by the late Dr. Leonard T. Troland, of Harvard. It might be that there is a division of labor among the nerve fibers. Although no single nerve fiber could respond to the higher frequencies, it might be that a single fiber would respond to every other sound wave or every third wave. Other fibers alternating with them would make it possible for the whole bundle of fibers to transmit the sounds of higher frequencies.

New light has just been thrown on this problem by Drs. H. Davis, A. Forbes, and A. J. Derbyshire, of Harvard Medical School. They picked up the action currents from the auditory nerve of an anesthetized cat by a sort of "listening in" arrangement and measured them on a cathode ray oscillograph. They found with this apparatus that when the sound reaching the ear of the cat was of a frequency of 700 or lower—that is, below the upper limit of the 'cello or alto singing voice—the frequency of the action currents of the auditory nerve was exactly the same.

Between 700 and 900 cycles, however, a sharp change occurs in the amplitude of the waves picked up. It drops to approximately half the size of those produced by equally loud sounds of lower frequencies. This bears out the "volley" theory—the hypothesis that the nerve fibers alternate in carrying the higher frequencies. The sharp drop in amplitude of the waves to half size was interpreted as meaning that at 700 to 900 cycles the nerve fibers had reached their speed limit and were now responding to only one of each two successive waves. Since only half the fibers responded to any one wave, the size of the response was only half as great as when all were working.

At a frequency of 1,700—somewhere among the high notes of the flute and violin and above the limit of the clarinet—another drop occurs, indicating a breaking up of the nerve fibers into three groups, each responding to every third wave. At a frequency of 2,800, however, the responses become completely irregular. Here the "volley" theory, too, falls down. Psychologists must seek further for an explanation of how we become aware of the shrill sound of the peanut whistle, or even the highest notes of the violin. The auditory nerve even by means of rotated activity among the fibers cannot transmit frequencies above 2,800.

The frequency theory, or its "volley" modification, may still be true as explaining the hearing of low pitches, or it may be that some other mechanism makes possible the hearing of both high and low tones.

Scientific knowledge grows chiefly because of investigation started by those who refuse to accept current theories, the doubting Thomases of their profession. While the psycho-physiologists have been busy modifying accepted theories of hearing, an educational psychologist has raised his voice in protest against the idea generally held by many psychologists, that intelligence is something fixed in the individual and not to be changed by education or environment.

It has been a widely accepted supposition that intelligence depends upon heredity. If a child is born bright, you may separate him from his parents, send him to school, or keep him at home, surround him with culture or let him live in a hovel, and still he will remain intelligent. His education will of course be defective if he is deprived of all educational opportunities, but his native ability will remain—his ability to reason, to solve problems, to meet situations as they arise.

This idea is challenged by Dr. Frank N. Freeman, of the University of Chicago. Intellectual training does improve intelligence, he believes. Ability to concentrate the attention, to think effectively, to avoid fallacies, and to grasp difficult relationships between thoughts, are among the aspects of intellectual ability which Dr. Freeman declares can be improved or controlled as a result of proper education. This conclusion he bases on the results of intelligence tests given to children of defective parents who were adopted into superior homes, and to children of the same family separated and adopted into families of differing advantages, and to identical twins who had been brought up separately.

In this conclusion he is supported by evidence obtained

by Prof. Edward A. Lincoln, of Harvard University, showing that intelligence is not a static thing, but changes as children grow older. Prof. Lincoln sought out a group of students who had been given psychological tests five years ago, and reëxamined them. He found that the superior pupils, the exceptionally bright children of the group, had failed to keep their great intellectual advantage over their fellows. Their IQ (mental age as compared with chronological age) had dropped substantially during the five or more years. The girls lost more than the boys. Does this mean that the ordinary school tasks are not as stimulating to the intelligence of the supernormal as to the children of more nearly average mentality?

Theories of learning or habit formation have also received serious upsets though recent research.

Habits—Good and Bad

ONE SUCH THEORY is that in learning a skill such as piano-playing you are at first guided by certain visual and auditory signals, but that as your playing becomes more of an automatic habit, the mere movement of your fingers in the playing of one note is sufficient to evoke the next movement for the next note, or in psychologists' language "the stimulus control is turned over to proprioception." Another theory is that when the habit becomes well enough learned, your "consciousness lapses" and you are actually not aware of which notes you have played.

Evidence against both these theories was found by Dr. Walter S. Hunter, of Clark University, in a complicated experiment. The subject in this experiment traced with a pointer a narrow black line which moved in a zigzag manner behind a slit. Whenever the pointer left the line, the subject received a slight electric shock from the pointer. Along the line and at varying intervals were certain numbers from one to five, each number corresponding to a finger of the left hand. The subject signaled the appearance of each number by pressing a key with the appropriate finger. All during this procedure the subject was also busy repeating a passage of prose after the experimenter.

Training brought no decrease in the subject's ability to report afterwards what he had recited, even when slight differences were introduced in the prose passage. The recitation, however well learned, never became mere "unconscious" parroting.

Dr. Edward L. Thorndike, of Teachers College, Columbia University, famous for his research on learning processes on which he has been engaged intensively for many years, has recently contributed a new step to his theories.

Many years ago, he found evidence that a reward given at the end of a desired action has a retroactive effect in strengthening the learning process. When the child spells cat, c-a-t, and the teacher smiles her approval, the child has a feeling of satisfaction that aids him in remembering the letters. If, however, he says k-a-t, and the teacher frowns or scolds, he tries another spelling and tends to forget that one.

Other psychologists have disagreed with Dr. Thorndike, maintaining that the strengthening of learning is due to forces operating during the learning or previous to it. When he is able to say c-a-t, the learning is already complete, they contend, and the reward is not necessary to explain the learning.

In his new experiments, Dr. Thorndike attached numbers arbitrarily to a series of simple words. When the experimenter pronounced a word, the subject was to give the correct number. The words were given in quick succession —only 2.2 seconds being allowed between words. Punishment followed the giving of a wrong number; reward was given for correct response.

An error that was made close before or after a rewarded correct answer was likely to be persisted in despite the punishment, Dr. Thorndike found. If the subject said 2 for the word "deduce," and was punished for his mistake, and then immediately said 5 for "early" and was rewarded, on the next trial he would be likely to persist in saying 2 for "deduce."

The moral of this experiment seems to be that spanking Johnny for pulling the tail feathers out of the canary will not be effective if he is immediately picked up and petted and praised for some cute saying.

An experimental study of great thoroughness to determine how we remember and why we forget was recently conducted by a British psychologist, Dr. F. C. Bartlett, of Cambridge. Using tests, some of them not greatly unlike the old-fashioned game of "gossip," except that here the object was not to distort the story repeated but to reproduce it as exactly as possible, Dr. Bartlett found that the material remembered depends not alone upon the personality and history of the individual, but also upon the race history of the social group to which he is attached. The Swazi people of South Africa, he found, have exceptionally perfect memories for everything connected with cattle, for their culture centers around the possession and care of cattle. What we "perceive" is largely built up in our minds from mere clues or general impressions given us by our senses, and what we remember is influenced greatly by the word labels we mentally attach to what we see. Thus, when an ambiguous drawing was thought of by the subject as an anchor, that person "remembered" long points on one end and a ring on the other; others who called it a turf-cutter remembered a smooth round blade; only one remembered it as it actually was—he had named it a prehistoric battle-ax.

Group Attitudes

THE ATTITUDES OF PEOPLE, both individually and as members of a group, have received an increasing amount of study from psychologists. They are vitally important for the understanding of human nature and for the furtherance of any dealings with others in this world.

It is a curious quality in the human make-up that one's attitudes as an individual, his "private" attitudes, may be entirely different from his attitudes as a member of a church, lodge, or other social group. The man who, as a church member, is completely opposed to card playing, may privately have no objection to it, may even play a quiet game occasionally at home. The striking character of this dual way of looking at things was disclosed by Dr. Richard L. Schanck, in a study of persons in a rural community and what they thought, publicly and privately, on controversial matters. It is an error to think of the private attitude as being more real or true than the public attitude, Dr. Schanck warned those who would jump to a conclusion that all men are hypocrites. Both attitudes are genuine, but the public attitude may be the more important because it is more likely to determine behavior.

Tests of attitudes have recently been developed, and these are now being used to measure the effect of movies, or lectures, or the radio, on the attitudes of the audience toward other races, toward crime, and other such matters. They are also being used to reveal trends in the sentiments of the public. The American voter, although not supporting the Socialist party, is inclining more toward socialistic doctrines, it was discovered by Dr. Edward S. Robinson, of the Yale Institute of Human Relations. This survey also revealed that much of the New Deal legislation was not revolutionary in the sense that it opposed the attitudes of the general run of voters. Rather it has followed a growing sentiment among the people instead of leading that sentiment.

Mathematics has been brought to bear on this complex problem of human nature. So that today psychologists are likely to avoid the old way of describing men as good or bad, loyal or false, reliable or untruthful. Instead you may hear in their discussions such terms as: multiple factor analysis, correlation coefficients, tetrad differences, tetrachoric coefficients, index of specificity, or orthogonal axes.

An American psychologist-mathematician-statistician, Dr. L. L. Thurstone, applying mathematical technique to the study of personality found that when the characters of individuals are described, certain traits tend always to appear together in "constellations." If a man is friendly, he is also likely to be congenial, broad-minded, generous, and cheerful. If he is capable, he is also likely to be frank, self-reliant, and courageous. If he is grasping, he is probably also self-important, sarcastic, haughty, cynical, and quick-tempered. Statistical treatment of these results revealed certain common factors underlying the personality make-up. There are not two, however, as some might expect—goodness and viciousness, or self-centeredness and interest in others. There are probably five, at least, and these have not been given names.

The study of personality also leads back to physiology, for a new link between the mind and the body has been observed by Dr. W. R. Miles and his wife and co-worker, Dr. Catharine C. Miles, of the Institute of Human Relations, Yale University. The minute quantities of weight lost from your body when you are lying quietly at rest in a room of ordinary comfortable temperature have been found to serve as an index to the sort of person you are. Individuals who lose weight rapidly under such circumstances have, in general, some different personality traits from those who lose weight slowly.

The weight loss is due to water loss from the body in vapor on the breath, which can be easily seen in cold weather but which is present at all times, and in the invisible perspiration which is constantly keeping the skin of hands and feet soft and slightly moist. The average rate of such weight loss is about an ounce and a half an hour. But one section of the experimental group of subjects lost at a rate almost twice as high as the average for the others.

The following personality traits were found to be characteristic of the high-loss group: They let others do the entertaining, daydream, are self-conscious before a crowd, prefer writing to talking, tend to obey, and tend to regard themselves as slightly below average intellectually. On the other hand, the following traits were found in the low-loss group. They plan but do not daydream, get acquainted easily, seldom blush, rarely forget, tend to be cautious themselves, and consider reasons before obeying.

Thus does the psychologist draw upon physiology, mathematics, physics, and chemistry, and all the other sciences in his study of the complex problem of man and his elaborate mental equipment and processes. Underlying all the sciences there is the human element of man's thought. And intimately associated with man's thought are all the physical facts of his environment.

CHAPTER 26
UNEARTHING THE OLD WORLD'S PAST

ARCHÆOLOGISTS have never been plagued by Alexander's famous complaint—no more worlds to conquer. For the archæologists' worlds are buried seven deep, sometimes deeper. Layer below layer, the remains of past cities and countries are packed under foot.

Scientists have been at work salvaging the buried past for about a century now. And although a hundred years of digging have brought some wonderful things into the light of day, there are plenty of surprises still left in the earth. No archæologist doubts that, in the least.

Finding a lost country—an important country—is one of the surprises that can still happen. This achievement was won by Prof. Raymond P. Dougherty of Yale University. Ancient history will have to be revised to make room for the neglected country, its kings and its people.

In Arabia, of all unexpected regions, Prof. Dougherty established the location of this country, which in ancient times was known as the Sealand. Scholars who read Babylonian texts had known something about such a place as the Sealand. It was mentioned vaguely in old writings, but it appeared to be merely a minor kingdom on the fringe of Babylonia.

Prof. Dougherty gave the Sealand back its identity, not by digging up the ruins, but by sitting at a study desk and poring over the hen-track writings on baked clay tablets. Whole libraries of clay books and documents of Babylonia and Assyria have been coming to light in recent years, as ruined cities in Mesopotamia are explored. These "new" books added helpfully to the references on the Sealand. By examining every scrap of disconnected evidence he could find, old and new, Prof. Dougherty brought order out of

chaotic ideas on the subject. He showed that the Sealand
was a great country in its own right and that it must
have been in Arabia. The name Sealand may have referred
to the desert sands which then, as now, reminded people
of billowing waves.

Prof. Dougherty, who unfortunately died shortly after
making his ingenious contribution to history, was even able
to outline the career of the Sealand in three main epochs.
The first, lasting from about 2500 to 1000 B.C., was notable
because the Sealanders intruded on the affairs of Babylonia.
The second, from 858 to 626 B.C., was during the height of
Assyria's power, and the Sealanders, far from quaking at
mighty Assyria, fought back hard and repeatedly. The
third epoch, running late into the sixth century B.C., was the
time of the Chaldean Empire. The last Sealand dynasty
contributed to Assyria's downfall, thus winning the long
rivalry. People of the forgotten Sealand appear to have
been a melting-pot race. Some of their kings had Semitic
names. Others were Sumerian.

In the Sealand, scholars may find the origin of some of
the Hebrew religious ideas which appear without background in the Bible; for the Sealanders were as dynamic
in their religion as in their politics. In an early day, when
most gods were far from godlike, and when temples were
scenes of dreadful sacrifice and emotional orgies, the
Sealanders in Arabia held a notion of divinity with such
attributes as mercy, beneficence, and absoluteness. Their
first known king bore the solemn name Iluma-Ilum, "verily
god is god." Existence of such ideas, declared Prof.
Dougherty, constitutes a source and an influence which must
be taken into account in attempts to trace the origin of
early Hebrew religious concepts.

In the unfolding evidence, the Sealand has so far spoken
only through its rivals and neighbors. Few, if any, of the
cuneiform inscriptions that mention it were written by
Sealand scribes. Archæologists still have to search for the
buried cities and records of the country itself beneath
Arabian sands. That is easy to suggest. But the Sealand
might be more quickly found if it were in the depths of the
sea instead of the desert. Vast stretches of Arabia have

never been explored even on the surfaces. And scientific
expeditions are not welcomed by suspicious desert tribes.
The Sealand may have to remain a paper country for some
time to come.

Finding a lost country is extraordinary. Finding forgotten kings is a frequent occurrence. It happens a number
of times in every archæological year. Many a monarch,
whose name was a terror or a blessing to thousands of
people, owes his entire historic identity today to some
twentieth-century scientist with a spade and a trained
mind capable of understanding what the earth yields. If
those ancient kings of the earth, wherever they are, take
any interest in their enduring fame, they may well be grateful to modern science.

It was a big day for the kings when an expedition from
the Oriental Institute of Chicago was digging at the ruins
of Khorsabad, north of Nineveh, in 1933, and someone uncovered a large clay tablet. On both sides of the tablet were
long lists of names—93 names. Those who could read the
cuneiform writing set to work eagerly, and read the names
of 93 Assyrian kings who reigned from about 2200 B.C.
to about 730 B.C. In the list were eight names entirely unfamiliar to anyone living today. And the earliest part of the
royal list showed the keenly interested excavators the exact
place in history for several Assyrian kings who had been
vaguely detached from any known period of their nation's
career.

Jewish History

WHEN THE ARCHÆOLOGIST cannot find written records in
ancient languages, to help explain forgotten history, he
depends on whatever scraps of evidence he can find. This
branch of science is famous for its sleuthing abilities, de-
servedly. In a great array of broken and rusted objects
gathered from some ruined city, the keen eye of the expert
roves over the lot, and picks out some small, significant
thing. Who but an archæologist would expect a heap of
broken clay dishes to put a new light on the Jewish exile
from Palestine? That piece of detective work was achieved

in 1933 by British archæologists, exploring the ruins of Lachish, in Palestine.

The exile of the Jews from their Promised Land, when King Nebuchadnezzar carried them off to Babylonia, is sometimes interpreted as a captivity of many people. But if the discoveries at Lachish are significant, the number of Jews carried off was small. The new clue to Jewish history is 700 pieces of pottery, found in a number of tombs. The discovery was made by chance, when a workman was digging up clay to use as plaster in building the archæologists' living quarters. The hundreds of pieces of pottery form an unbroken series, showing the kind of clay wares made in Palestine from the ninth century B.C. down through the exile period three hundred years later. The Jewish history told in clay dishes proceeds in orderly fashion with no dramatic breaks in style or technique, such as would be expected if the national life was rudely disrupted by foreign conquerors and deportation of all or most of the people. Hence it is believed that comparatively few captives were taken.

Discoveries that shed light on the Bible attract the interest of a wide public. So there was excitement among laymen, as well as archæologists, when the ruins of Dura-Europos on the Euphrates River yielded paintings showing how artists first pictured Old and New Testament events.

In 1932, a joint expedition from Yale and the French Academy of Inscriptions was exploring the ruins of Dura. The city was revealing itself as an extremely religious place. In various levels of earth there emerged temples to Greek and Roman gods, Assyrian, Babylonian, and Persian deities. But no trace of a Christian church could the excavators find, though they reminded themselves that Dura lasted until A.D. 256, and that surely so religious a city would have entertained the new faith. And then they came upon what they were seeking. In a house, perhaps the residence of a bishop, were the ruins of a little Christian chapel, built about A.D. 200.

To their delight and amazement, the discoverers found the walls and the apse covered from top to bottom with frescoes. Here were Bible characters as people thought of them within 200 years of Christ's own time. The artist painted Christ healing the sick, Peter trying to walk on the water, the Good Shepherd and the twelve sheep, and other scenes.

Most impressive of all, he painted the scene of the Resurrection. A beautiful description of this painting was given by Prof. Michael Rostovtzeff of Yale:

"We see the majestic front of the grave with two shining stars above it and the procession of the myrrhophores, the three Marys with their companions moving slowly and solemnly towards the grave with lighted torches and bowls full of myrrh in their hands. It is a beautiful composition painted with a gorgeous display of colors."

Since the finding of the chapel, the paintings have been brought to the United States. The chapel they adorned has been partly reconstructed at the Yale Gallery of Fine Arts, to show some of the earliest Christian art in its own and proper setting.

The following year, 1933, Dura disclosed more religious art, this time on Old Testament subjects. A Jewish synagogue was unearthed. Before the walls were fully uncovered, the excited workers reported the discovery that the walls as far as could be seen were completely covered with a magnificent series of frescoes. With the art of the catacombs, these paintings are the oldest pictures of Old Testament scenes ever discovered. Worshipers in the synagogue looked up at pictures of Moses beside the burning bush and Pharaoh pursuing the Israelites into the Red Sea. Another dramatic scene showed the return of the Hebrew ark of the covenant to the Hebrew camp after the Philistines had captured the ark in battle and had found it a disastrous piece of property for them to hold. That story is told in Samuel, first book, fourth chapter.

Again Prof. Rostovtzeff commented vividly on the historic value of such early religious art. It had been a common belief among some students, he said, that Jewish religion forbade decorating religious buildings with paintings, though late discoveries undermined this theory. Now

Dura's synagogue, built in A. D. 244, revealed something that few scholars had even suspected. Christian art, these paintings clearly showed, must have borrowed from Jewish pictorial art in style, composition, and subject matter.

Said Prof. Rostovtzeff:

"This sensational discovery at Dura is of great importance for the study of the Bible, the history of Judaism in the days following the destruction of the Temple, and, first and foremost, for the history of the early development of Christian art."

Ancient Buildings

THE SURPRISES of every archæological year include remarkable long-lost buildings, some famous, some unheard of by us moderns until a lucky turn of the spade reveals the ancient walls. The year 1933 yielded its quota of these buildings, some of which may become "sights" that travelers will journey to see.

In Persia, at Persepolis, the sands gave up the beautiful stairway and walls of a king's palace.

A scene of pomp and ceremony, such as living people once enacted, was found carved on the palace stair. Up the grand stairway moved a long line of ambassadors from twenty-two subject nations, carrying in their arms tribute to Persia. Down the stair on the opposite side were ranged the brilliantly uniformed palace guards. So beautiful was the finish of the sculptor's work, when they carved this scene, that even chariot nails were embellished. Copying real bronze nails, the sculptors carved nail heads into female figures, achieving delicacy of cameo in stone work no larger than a postage stamp. Colors once added to the splendor of the palace carvings. But no color is left except on a portrait of the emperor, showing him in a robe bordered with scarlet and purple, scarlet shoes, and other regal adornments. Tradition says that the palaces of Persepolis were destroyed with fire by Alexander the Great as a climax to a drunken feast, in 330 B.C.

Of special interest to archæologists was the discovery

"WHITE RUSSIAN" DEATH MASK

GRAVES of a mysterious blond and chestnut-haired people, who had a strange custom of making painted plaster masks for the dead, have been found in Siberia. The graves date from the first centuries of the Christian Era. The inside of the masks record the complete facial characteristics of the dead, even to wrinkles of face and neck. These impressions reveal a beak-nosed, long-headed, narrow-faced race with blond and brown hair. Whence this race came and whither it vanished are not known.

"ROSETTA STONE" (below)

THIS small bowl of unusual shape and intricate design has been hailed as a possible Rosetta Stone of the United States. Frank M. Setzler of the Smithsonian Institution, who discovered the bowl at Marksville, Louisiana, is shown leaning on a reproduction of the real Rosetta Stone which enabled archæologists to read the Egyptian hieroglyphics because it bore the same inscription in known and unknown written languages. The bowl, similarly, bears a known and an unknown type of decoration and links the well-known Hopewell Mound builders with a hitherto unplaced race in the south.

BAS RELIE
STAIRWA

AN ARCHÆOLOGICAL fin ever made in Western As bas relief in a palace : ing a stairway, are amb from twenty-two nation palace was sent up Great in 330 B.C., as

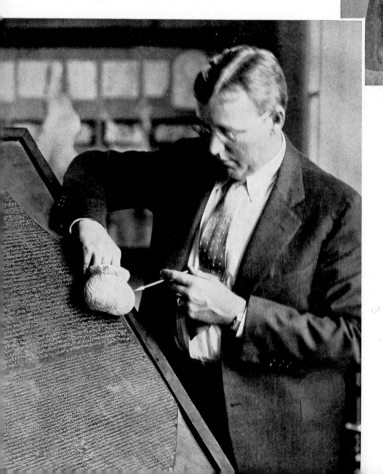

ADAM AND EVE (below)

THAT "Adam and Eve" and the serpent were known at least two thousand years before the oldest portions of the Bible were written is proved by this clay seal dug up in Mesopotamia. The pair, who are shown bent and stumbling, and aiding each other forward, wear no clothing except headdresses. Behind the woman looms the serpent. Found in the city of Tepe Gawra, and made by an artist in 3700 B.C., the seal pushes the "Adam and Eve" story far back into antiquity and forms one more link between the Hebrew Bible writers and the civilization of Babylon.

ROM A
N PERSIA

at ranks with the greatest
earthed this splendid
rsepolis. The figures, lin-
dors bringing tribute
adition says that the
mes by Alexander the
max to a drunken feast.

NORSE RECORD ON STONE

If Norsemen and Goths actually carved this stone and left it behind them in the Minnesota wilderness in 1362, it is the most important record of white men in America yet discovered. Originally found in 1898, many have branded it as fake, but new evidence now tends to prove its genuineness. It may require that a new chapter in American history be written. Scientists hardly dared believe that the story told on the stone of an expedition down through Hudson's Bay into northern Minnesota could be proved true.

TEXAS MUMMIES

Seven mummies of the cave dwellers of the Big Bend region of Texas, dating from prehistoric times, have recently been unearthed. Nearly all the skeletons had fractured arms or legs which had healed without benefit of setting. The cave being on a high cliff, it is thought that the ancient people suffered frequent falls.

at Lisht in 1933 of a tomb built by one of their own clan —an Egyptian antiquarian who lived 1900 years before Christ. As has been said earlier in this chapter, scientific archæology with its techniques and training is one of the newer sciences. Yet, it is true that as far back in history as old Egypt and Babylonia there were people who took an intelligent interest in the past. Ur of the Chaldees, for example, had a museum of local antiquities in the sixth century B.C. It was kept by a Babylonian princess, daughter of King Nabonidus, who took an almost eccentric delight in his royal ancestors. When the princess' museum was discovered, at Ur, the archæologists picked up half a dozen museum exhibits. Not one of these statues or inscriptions was less than seven hundred years old when people of Ur came to visit their museum. Even a museum label was found in the room.

The Egyptian archæologist who gained a new belated fame in 1933 was a specialist in royal tombs and their inscriptions. In his era, about 1900 B.C., there was a revival of interest in old traditions. The Pharaohs aspired to model their tombs like some that were built by Pharaohs five hundred years earlier. Officials were accordingly engaged to study up on fifth and sixth dynasty pyramids, and probably told to visit and copy the plans and inscriptions. In short, the officials did research and were archæologists. Among these, apparently, was S'en-Wosret-'ankh.

S'en-Wosret-'ankh liked the old-fashioned customs. When he planned his own tomb, he did not quite dare to build a kingly pyramid. He was satisfied with a flat-topped mastabah, such as lesser Egyptians had. But inside he reproduced the plan of a royal tomb, and column after column of inscriptions was copied from tombs of departed kings. Of 296 columns of writings painted on the walls of the burial chamber, all but one column was from the royal pyramids. The caliber of the research back of this "reproduction" was good. Modern archæologists who entered the tomb of their fellow worker paid due respect to his carefulness and knowledge.

CHAPTER 27
UNEARTHING AMERICA'S PAST

IT IS A HERCULEAN TASK to dig up the buried remains of prehistoric America, and, using them intelligently, to write an orderly ancient history for the New World. But this is the task to which American archæology is dedicated. There is practically no archæological exploration in this country deserving to be called scientific which does not have for its goal the discovery of *facts* to be added to the history. Discovery of *things* is far less important, however curious or beautiful the objects thus found may be.

The hardest, most intriguing problem of all is to write the genesis chapter of human events in America. The first American is still an unknown figure. Presumably he was someone who ventured across Bering Strait with other straggling wanderers seeking a better hunting field or a more friendly country than bleak Siberia. But how long ago was it when he set foot on New World soil? That is still an archæological puzzler. In fact, scientific disagreement has waxed intense over every clue suggesting that man has been in America more than a mere four or five thousand years.

The earliest chapter of American life that science has so far pieced together with any completeness deals with Basket Maker Indians. Basket Makers were farmers, living in caves in the Southwest during an early stage, and later building houses. Their arrival in the Southwest is put at about 1500 B.C. Archæologists can tell you how they looked, what they wore, and the sort of lives they lived.

But 1500 B.C. is no great depth for ancient historians to probe. There were assuredly American inhabitants earlier than this, and their story must be unearthed and written. Evidence belonging to these earlier chapters has been coming to light for years. It is singularly hard, however, to interpret the meaning of stone spearheads found beside mammoth bones, or stone tools embedded in layers of earth pronounced geologically to be thousands of years old. Cautious scientists have greeted these discoveries with a demand for proof that spearhead and mammoth bone did not come together by coincidence. They asked proof that a buried tool was not pushed down into a layer of earth far older than itself.

The problem calls for proof by a sort of scientific triangulation. If an eminent jury of three sciences—geologists, paleontologists, and archæologists—could jointly make one of these "ancient man" discoveries, or could reach a discovery site before a grain of earth was removed, and if they agreed that the evidence pointed to existence of ancient men, that would be a verdict carrying weight.

In the summer of 1933, a notable field convention of experts was achieved. Edgar B. Howard, excavating for the University of Pennsylvania Museum and the Philadelphia Academy of Natural Sciences, had been digging into old lake beds near Clovis, New Mexico. The beds had yielded matted masses of bones of mammoth, extinct species of horses and bison, and probably also camel. Mr. Howard reconstructed the scene as a mad rush of animals for water and their trampling one another into the mud. No human bones were discovered, but numbers of stone spear points, knives, and scrapers lay in the lake beds near the ancient animals. In one of the beds, an expedition helper had found a layer of charcoal several feet in extent and half a foot thick. In it were burned bones of mammoth and bison and more than twenty flint knives and scrapers, all showing signs of fire. Only man makes hearth fires and cooks his food.

On August 2d, a group of eminent scientists dug and inspected together at the desert site. The group included Dr. John C. Merriam, president of the Carnegie Institution of Washington and an authority on paleontology; Sir Arthur Smith Woodward, formerly geologist of the British Museum; Dr. Chester Stock, paleontologist of the California Institute of Technology; Dr. V. Van Straelen, director of the Royal Museum of Natural History in Brussels;

and Mr. Howard, anthropologist. The group watched Dr. Merriam probe into a sand bank and uncover the charred remains of a fire. In the blackened mass he found the half-burned bones of an extinct form of bison and a handful of flint weapon points.

Each scientist examined the evidence from his own specialized viewpoint, and all agreed with Mr. Howard when he said:

"It is about time for us to recognize a culture in this country older than the Basket Maker, more than likely a hunting culture following large herds of animals frequenting the open country of the West and Southwest, and perhaps extending to other parts of the country. It should not stretch our imagination too much to picture a people living at a time when the elephant, ground sloth, and other animals now extinct, lived."

Mr. Howard, you notice, does not yet ask science to accept a theory that man lived in America as early as the Ice Age, which was the real era of the animals found at Clovis. Perhaps there were men here then, 15,000 or more years ago. On the other hand, perhaps the men came later. They might have met the Ice Age animals, only because the animals lingered on for several thousand years after the great ice sheet retreated toward its polar base. Whichever alternative is correct, Mr. Howard simply calls upon scientists to accept the existence of man contemporaneous with the elephant in America and thereby clarify scientific thinking on that major point.

Another discovery, strengthening this scientific position, was made near Las Vegas, Nevada. In a deeply buried charcoal bed, Fenley Hunter of New York found bones of extinct horses, bison, and camels, and a flake of obsidian, or dark volcanic glass, apparently shaped by human hands. Through coöperation of the Carnegie Institution, M. R. Harrington, of the Southwest Museum, visited the region in December, 1933, and half a mile from the charcoal beds he found a new series of similar beds, like an old camp ground. Most interesting to him was an ash dump where the camp refuse was thrown into a gully. In the dump he found hundreds of fragments of bones, many split for the marrow while green and many scorched as from cooking. Among the animals thus apparently prepared for man's cooking and eating were extinct camel and bison.

From such discoveries as those described, and from earlier discoveries, notably those made by Mr. Harrington at Gypsum Cave, Nevada, the ancient story of America is pushed back one step at least. There seems no longer reason to doubt: there *were* men in the New World in the days of the mammoths.

Weapons used by the early hunters have received close attention. They are distinctive, unlike blades made by Plains Indians, Basket Makers, Aztecs, or other Indians of the long period of prehistory that preceded the coming of white men. Folsom points and Yuma points, archæologists call the blades, after the sites where they first attracted attention. A young student of anthropology at the University of Denver made a careful survey of these weapons, classifying into 9 types all that have been reported by discoverers. His results, reported in a thesis in 1933, show that no less than 343 specimens are known to archæologists, and the specimens were found in no less than 30 states. From New Hampshire to Oregon across the country, and from North Dakota to Louisiana, ranged the hunters who tipped their spears with these distinctive blades of stone. If the story that the weapons seem to tell is true, then the ancient hunters were scattered practically throughout the United States.

That picture points to another, more remote chapter of America's past. For if wandering hunters of the Yuma and Folsom age were so widely established, they cannot well have been fresh immigrants in the continent. The magnificent distances of North America were never traversed rapidly by the pioneers in the Stone Age of culture.

More Modern Americans

IT IS A JUMP IN PROGRESS from a ring of primitive hunters huddled over a fire and gnawing bones of mammoths and camels to the colorful pageantry of Indian civilization that later sprang up in the American tropics and Peru. The beautiful trappings of these civilizations have already revealed a great deal of information about the attainments of the native Americans. But we are still a long way from knowing how Folsom hunters or other waves of wandering immigrants were changed into farmers, goldsmiths, weavers, astronomers, architects, and priests.

When an expedition from the Peabody Museum of Harvard University went into the province of Cocle, Panama, and found graves of chieftains there, the first news reports early in 1934 stressed the glittering display of gold worn by the buried dignitaries. A great man's funeral was so spectacular that even the long-buried remnants could arrest the world's attention. A dead ruler in ancient Panama —even as in Ur of the Chaldees and the first Egyptian dynasties—took to the grave with him not only a load of useful and valuable articles for his future life but his wives and attendants. It was their lot to die with him. Dr. S. K. Lothrop, director of the expedition, told of one grave containing 20 bodies and more than 2,000 objects. Among the 2,000 objects Dr. Lothrop counted 96 gold necklaces, bracelets, and other golden jewelry, which lay piled over and around the bones of the dead. There were 225 pottery dishes for ceremony and for the homemaking of the ruler. There were 188 arrowpoints, axes, and knives, quite a store of hardware, and all of stone, for America down to the arrival of Columbus was almost entirely a land of the New Stone Age. There were 9 mirrors of hematite, and gilded copper ornaments, and a host of other things laid in this one grave. Said Dr. Lothrop: "A very brilliant civilization has come to light in a region previously considered barren of higher culture."

The real treasure of the graves, archæologically, is not the gold, but the wealth of designs on the pottery ware and the gold ornaments. These designs, some pronounced superb, reveal the artistic sense of the people and also their relationships with other parts of America. Archæologists are always looking for evidence showing which tribes of ancient America had contact with other tribes. It is not yet known how far the influences of the great Indian civilizations of North and South America spread in widening circles. The graves of the chiefs in Cocle point south. On many of the metal ornaments, Dr. Lothrop found designs related to the jaguar god of Colombia and Peru. By this and other clues he links the new-found civilization of Panama with the Chimu Indian culture which once raised great cities of adobe along the sandy coast of northern Peru.

Mexican Finds

PERHAPS THE LIVELIEST AREA of activity in the excavating for American history recently has been in Mexico. Even through economic depression, Mexico has forged ahead, adding to its official list of more than 1,200 known archæological sites, repairing its famous ruined temples, digging others out of their hiding places.

In 1932, Mexican archæologists ventured to explore the greatest of Mexican pyramids, that at Cholula. For more than a year, indoor work of tunneling under the mound has continued. To avoid disturbing the church, the archæologists resorted to mining methods. They have dug more than a thousand feet of tunnels penetrating the pyramid at different levels, and have lighted the underground passages by strings of electric lights. The visitor may ascend from one "floor" to another by walking up ancient stone stairways found within. One is the widest stair known among the ruins of ancient America. On buried walls of the pyramid are mural paintings, badly blurred.

One terrace has yielded several skeletons which appeared sitting upright, knees to their chins and arms hugging their knees. So placed, the dead were considered ready for the next world as soon as they arrived. The Mexican archæologists who found these skeletons examined with special interest the incisor teeth, filed to points. Off in Yucatan, the Mayan Indians were accustomed to mutilate the teeth, but it was not the usual fashion among Aztec tribes on the central plateau of Mexico, where Cholula stands. By charting such points of likeness, the relationships of the ancient tribes are being slowly better understood.

Proof that Indians in Mexico build pyramids to serve

as astronomical timepieces was obtained in 1933 by Sr.
Ignacio Marquina, chief of the Mexican Direction of Pre-
hispanic Monuments. Thus, the pyramids of America have
been awarded a significance which researchers have vainly
tried to attach to Egypt's pyramids. Egypt's pyramids are
tombs but not timepieces, Egyptologists almost universally
admit. Mexico's pyramids, on the other hand, are pedestals
for high temples, and some at least are oriented to mark
the passing of the sun and certain stars.

When Sr. Marquina was surveying archæological sites
of Mexico, his attention was drawn toward a possible relationship of the structures with the sun. He noticed that
the angle at which principal pyramid-temples faced was
apt to be followed by monuments and buildings throughout a city. This seemed to be an intentional arrangement.

He also observed two ideas in orientation in the cities.
In southern Mexico and Guatemala and southern Yucatan,
the buildings were generally square to the four world directions and faced astronomically west, exactly between the
two points where the sun sets in the summer and winter
solstices. But farther north in places built by Toltec Indians
and their cultural allies, he found the main pyramids
skewed a little from facing west. They faced slightly
northward, the angle of deviation varying with the latitude
of the city. This was the case at such widely separated
cities as Chichen Itza, Uxmal, Teotihuacan, Tenayuca, and
Cholula.

At Tenayuca, Sr. Marquina made elaborate tests to see
whether this constant arrangement at cities so far apart
obeyed some astronomical rule. He measured the angle
which the setting sun makes with the center of Tenayuca's
pyramid. He measured it for summer and winter solstices,
for spring and autumn equinoxes, and for the two times
in the year when the sun passes straight overhead. He
found the highly significant fact that the Tenayuca pyramid looks straight into the setting sun on May 16th and
July 26th of every year. Those are not important dates
in our calendar, but they were great days in the Mexican
year. They were the days when the priests watched the sun
cross overhead in the zenith, and for one great moment

every upright monument lost its shadow completely, because the sun stood directly above it. This sign, so easily observed, marked the passing of the year, and the Mexicans celebrated their New Year's Day on July 26th.

From demonstrating that Tenayuca pyramid was oriented to mark the year's most important solar event, Sr. Marquina proceeded to test the pyramid's relationship to the stars. He found that the stars important to the Indians in their religion were precisely those stars whose lines of sight coincided with the sun on important dates— the solstices, equinoxes, and the sun's zenith. It appears that those stars were important in Mexican religion and astronomy because they did coincide. The leading star was Aldebaran, called in Aztec lore Lord of the Night. Aldebaran was on the line of sight of the setting sun on the two days when the sun crossed the zenith. Thus, in building the pyramids, the Indian architects could use Aldebaran as a daily guide in figuring the right angle for the structure's facing. They did not have to wait for the two days in the year when the sun itself would show them the temple's correct orientation.

Monte Alban

At the mountain-top city of Monte Alban, a Mexican expedition continued exploration of what is surely a most remarkable place. Monte Alban has yielded no new flashes of funereal treasure since Dr. Alfonso Caso opened Tomb Seven early in 1932 and removed 500 pieces of Indian jewelry, of gold and jade and turquoise, and, most interesting of all archæologically, bones exquisitely carved with pictured events and written inscriptions in Zapotec hieroglyphics.

The winter season of excavation at Monte Alban, ending March, 1934, saw Dr. Caso's expedition at work again in the cemetery and on the acropolis of the city, which contains some of the best preserved examples of early Zapotecan Indian architecture known. Comparatively complete reconstruction of some buildings is possible, and this will give an excellent idea of how the mountain city looked. The cemetery begins at the northern end of the acropolis, where the hills roll down from Monte Alban's heights. The treasure tomb Number Seven and several more tombs have unexpectedly showed themselves as mere cellars of more important buildings which are now being unearthed. So completely had earth covered these edifices from centuries of weathering that the tops formed mere bulges.

The rite of child sacrifice may have been one of the darker scenes of life in Monte Alban. So it appears, at least, from the arrangement of Tomb Forty-three, which is one of the latest entered in the cemetery. The adult owner of the tomb was found stretched the length of the floor. At his feet were the sets of bones of two children, not buried as whole corpses. There were bones of birds, also, and those of small animals, in the tomb. The two children, girls, are the only female occupants so far found in the entire cemetery.

Placing Monte Alban in the ancient history of Mexico is difficult. At the "Treasure Tomb" Number Seven and elsewhere there are two distinct kinds of prehistoric culture in evidence. One is Zapotec and the other is Mixtec. The Zapotec shows many resemblances to Mayan relics, and the Mixtec is strikingly like Aztec relics. Hence, it is thought likely that Monte Alban may contain in its ruins a long-sought link between the old civilization of the Mayan Indians to the south and that which the Aztec Indians evolved in the Mexican highland.

The age of the city of Monte Alban has unexpectedly been shown by the evidence of its ball games. Tlachtli was an Indian game widely played in tropical America, apparently for religion as well as sport. The game changed somewhat in the course of ten or fifteen centuries, to judge by courts that have been found. All courts have an H-shaped playing area. Very old courts of the south had several round altars in the center, and the side walls enclosing the field sloped. Northern courts lost their altars as centuries went by, their side walls became vertical, and big stone rings were placed in the walls for the ball to be shot through. Now the Monte Alban court belongs between these two types, for its walls slope and are without a stone ring, although it had already lost all but one of its central altars. It is therefore likely that Monte Alban's ball court, and the city itself, belong to a period about a thousand years ago. When the city actually had its beginning, or when it ceased to be, are questions still to be answered. Dr. Caso believes that the Monte Alban ball games are evidence of the northern spread of the great Mayan civilization, and that the brilliant Mayas throughout their rise were an inspiration to other cultures about them, far and near.

Excavations in the heart of Mexico City under the ground of Cathedral Square were begun in the summer of 1933 by archæologists of the Mexican National Museum. They were probing for ruins of the old Aztec capital which stood on the site of the modern city. They found walls and a stairway which are thought to be part of the Great Teocalli or Aztec God-House.

In a hitherto unexplored region of southeastern Campeche, Mexico, the discovery of ruins was reported early in 1934 by an expedition from the Carnegie Institution of Washington. The explorers, led by Karl Ruppert, staff archæologist, set out from Chichen Itza in Yucatan to investigate rumors that natives seeking new sources of chicle, chewing-gum raw material, had found an unknown ruined city in a wild region. They found the ruins and twenty sculptured stone monuments. Reading the picture writings on the monuments, they learned that the lost city was inhabited during the Old Mayan Empire of Mexico's history, which ended in the seventh century A. D. Many cities of the Empire were abandoned in the seventh century, in mysterious waves of northern migration. The ruined city found by the explorers has the importance of filling in a blind spot in Mayan history, because of its geographic position between Old Empire centers in southern Yucatan and the New Empire cities farther north.

Archæology at Home

IN THE UNITED STATES, economic restrictions drove many an archæological expedition out of the field. The same de-

pression put new expeditions into the field, advancing research notably in Southeastern states. While the story of
the Southwest has been pieced together remarkably from
exploration of Pueblo and Basket Maker settlements, the
ancient Indian story of the Southeast is much less fully
known.

Construction work on the dams in the Tennessee Valley
aroused archæologists to the realization that large areas,
that they had never studied, were soon to be flooded by
the Wheeler and Norris reservoirs. They hastened to see
what could be done, so that they might rescue some of the

OUTSTANDING DATES IN AMERICA'S ANCIENT HISTORY

As given by the natural calendar of the tree rings

FIGURE 20

660 A.D.
Earliest established date in United States history. A timber cut that
year marks the building date of an Indian dwelling in northern
Arizona.

919
Building of Pueblo Bonito, the "city beautiful," of New Mexico. It was
abandoned sometime after 1130, the latest date detected in its beams.

1073–1272
Building times at the great cliff dwelling of Mesa Verde, Colorado.

1274
Earliest date found at Keet Seel, one of the biggest and latest of the
ancient cliff-dwelling communities. It is in northern Arizona.

1276–1299
Great drought in the Southwest, persisting over two decades, and
causing Indians to abandon many towns.

1348–1838
Dates known from Pecos' tree-ring record. This New Mexican pueblo
was visited by Spanish explorers in 1540 and picturesquely described.

1370
Earliest tree ring date found at Oraibi, Arizona. This pueblo, still in
use, has been called the oldest continuously inhabited site in the United
States.

1507–c. 1565
Dates from Puye, New Mexico, a late Indian town that may have run
its entire course briefly after America's discovery.

A few years ago, Dr. A. E. Douglass of the University of Arizona
arranged in unbroken sequence a calendar of tree rings from A.D. 623 to
the present. Archæologists can match to this calendar the tree ring "dates"
they find in cross-sections of beams from Indian dwellings, and thus prehistoric settlements are added to the dated records of history. The outer-
most ring shows the year a piece of timber was cut for building purposes.
Seventy-five pueblos and cliff dwellings have so far been dated.

prehistoric data in the few months that remained before the land was turned to water. For this emergency rescue work the Carnegie Corporation granted some funds. The Civil Works Administration paid salaries and lent squads of workmen for the digging. Prof. W. S. Webb left his post at the University of Kentucky to direct the work.

It was hoped that the Yuchi Indians, who are little more than a name, would come to light as real people from this investigation. Early Spanish narratives mention the Yuchi as having superior intelligence, but no homes or graveyards have ever been identified as belonging to the superior Yuchi. Cherokee Indians are known to have pushed down into southeastern Tennessee in fairly recent times. In northern Tennessee were Chickasaws; and Siouan peoples also spread in that direction, coming from Ohio. Earlier than these, there may have been wandering hunters who sheltered themselves in Tennessee caves.

One of the earliest reports from Prof. Webb's work, announced in February, 1934, tells of exploring a mound on a farm in Catham Bend. The mound was once an important high place in the center of an Indian village. In this mound he identified the construction work of two sets of builders. The later Indians set up a wooden structure thirty feet square made of posts driven into the earth and completed by wattle work woven between the posts to form walls. No trace of white man's goods could be seen in the earth of the mound, and that is a reasonably sure sign that the village dates back to the days before Spaniards began trading iron knives and glass beads as they went through the New World seeking gold, new lands, and adventure. But whether the Indians of the village were early Cherokee or some other people, the excavations have not yet shown.

Two miles north of the mound, on Powell River, Prof. Webb explored a series of open-front caves, and in one cave found eight skeletons of an ancient people. They lay buried in ash-filled hollows lined with bark, and around the bones hung the remnants of a roughly woven twine fabric that had wrapped the bodies. These eight apparently represent some of Tennessee's inhabitants older than those of the near-by village.

One Federal Civil Works project, initiated in December, 1933, set a thousand men to disinterring aboriginal history in five states. The Smithsonian Institution coöperated by selecting sites that were likely to prove key points in Indian history. With the exception of a site in California, all the work centered in Southeastern states, where digging could proceed in winter weather. The Smithsonian also made arrangements for archæologists from its own staff or other institutions to go out to the sites to direct the digging. Toward spring the work was partly transferred to local charge, and the final results are not yet fully evident.

Reports from the various sites tell of discoveries of historic significance. At Macon, Georgia, Indian mounds are being explored which may prove to be the ancient capital of Creek Confederacy. One of the hillocks of earth when opened up yielded the remains of a round building which agrees in most particulars with the written accounts of a Creek "hot house," the clubhouse and ceremonial building where Creek men foregathered. No less than three or four levels of Indian occupancy have been distinguished in some of the Macon mounds, indicating a long history for the site, and, from the carpet of flint chips and potsherds on the ground in some places, there was a dense population in this locality.

The site chosen for excavation in North Carolina was one best fitting the description of the flourishing Indian town of Guasili, visited by De Soto in 1540. The biggest mound which marks the site does indeed tell a story of some white man's coming, but not conclusively the famous De Soto expedition. Glass beads and scraps of iron have been found in the top layer of the big mound, all mingled with Cherokee pipes, pottery, and other Indian-made articles. Deeper in the mound are only the Indian objects, marking sharply the pre-Spanish era from the era of exploration and conquest.

California's part of the project has gained added interest through the unexpected chance of fixing some new dates in American ancient history. The unemployed men were set digging into an old Indian burying ground in Kern County. The Indians who lived in the region abandoned it completely

soon after the Spaniards arrived. Before that, the Indians
had been there for a long time, extending indefinitely into
the past. In the hillside graveyard the men were able to find
parts of 350 skeletons wrapped in cloth and matting, and
showing the physical type of the people, and something of
their simple way of living. The outstanding feature of the
excavations, however, is finding old grave posts of cedar or
juniper wood so well preserved that the annual rings can
be seen. This means that the rings may be compared with
the long calendar of annual rings shown in California red-
wood trees, and perhaps the years when the grave posts
were cut may be learned.

A similar calendar of Southwestern tree rings constructed
in unbroken sequence from the seventh century to the present has become famous in American archæology in the past
few years. With this calendar, worked out by Dr. A. E.
Douglass with the help of archæologists, more than seventy-
five pueblos and cliff dwellings are definitely dated in terms
of our own calendar system. Each year sees new ruins dated
by the system, and the "oldest dated event in the United
States" is pushed back a little farther into the dark centuries. In 1933, Dr. H. S. Colton of the Museum of Northern Arizona made a new record and then broke it with
another, a week later. He first reported that United States
dated history had been set back seventy-six years by the
discovery of an Indian dwelling in Arizona containing a bit
of a beam cut in A.D. 708. Then he found another bit of
charred timber in an Indian ruin and read the date A.D.
660. The building of this house in 660 is thus established
as the oldest dated event in the United States—until some
archæologist sets a new antiquity record.

From one of three Indian mounds unearthed by the unemployed at Marksville, La., was taken a little clay bowl
of exceptional historic importance. Frank M. Setzler, of
the Smithsonian, who discovered the bowl, realized that he
had found a "Rosetta Stone" of Mississippi Valley history.
The Rosetta Stone of the Nile bore the same inscription
in known and unknown writing, thus aiding Egyptologists
to decipher the hieroglyphics of Egypt. The Louisiana
"Rosetta Stone" bears two kinds of art designs—known

and unknown. One is the art style of the Hopewell Mound Builders who were the most advanced people of the ancient Mid-West. Their busy, prosperous villages lay chiefly farther up the valley, in Ohio. The other art style is new to archæologists. It had been found on a few objects in the South before, but it was like an unknown language, in that no one knew definitely what sort of people made such art or where they belonged in the ancient story of the Indian. Finding the known and unknown art on one bowl is evidence that the unknown people represent a southern variation of the Hopewell culture existing at the same time, and closely allied. The "Rosetta Stone" clay bowl has an odd shape. It looks as if the potter had made two generous halves of vases, decorated each in a distinctive manner, and then joined them in a twin form.

The vase with dual decoration scheme was found in a mound containing about 30 graves. The skeletons, almost disintegrated, were mostly those of young children. It is Mr. Setzler's opinion that the pipes, pottery, and other articles being assembled to show the new "Marksville" variant of the Hopewell culture might prove to be older in type than Mound Builder relics from farther up the valley. The Gulf coast may have been the original center from which spread the great complex of arts and customs now labeled "Mound Builder." At their highest point, the Hopewell type of Mound Builders had great skill at carving in stone, weaving cloth and dyeing patterns in it, hammering copper into many ornamental objects, growing farm crops, and what materials they did not conveniently have they obtained by trade, even from across the Rocky Mountains, a distance of over a thousand miles.

So spectacular was the culture of the Mound Builders that many people have thought of a Mound Builder as some strange, superior race distinct from the Indian. Scientific excavations long since proved this theory unwarranted. Mound Builders were Indians. Linking the Mound Builders with known historic tribes has been harder to achieve. But with recent discoveries, the cultural events in the Mississippi Valley are beginning to fall into shape. Marksville appears to show very early Mound Builders who seem to merge with the famous Hopewell culture in Ohio. Another Louisiana site carries the sequence farther toward modern times. At this site, James Ford, a Mississippi archæologist, found evidence of Hopewell pottery followed by what is known as Coles Creek type of pottery, and thence in Mississippi he linked that with prehistoric Tunica Indians, and finally with Tunicas of historic times. The family tree of the Mound Builders is thus pushed back into antiquity, perhaps fifteen centuries long, which remains undated until some ingenious research worker finds a dating device for the Mid-West as effective as the tree-ring calendar is for the Southwest. Efforts to construct an oak tree-ring calendar for this region are now being made.

CHAPTER 28
OUR ANCESTORS—AND OTHERS

IF THERE WERE ANY WAY of turning back the time clock and seeing the men and women of 50,000 or 500,000 B.C.! Anthropologists studying the dry bones of man's past would give their last skull for one glimpse of those living and breathing forerunners of ours.

But that sort of magic is beyond science. There is only the lesser magic that works slowly, though impressively. That is to rebuild those vanished men out of scrappy portions of anatomy and place them against their proper background of time and country. It is a slow process, today perhaps a third complete.

One certainty on which we can build is that a number of experimental types of mankind emerged in the dawn ages. The sole survivor today is our species which we modestly call *Homo sapiens,* meaning wise or intelligent man.

Some of the experiments which nature tried have been unearthed. They are recognized and dated in a vague way by such clues as the ancient geological layers in which they lie buried, by remains of long-ago animals found with them, and, most definitely of all, by the different look of the bones. They differ from us in such features as skull form, posture, angle of jaw, or other details of structure. In their relationship to *Homo sapiens* they have as a rule been called mere cousins. Placed on the family tree of man, they have generally been shunted off to branching limbs away from the branch that designated our own direct ancestry. However, there again scientists disagree. Some scientists suspect that some of the ancient forms were our ancestors, after all, much as the pattern has changed.

As experiments, the earliest men seem like discouraging material. In thousands and thousands of years, those slow-witted men and women showed their capacity to use their

330

hands skillfully and creatively, and to use their voices in systematic communication. Those were fundamental advances, but not a great deal to show for so long a lease of the earth. We can admire their endurance, for it was nip and tuck with them to hold their own against cold, hunger, and wild beasts. But we hardly see them as lords of the earth. Eventually, *Homo sapiens* emerged and pushed ahead into civilization, alone.

Among the vanished types was *Pithecanthropus erectus,* or, as he is called in plain, uncomplimentary English, the Ape Man of Java. His fragmentary remains came from a fossil bed by a Javanese stream. They are the most famous bones in anthropological science, because of their reputation as the oldest human-like bones known. Some anthropologists are inclined to dislodge old *Pithecanthropus* from his distinctive rôle of the oldest man. They consider other specimens of mankind older. In his lifetime, usually put at several hundred thousand years ago, perhaps more than 500,000, *Pithecanthropus* was a low-browed, thick-necked creature. But he walked entirely erect, as his scientific name emphasizes. And judging from the development of "Broca's area" in his brain, he was capable of speech, though it may have been scarcely more than rough grunting noises.

Another experiment was *Eoanthropus,* or the Dawn Man, better known as Piltdown Man, after the place in England where the remains were unearthed. The jaw and cranial bones which represent Piltdown Man were broken and scattered when they reached the scientific laboratories. Hence, there has been room for endless argument over the age of the Dawn Man, and also whether the parts recovered really belong to the same being, after all. The most recent verdict is that the ape-like jaw and the really good forehead do belong to the same individual. The restoration of the skull shows a man not so primitive as the scattered parts had first indicated. The portion of brain which controls speech was essentially human in its development. Moreover, Dr. Hans Weinert of the Kaiser Wilhelm Institute, who examined the original specimens in England, gave a report early in 1933 to the effect that the teeth of Piltdown Man are human. What appears to be ape-like about the teeth can be found in other human teeth as well, he declared. Dr. Weinert is convinced that Piltdown Man was not a contemporary of the ancient animals found near him at all. Piltdown Man has sometimes been called older than *Pithecanthropus*. Dr. Weinert's verdict, if accepted, will bring Piltdown Man farther up in the world toward modern times and make a more human being of him.

Another of Nature's experiments was Heidelberg Man, revealed so far only by a jaw found near the university town of Heidelberg, Germany. No less than twenty-four strata of earth lay piled above this jaw. And the jaw itself is a most extraordinary object, it is so big and powerful and yet definitely the jaw of a man.

Then there was *Sinanthropus Pekinensis,* meaning the Chinaman of Peking. Two skulls and an assortment of other bones of this Eastern type were found in a cave forty miles from Peking. The antiquity and the anthropological significance of this oldest Celestial are still being discussed all over the scientific world.

The last to struggle for survival was Neanderthal Man. A good deal is known about him and his way of living. Neanderthalers made their homes in caves, and the men seem to have been the first to seize a woman and protect her from animals and other men. Family life was being tried.

The Neanderthalers

ANTHROPOLOGISTS are often asked: "When did mankind first subdivide into races?" From recent discoveries, it is beginning to appear that this happened at least as early as the Neanderthal times. Racial differences in those days were not necessarily like the differences between a present-day Oriental and a European. Neanderthalers were different in their own way, and that was so peculiar that when the first of them was dug up in modern times, everyone thought something was wrong with him. He seemed misshapen by some dreadful disease. Surely, exclaimed those who examined the bones, men like this never walked the earth! But more of the grotesque men came to light, whole skeletons. The type had to be acknowledged as real.

The Neanderthalers thrust their heavy heads forward and looked out from under jutting brows as they shambled along. Their foreheads receded and their chins were weak and their noses were bulbous. The joints of their bodies were thick and clumsy. They looked as though some glandular irregularity was mischievously at work, and maybe it was.

In Germany, France, Spain—all European countries—this sort of man was unearthed. Then variations, like racial differences, began to be found.

In 1932, the skull-top of a Javanese was found and given the name Solo Man (after the Solo River, where he lay) and assigned to the same prehistoric antiquity as Neanderthal Man. The Javanese had the unforgettable beetling brow ridges of the Neanderthalers and the same massive frame. But he was set apart by racial differences. He had a flatter skull and forehead than his European relatives, though they had none too much forehead to boast of. There may also have been outer differences of hair and coloring, but we can never know about those.

More spectacular than the appearance of the Javanese variation was the discovery in Palestine in 1932 and 1933 of a whole group of Neanderthalers who looked strangely foreign as compared with the European Neanderthalers that science had grown accustomed to seeing. A joint British and American expedition digging in caves near Mount Carmel found these cave dwellers of Palestine. The initial find was made by young Theodore McCown of the American School of Prehistoric Research. In the months following the first discovery, the hard-working expedition dug out skeletons of men, women, and children of the ancient race. So firmly were the bones embedded in limestone and breccia that whole blocks of the matrix were removed from the caves.

Mr. McCown reported that the new-found people had some of the Neanderthal features, such as heavy brow ridges, slight curvature of the thigh bones, powerful bodies, and protruding upper teeth. But they had higher foreheads, and, as near as could be determined by examining bones so embedded in rock, the Palestine Men had fairly well-developed chins. A dozen of the valuable skeletons, still in their rocky beds, were shipped to the Royal College of Surgeons in London, where late in 1933 the task of drilling the bones out with pneumatic chisels began. One skull already detached from its matrix had proved to have the receding chin of the Neanderthalers. This has raised a question as to whether Palestine Man will prove to be so distinctive from his European neighbors as was expected. But there seems little doubt that he will be a "foreigner."

Peking Man is also considered a variant of the Neanderthal pattern. This is the conclusion, at any rate, of Dr. Eugene Dubois, famous as the discoverer of *Pithecanthropus*. Dr. Dubois linked Peking Man with the Neanderthalers after a careful study of the brain cast made inside the first-found Peking skull. The skull is that of a youth with very small head.

Bones of the horses, deer, elephants, and other wild beasts that Peking Man hunted and ate have been examined closely to establish their age and his. Père Teilhard de Chardin tells of scrutinizing four tons of remains from the cave. The result of this sifting of a little mountain can be summed up in a brief statement: the animals known to Peking Man were of an age older than the Middle Pleistocene. (Pleistocene is the geologic name for the long stretch of earth history when a series of ice ages ocurred and when man was culturally in the Old Stone Age. The middle of the Pleistocene was the time of the Neanderthalers in Europe.)

Tools of stone wielded by the oldest men of China have been studied with equal care by the same French geologist and paleontologist. The tools buried in the lowest zone are of green sandstone, quartz, beautiful transparent quartz crystal, and several other materials. Some of the implements are merely roughly chipped blocks. Others are choppers, quartz cores, pointed implements, and scrapers. It is clear, Père Teilhard has reported, that these implements are the work of men who had arrived at methods of selecting, breaking, and adapting stones to various uses; but they obeyed and had not mastered their material.

THE AGE OF MAN

FIGURE 21

GEOLOGI-CALLY	ANTHROPOLOGI-CALLY	ARCHÆOLOGICALLY		IN YEARS (Estimates vary greatly)
Holocene Period (Recent)	Modern Races	Neolithic or New Stone Age	First Potters and Others	8,000
Upper Pleistocene Period	Cro-Magnon Man and Other Races	Mesolithic or Middle Stone Age	Campignian Natufian Azilian-Tardenoisian	15,000
		Paleolithic or Old Stone Age — Upper	Magdalenian	20,000
			Solutrean	25,000
			Aurignacian	30,000
	Neanderthal Man, Solo Man, Palestine Man, Kanjera Man	Middle	Mousterian	60,000
Lower Pleistocene Period	Piltdown Man (?), Peking Man, Kanam Man, Heidelberg Man, Java Man	Lower	Acheulian	100,000
			Chellean	500,000
			Pre-Chellean (transition)	800,000
Pliocene Period		Eolithic or Dawn Stone Age		
Miocene Period	Origin of Man (?)			10,000,000

You can talk about ancient man in any of four or five scientific "languages." For example, the geologist would tell you that Neanderthal Man belonged to the Middle Pleistocene period of earth history. The archæologist, thinking in terms of cultural history, would say that the Neanderthaler was a Mousterian, that being the name for the Neanderthaler's particular type of stone industry. The anthropologist, speaking in terms of human development, would speak of the Neanderthal Age.

When laymen tackle the subject, they like best to translate into terms of years, and for them it seems clearest to say that the Neanderthalers lived 50,000 to 75,000 years ago. Scientists like that designation least of all, because there is still much difference of opinion about the years of ancient man. In the chart above, the figures on the right offer the reader some idea of a time scale. But it should be kept in mind that some anthropologists might stretch or shorten the time intervals.

From the geologic evidence and the identity of animal bones around him, Peking Man lived early in the Pleistocene period. If he was a Neanderthaler of a sort, he was a remarkably early appearance of that breed. One of his most interesting attainments was the use of fire. His hearth fires have left their charcoal mark unmistakably in the old cave home, showing that fires for warmth and cooking were among the comforts of life so very long ago.

From these and other recent discoveries of Neanderthalers and their kin, several important ideas about the past can be gained. It is clear that ancient man was widely scattered over the Old World. It also begins to appear that the Neanderthal type was not limited to the Middle Pleistocene period of earth history but made an appearance far earlier. Most remarkable of all, it may turn out that the un-beautiful Neanderthalers were some of our own ancestry. This has been a theory advanced by Dr. Ales Hrdlicka, of the Smithsonian Institution, though most anthropologists have leaned to the opposing view that the Neanderthalers died out—perhaps were extinguished in an epic struggle with the tribes of the rising *Homo sapiens*.

As evidence pointing toward direct inheritance from the Neanderthal line, two Oxford anthropologists, called attention to the fact that a child of Neanderthal race in Europe had significant "modern" characteristics not found in the adults. They detected this in the skull of a child found at Gibraltar. In a note to the British scientific journal *Nature* they wrote:

"The resemblance between *Homo sapiens* and *Homo neanderthalensis* suggests that the former may have been descended from the latter by a progressive retention into adult life of characters present in the young stages of the ancestor."

Another suggestion pointing in the same direction— toward Neanderthal Man as the ancestor of Modern Man —comes from Prof. George Grant MacCurdy of Yale University, and Director of the American School of Prehistoric Research. In a lecture at Brown University he

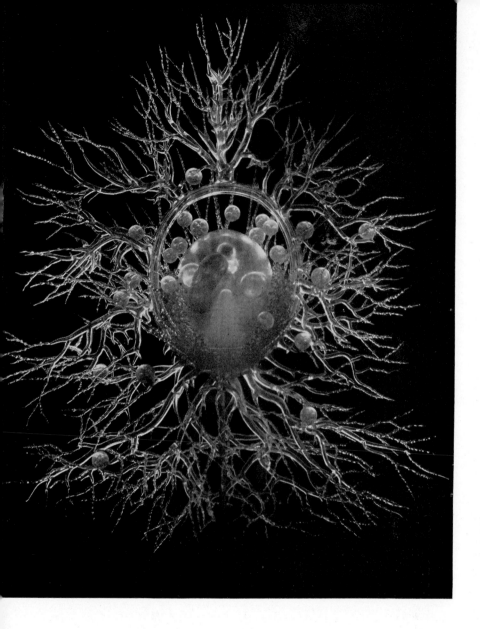

LIVING JEWEL

MANY species of radiolaria, marine animals of miscroscopic size, are infinitely beautiful. Made by Herman Mueller of the American Museum of Natural History, this model is in itself something for science to marvel over, for it is entirely hand-blown glass.

TREE OF LIFE

MAN'S position on this tree of life, constructed by Dr. W. K. Gregory of the American Museum of Natural History, is among the primates, and his branch is next to that of the anthropoid apes. Starting at the topmost branch of the tree of life: 1. White race. 2. Yellow race. 3. Red race. 4. African race. 5. Cro-Magnon man. 6. Australian race. 7. Neanderthal man. 8. Pithecanthropus or Java man. 9. Sinanthropus or Peking man. 10. Piltdown man of England. 11. Taungs fossil ape of South Africa (Australopithecus). 12. Chimpanzee. 13. Gorilla. 14. Orang-utan. 15. Siamang. 16. Gibbon. 17. Horse-tailed monkey. 18. Langur. 19. Snub-nosed langur. 20. Proboscis monkey. 21. Macaque. 22. Black ape. 23. Gelada. 24. Baboon. 25. Guenon. 26. Red ground monkey. 27. Mangabey. 28. Squirrel monkey. 29. Capuchin monkey. 30. Uskari. 31. Saki. 32. Spider monkey. 33. Woolly monkey. 34. Howler monkey. 35. Night monkey. 36. Titi monkey. 37 Marmoset. 38. Tarsier. 39. Bush baby. 40. Loris. 41. Potto. 42. Sifaka. 43. Indris. 44. Awahis. 45. True lemur. 46. Gentle lemur. 47. Dwarf lemur. 48. Aye-aye. (Chart from *Man's Place Among the Anthropoids*, by William K. Gregory; Clarendon Press, 1934.)

MAN AMONG THE PRIMATES

Man's position on the tree of life is among the primates and his branch is next to that of the anthropoid apes.

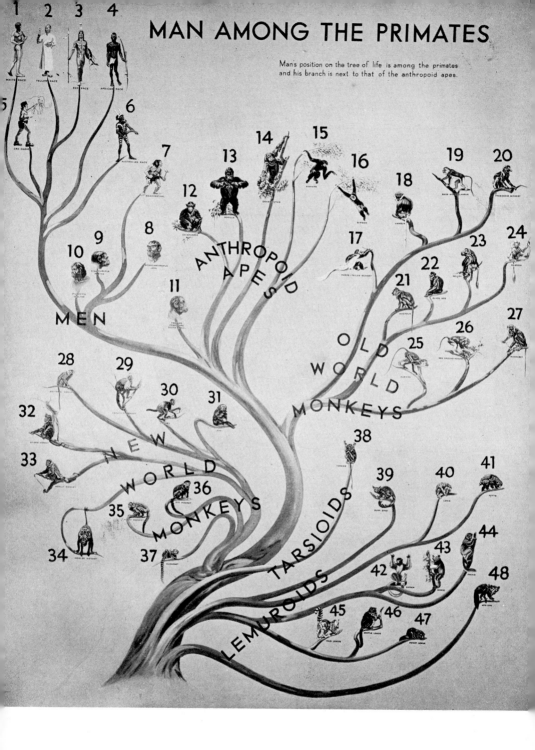

GOLD FROM SEA WATER

SEA WATER may some day yield gold, but no one has yet found a way to extract it economically. Meanwhile man has begun to make his first direct profit from sea water by blowing out of it bromine used in ethyl gasoline. At Wilmington, N. C., enormous quantities of water are sucked in between these dikes, allowed to warm (because bromine is more easily secured from warm water) in a depression possibly made by a meteorite ages ago and then treated with the chlorine that dislodges the bromine.

GREAT WALL IN PERU

IT SEEMS almost impossible that this great wall in Peru remained undiscovered until very recently. Many must have crossed it, never realizing its great length (it has been traced for forty miles), until an airplane expedition accidentally discovered it. It was built by the Chimu Indians, probably about eight hundred years ago and possibly as a defense against the Incas. It will rank in importance with the Great Wall of China and Hadrian's Wall in Great Britain. The wall was found and photographed by the Shippee-Johnson Peruvian Expedition.

outlined four stages of man that appear to have followed in evolutionary series in the Far East. The four are: *Pithecanthropus* of Java; then Peking Man, an early Neanderthal-like form; then Solo Man of Java, also considered a Neanderthal; and last, the modern primitive Australian.

It has been generally assumed that the modern pattern of man, *Homo sapiens,* took shape toward the end of the Neanderthal age. That is to say, men with our sort of skulls, teeth, facial contour, and general appearance emerged some thirty thousand years ago.

Recent discoveries, however, have cast doubt on the relative youthfulness of Modern Man. British anthropologists have been especially keen to discuss arguments favoring greater antiquity for intelligent man. Men and women of our look and build may have been inhabiting the earth for 75,000 years, it has been asserted. Some of the evidence would even add another cipher to the figure. Not all anthropologists have accepted these views, but we present them here, for they are much discussed in the world of science.

The Missing Link—At Last?

THE SKULL OF A WOMAN found in London in 1925 and nicknamed the Lady of Lloyds (after the building under which workmen found her) has been nominated for the title "oldest known example of Modern Man." Prof. G. Elliot Smith, British anthropologist who has taken this view of the lady's importance, has concluded that she lived in the early days of Neanderthal Man. Yet he considers her a modern in type. If this view is correct, it more than doubles the lifetime of our species on earth, as formerly known.

If the age of the early Londoner is generally accepted by science, she may nevertheless lose her distinction of being the oldest of the moderns. Her rivals, recently found, are Kanam Man and Kanjera Man, named as usual after places where science first encountered their kind. They have come to light from fossil beds abounding in animal remains, near the shores of Lake Victoria, in Kenya, East Africa.

Great age is claimed for these two by their discoverer, Dr. J. S. B. Leakey, a young British anthropologist. And a conference of the Royal Anthropological Institute, called in the spring of 1933 to hear Dr. Leakey's report and to examine the fossil bones from Africa, gave a verdict that Dr. Leakey had not exaggerated the antiquity of the specimens. The conference then congratulated the young man on the exceptional significance of his discoveries and adjourned.

If Kanam Man and Kanjera Man are indeed what Dr. Leakey believes, they reveal Africa as the cradle home of our ancestry. Charles Darwin would have been keenly interested in these African discoveries, for in 1871 he wrote in prophetic vein:

"It is somewhat more probable that our early progenitors lived in the African continent than elsewhere."

Following the spring conference, Dr. Leakey made a careful study of the fossil remains he had discovered. In October he reported to the Royal Anthropological Institutute that Kanam Man bears evidence of being one of our ancestors, but in almost pre-human form. So great is his antiquity, according to the geologic testimony of the site, that Kanam Man may have been a contemporary cousin of old *Pithecanthropus* himself. All that is left of him, or all so far recovered, is a portion of jaw with several teeth intact. But from examination of this fragment Dr. Leakey reported that the chin is typical of modern man, and the teeth arranged like ours. And yet, he found that X-ray examination showed up differences in structure. From this, he considers Kanam Man to be an early member of our own genus, but a different species. He is, in other words, said to be one of the much sought missing links in our remote ancestry. His tools were roughly chipped products of a pebble industry.

Kanjera Man is pronounced younger, and a true member of the species *Homo sapiens*. Kanjera Man may have been one of the great-great-etc.-grandchildren of Kanam Man. He was living in Africa at least as early as the middle of the Pleistocene era, by the geologic evidence. That fits him into the middle of the Old Stone Age and makes him a contemporary of Europe's Neanderthalers and perhaps the Lady of Lloyds. Kanjera Man has been widely heralded as the oldest of the moderns. Will he share the title with the London lady?

Kanjera Man is represented by three skulls and some skeletal fragments. The femur shows that this type of man walked nobly erect, not shambling like the clumsy Neanderthalers. And he lacked the beetling brows that made the Neanderthaler such a glum and glowering person. His characteristic weapon was a hand ax of a type that corresponds to the Chellean industry of Europe.

Kanjera Man is shown to us as a superior type for the age in which he lived. And Kanam Man, hundreds of thousands of years older, by report, was a superior type to old *Pithecanthropus* of the other primitive experiments.

If Dr. Leakey's African men are as old as he believes, then some adjustment must be made to fit them into the evolutionary picture of Man. Two possible ways may be suggested. One is to assume that the appearance of *Homo sapiens* was not a single historic event, but that at several times and places Modern Man developed from ancestral forms. Thus, Solo Man of Java may, as Dr. MacCurdy has suggested, be the ancestor of living Australian natives. The African remains found by Dr. Leakey would represent another line, with modern representatives as yet untraced. And in Europe there might be still another evolutionary series. The other way of fitting the Africans into the picture in the rôles Dr. Leakey assigns them would be to discount the theory that Modern Man is a child of the Neanderthalers, and to accept without reservation Africa as the cradle land of Modern Man.

An ingenious theory has been advanced to account for early superiority of *Homo sapiens* in the struggle toward civilization: He may have had better tools. In Tanganyika, East Africa, Dr. Leakey found very old tools made from cores of large stones. The men who made these tools knocked off flakes from a chosen stone until they had a core left that was a good shape for a hand ax. This method, Dr. Leakey suspects, was first invented in Africa and was followed consistently by *Homo sapiens*. The Neanderthalers, on the other hand, preferred to strike off flakes from a stone and finish the flakes into weapons, throwing aside the core. It is merely a theory, that the two types of technique played any important rôle in the dominance or weakness of early types of mankind, but it is an interesting possibility, worth checking up to a conclusive point.

1,000,000-Year-Old Men

ONE MAN IN ENGLAND has spent years hunting for dawn tools. About 1910, this man, J. Reid Moir, startled conservative scientists by showing some queer-shaped flints that he had dug up near his home in Suffolk. He called these stone objects the handiwork of men living in the Pliocene period of pre-history. If true, that would mean that man was using his hands and brain to make tools earlier than had ever been demonstrated.

Very slowly, scientific incredulity regarding these "tools" changed to scientific coöperation. Mr. Moir's flint objects, which he continued to unearth in East Anglia, came to be accepted rather generally as true works of man. Examples of these old, old stone implements are among the exhibits of early man in the American Museum of Natural History in New York, the Field Museum of Natural History in Chicago, and the British Museum in London.

So Mr. Moir has proceeded to the next stage in his task and doubtless to a new controversy. He began recently to sort out the oldest recognized relics of man in England with a view to determining more accurately how old they are.

In a report to the British scientific journal *Nature*, in January, 1934, he announced "certain unexpected and far-reaching conclusions." This scientific bombshell is that when the flint pieces are laid out in rows, Mr. Moir finds it possible to point to "four distinct and different groups of implements."

Why is that a bombshell of an idea? Simply because Mr.
Moir says the progress from one to another of those four
kinds of stone tools may be measured by tens, perhaps hundreds, of thousands of years. The men who made the four
kinds represent possibly several hundred thousand years
of progress.

The age ends in the Late Pliocene, which is a time estimated to be at least a million years ago. But it is the beginnings that are more dramatic. Mr. Moir assigns one
well-made curved implement, of the kind called an eagle-
beak because of its hooked point, to an age older than
the Lower Pliocene stratum of the site. And this eagle-
beak is not so old as the implements that Mr. Moir considers the earliest. And there Mr. Moir has temporarily
left his problem, having pushed his old weapon makers
back into an age which he calls "at present unspecified."

Who made the dawn tools is not certain. Probably not
Pithecanthropus. He is usually assigned to a higher cultural stage, the pre-Chellean type of tool-making. Some
anthropologists, who take the oldest-seeming clues of Piltdown Man as being the real index of his age, consider
Piltdown Man an eolith maker. Others, however, class him
as a pre-Chellean, and others think him not so old as that.
Piltdown Man's age and abilities, as we have seen, are
highly variable quantities, at present ratings.

In any case, some paleontologists tell us that beings entitled to be called human must have lived in Pliocene times.
These more than a million-year-old men, the makers of the
dawn tools—perhaps yet to be revealed—must have been
real dawn men of civilization.

CHAPTER 29
LIVING RACES

THERE IS ONE GROUP OF SCIENTISTS that might be called dramatically Men of the Last Chance. A good deal of their best material is vanishing before their eyes. What they fail to learn from this vanishing material may be lost knowledge forevermore. These are the scientists studying living races of the earth. They are the anthropologists, concerned with man's physical traits, and the ethnologists, concerned with his forms of culture.

We read now and again about some Indian tribe that is passing. Only one old woman, perhaps, is keeping alive in her memory the customs of her people. When she dies, the language and traditions of a tribe will die with her. The same dying-out process can be observed in jungle lands, tropic islands, and Arctic wastes. It is not always a matter of a group dwindling to actual extinction. Sometimes a people loses its customs and its own distinctive language by absorption into a stronger, more vital group. Sometimes a primitive people acquires so much civilization that its own cultural heritage is obscured in the new blend. Whatever the local cause, the fading of interesting and picturesque peoples from the earth is happening in so many places that science cannot hope to reach them all in time to fit their story into man's cultural record.

A strong effort to capture some of the vanishing evidence was made when the Field Museum of Natural History in Chicago called upon the well-known sculptor, Malvina Hoffman, to travel round the world and make portrait sculptures of representative types. Results of her work are displayed in Chauncy Keep Memorial Hall, which was opened to the public in June, 1933.

Around this hall is a bronze assembly such as never has

gathered anywhere in the flesh. Over seventy figures were on display when the hall opened, and some have since been added. A native of the Australian bush stands aggressively ready to hurl his death-dealing spear. A bronze Hawaiian balances lightly on his surf board. A lady of India shows in her calm face the reserve of her class and culture. Farther on is an "untouchable" old woman of India, in striking contrast. A slender negress of the Sara tribe stands in a dancing pose that would do credit to any dancer. Sir Arthur Keith, British anthropologist, pronounced the bronze gathering "The finest racial portraiture that the world has seen."

In an introduction to a guide book to the hall, Sir Arthur Keith gives us a good idea of what an anthropologist sees in such an array of faces. In his rôle of guide, Sir Arthur shows that as we pass round the hall and make the acquaintance of representatives of living races, there emerge from what first looks to be confusion three main types of humanity. These are the white or European, the yellow or Mongolian, and the black or Negro. These three, of which all others are variations and blends, are portrayed in a central group in the hall. They stand with their backs to a bronze pillar, portraying the highest qualities of the Nordic, East Asiatic, and African. In their grouping, they symbolize the unity of mankind.

How Man Becomes Civilized

IN OUR OWN HALF OF THE WORLD—the Americas—some of the most interesting studies of living man are being made. In Yucatan, for example, one group of ethnologists is watching how civilization develops. Taking city, town, and village for his laboratories, Dr. Robert Redfield of the University of Chicago has been walking about and observing for himself how people become civilized. Yucatan offers excellent material for this study because not only do the living Mayan Indians represent the entire range of social development from primitive tribe to modern city, but these groups in their varying stages of advancement are, right now, being influenced by civilizing factors.

In isolated villages of Quintana Roo an ethnologist may find Mayas who are still maintaining an independent semitribal organization, and whose primitive customs are scarcely challenged by modern ideas. Less isolated, only thirty miles in the bush, may be found such a village as Chan Kom, which Dr. Redfield chose to represent a slightly more complex stage. The population of this village is 250 Mayas of nearly pure Mayan blood. Chan Kom combines the old and new, often incongruously. A town on a branch of the railroad was chosen to show a more advanced stage of Mayan modernization. The town has many persons with much white blood. And to see what real city life does to the Indian, Dr. Redfield took the capital city of Merida for his most advanced laboratory.

In a progress report to the American Association for the Advancement of Science in 1933, Dr. Redfield told some of his observations.

One of the most striking changes he observed in Yucatan, in the transition from simple community life to the more complex, is a diminishing importance of religious belief and ritual. In the village, he explained, all the Indians are farmers, and every house is anxious about the problems of drought and harvest. Religion, a mixture of Catholic faith and old native beliefs, is close to their daily lives. They follow understandingly what the shaman-priest says and does to insure a harvest. If anyone falls sick, the villagers trace it to failure to perform the proper rituals. Illness is proof of lapse from piety.

"But in the town and in the city," he continued, "there are the very Catholic and the less Catholic, as well as Protestants and skeptics. And there are men in the community—few in the town and many in the city—who are not agriculturists and for whom therefore the anxieties of sowing and drought are not acute.

"In the village the agricultural rites are acts of piety; in the town they are acts of safeguard. They become less the direct responses to crises, and more matters of traditional performance. In the village the forms are still full of meaning. The layman understands and follows what the shaman-priest says and does. In the towns this is less true. The shaman-priest is not a member of the town community. He is brought in from a village, and the symbolism of what he does is less understood. It is simply an act of prudence to have him perform his ceremonies: otherwise, the crop might fail. In a word, this functionary becomes less of a priest and more of a magician."

Dr. Redfield's materials point to the conclusion that black magic gains in potency in the Indian circles as life becomes more complex. Fear of black magic as a cause of sickness and death appears to be commoner in city than town; and commoner in town than in village. This curious trend—not what we should expect in a people acquiring modern civilization—may possibly be explained, Dr. Redfield suggests, by the fact that village life moves in simple, familiar patterns, with everyone knowing his neighbors and understanding them. In the city and town, life seems more fearfully insecure, and the old religious authorities no longer offer such reassuring support. Hence the Indian turns to magic which seems to offer protection. Cubans who come to Yucatan are believed to be bringers of much West Indian magic.

From Dr. Redfield's study of the patterns of life in Yucatan, he is already beginning to formulate generalizations as to the civilizing process. The Mayas' experiences with civilization are not unique. What they are experiencing can be compared with the effect of white civilization upon peripheral peoples in other parts of the world, the ethnologist explains. It can be compared with the gradual civilization of Europe, as known to us from history.

Objects that come into a museum for exhibition, from distant places, sometimes give ethnologists a vivid glimpse into the ways that man may acquire a new thought of cultural importance. How Tule Indians of Panama acquired a new god was shown when the U. S. National Museum received about a dozen wooden canes such as Indian medicine men carry. Every one of the canes is carved with the unmistakable features of a Scottish doctor who has become the Tule god of medicine.

This white man who attained so unusual a brand of immortality was Dr. William Patterson, leader of a seventeenth century colonial venture to Panama. His colony came there intent on trading and making money. But Spaniards objected to the Scottish traders, feeling that the colony was an encroachment on Spanish preserves. After two years, Dr. Patterson and his followers gave up the battle and departed.

In those two years, Dr. Patterson had made friends with the Indians by his power to cure their diseases. He left them the memory of the greatest medicine man they had ever known, and in time they came to think of him as a god who spent a short time in their midst. His long-nosed, sharp profile carved in wood became magic to aid Tule doctors in their work. His cult is now spreading even to Indians of northern South America, for some of the magic canes in the Smithsonian collection are from that region. Some of the canes picture him in his Sunday outfit of top hat and long blue coat. Other canes show him wearing a golf cap, walking suit, and heavy stick. Indian god though he is, Dr. Patterson remains very much the Scotsman in his images.

Some of the primitive peoples of America that are familiar names to the reading public are almost "unknown" so far as scientific data about them are concerned. When an expedition does have the opportunity to live among one of these groups, get their point of view, and compare them with other peoples, surprising discoveries are made.

Head-Hunters

JIVARO HEAD-HUNTERS of Ecuador and Bolivia are a case in point. Famous as bloodthirsty fighters, known everywhere for their custom of hunting a feudal enemy to the death and then shrinking his head to make a belt trophy the size of an orange, the Jivaros have nevertheless remained an unknown quantity as specimens of the human race. After all, there must be more to a head-hunter than his hunting, however important that activity may be to him. But few explorers ventured close enough to learn very much about the head-hunters. And scientists seemed a bit reluctant to visit Jivaros in their jungle homes. Perhaps, however, the scientists were only waiting a good chance. For certainly when his chance came, Matthew Stirling, chief of the Bureau of American Ethnology, seized it. Joining the Latin-American Expedition, Inc., which departed in 1931 and 1932 to explore the little-known regions of Ecuador and Colombia, Mr. Stirling set out with the intention of making friends with the Jivaros and studying them for science. His philosophy of friendliness stood the test, for the Jivaros, like the "fierce" pygmies he had studied in New Guinea, accepted him as a friend and helped him to gather the information he was seeking.

He found a paradox. The fierce Jivaro warriors are so feminine in appearance that it is hard to tell a man from his wife or sisters. A Jivaro fighting man wears long hair. He wears a skirt so like his wife's skirt that it takes a Jivaro or a fashion expert to detect the slight difference. The warrior paints his face, not in bold streaks of war paint, but in a feminine fashion. And when he speaks he has a soft voice. Mr. Stirling, introduced to this strange society, could feel a sort of femininity in the very atmosphere. He had for some days the vague, subconscious feeling of living in a woman's world.

It is the young men of the Jivaro warrior class who look most gentle and feminine. The Jivaros have, moreover, to an unusual degree, the smooth muscles and almost hairless bodies that Indians generally possess.

But, reported Mr. Stirling emphatically, when he returned to civilization, there is nothing sissy about a Jivaro except his appearance. And a Jivaro has strong ideas of what is right and fitting for a man and what is suitable for a woman. A Jivaro maiden would be shocked at the idea of herself as a warrior. Not that she has any aversion to carnage, but she is guided by tribal beliefs in sex differentiation, which permeate everything a Jivaro does. Every object in nature is male or female, the Jivaros informed Mr. Stirling, and every object must be treated accordingly.

Weapons of warfare are male, and a woman who would take them up in battle would bring down calamity upon herself and her entire family. On the other hand, the soil is feminine, and woman only may till it. The soil would resent interference by a man. Clothing materials are male. Hence the warrior must make not only his own clothes, but those for his wife and children, too.

From such revelations, it begins to be clear how much there is to be learned from a people whom the world has simply summed up "head-hunters."

Incidentally, how the Amazon River got its name can now be understood. The Spanish explorers who encountered Jivaro warriors thought they had found girl fighters, like the Amazons of old Greek literature.

Slave Trade

ETHNOLOGICAL RESEARCHES often clear up obscure points of geography and history. One supposedly unsolvable mystery—from what parts of Africa came the Negroes of America—is being cleared up by the aid of ethnology. A progress report on this task was given before the American Association for the Advancement of Science in 1933, by Dr. Melville Herskovits, of Northwestern University. His report made clear that the regions of Africa where slave traders captured natives were not nearly so vast and vague as popular fancy has believed. That some slaves came from the deep interior of the Dark Continent or from East and South Africa is not to be denied, he explained. But by far the major portion of the slaves were drawn from a region comprising only a fraction of the vast bulk of Africa. This area was the West Coast from Loango to Gambia and the forested belt that stretches a hundred or so miles inland.

Several kinds of evidence are being focused on the problem of tracing the origin of the American negro, Dr. Herskovits explained. One is the testimony of writers who referred to slave-trading operations at the time when the trading was at its height. A great mass of letters, books, and other literature is available from that period, but the fact seeker, delving into the pages, finds African names and places so poorly recorded that it is no simple matter to elicit definite historic facts. Yet the literature displays a new historic usefulness when it is checked against information from ethnological sources. These ethnological sources are Negroes in Africa and Negroes in America.

Old men who actually participated in the slave trade can be found living in Africa today. From several of these, during African trips of scientific investigation, Dr. Herskovits obtained details of the slave trade and the routes that were taken. He has also begun study of Africanisms that have survived in Negro life in America. All of the evidence points to West Africa as the home land of the majority of Negroes in America today.

In South America and islands of the Caribbean, for example, Dr. Herskovits found customs and lore of Africa occurring, over and over. Names of gods, place names, and ideas of religion can be identified as coming from the Gold Coast, Dahomey, Togoland, Nigeria, all West African sections. In the United States most Negro memories of Africa can be identified as generalized West Coast Africanisms. Describing some of these, the ethnologist said:

"Negroes in the United States are Christians. Yet their dead must 'cross the River Jordan' in a manner that is exactly parallel to that in which the West African dead must cross their rivers before they reach the spirit world. We find the African importance attached to wakes for the dead. And we observe an entire complex of ritual surrounding burial so akin to West African funeral customs, even to 'burying shallow' until arrangements can be made for a proper funeral, the passing of small children over the coffin as they do in the Suriname bush, and the inclusion of food and money in the coffins."

Declaring that peculiarities of speech of southern Negroes have been mistakenly accounted for, Dr. Herskovits reported:

"Any grammar of a West African people explains the grammatical oddities which it has become customary to ascribe to the influence of Elizabethan English on the early slaves, or to the grammatical perversions of child-like folk taught the language of the masters in a manner that children are spoken to."

Who Is a Nordic?

THERE IS NO DOUBT that the anthropological topic most widely debated in recent months is a topic that has little or no scientific meaning. This is the burning question: Who is a Nordic and how important is it to be one? No new scientific knowledge (except psychological) has come from the current excitable discussions of Germany's Nordic movement.

Nordicism was evolved as a theory years ago. Dr. K. Holler, well-known German eugenist, credits a Frenchman and a German with awakening the movement in Germany. The Frenchman, Prince Gobineau, obtained little recognition in his own country but was well received in Germany when his work on the inequality of human races was translated into German about the turn of the century. At about the same time Houston Stewart Chamberlain's *Foundations of the Nineteenth Century* appeared and exercised a profound effect on German thought. It was after the European war and the revolution, however, that the movement took its decided advance. In 1922, a German anthropologist, Dr. Hans F. K. Gunther, published a book on racial traits of the German people, which proved to be a best seller of its kind. The author expounded the text that "foundation and maintenance of German culture, as indeed of all European and west-Asiatic cultures, rests on the blond Nordic race, and by its disappearance German and European culture is threatened." Gunther's Nordicism was intended not to divide but to unite the German peoples. Nordic blood is the only kind common, more or less, to the Germans, he contended. All other racial strains there are more or less local.

This Nordic philosophy of Dr. Gunther was taken up by Adolf Hitler, Chancellor of Germany, as a rallying point for political and cultural nationalism. Used as a lever against the Jews, it aroused a world-wide controversy. Nordicism, as applied by German nationalists, fits no recognized anthropological classification. It has become a purely psychological matter, to be a Nordic. It is a state of mind, or more perhaps a state of the emotions. A Nordic first and foremost is a fighter. He should be blond, long-headed, and blue-eyed, or have such traits displayed in the ancestral portraits. But many of the most enthusiastic Nordics of Germany lack the supposedly essential blondness. They never lack, however, the psychological traits.

From an anthropological standpoint, the Jews are not, properly speaking, a race. They are a people of mixed racial origin, and may even trace part of their ancestry to the fair Nordics. It is no more correct to speak of the Jewish race than it would be to refer to the French race. According to a British anthropologist, Dr. A. C. Haddon, of Cambridge University, the Jewish people were originally a Semitic people who even in very early times mixed with Amorites, Hittites, and Philistines. The so-called Jewish nose is a heritage from the Hittites. From the Amorites, modern Jews derive their claim to Nordic descent. The Amorites were fair, and representations of them in frescoes in the tombs of Abu-Simbel show some of the Amorites as having blue eyes and red beards.

Jews of Germany, and of northern and eastern Europe generally, are by no means purely of the old Palestinian stock, mixed though even that was. They represent a dispersal of the old stock northward and westward by way of the Black Sea and the river valleys that slope towards it. They represent also a vigorous and successful missionary effort on the part of Judaism at about the beginning of the Christian era, which brought into the fold of Abraham considerable numbers of aliens, mostly Slavic, around the Black Sea coasts.

It is perhaps the bitterest piece of irony in the tragic situation of the Jew in Germany that Hitler, leader of "Nordics," is himself a non-Nordic, and that the Jews who have been hazed by his partisans have a strong strain of his own Alpine blood in their veins.

The American Race

THE MINGLING OF RACES AND SUB-RACES is proceeding so rapidly in some parts of the world that new types can fairly be seen emerging. This is particularly true in America, where almost every part of the world has poured its contribution into the melting pot, and the mixing has been rapid. Anthropologists are taking great interest in the American type that will, sooner or later, emerge. Various efforts have been made to measure and observe Americans of successive generations, to see what the trend is.

The opportunity afforded by the Century of Progress in Chicago for measuring a cross-section of the American public was used to advantage by the Harvard Anthropometric Laboratory. An anthropological station was set up in the Hall of Social Sciences, with C. W. Dupertuis in charge, and 3,100 visitors paused long enough from sightseeing to permit the recording of 125 statements as to their measurements, physical traits, and sociological background. Prof. E. A. Hooton, director of the Harvard laboratory, was well pleased with the material obtained, calling it "undoubtedly the best anthropological cross-section of the American public ever made."

Complete analysis of the facts and figures recorded would require at least two years of statistical work. But Prof. Hooton has already announced the results of some preliminary tabulations of the first 1,565 individuals measured at the Fair.

The figures show that the Pure Nordic, tall, blue-eyed, blond, and long-headed, is rare among the men in America and rarer among the women. Pure Nordics make up less than 8 per cent of the male population and just 5 per cent of the female. Other pure racial types are even less numerous.

The figure of man most commonly found in America today appears to be tall, with long head, hair of medium or light brown, eyes of mixed color (some brown pigment on a light ground), and a narrow nose. Prof. Hooton calls this mixed type Predominantly Nordic. He believes it to be the most prevalent type in native-born Americans of native parentage, for it prevails among the large number of criminals that he has measured no less than among the crowds of the Fair. About one third of the men measured at the Fair were Predominantly Nordic. So were about one fourth of the women.

A different mixed type, however, was found the most prevalent among the women of this country. Nearly one third, 32 per cent, of the women measured at the Fair were what Prof. Hooton calls Nordic-Alpine. The Nordic-Alpine woman is tall and of medium or lightish coloring with eyes of mixed color. Her head is round or inclined to the Alpine broadness, not long like a Nordic head. About 16 per cent of the men measured were of the Nordic-Alpine type.

Third in numbers is a type classed as Nordic-Mediterranean. People of this appearance have long heads, dark hair and eyes, but are much taller and bigger than pure Mediterraneans. About 16 per cent of men and 19 per cent of women in this country fall in the Nordic-Mediterranean class.

To sum up, the present native-born American is thus shown as fitting into one or another of three mixed racial types, in all of which Nordic is the most prominent element.

"When all of the material is worked out in detail," Prof. Hooton commented, "we shall know a great deal about the relation of physical types to education, occupation, marital state, place of birth. We ought to be able to settle the question as to whether gentlemen really prefer blondes, and a great many other questions which are infinitely more important."

CHAPTER 30
THE FUTURE OF MAN

EVER SINCE DARWIN popularized the doctrine of evolution, and as a consequence thereof extended man's history into the past a hundred times as far as people were used to thinking it had gone, a favorite pastime of prophets of the romantic school has been to project man's history-to-be into imagined future centuries. Some very fascinating and fantastic pictures have thus been drawn of what humanity will be like, but they have been almost wholly the work of imagination; most scientists have for the most part shied off, denying that they were prophets or the sons of prophets.

Nevertheless, some kind of a provisional peep into mankind's future can really be made, and that without violating the principles of sound science. A modest forecast of what man may be like 500,000 years from now has been made by Dr. H. L. Shapiro, associate curator of physical anthropology at the American Museum of Natural History. The suggestions he put forth, somewhat provisionally, were not just guesses; they were based on careful study of the fossil remains of early races of man and of his nearest cousins among the lower animals, together with observations of what seem to be present trends of physical development among modern men. In other words, Dr. Shapiro's prophecy was the application of a common method of science—the projection of the more or less solid line of the known past as a dotted line into the unknown future.

There is good reason for taking as long a focus as Dr. Shapiro's into the future. Any prophecy at a much shorter range, say ten or fifty thousand years, he said, might not be particularly interesting, for evolution moves so slowly that nothing much is likely to happen to man's physical being in such short periods as those. Present-day man is very little changed from the men of the later days of the Old Stone Age, if indeed he is changed at all. But half a million years gives man time enough to change his make-up and emerge with at least a slightly different face and figure.

Before launching into his prophetic career, Dr. Shapiro also took another precaution, as a proper scientist should. He covered up contingencies with a solid, protecting "if." Man is to a considerable extent the creature of his environment. If major changes should take place in the earth's astronomic behavior, or if its climate, geology, or other factors that influence man should become radically different in his 500,000 years, then naturally all bets are off. But if conditions remain substantially as they are today —and Dr. Shapiro held this to be as likely as any other possibility—then a forecast can be ventured.

"The earth, we have no reason to doubt, will continue in its orbit at a speed not perceptibly different," said Dr. Shapiro. "Nature, perhaps rather more under control than now, will function in the accustomed way, with occasional eruptions to warn man of his human and finite powers. Inevitably in this long period of time civilizations will have declined and new ones will have arisen to take the lead for a time. Perhaps on several occasions civilization will come perilously near to barbarity, but it will ever spring anew and to dizzier heights. There is nothing in human history inconsistent with this view.

"Nor, on the other hand, do I share the opinion of some that man will have become so enmeshed in machines that he will have lost the function of his appendages through disuse. No, the use of our arms and legs, even though it be only for sport, will be vigorous. In this I agree with Aldous Huxley, in whose brave new world man employs machines to his enhanced satisfaction but nevertheless enjoys the exercises of his body."

That eugenics will greatly influence the physical development of the race Dr. Shapiro expressed doubt. It is conceivable, even inevitable, he said, that its principles will be applied, but "it will not deflect the stream of evolution very far from its course."

Our Gigantic Grandsons

THE FIRST THING you might notice, if you saw your great-grandson-16,666-times-removed approaching from a distance, would be his great height and corresponding bulk. Even in recent measured times, people of the same stock, of the same line of descent, have been growing taller and heavier. Dr. Shapiro cited the close physical measurements that have been made on three generations of Harvard men. The present generation in this group is about 3.55 centimeters (1⅜ inches) taller than their own fathers, younger sons are somewhat taller than their elder brothers, and the fathers are taller than the grandfathers.

The increase in height will entail an increase in girth, as well, probably. Such has been the tendency in all lines of animal descent. That is what happened in the long descent of the horse from the little Eohippus.

This taller, heavier, many-times-removed great-grandson will of course require nutriment for his bigger body. Dr. Shapiro is not one of those who expect future man to have a much-reduced digestive system, sufficient only to absorb highly concentrated food pills with which they fancy man will content himself. He made mock of such dismal forecasters:

"Perhaps even such a vestigial digestive tract may be dispensed with altogether if man ever becomes indifferent to food. In that sad day the essential nutriment of life might then be injected directly into the blood stream.

"But I cannot accept this dismal future. The delights of the table are too pleasant to be lightly eliminated in favor of the sterile and joyless consumption of food pills. I can perceive no diminution in man's appetite—if anything, he eats more than primitive man—and certainly I have yet to know a healthy man who shows even the faintest inclination to relinquish the sensuous and delicate enjoyment of solid foods. Therefore I leave you your stomach and its appurtenances."

But even though the digestive system remains intact, one adjunct to it is undergoing modifications and will continue to do so, Dr. Shapiro warned. This is our dental equipment. No vertebrate is afflicted with such extensive dental decay as man, he says. Our jaws have shortened amazingly since the happy forgotten tree-dwelling days—indeed, many modern men never get the use of their third molars, or wisdom teeth. A whole new branch of dental surgery— orthodontia—has been developed to take care of the many ills of overcrowded, badly arranged, ill-erupted teeth. So when our future man eats he will have to manage his pleasures of the table with even poorer and smaller teeth than we have now, and perhaps fewer of them.

Even more significant, however, may be the changes taking place in the top of man's head during the half-million years to come. His brain may be expected to increase in size—although Dr. Shapiro hedges his prophecy at this point with the reminder that cerebral evolution may be accomplished by an improvement in the quality of the brain without an accompanying increase in size. But, in spite of certain exceptions to be noted, the human brain has steadily grown larger, from the most ancient to the most modern specimens. Dr. Shapiro gave 900 cubic centimeters for Java Man, 1,00 cubic centimeters for the somewhat later Peking man; for the modern European, 1,450 cubic centimeters. Projecting the line into the future would give a brain-size of 1,725 cubic centimeters 500,000 years from now.

"But this need not call up a picture of a balloon-headed individual," he continued. "There are men to be met without special comment on the streets today whose skull capacity reaches and even exceeds this figure."

Nevertheless, we may expect the human head to become more dome-like as the brain becomes larger. For the bottom of the skull, as indicated by past developments, can be expected to become shorter. The very shortening of the upper jaw, as the teeth became more poorly developed, has helped in the pulling in of the facial angle to a more and more nearly vertical slope. Although they are probably not at all on the same line of descent, the gorilla, the Australian native, and the European white man illustrate the development of facial steepness very well indeed. The great ape's face slopes like a roof; the Australian's face is human,

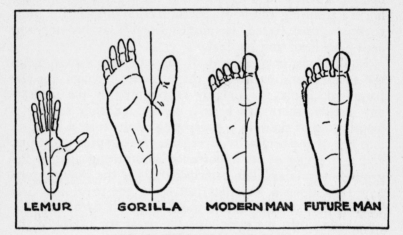

PEDAL EVOLUTION OF MAN

FIGURE 22

THREE steps in the evolution of the primate foot, and a possible fourth.
Courtesy American Museum of Natural History.

though he still has a decided "mug"; the European is straight-faced, and we even encounter actually dish-faced individuals.

Another cranial change that past ages have brought, and future ages may continue, is the smoothing of the skull. Apes develop a crest of bone and tremendous eyebrow ridges. Primitive man had heavy eyebrow ridges also, and these ridges survive, reduced, in many moderns. But on the whole there has been a smoothing off of angles, an evening out of curves.

In this feature, the females have always kept ahead of the males, in apes, in primitive men, in moderns. If the refinement of the skull continues along the lines of the past, we may expect the men of 500,000 years hence to have "feminine" skulls. Meantime the women will have achieved still rounder skulls and smaller faces—their crania will have become infantile.

It has been observed that although man is rated as the highest of evolution's products, he is in many respects still relatively little evolved, still to a considerable extent unspecialized. This appears when we compare the human hand and arm with the bat's wing, the seal's flipper, or the horse's front leg and hoof. Specialization in man, the same scientists have stated, is most noticeable at his opposite ends—his head and his feet.

In the long development of modern man's foot, from the smallest and earliest of the primates through ape-like forms which may be roughly represented by the present-day gorilla, there has been a steady tendency toward a lengthening of the sole, a shortening of the toes, a bringing into line of the originally divergent, tree-adapted great toe, and a stressing of its importance in thrusting against the ground in walking. The principal push of the walking foot now falls along a line that just edges the great toe; Dr. Shapiro expects that line to move over, bit by bit, until it runs right down the middle of the great toe itself. At the same time the little toe, already not much more than a vestige in many human beings, and with a toenail hardly recognizable as such, will become even more reduced and may disappear altogether. The man of the future, *Homo futurus* as Dr. Shapiro nicknames him, will sum up as a giant with a big, powerful head at one end and big, powerful toes at the other.

CHAPTER 31
THE FUTURE OF OUR POPULATION

W HAT WILL THE UNITED STATES be like fifty years from now? Will the character of its population change; and if so, how? Will Americans remain, as they are now, a nation of comparative youngsters? What effect will our mode of life have on the span of our years? And what about the size of the nation? Will the United States continue its phenomenal growth indefinitely in the future, or will the declining birth rate and the bars against immigration from abroad produce a stationary population or an actually diminishing number in the years that are to come?

All these questions have a vital import for those who are planning any long-time program of industrial recovery or expansion for the nation. They have been given the most serious thought by statisticians, biologists, and economists, with the result that predictions have been made of what is likely to occur in the next few decades. Momentous economic and social changes are foretold. The way of the future is suggested in part by the study of what has happened to the population in the past.

The growth of America's population has been extraordinary. From about 2,500,000 in 1776, the United States population increased to over 122,500,000 in 1930—almost fifty-fold in a little more than a century and a half. In the present century, since 1900—a period of only 30 years— the population increased about 47 millions or nearly two thirds as much as it did in the 125 years preceding.

Nevertheless, scientists warn us not to expect this phenomenal growth to continue indefinitely. Already signs have appeared to tell the discerning that Nature's brakes are being applied, and that each future census is likely to show a smaller growth than the preceding one. For the growth of peoples is like the growth of animal species or

360

even like the growth of an individual child. It is rapid at first. A child doubles his birth weight in six months. If he kept on at this rate he would soon reach the proportions of a fairy-tale giant. But, except for the spurt at adolescence, his growth each year is slower than it was the year before, until it is not even enough to replace the wear and tear of life processes.

A similar process is observed when a plant or animal species is introduced into a new environment. Since the English starling was introduced into the United States, these birds have multiplied with such amazing rapidity that they have reached the proportions of a pest in many Eastern cities. Yet the biologist gives us the hope that finally the saturation point will be reached, and the starling will take his place among the other birds and cease to be more favored than they in rate of increase.

The beginning student in biology is impressed with the rate at which a new yeast colony grows. If yeast and bacteria and germs propagate at such a rate, why is there room in the universe for anything else? he asks. However, his instructor can tell him that this growth will not keep up indefinitely; it will continue until the flask is pretty well filled, but after that the increase would be just about enough to keep the population at the same total.

The changing rate of growth of yeast, and fruit flies, and human populations can all be expressed mathematically by similar formulæ, it has been found by the biologist, Dr. Raymond Pearl, of Johns Hopkins University. When it is shown graphically by a curve the height of which increases with increasing rate of growth, the result looks something like the back of a stream-lined automobile. The line starts out somewhat slowly, rising at a not very steep angle, then the incline becomes more and more precipitous for a while, but soon it becomes less steep again and at last flattens out completely. In the case of the population of the United States, Dr. Pearl reasons that the upper limit will be reached when the population is 197,274,000, and this will occur early in the next century.

Other statisticians have put the maximum at an earlier time and a lower number. Dr. O. E. Baker, the U. S. Department of Agriculture's senior agricultural economist, believes the population of the nation is unlikely to exceed 150 million.

Others have made even more extreme estimates. Drs. Warren S. Thompson and P. K. Whelpton, of the Scripps Foundation for Research in Population Problems at Miami University, Oxford, Ohio, who devote themselves primarily to a study of population problems and have given particular attention to estimates of future population, set about 145 million as the peak for the population of the United States to be reached in 1970. By 1980, they consider that the total population of this nation will be well on the down grade in numbers. Dr. Louis I. Dublin, actuarian and statistician of the Metropolitan Life Insurance Company, sets the population for 1970 at 150 million and adds that then the population will be practically at a standstill, gaining only the small number which the immigration laws will then permit. Most of these estimates are made on the basis of the population figures and birth and death rates available up to and including the 1930 census.

The principal reason for the slowing of America's growth is to be found in the rapidly declining birth rate. The white infants born in 1800 numbered nearly 28 for every 100 women of child-bearing age; in 1930 there were born fewer than nine babies to each 100 women, less than a third the rate in 1800. This drop has not occurred suddenly in the last few years; it has been a steady decline for more than a century.

Fewer children and more old people live in America now than in the past, and this change in age make-up of the population has had its effect on the birth rate, too. At first, America was a pioneering country, and land is settled not by the aged or by the very young, but by people in the prime of life. Immigrants to a new land are of the productive age groups, and the United States in the past has been a Mecca for immigration. Today the picture has changed. The tide of immigration has now reversed, so that more are leaving our shores than are seeking new homes here. The movement is no longer to the open country for the founding of homes but to the cities for the founding of

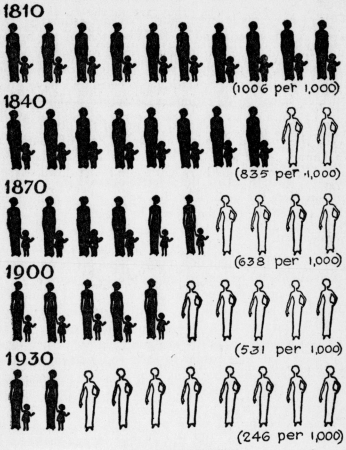

1810 (1006 per 1,000)

1840 (835 per 1,000)

1870 (638 per 1,000)

1900 (531 per 1,000)

1930 (246 per 1,000)

CHILDLESS WOMEN

FIGURE 23

In 1810 the United States had 1,006 children under five years of age for each 1,000 women of child-bearing age, or about a child for each woman. In 1930, we had 246 children for each 1,000 women of child-bearing age, or a little more than 2 children for each 10 women.

fortunes. Still it is the young men and women who are moving, but they are moving to the cities where the birth rates are far below what they are in the rural districts. Yesterday's group of parents was recruited from day-before-yesterday's children plus many new voyagers to our shores. Today's group is mainly just the survivors of yesterday's children. If present trends continue, it is estimated by Drs. Thompson and Whelpton that the birth rate in 1980 will be but 6.4 for every 100 women of child-bearing age or 13.5 for each thousand of the population.

Will the present trends continue? That, of course, no man knows. Some scientists think that some change must come. The immigration bars will again be let down. Larger families will again become fashionable, perhaps through political propaganda such as is being attempted in Germany and Italy at the present time. Or the "back to the land" movement started to some degree by the depression will have the effect of again increasing the birth rate.

Others disagree. They point to the likelihood of war with its devastating consequences on human numbers and human reproduction. Immigration is not likely to be encouraged, they argue, while unemployment is prevalent, and Americans have shown no wholesale tendency to return to the farm so far. Although the growth of yeast colonies and other subhuman populations is controlled entirely by the physical conditions of their environment and their own innate tendencies to reproduce, a new element enters more and more into the situation for human populations. Human beings are learning to apply intelligence in the control of their own numbers; human ideals, standards of living, and affection for the young are causing many voluntarily to refrain from parenthood and to limit artificially the size of families.

Thus birth control, and the gradually increasing spread of information concerning it, is an extremely important factor in controlling the population growth. A recent survey conducted by Dr. Pearl for the Milbank Memorial Fund showed that of nearly 5,000 city-dwelling married women of all ranks of life, birth control was practised regularly or intermittently by 45 per cent of the white women and 26 per cent of the Negroes. Among the well-to-do white women, over 78 per cent had practised birth control. The survey indicated that the innate natural fertility of married couples is probably substantially similar in all economic classes and in the white and colored races; the larger family of those of humbler means is not due to any superiority of health and vitality among this group, it is due almost wholly to artificial alterations of natural biological fertility. By the intelligent practice of birth control among the well-to-do white women the average birth rate was lowered some 73 per cent below its natural level under present-day conditions of life. Among the poor and very poor classes of white women, all the birth control practised succeeded in lowering the average birth rate only 57 per cent below the natural biological level. In these unfortunate classes, only a few more than a tenth practised birth control really intelligently, it was found.

The second great factor affecting the rate of growth of a nation is the death rate. Owing to the efficient public health program, death rates in the United States have been falling with great rapidity. If the large and populous state of Massachusetts may be taken as typical of the country as a whole, the rate has fallen from the high figure of 27.8 deaths per thousand of population in 1789 to only 11.4 in 1931. During the same period, the expectation of life at birth has been raised from about 35 years to nearly 60 years.

This does not mean, however, that the span of human life will be much longer. The average length of life has been raised, not by prolonging the lives of the aged to a later demise, but by saving the lives of hundreds of infants from extinction by preventable children's diseases. Despite the fact that the 1934 infant looks forward to a life much longer than that likely for the new-born in 1790, the man of forty years has no greater expectancy than had his predecessor a century and a half ago.

Death is something that can be deferred but cannot be prevented. A decline in deaths from diphtheria, scarlet fever, tuberculosis, and other diseases of youth must necessarily be paralleled by an increase in the deaths from heart disease, cancer, arteriosclerosis—afflictions of the old. For persons older than sixty-two, the death rate has increased, not decreased, and has increased a considerable amount since 1790. Unless some means is found for reducing the death rate among the older people, the gradual increase in the proportion of old people in the United States will perforce lead to a future increase in death rate for the whole population.

Thus the scientific prophets of population see for the United States of the future a rapidly declining birth rate, an increasing death rate, an older citizenry, and a population without growth, perhaps actually dwindling in numbers.

More important than mere numbers, however, is the rapidly increasing number of older persons that will come with America's population stagnation. This is not entirely a problem of the future, for there were 34 per cent more people over 65 in the United States in 1930 than in 1920, and the increase is continuing. The unemployed are growing older, and many are becoming unemployable.

The dependent old, already a burden on the public, will become a problem of greatly magnified proportions. As the abolishing of child labor and the lengthening of the school period delay the beginning of the earning period, and as the practise of early retirement or dismissal from industry of men and women of middle age curtails the productive period at its latter end, the burden of support for the young and the old is being placed on the shoulders of a constantly decreasing number.

HOW AMERICA WILL GROW OLDER
Figure 24

Drs. Thompson and Whelpton predict the age-group distribution over fifty years.

Ages in Years	Number in Age Group out of Each 100 in Population	
	1920	1980
0 to 19	41.0	26.1
20 to 49	43.6	43.1
50 to 69	12.6	24.1
70 and over	2.8	6.7
All ages	100.0	100.0

UNCLE SAM'S FAMILY

For each ten people —
In 1880

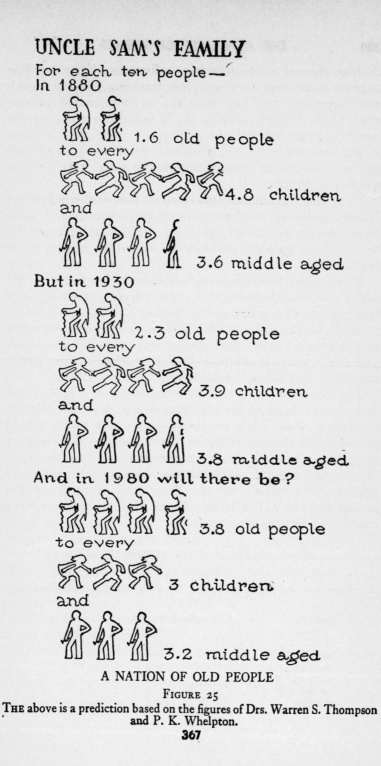

1.6 old people

to every

4.8 children

and

3.6 middle aged

But in 1930

2.3 old people

to every

3.9 children

and

3.8 middle aged

And in 1980 will there be?

3.8 old people

to every

3 children

and

3.2 middle aged

A NATION OF OLD PEOPLE

FIGURE 25

THE above is a prediction based on the figures of Drs. Warren S. Thompson
and P. K. Whelpton.

A glimpse into the future as reflected in the prognostic charts of statisticians is of great interest. Let us compare the population of 1920 with the probable inhabitants of the America of 1980, using the data of Profs. Thompson and Whelpton.

The percentage of those in their prime of life, from 20 to 49 years of age, will be almost the same, about 43 out of every 100 of the total population. But the youth below 20 in 1920 will constitute only 26 per cent of the population compared with 41 per cent as now. The percentage of those from 50 to 69 years of age in 1920 will nearly be doubled in 1980, an increase of from 12 out of each 100 of the population in 1920 to 24 out of each 100 in 1980. There will be some 6,500,000 more old men and women of 70 and over in 1980 than in 1920, a 1980 percentage of 6.7 compared with a 1920 percentage of 2.8.

Added to the economic troubles of a decreasing numerical population in 1980, the United States will be a land of more old people and fewer children. That is the kind of America in which our children and children's children must live.

In thus looking into the future through the glass of statistical trends, it is necessary to keep in mind the fact that the most careful and best founded of predictions can fail. Predictions are based in part upon the trends of the past, and in part upon factors such as the biological make-up of mankind, habits, ideals, and customs that have a certain continuity carrying them over from age to age, from past to future.

Wars, economic or military, plagues, great peaceful movements of peoples, changes of human minds and emotions may give new orientations or new directions to the trends of human growth. Yet for the most part such occurrences have caused but a temporary interruption to the great general trend; soon the stream of life has returned to its customary pathways. Powerful as is science in its effect on mankind, it cannot yet guide destinies to such an extent as to change materially our population's course: nor can the accidents of fate long delay or divert the peopling of the earth.

CHAPTER 32
SCIENCE AND CIVILIZATION

THE REMAKERS OF CIVILIZATION, the true molders of history, whose names so seldom are found in the chronicles of history, are the investigators engaged in scientific research. They are the catalysts of civilization. So often not a part of the everyday beehive of routine living, so often apart from the applications of their discoveries, the scientists are the most powerful agents in the continual rebirth of our community, national and international existence.

Numerically few, their works bulk large in the fundamental reckoning of progress. Perhaps 10,000, less than a hundredth of 1 per cent of the U. S. population, strike with the flint of genius from the steel of learning the sparks that continually kindle anew the forward-moving torches of science. Most strike fire only once or twice; a few flare forth repeatedly. Occasionally intellectual warmth and light are created which will illumine the ages.

So seldom is it possible or necessary to have individual contact with these creative scientists. When illness comes, the physician who is an applier of science prescribes and treats, using the accumulated tested scientific methods and techniques created in thousands upon thousands of investigations. When a new machine is needed or a new building must be erected, the engineer who is an applier of science fashions the mechanism or structure with the aid of accumulated experience and inquiry. The creative scientist usually works about a decade or more in the vanguard of civilization, laying today the foundations for the material and intellectual progress of tomorrow.

Unless there is constant contact with the scientific pioneer, unless the facts and the implications of his work are transmitted to the world at large, there is grave danger that the gains of knowledge made will not come to material or intellectual fruition. This book has been written in an attempt to peer in upon the activities of the creative scientists on the frontiers of civilization. The seeing is often difficult, and the language is not always familiar.

What is the purpose of science? To cure our ills? To make new machines? To forecast the weather? To fashion engines of war? To formulate understandings of peace? To discover whether other planets are inhabited? To provide more creature comforts in return for fewer hours of work? To make transport faster and faster?

The practical and material results of science are important in their sociological applications. More important is the attitude of mind that science engenders. The greatest purpose of science is to have people think straight. Straight thinking, that is to say, scientific thinking, applied to any problem will give its solution, provided the facts are sufficient. Method of analysis and thought are far more important than the so-called facts, because these facts often change as the amount of information and experience obtained becomes more comprehensive.

A large proportion of our present-day ills and troubles may be blamed upon false, prejudiced, and unscientific thinking. There are still mediums, soothsayers, phrenologists, palmists, mind readers, and astrologers patronized and believed by persons from all levels of our civilization. Millions of dollars are spent annually on quack remedies and beauty aids that are worthless or harmful. Millions of dollars were invested during the boom years in enterprises about which the investors knew little or nothing. In everyday life, straight thinking is not often recognized and seldom practised.

It is one of the great hopes of education that the people as a whole can be taught to think straight and scientifically. Dr. Victor H. Noll, of Teachers College, Columbia University, has listed six fundamental habits of thinking characteristic of the scientific attitude:

1. Habit of accuracy in all operations, including calculation, observation, and report.

2. Habit of intellectual honesty.

3. Habit of openmindedness.
4. Habit of suspended judgment.
5. Habit of looking for true cause and effect relationships.
6. Habit of criticism, including self-criticism.

Concerned as it is with our mode of thinking, it is evident that science today as in the past must have profound repercussions upon our systems of economics, philosophy, and religion. Just as it changes the way we travel about the surface of the earth, the food upon our dinner tables, and the way in which we combat the specter of death, so science affects, subtly and slowly, the forms of our governments and the codes that govern our emotional life and our relations with our fellow men.

It is fortunate that science as a body of method and knowledge is so often aloof from the exigencies of economic, political, and religious matters. The torch is carried on through revolutions, political and intellectual. The light may dim for a time as one structure topples and another is reared. The new reigning order will need the services of science, or the intellectual flame is carried to other geographical areas where the fuel is more plentiful. We do not need to turn to the uncertain present for examples. Dr. George Sarton, whose researches as Carnegie Institution of Washington associate have lifted the curtain which has hidden the history of science in its early years, has found that the Moslem world writing in Arabic carried and kindled science's torch during the so-called "dark" Middle Ages, an era that Latinists found barren because they could not read Arabic which was then the language of science.

Contemporaneously, there is being enacted in Germany a significant drama of intellectual intolerance. Of all the passions common to man, intolerance has no doubt had more to do with retarding man's march toward his ultimate destiny than any other. Hitler's government is not the first example, nor will it be the last.

Economic depression, as well as political upheaval, sometimes singles out science as the devil causing civilization's growing pains. Occasionally there is a loud voice raised demanding that the progress of science shall be stopped to allow the world to catch up. Others charge that science destroys jobs and that it is at the root of our economic and social ills.

Scientific leaders condemn as insidious and dangerous to the nation the idea that science is to blame for unemployment and the depression. America will be barred from rising to a higher level of living, and we will suffer from industrial advances in foreign countries, if further technical improvements in manufacturing are stifled, or if propaganda against science reduces public support of scientific work.

For example, Dr. Karl T. Compton, president of the Massachusetts Institute of Technology and chairman of President Roosevelt's Science Advisory Board, finds that if thirty years ago there had been a successful attempt to restrain so-called "technological unemployment" in the carriage and wagon industry and the rise of the automobile had been prevented, the source of income that now supports about 10,000,000 of our population would have been eliminated. Previous to the days of the automobile the 1900 census lists 976,000 individuals employed in the carriage and wagon industry, as manufacturers, drivers, draymen, livery-stable managers, blacksmiths, etc. Thirty years later, with the advent of the automobile, based on innumerable scientific discoveries and engineering developments, the census lists 2,405,000 individuals engaged in this industry, exclusive of those involved in oil production. These are figures corrected to allow for the increase in general population in the same interval. They show that while the advent of the automobile produced technological unemployment among carriage and harness makers, yet the net result for labor has been a 250 per cent increase in the number of jobs. There is a widespread idea that use of labor-saving machinery on highways has thrown out of work men who would otherwise be employed in road construction. The 20 years from 1910 to 1930 which witnessed development of most of the road-building labor-saving machinery show an increase in the number of employees in road construction and repair from 203,000 to 339,000 individuals, with figures corrected for increase in general population.

If scientific research is evaluated in terms of dollars and cents, the costs are low and the returns are high. In some cases investment in research pays dividends of thousands per cent contrasted with the conventional six per cent of finance. The funds to support research are expended through universities, governmental laboratories, research institutions, and industrial laboratories. They come from a very small slice of our taxes, from foundations, and from the wise investments that industrial concerns make in fundamental research.

The pursuit of new knowledge in the sciences and creative activities in higher education are in considerable part supported by the surplus wealth of rich men who, having accumulated more than they and their families need, establish philanthropic foundations.

In times when accumulated wealth, or rather those debt liens upon the energy and materials of the future that we are in the habit of calling wealth, undergoes shrinkage or devaluation, the lessened power of foundations to support research, scientific, and educational activities is of great concern to the future of the intellectual world. This probably means that government in this country will need to take a larger part in the support of scientific research than it has in the past.

In the past few years the federal expenditures for science have been reduced until they total less than 30 million dollars, which is a mere three tenths of 1 per cent of all of Uncle Sam's general and emergency expenditures, not including public debt retirements. The expenditures by the foundations for science probably amounted to about the same figure, perhaps somewhat more. And the expenditures in industry and universities probably bring the total of America's annual expenditures for science to less than 100 million dollars. In very round figures, the cost of science for every United States inhabitant is less than a dollar a year.

Earning its way manyfold in service to civilization, science is dependent for financial support upon the wisdom of rulers of the state, the beneficence of millionaires, and the farsightedness of industrialists. Money there must be to pay scientists' salaries and purchase their apparatus. But money is the least ingredient of investigation. More important is the spirit of inquiry and the tradition of service to mankind that actuate the investigator.

Bountiful and exciting has been the progress of science, especially in the last few years. The bonanza days of science are with us still. The advance is swift; the tasks are difficult and complex. But pioneers can still push outward the frontiers into unknown or dimly seen fields.

Some of the problems of science are undoubtedly destined to defy solution for many years to come. What is life? How does the living differ from the non-living? Whence came the first life? Does life exist in other parts of the universe? Brave attempts are being made and will be made to answer, but can we hope for more than a few hints as to the ultimate truth?

More hope of satisfactory understanding surrounds more immediate and practically useful scientific attacks, such as the studies directed toward the discovery of the cause and cure of cancer. Diseases as baffling and deadly have been conquered. As knowledge grows, a problem like that of cancer grows more complex, but with complexity comes better understanding and hopeful methods of attack. One problem becomes many, some of which are solved.

In the physical sciences, multiplex as the fundamental units of matter and energy have become, and vast as the universe is revealed, the scientist seems closer to understanding the fundamentals because the stuff with which he works seems simpler in organization.

The investigator in biology, taking phenomena at their simplest, still must work with units of immense complexity as compared with the atoms of physics.

In the field of human biology, the study of man in relation to the rest of the world, complexity reaches a peak from which the ways down into the valleys of understanding are shrouded in clouds. The physiologist has made important beginnings in understanding the functioning of the body and its relation to the brain. But they are only beginnings. The psychologist and the psychiatrist understand that their studies of human behavior are as yet embryonic.

Least advanced of all, perhaps, are the sciences of man's relations with his fellow men, the broad field of the social sciences which are only now beginning to adopt the scientific methods that have proved so fruitful in the physical and natural sciences.

Often the specific achievements in science that seem most imminent do not materialize. Then out of a rather dormant line of attack there may come brilliant achievements, seemingly born of an instant. Always in the line of inheritance of these epochal discoveries there are many who have gone before, blazing new trails, labeling blind alleys, building the steps which the conquering scientist mounts to unlock the gate to new progress.

Science is a grand procession through the ages. Blaring trumpets, waving flags, and pomp are not its accompaniment. It travels the quieter roads of the intellect. Martial noise and commercial strivings often delay it. Curiosity often gives new energy to flagging scientific spirits. Like all great causes, science cannot be stopped permanently by lack of support, intellectual or financial, although it may suffer severe losses.

Shall we join the procession, traveling with it as best we may according to our personal endowments? The least we can do is to lend encouragement and give understanding. We can watch the progress and make sure that the world utilizes the gains achieved.

NEW WORDS IN SCIENCE

Aërodyne: A generic term for aircraft that derive their lift in flight chiefly from aërodynamic forces.

Air-mass analysis: Method of meteorological research involving study of moving of masses of cold air from polar regions and warm air masses from the tropics, with the "weather-making" inter-actions of their encountering fronts.

Anti-neutrino: See Neutrino.

Autogyro: A type of rotor plane whose support in the air is chiefly derived from airfoils rotated about an approximately vertical axis by aërodynamic forces, and in which the lift on opposite sides of the plane of symmetry is equalized by the vertical oscillation of the blades.

Automatic pilot: An automatic control mechanism for keeping an aircraft in level flight and on a set course. Sometimes called "gyro pilot," "mechanical pilot," or "robot pilot."

Azochloramid: A chlorine-containing antiseptic.

Boundary layer: A layer of fluid, close to the surface of a body placed in a moving stream, in which the impact pressure is reduced as a result of the viscosity of the fluid.

Civilian Conservation Corps (C. C. C.): Established April, 1933, by U. S. government as work project for unemployed young men. Engaged in reforestation, road building, and other conservation activities in national parks and other public areas.

Cyclogyro: A type of rotor plane whose support in the air is normally derived from airfoils mechanically rotated about an axis perpendicular to the plane of symmetry of the aircraft, the angle of attack of the airfoils being always less than the angle at which the airfoils stall.

D: Chemical symbol for deuterium (diplogen), as used by British and American scientists. *See also* H^2, Hd.

Deuterium: Heavy hydrogen. Hydrogen isotope mass two. Component of heavy water. Name proposed by Urey, Brickwedde, and Murphy. Diplogen (British). Deuton is deuterium nucleus.

Deuton: Nucleus or kernel of deuterium atom. Particle used in atomic disintegration experiments. Diplon (British).

Diplogen: British term for deuterium.

Diplon: British name for deuton.

Feather: In rotary wing system, to periodically increase and decrease the incidence of a blade or wing by oscillating the blade or wing about its span axis.

Flap: A hinged or pivoted airfoil forming the rear portion of an airfoil, used to vary the effective camber.

Gyroplane: A type of rotor plane whose support in the air is chiefly derived from airfoils rotated about an approximately vertical axis by aërodynamic forces, and in which the lift on opposite sides of the plane of symmetry is equalized by rotation of the blades about the blades' axes.

H^1: Chemical symbol for ordinary hydrogen of mass one (protium) to distinguish it from naturally occurring mixtures of protium and deuterium, designated by H. *See* Hp.

H^2: Chemical symbol for deuterium (diplogen). *See also* D, Hd.

H^3: Chemical symbol for tritium, triple-weight hydrogen, isotope of mass three.

Hd: Chemical symbol for deuterium. *See* D, H^2.

Hp: Chemical symbol for ordinary hydrogen mass one (protium). *See* H^1.

Heavy water: Water which contains an unusually large percentage of heavy hydrogen (deuterium).

Hodoscope: An assemblage of cosmic ray tube counters each attached to a neon lamp, which signals the passage of an ionizing particle by lighting when the corresponding tube is traversed by a particle.

Meteoritics: The study of meteorites.

Micro-vivarium: Device combining microscope and stereopticon lantern, which makes possible the direct projection of the images of living microörganisms on a screen.

Negatron: Name proposed for electron (negative electron) to differentiate it clearly from positron (positive electron).

Neuton: Name suggested for element of atomic number zero by Prof. William D. Harkins of University of Chicago. The element neuton would be composed of neutrons, the "atoms" in it.

Neutrette: See Neutrino.

Neutrino: Neutral electrical particle, having properties of a neutron but the mass of an electron. Prof. E. Fermi, Italian physicist, suggested the name meaning little neutron. Some experimental evidence for its existence has been found. English name is neutrette. To account for magnetic properties of atoms it has been necessary to associate with the neutrino another particle, the anti-neutrino, having the same identical properties but which spins in reverse direction.

Neutron: Electrically neutral particle of matter having approximately the same mass as a hydrogen atom. May be composed of proton and electron in close combination. Discovered by Prof. J. Chadwick of Cavendish Laboratory of Cambridge University in 1932.

Oceanograph: An instrument, built on the same principle as the meteorograph for recording upper atmosphere conditions, devised for the purpose of measuring the temperature of the sea down to a depth of 600 feet.

Oleo gear: A type of oil-damping device that depends on the flow of oil through an orifice for its shock-absorbing effect in a landing gear.

Oreston: Alternate (British) name proposed for positive electron (positron).

Positron: Positive electron. Anti-electron (Dirac). Particle of positive charge with mass same as electron, $1/1850$ of mass of proton. Discovered August, 1932, by Dr. Carl D. Anderson, California Institute of Technology. Christened by discoverer. Formed when cosmic rays bombard matter. Average life of a positron is a hundred thousandth of a second. (Common mistake is to misprint "position.")

Psychodietetics: The branch of therapeutic science that deals with the relation of mental conditions and diet.

Rotenone: Active principle of new types of insect poisons, derived from tropical legumes.

Science Advisory Board (S. A. B.): Founded by President Roosevelt's executive order of July 31, 1933, to advise on organization, functioning, and programming of scientific and technical work.

Seismometer: An instrument that registers the amplitude or force of earthquake waves.

Servo control: A control devised to reinforce the pilot's effort by an aërodynamic or mechanical relay.

Sono-chemistry: The speeding of chemical reactions by means of intense sound waves in liquid.

Stoss (pl. Stösse): An atomic explosion or burst of ionization, such as those produced in gases by cosmic rays. Term first used by German physicist Hoffmann.

Tab: An auxiliary airfoil attached to a control surface for the purpose of reducing the control force or trimming the aircraft.

Tiltmeter: An instrument that measures changes in the ground level, used in studying conditions preceding or following earthquakes; of possible future use in earthquake prediction.

Triplogen: British term for tritium.

Triplon: British term for triton.

Tritium: Triple-weight hydrogen. Hydrogen isotope mass three. Triplogen (British). Triton is tritium nucleus.

Triton: Nucleus of tritium atom. Triplon (British).

Vinyl: Chemical group, or radicle, of the formula CH_2CH, compounds of which are used in artificial gums and resins.

DIAMETERS OF MATERIAL SYSTEMS
FIGURE 26

	Centimeters
Proton	10^{-13}
Atom	10^{-8}
Molecule	10^{-7}
Colloid	10^{-6}
Comet and meteor stream	10^{8}
Earth-moon system	10^{11}
Solar system	10^{15}
Galactic cluster	10^{19}
Globular cluster	10^{20}
Star cloud and galaxy	10^{22}
The galactic system	10^{23}
The metagalaxy	less than 10^{27}
The universe (hypothetical radius)	10^{29} (?)

The vast spread of sizes is shown in the above table. Expressed in centimeters ($2\frac{1}{2}$ centimeters make an inch), it is convenient to make use of the exponential method of expressing large and small numbers. For instance, the proton is 0.0000000000001 cm. in diameter, while the hypothetical radius of the universe is 100 octillion cm. in diameter. This table is taken from Dr. Harlow Shapley's *Flights from Chaos* (McGraw-Hill Book Co.) by permission.

NUMBERS OF PARTICLES
FIGURE 27

Hydrogen atom	2
Mercury atom	400
One gram	10^{24}
Comet	10^{44}
Earth	10^{52}
Sun	10^{57}
Globular cluster	10^{63}
Galaxy	10^{66}
Supergalaxy	10^{68}
The universe	less than 10^{73} (?)

Dr. Harlow Shapley in his book, *Flights from Chaos* (McGraw-Hill Book Co.), gives the above census of the universe, based on the idea that fundamentally proton and electron are the particles that make up everything in the universe. To express the extremely large numbers, it is convenient to use the exponential system. For example, the number of particles in a gram (1/30 ounce) is 10^{24} or 1 septillion.

ATOMIC WEIGHTS, 1934

From the Report of the International Committee

FIGURE 28

	Symbol	Atomic Number	Atomic Weight		Symbol	Atomic Number	Atomic Weight
Aluminum	Al	13	26.97	Molybdenum	Mo	42	96.0
Antimony	Sb	51	121.76	Neodymium	Nd	60	144.27
Argon	A	18	39.944	Neon	Ne	10	20.183
Arsenic	As	33	74.91	Nickel	Ni	28	58.69
Barium	Ba	56	137.36	Nitrogen	N	7	14.008
Beryllium	Be	4	9.02	Osmium	Os	76	191.5
Bismuth	Bi	83	209.00	Oxygen	O	8	16.0000
Boron	B	5	10.82	Palladium	Pd	46	106.7
Bromine	Br	35	79.916	Phosphorus	P	15	31.02
Cadmium	Cd	48	112.41	Platinum	Pt	78	195.23
Calcium	Ca	20	40.08	Potassium	K	19	39.096
Carbon	C	6	12.00	Praseodymium	Pr	59	140.92
Cerium	Ce	58	140.13	Radium	Ra	88	225.97
Cesium	Cs	55	132.91	Radon	Rn	86	222
Chlorine	Cl	17	35.457	Rhenium	Re	75	186.31
Chromium	Cr	24	52.01	Rhodium	Rh	45	102.91
Cobalt	Co	27	58.94	Rubidium	Rb	37	85.44
Columbium	Cb	41	93.3	Ruthenium	Ru	44	101.7
Copper	Cu	29	63.57	Samarium	Sm	62	150.43
Dysprosium	Dy	66	162.46	Scandium	Sc	21	45.10
Erbium	Er	68	165.20	Selenium	Se	34	78.96
Europium	Eu	63	152.0	Silicon	Si	14	28.06
Fluorine	F	9	19.00	Silver	Ag	47	107.880
Gadolinium	Gd	64	157.3	Sodium	Na	11	22.997
Gallium	Ga	31	69.72	Strontium	Sr	38	87.63
Germanium	Ge	32	72.60	Sulfur	S	16	32.06
Gold	Au	79	197.2	Tantalum	Ta	73	181.4
Hafnium	Hf	72	178.6	Tellurium	Te	52	127.61
Helium	He	2	4.002	Terbium	Tb	65	159.2
Holmium	Ho	67	163.5	Thallium	Tl	81	204.39
Hydrogen	H	1	1.0078	Thorium	Th	90	232.12
Indium	In	49	114.76	Thulium	Tm	69	169.4
Iodine	I	53	126.92	Tin	Sn	50	118.70
Iridium	Ir	77	193.1	Titanium	Ti	22	47.90
Iron	Fe	26	55.84	Tungsten	W	74	184.0
Krypton	Kr	36	83.7	Uranium	U	92	238.14
Lanthanum	La	57	138.92	Vanadium	V	23	50.95
Lead	Pb	82	207.22	Xenon	Xe	54	131.3
Lithium	Li	3	6.940	Ytterbium	Yb	70	173.04
Lutecium	Lu	71	175.0	Yttrium	Y	39	88.92
Magnesium	Mg	12	24.32	Zinc	Zn	30	65.38
Manganese	Mn	25	54.93	Zirconium	Zr	40	91.22
Mercury	Hg	80	200.61				

THE METRIC SYSTEM

The fundamental unit of the metric system is the METER (*the unit of length*). *From this the units of mass* (GRAM) *and capacity* (LITER) *are derived. All other units are the decimal sub-divisions or multiples of these. These three units are simply related, so that for all practical purposes the volume of one kilogram of water (one liter) is equal to one cubic decimeter.*

PREFIXES	MEANING			UNITS
MILLI-	= one thousandth	$\frac{1}{1000}$	.001	
CENTI-	= one hundredth	$\frac{1}{100}$	.01	
DECI-	= one tenth	$\frac{1}{10}$	.1	METER *for length*
unit	= one		1.	GRAM *for mass*
DEKA-	= ten	$\frac{10}{1}$	10.	LITER *for capacity*
HECTO-	= one hundred	$\frac{100}{1}$	100.	
KILO-	= one thousand	$\frac{1000}{1}$	1000.	

The metric terms are formed by combining the words "METER," "GRAM," and "LITER" with the six numerical prefixes.

LENGTH

10 milli-meters	mm	= 1 centi-meter	cm
10 centi-meters		= 1 deci-meter	dm
10 deci-meters		= 1 METER (*about 40 inches*)	m
10 **meters**		= 1 deka-meter	dkm
10 deka-meters		= 1 hecto-meter	hm
10 hecto-meters		= 1 kilo-meter (*about ⅝ mile*)	km

MASS

10 milli-grams	mg	= 1 centi-gram	cg
10 centi-grams		= 1 deci-gram	dg
10 deci-grams		= 1 GRAM (*about 15 grains*)	g
10 **grams**		= 1 deka-gram	dkg
10 deka-grams		= 1 hecto-gram	hg
10 hecto-grams		= 1 kilo-gram (*about 2 pounds*)	kg

CAPACITY

10 milli-liters	ml	= 1 centi-liter	cl
10 centi-liters		= 1 deci-liter	dl
10 deci-liters		= 1 LITER (*about 1 quart*)	l
10 liters		= 1 deka-liter	dkl
10 deka-liters		= 1 hecto-liter (*about a barrel*)	hl
10 hecto-liters		= 1 kilo-liter	kl

The square and cubic units are the squares and cubes of the linear units. The ordinary unit of land area is the HECTARE (about 2½ acres).

LENGTH

Centimeter	= 0.3937	inch
Meter	= 3.28	feet
Meter	= 1.094	yards or 39.37 inches
Kilometer	= 0.621	statute mile
Kilometer	= 0.5396	nautical mile
Inch	= 2.540	centimeters
Foot	= 0.305	meter
Yard	= 0.914	meter
Statute mile	= 1.61	kilometers
Nautical mile	= 1.853	kilometers

AREA

Sq. centimeter	= 0.155	sq. inch
Sq. meter	= 10.76	sq feet
Sq. meter	= 1.196	sq yards
Hectare	= 2.47	acres
Sq. kilometer	= 0.386	sq. mile
Sq. inch	= 6.45	sq. centimeters
Sq. foot	= 0.0929	sq. meter
Sq yard	= 0.836	sq. meter
Acre	= 0.405	hectare
Sq. mile	= 2.59	sq. kilometers

VOLUME

Cu. centimeter	= 0.0610	cu. inch
Cu. meter	= 35.3	cu. feet
Cu. meter	= 1.308	cu. yards
Cu. inch	= 16.39	cu. centimeters
Cu. foot	= 0.0283	cu. meter
Cu. yard	= 0.765	cu. meter

CAPACITY

Milliliter	= 0.0338	U. S. liq. ounce
Milliliter	= 0.2705	U. S. apoth. dram
Liter	= 1.057	U. S. liq. quarts
Liter	= 0.2642	U. S. liq. gallon
Liter	= 0.908	U. S. dry quart
Dekaliter	= 1.135	U. S. pecks
Hectoliter	= 2.838	U. S. bushels
U. S. liq. ounce	= 29.57	milliliters
U. S. apoth. dram	= 3.70	milliliters
U. S. liq. quart	= 0.946	liter
U. S. dry quart	= 1.101	liters
U. S. liq. gallon	= 3.785	liters
U. S. peck	= 0.881	dekaliter
U. S. bushel	= 0.3524	hectoliter

WEIGHT

Gram	= 15.43	grains
Gram	= 0.772	U. S. apoth. scruple
Gram	= 0.2572	U. S. apoth. dram
Gram	= 0.0353	avoir. ounce
Gram	= 0.03215	troy ounce
Kilogram	= 2.205	avoir. pounds
Kilogram	= 2.679	troy pounds
Metric ton	= 0.984	gross or long ton
Metric ton	= 1.102	short or net tons
Grain	= 0.0648	gram
U. S. apoth. scruple	= 1.296	grams
U. S. apoth dram	= 3.89	grams
Avoir ounce	= 28.35	grams
Troy ounce	= 31.10	grams
Avoir. pound	= 0.4536	kilogram
Troy pound	= 0.373	kilogram
Gross or long ton	= 1.016	metric tons
Short or net ton	= 0.907	metric ton

THE METRIC SYSTEM

FIGURE 29

FIGURES furnished by the United States Bureau of Standards.

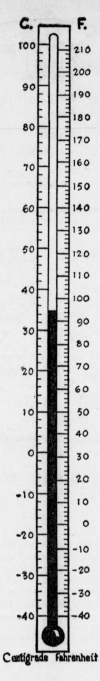

Centigrade Fahrenheit

COMPARISON OF
CENTIGRADE AND
FAHRENHEIT
SCALES

FIGURE 30

384

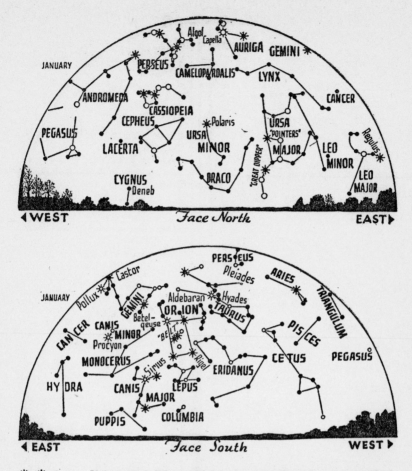

* ✳ ○ ● SYMBOLS FOR STARS IN ORDER OF BRIGHTNESS

THE HEAVENS IN WINTER

FIGURE 31

THESE figures are correct for January 1 at 8 P.M. Planets are not shown. Looking south one sees Orion. The three bright stars that form the warrior's belt are easily identified. Above and to the east is the red star Betelgeuse, while below and directly opposite is the star Rigel. Higher than Orion and to the west is the red star Aldebaran in Taurus. Below Orion is the most brilliant star in the sky, Sirius, in the constellation of Canis Major. Canis Minor is farther to the east, with its brightest star, Procyon.

Looking north one sees the second brightest star now visible, Capella, in Auriga. Below Auriga to the east, and also seen near the zenith when facing south, are the two bright stars, Castor and Pollux in Gemini. Lower in the east is the familiar Sickle, part of the constellation of Leo, its handle downwards and the blade curving upwards. Low in the northwest may be seen the bright star Deneb in Cygnus, although most of the constellation which marks the Northern Cross may be below the horizon.

385

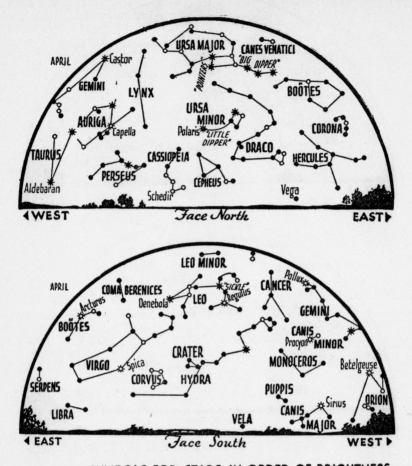

☼ ✳ ○ ● **SYMBOLS FOR STARS IN ORDER OF BRIGHTNESS**
THE HEAVENS IN SPRING

FIGURE 32

THIS chart is correct for April 1 at 8 P.M. Planets are not shown. Facing south one still sees the brightest star in the sky, Sirius in Canis Major. High in the south is Leo, easily identified by the Sickle, with the blade now pointing to the southwestern horizon. To the southeast of Leo is Virgo, marked by the bright star Spica. Directly west, halfway from the horizon to the zenith, is Gemini with the bright stars Castor and Pollux. Below the twins is Procyon in Canis Minor, and farther below it, Sirius in Canis Major. To the left of Virgo is the bright star Arcturus in Boötes, and low in the northeast, mounting higher and higher each night, is bright Vega in the constellation of Lyra.

Looking north one sees the Big Dipper, a part of Ursa Major, high up. Following the two "Pointers" in the bowl one sees Polaris, the Pole Star, in Ursa Minor, which is almost directly over the North Pole. Cassiopeia is easily spotted near the horizon by the great W which its stars form.

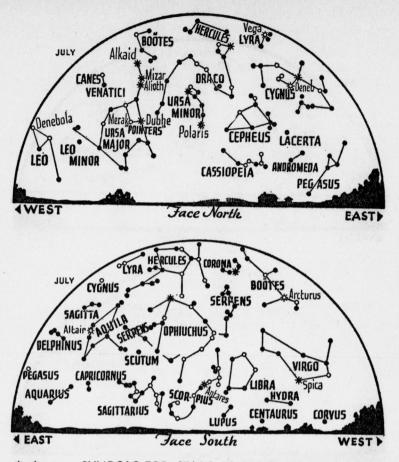

☼ ✳ ○ ● SYMBOLS FOR STARS IN ORDER OF BRIGHTNESS

THE HEAVENS IN SUMMER

FIGURE 33

THIS chart is correct for July 1 at 8 P.M. Eastern Standard Time. Although the sky is still light at this time of year, the position of the constellations is not greatly changed when viewed later in the evening. Planets are not shown. The summer constellations are now in all their glory. In the eastern sky, almost overhead, is Lyra with the brightest star now in the sky, Vega. Below Lyra is Cygnus, sometimes called the Northern Cross. South of Cygnus is Aquila, with bright Altair, then Scorpius with the red star Antares. High up in the west is Boötes with Arcturus, the light from which, after a journey of forty years, was used to inaugurate the Chicago Century of Progress Exposition in 1933. Lower down is Virgo and the bright star Spica.

In the north is the big W in Cassiopeia, and in the west Ursa Major with the Great Dipper and the "Pointers." High overhead is Hercules, in which one can see, under favorable conditions, a faint patch of light making a great cluster of one hundred thousand stars each comparable in size with our own sun. Light, traveling at the rate of 186,000 miles per second, takes 36,000 years to come from this cluster, so great is its distance from the earth.

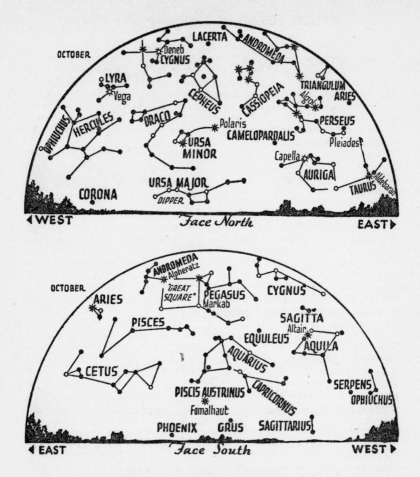

✦ ✹ ○ • SYMBOLS FOR STARS IN ORDER OF BRIGHTNESS

THE HEAVENS IN AUTUMN

FIGURE 34

THIS chart is correct for October 1 at 8 P.M. Planets are not shown. Facing south one sees low down a star that is visible only during a few months of the year, Fomalhaut in Piscis Austrinus. The Northern Cross, part of Cygnus, is now high in the west with Deneb at its top. To the east is the constellation of Pegasus, and the great square which it forms with the star Alpheratz in Andromeda is easily seen.

Looking north one sees Lyra, with bright Vega, fairly high in the west. Above it is Cygnus, and just below the zenith to the east, great Andromeda. Taurus is far down on the horizon, with Aldebaran almost invisible, and equally far down, directly north, is Ursa Major and its familiar Great Dipper with its two stars pointing to the Pole Star in the Little Dipper of Ursa Minor.

FUTURE TOTAL ECLIPSES OF THE SUN
FIGURE 35

A total eclipse of the sun is a rare event attracting astronomers from all over the world. During eclipses, the corona of the sun is especially studied.

The eclipse of June 19, 1936, will be visible along a path crossing Europe and Asia from the vicinity of Istanbul in Turkey to China and Japan. The following year, on June 8, astronomers will observe an eclipse from the South Pacific Ocean. If it is found that there is an island near the center of the path, it will be a suitable station, for this eclipse will last, at its maximum, over seven minutes.

The longest an eclipse can last is 7 minutes, 40 seconds, but this almost never happens. However, the end of the 1937 eclipse will be seen from Peru, and even there it will last several minutes, so some astronomers will probably observe it from South America.

In 1940, on October 1, an eclipse track will start in Brazil and cross the South Atlantic to Africa. Then comes one in 1941, on September 21. This will be seen along a path starting east of the Caspian Sea, passing over Asia to Indo-China, and out into the Pacific Ocean. February 4, 1943, will bring one with a track starting in China and crossing the North Pacific Ocean to Alaska. On July 9, 1945, one will start in the northwestern part of the United States at sunrise and will pass over into Canada a few minutes later. Then it will pass over Hudson Bay, Greenland, Norway, Sweden, and Russia. The United States will not be a good place from which to observe this, but doubtless astronomical parties will attempt it from northern Europe.

September 1, 1951, will see an eclipse start at sunrise along the coast of North Carolina, then pass across the Atlantic, but this will probably not be successfully observed. It will not be total, but annular, in which a ring of sunlight remains visible around the moon's disk. Such an eclipse is of slight scientific value. In 1954, on June 30, one starts in the Middle West at sunrise, then passes northeastward, over Canada, James Bay, Labrador, southern Greenland, Iceland, Norway, Sweden, Poland, and Russia. Like the 1945 eclipse, this will be unfavorable from the United States, but will be fairly satisfactory from the Scandinavian peninsula and central Europe.

Probably the eclipse most eagerly awaited, and certainly the best during the twentieth century, is scheduled for June 20, 1955. This is the repetition, after the 18-year and 11-day period called the "saros," of the 1937 eclipse, and it lasts even longer. It starts in the Indian Ocean, crosses the southern tip of India, Indo-China, Siam, and the Philippine Islands. Then it goes out into the Pacific Ocean. In the Philippines it passes close to Manila, and there it occurs at noon, with the sun almost in the zenith. Conditions could hardly be better, and the total phase will last for 7 minutes and 10 seconds. If the present scientific interest in eclipses continues unabated, this should witness a greater concentration of eclipse observers than ever before.

The next American eclipse will be on July 20, 1963, in eastern Canada and New England.

After the 1963 eclipse, the next in the United States will be in Florida, on March 7, 1970. Then will come one on February 26, 1979, passing across Washington, Montana, and North Dakota, Canada, Hudson Bay, and northern Greenland. The next is on August 21, 2017, when one crosses the United States from California to North Carolina.

389

INDEX